Hindi–English English–Hindi Concise Dictionary

Todd Scudiere

Hippocrene Books, Inc.
New York

Second printing, 2011

For information, address:
Hippocrene Books, Inc.
171 Madison Avenue
New York, NY 10016
www.hippocrenebooks.com

Library of Congress Cataloging-in-Publication Data

Scudiere, Todd.
Hindi-English/English-Hindi concise dictionary / Todd Scudiere.
p. cm.
ISBN 978-0-7818-1167-5 (alk. paper)
1. Hindi language—Dictionaries—English. 2. English language—Dictionaries—Hindi. I. Title. II. Title: English-Hindi.
PK1936.S413 2009
491.4'3321—dc22
2009032051

FSC
MIX
Paper
FSC® C011935

Printed in the United States of America

Acknowledgments

Heartfelt thanks to my family, friends, and to Michael Carroll, Monica Bentley and Barbara Keane-Pigeon at Hippocrene for all of their support throughout this project. Special thanks to Lauren Prince for her invaluable help with Excel. Special thanks to Sapna Sharma for her expert formatting and copyediting.

Todd Scudiere
San Diego, CA

CONTENTS

INTRODUCTION

Hindi is an Indo-European language that is spoken extensively in various parts of India, where it is one of two official languages. It is primarily spoken in the north of the country. The standard Hindi dialect is known as *Kharībolī*. In the north of India one often hears what is termed *Hindustāni* which is essentially a mix of Hindi and Urdu. Urdu is the official language of Pakistan, is written in the Arabic script, and a large portion of its vocabulary is Perso-Arabic in origin. Hindi is written in the *Devanāgarī* script and derives much of its vocabulary from the ancient language of Sanskrit. These languages are extremely similar in grammar and are primarily differentiated by cultural and political agendas.

Hindi is also widely spoken by the Indian diaspora in Mauritius, Fiji, the United Arab Emirates and neighboring Gulf countries, Germany, the United Kingdom, Uganda, Kenya, South Africa, New Zealand, Canada, the United States, and many others. According to the *Time Almanac 2008* Hindi is the third most widely spoken language in the world, after Chinese and English. Combined with Urdu, it ranks as the second most widely spoken language on the planet.

PRONUNCIATION GUIDE

Vowels

These vowels are shown written in their "full form" along with pronunciation. This is how they appear when at the beginning of a word. When following a consonant, vowels appear in short form known as a *mātrā*. To illustrate this, the letter म will be shown in parenthesis at the end of each entry. Note that the first vowel does not have a *mātrā*.

अ	**a**, like *u* in the English "b**u**s" (म = ma)
आ	**ā**, like *a* in the English "f**a**ther" (मा = mā)
इ	**i**, like *i* in the English "p**i**n" (मि = mi)
ई	**ī**, like *ee* in the English "sl**ee**ve" (मी = mī)
उ	**u**, like *u* in the English "p**u**t" (मु = mu)
ऊ	**ū**, like *oo* in the English "f**oo**l" (मू = mū)
ए	**e**, like *a* in the English "g**a**me" or "c**a**ke" (मे = me)
ऐ	**ai**, like *e* in the English "m**e**n"; for some speakers in different regions, **i** like *i* in the English "sm**i**le" (मै = mai)

ओ **o**, like *o* in the English "m**o**st" (मो = mo)

औ **au**, like *ou* in the English c**ou**gh; or sometimes stronger like *ou* in the English "c**ou**ch" (मौ = mau)

ऋ **ṛ** ,*ri* like in "**ri**p" (*occurs only in Sanskrit loan words*) (मृ = mṛ)

Consonants

क **k**, like *k* in the English "s**k**irt"

ख **kh**, like *kh* in the English "**kh**aki" (*aspirated*)

ग **g**, like *g* in the English "sprin**g**"

घ **gh**, like *g* in the English "**g**um" (*aspirated*)

ङ **ṅ**, *To make this sound, roll the tip of your tongue quickly across the roof of your mouth while pronouncing the English sound na. This will produce the required "flapping" sound unique to this letter.*

च **c**, like *ch* in the English "ri**ch**"; or the final *ch* sound in "chur**ch**"

छ **ch**, like *ch* in the English "**ch**arm"; or the initial *ch* sound in "**ch**urch" (*aspirated*)

ज **j**, like *ge* in the English "brid**ge**"

झ **jh**, like *j* in the English "**j**ump" (*aspirated*)

ञ **ñ**, like *n* in the English "i**n**jury"

ट **ṭ**, like *t* in the English "plan**t**" (*retroflex*)

ठ **ṭh**, like *t* in the English "**t**able" (*retroflex and aspirated*)

ड **ḍ**, like *d* in the English "blan**d**" (*retroflex*)

ढ **ḍh**, like *d* in the English "**d**am" (*retroflex and aspirated*)

ण **ṇ**, like *n* in the English "**n**ine" (*retroflex*)

ड़ **ṛ**. *To make this sound, place the tip of your tongue on the roof of your mouth and say "da," flapping the tip of your tongue slightly.*

ढ़ **ṛh**. *Make this sound the same as above letter, but aspirated as well (exhale slightly)*

त **t**, like *t* in the English "**t**ip" with the tip of your tongue behind the front teeth

थ **th**, like *t* in the English "**t**alk" (aspirated)

द **d**, like *d* in the English "**d**ip"

ध **dh**, like *d* in the English "**d**onut" (*aspirated*)

न **n**, like *n* in the English "bea**n**"

प **p**, like *p* in the English "cu**p**"

फ	**ph**, like *p* in the English "**p**arty" (*aspirated*) (*Note: although there is no* h *sound in words such as party or pot, when we say these words there is a slight aspiration which makes a* "puh" *sound. This is similair to* ph *in Hindi.*)

ब	**b**, like *b* in the English "la**b**"

भ	**bh**, like *b* in the English "**b**akery" (*aspirated*)

म	**m**, like *m* in the English "**m**other"

य	**y**, like *y* in the English "**y**ard"

र	**r**, like *r* in the English "**r**ap" but rolled or trilled slightly

ल	**l**, like *l* in the English "**l**ove"

व	**v**, like *v* in the English "lo**v**e"; sometimes like *w* in the English "**w**ater"

श	**ś**, like *sh* in the English "ca**sh**" or "**sh**opping"

ष	**ṣ**, like *sh* in the English "ca**sh**" (*retroflex*)

स	s, like *s* in the English "soap"

ह	**h**, like *h* in the English "**h**ouse"

Perso-Arabic Sounds

फ़ **f**, like *f* in the English "**f**ake"

ज़ **z**, like *z* in the English "**z**ebra"

क़ **q**, like *k* in the English "s**k**irt," but said in the back of the throat

ख़ **qh**, same has **kha**, but said in the back of the throat

ग़ **qg**, same as *g* in the English "son**g**," but said in the back of the throat

Nasalized vowel sounds in this dictionary will be transliterated as **ṁ**. This is not to be pronounced as a hard "m" sound. For an example of the sound, say the English word "hay" aloud. Now, holding your nose closed, say it again. The sound you are now hearing would be represented by "hayṁ"

Aspirated sounds require a slight exhalation when they are pronounced. In this dictionary, whenever you see an "**h**" immediately after a consonant, you will know that the word requires a slight aspiration.

Retroflex sounds, represented in this dictionary by dots underneath letters such as **ḍ** and **ṭ** are formed by placing the tip of the tongue on the roof of the mouth. For instance, for the **ṭ** sound, place the tip of your tongue on the roof of your mouth and voice **ṭ**. For a sound that is both retroflex and aspirated, such as **ṭh**, follow the same instructions but this time exhale slightly to produce a "ha" sound after the consonant.

The transliteration scheme shown above has been followed in the dictionary, with some exceptions. In some cases slight substitutions were made in order to provide the reader with a more common and understandable pronunciation.

Abbreviations

adj.	adjective
adv.	adverb
f.pl.	feminine plural
f.s	feminine singular
interj.	interjection
interr.	interrogative
m.pl.	masculine plural
m.s	masculine singular
n.	noun
n.f.	feminine noun
n.m.	masculine noun
num.	number
pl.	plural
pref.	prefix
prep.	preposition
v.aux.	auxiliary verb
v.i.	intransitive verb
v.t.	transitive verb

English–Hindi Dictionary

A

abandon *v.t.* परित्याग करना parityāg karnā
abbreviate *v.t.* संक्षिप्त करना saṅkṣipt karnā
abbreviation *n.* संक्षेपण saṅkṣepaṇ
abdomen *n.* पेट peṭ
ability *n.* योग्यता yogyatā
able *adj.* योग्य yogya
abnormal *adj.* अप्रसम aprasam
aboard *adv.* में सवार meṁ savār
abortion *n.* गर्भपात garbhpāt
about *adv.* लगभग lagbhag; *prep.* के बारे में ke bāre meṁ
above *adv.* के ऊपर ke ūpar
above all *adv.* सर्वोपरि sarvopari
abroad *adv.* विदेश में videś meṁ
absence *n.* अनुपस्थिति anupasthiti
absent *adj.* अनुपस्थित anupasthit
absolute *adj.* पूर्ण pūrṇ
absorb *v.t.* तल्लीन करना tallīn karnā
abstract *adj.* निराकार nirākār
absurd *adj.* बेतुका betukā
abundance *n.* बहुतायत bahutāyat
abundant *adj.* प्रचुर prachur
abuse *n.* दुरुपयोग durupyog; *v.t.* दुरुपयोग करना durupyog karnā
abusive *adj.* अपमानजनक apmānjanak
academic *adj.* शास्त्रीय śāstrīy
academy *n.* अकादमी ākādamī
accelerate *v.i.* चाल बढ़ाना cāl baṛhānā
accelerator *n.* त्वरित्र tvaritra
accent *n.* उच्चारण uccāraṇ
accept *v.t.* स्वीकार करना svīkār karnā

acceptance *n.* मंजूरी manzūrī
access *n.* प्रवेश praveś
accessory *n.* सहायक sahāyak
accident *n.* दुर्घटना durghaṭnā
accidental *adj.* आकास्मिक में ākāsmik meṁ
accommodate *v.t.* सहायता देना sahāyatā denā
accommodation *n.* आवास āvās
accompany *v.t.* साथ साथ sāth sāth
accomplice *n.* सहायक sahāyak
accomplish *v.t.* सफलतापूर्वक पूरा करना saphaltāpūrvak pūrā karnā
accomplishment *n.* उपलब्धि upalabdhi
according to *prep* … के अनुसार … ke anusār
account *n.* खाता khātā
accountant *n.* लेखाकार lekhākār
accounting *n.* लेखा कार्य lekhā karya
accumulate *v.t.* इकट्ठा करना ikṭṭhā karnā
accurate *adj.* सही sahī
accusation *n.* अभियोग abhiyog
accuse *v.t.* दोषी ठहराना doṣī ṭharānā
accustom *v.i.* अभ्यस्त बनना abhyast bananā
ace *n.* इक्का ikkā
ache *n.* दर्द dard
achieve *v.t.* सम्पादित करना sampādit karnā
achievement *n.* कार्यसम्पादन kāryasampādan
acid *n.* अम्ल amal; *adj.* अम्लीय amlīy
acidity *n.* अम्लता amlatā
acknowledge *v.t.* मान लेना mān lenā
acknowledgement *n.* प्राप्ति सूचना prapti sūcnā
acne *n.* मुँहासा muṁhāsā
acquaint *v.t.* परिचित करना paricit karnā
acquaintance *n.* परिचय paricay

acquire *v.t.* प्राप्त करना prāpt karnā
acquisition *n.* प्राप्ति prāpti
acre *n.* एकड़ ekaṛ
across *adv.* पार pār
act *n.* कार्य kārya; *v.t.* कार्य करना kārya karnā
action *n.* क्रिया करना kriyā karnā
active *adj.* सक्रिय sakriy
activity *n.* क्रिया kriyā
actor *n.* अभिनेता abhinetā
actual *adj.* वास्तविक vāstavik
acute *adj.* नुकीला nukīlā
A.D. ईसवी सन īsavī san
adapt *v.t.* अनुकूल करना anukūl karnā
adapter *n.* अनुकूलक anukūlak
add *v.t.* (*increase*) बढ़ाना baṛhānā; (*join*) जोड़ना joṛnā
addition *n.* संयोजन sanyojan
additional *adj.* अतिरिक्त atirikt
address *n.* पता patā; *v.t.* भाषण देना bhaṣhaṇ denā
adequate *adj.* पर्याप्त paryāpt
adhere *v.i.* चिपकना cipkanā
adhesive *adj.* चिपचिपा cipcipā; *n.* गोंद goṁd
adjacent *adj.* निकटवर्ती nikaṭvartī
adjective *n.* विशेषण viśeṣaṇ
adjoin *v.i.* आसन्न होना āsann honā
adjust *v.t.* समायोजित करना samāyojit karnā
administer *v.t.* प्रबन्ध करना prabandh karnā
administration *n.* शासन śāsan
administrative *adj.* प्रशासी praśāsī
admirable *adj.* प्रशंसनीय praśansanīy
admiral *n.* नौसेनापति nausenāpati
admire *v.t.* प्रशंसा करना praśansā karnā
admission *n.* प्रवेश शुल्क praveś śulk

admit *v.t.* प्रवेश देना praveś denā
adolescent *n.* किशोर kiśor
adopt *v.t.* गोद लेना god lenā
adoption *n.* गोद लेना god lenā
adore *v.t.* आराधना करना ārādhanā karnā
adult *n./adj.* वयस्क vayask
advance *n.* प्रगति pragati; *v.t.* प्रगति करना pragati karnā
advantage *n.* फायदा fāydā
adventure *n.* साहस sāhas
adverb *n.* क्रियाविशेषण kriyāviśeṣaṇ
adversary *n.* विरोधी virodhī
advertise *v.t.* विज्ञापन करना vigyāpan karnā
advertisement *n.* विज्ञापन vigyāpan
advice *n.* सलाह salāh
advise *v.t.* सलाह देना salāh denā
adviser *n.* सलाहकार salāhakār
aerial *n.* एरियल eriyal; *adj.* वायवीय vāyvīy
affair *n.* मामला māmlā
affect *v.t.* प्रभावित करना prabhāvit karnā
affection *n.* अनुराग anurāg
affectionate *adj.* स्नेही snehī
affirm *v.t.* निश्च्यपूर्वक कहना niścayapūrvak kahenā
affirmation *n.* अभिकथन abhikathan
afflict *v.t.* दुख देना dukh denā
affliction *n.* दुख dukh
afford *v.t.* खर्च कर सकना qharc kar saknā
afraid *adj.* डरा हुआ ḍarā huā
Africa *n.* अफ़्रीका afrīkā
African *n./adj.* अफ़्रीकी afrīkī
after *adv.* के बाद ke bād
afternoon *n.* तीसरा पहर tīsrā pahar
afterward *adv.* बाद में bād meṁ

again *adv.* दुबारा dubārā
against *prep.* … के खिलाफ़ … ke khilāf
age *n.* उमर umar
agenda *n.* कार्यसूची kāryasūcī
agent *n.* अभिकर्त्ता abhikarttā
aggravate *v.t.* भारी कर देना bhārī kar denā
aggressive *adj.* लड़ाका laṛākā
agile *adj.* फुर्तीला phurtīlā
agitate *v.t.* हिलाना hilānā
ago *adv.* पहले pahale
agony *n.* घोर व्यथा ghor vyathā
agree *v.t.* सहमत होना sahamat honā
agreeable *adj.* मनोहर manohar
agreement *n.* सहमति sahamati
agriculture *n.* खेतीबारी khetībārī
agricultural *adj.* खेत का khet kā
ahead *adv.* आगे āge
aid *n.* सहायता sahāyatā; *v.t.* सहायता देना sahāyatā denā
AIDS *n.* एड्ज़ eḍz
aim *n.* निशाना niśānā; *v.t.* निशाना बाँधना niśānā bāṁdhnā
air *n.* हवा havā
air-conditioning *n.* ए. सी. e. sī.
air force *n.* वायु सेना vāyu senā
airline *n.* हवाई कम्पनी havāī kampanī
airmail *n.* हवाई डाक havāī ḍāk
airplane *n.* हवाई जहाज़ havāī jahāz
airport *n.* हवाई अड्डा havaı aḍḍa
aisle *n.* गलियारा galiyārā
alarm *n.* चेतावनी cetāvanī; *v.t.* उत्तेजित करना uttejit karnā
alarm clock *n.* अलार्म घड़ी alārm ghaṛī
alcohol *n.* शराब śarāb
alcoholic *n.* शराबी śarābī; *adj.* मादक mādak

alcove *n.* आला ālā
ale *n.* बियर biyar
alert *n.* चेतावनी cetāvanī; *v.t.* चेतावनी देना cetāvanī denā; *adj.* सचेत sacet
alien *n.* विदेशी videśī; *adj.* अन्यलोकवासी anyalokavāsī
align *v.t.* सीधा मिलना sīdhā milnā
alike *adj.* समान samān
alive *adj.* जीवित jīvit, ज़िन्दा zindā
all *adj.* सब sab
allergic *adj.* एलर्जी संबन्धी elarjī sambandhī; *v.i.* (*to be allergic*) एलर्जी होना elarjī honā
allergy *n.* एलर्जी elarjī
alley *n.* गली galī
alliance *n.* एका ekā
allow *v.t.* अनुमति देना anumati denā
ally *n.* मित्र mitra
almond *n.* बादाम bādām
almost *adv.* लगभग lagbhag
aloft *adj.* ऊँचे पर ūṁce par, ऊपर ūpar
alone *adj.* अकेला akelā
along *adv.* साथ साथ sāth sāth
aloud *adv.* ज़ोर से zor se
alphabet *n.* वर्णमाला varṇamālā
already *adv.* पहले से pahale se
also *adv.* भी bhī
altar *n.* वेदी vedī
alter *v.t.* बदल देना badal denā
alteration *n.* परिर्वतन parivartan
although *conj.* हालाँकि halāṁki
altitude *n.* ऊँचाई ūṁcāī
altogether *adv.* पूरी तरह से pūrī tarah se
aluminum *n.* ऐलुमिनियम ailuminiyam

always *adv.* हमेशा hameśā
a.m. *adj.* मध्यान्ह पूर्व madhyānh pūrv
amateur *n.* अव्यवसायी avyavasāyī; *adj.* शौकीन śāukīn
amaze *v.t.* हैरान करना hairān karnā
amazing *adj.* विस्मयकारी vismayakārī
ambassador *n.* राजदूत rājdūt
ambiguous *adj.* अनेकार्थक anekārthak
ambition *n.* महत्वाकांक्षा mahatvākāṇkṣā
ambitious *adj.* महत्वाकांक्षी mahatvākāṇkṣī
ambulance *n.* अस्पताल की गाड़ी aspatāl kī gāṛī
amendment *n.* संशोधन sanśodhan
America *n.* अमरीका amrīkā
American *n./adj.* अमरीकी amrīkī
amid *prep.* बीच में bīc meṁ
ammonia *n.* अमोनिया amoniyā
among *prep.* में meṁ
amphibian *n.* उभयचर ubhayachar
amplifier *n.* प्रवर्धक pravardhak
amplify *v.t.* विस्तार देना vistār denā
amputate *v.t.* काट डालना kāṭ ḍālnā
amputation *n.* विच्छेदन vicchedan
amuse *v.t.* जी बहलाना jī bahalānā
amusement *n.* मनोरंजन manoranjan
analogy *n.* सादृश्य sādṛśya
analysis *n.* विश्लेषण viśleṣaṇ
analyze *v.t.* विश्लेषण करना viśleṣaṇ karnā
anarchy *n.* अराजकता arājaktā
ancestor *n.* पूर्वज pūrvaj
anchor *n.* लंगर laṅgar; *v.i.* लंगर डालना laṅgar ḍālnā
ancient *adj.* प्राचीन prācīn
and *conj.* और aur
anecdote *n.* किस्सा kissā

angel *n.* फ़रिश्ता faristā
anger *n.* गुस्सा gussā; *v.i.* गुस्सा दिलाना gussā dilānā
angle *n.* कोण koṇ
angry *adj.* नाराज़ nārāz, गुस्सा gussā
anguish *n.* वेदना vednā
animal *n.* जानवर jānvar
ankle *n.* टखना ṭakhnā
annex *n.* उपभवन upbhavan
anniversary *n.* जयन्ती jayantī
announce *v.t.* घोषणा करना ghoṣaṇā karnā
announcement *n.* घोषणा ghoṣaṇā
annoy *v.t.* परेशान करना pareśān karnā
annoyance *n.* खीज khīj
annual *adj.* वार्षिक varṣik
annul *v.t.* रद्द करना radd karnā
anonymous *adj.* गुमनाम gumnām
another *adj.* एक और ek aur, दूसरा dusrā
answer *n.* जवाब javāb; *v.t.* जवाब देना javāb denā
ant *n.* चींटी cīṁṭī
antenna *n.* ऐन्टेना ainṭenā
anti- *pref.* विपरीत viparīt
antibiotic *n./adj.* प्रतिजैविक pratijaivik
anticipate *v.t.* प्रत्याशित करना pratyāśit karnā
anticipation *n.* प्रत्याशा pratyāśā
antique *n.* पुरानी वस्तु purānī vastu
antiseptic *adj.* पूतिनाशक pūtināśak
anxiety *n.* चिन्ता cintā
anxious *adj.* चिंतित cintit
any *adj.* कोई koī
anybody *pron.* कोई भी koī bhī
anyone *pron.* कोई भी koī bhī
anything *pron.* कुछ भी kuch bhī

anytime *adv.* जब कभी jab kabhī
anywhere *adv.* कहीं भी kahīṁ bhī
apart *adv.* अलग alag
apartment *n.* कमरा kamarā
apathetic *adj.* उदासीन udāsīn
apologize *v.i.* क्षमा माँगना kṣamā māṁgnā
apology *n.* क्षमा-याचना kṣamā-yācnā
apparatus *n.* उपकरण upkaraṇ
apparel *n.* कपड़े kapṛe
apparent *adj.* स्पष्ट spaṣṭ
appeal *v.i.* पसंद आना pasand ānā
appear *v.i.* प्रकट होना prakaṭ honā
appearance *n.* दर्शन darśan
appendix *n.* (*book*) परिशिष्ट pariśiṣṭ; (*anatomy*) उण्डुकपुच्छ uṇḍukpucch
appetite *n.* भूख bhūkh
appetizer *n.* हल्का नाश्ता halkā nāśtā
applaud *v.t.* तालियाँ बजाना taliyāṁ bajānā
applause *n.* शाबाशी śābāśī
apple *n.* सेब seb
appliance *n.* यन्त्र yantra
application *n.* आवेदन पत्र āvedan patr; (*use*) उपयोग upyog
apply *v.t.* आवेदन करना āvedan karnā; *v.i.* लागू होना lāgū honā
appoint *v.t.* नियुक्त करना niyukt karnā
appointment *n.* नियोजन niyojan
appraisal *n.* मूल्यांकन mūlyāṅkan
appreciate *v.t.* सराहना sarāhnā
appreciation *n.* मूल्यांकन mūlyāṅkan
approach *n.* पहुँच pahuṁc; *v.i.* पास आना pās ānā
appropriate *adj.* ठीक ṭhīk
approval *n.* मंजूरी manzūrī
approve *v.t.* मंजूर करना manjūr karnā

approximate *n.* लगभग lagbhag; *v.t.* निकट आना nikaṭ ānā
apricot *n.* खूबानी khūbānī
April *n.* अप्रैल aprail
apron *n.* जामा jāmā
apt *adj.* उपयुक्त upyukt
aptitude *n.* क्षमता kṣamatā
aquatic *adj.* जलचर jalcar
Arab *n.* अरब arab
Arabic *adj.* अरबी arabī
arbitrary *adj.* मन-माना man-mānā
arch *n.* मेहराब meharāb
archaeological *adj.* पुरातत्वीय purātatvīy
archaeology *n.* पुरातत्त्वा purātattvā
architect *n.* वास्तुकार vāstukār
architectural *adj.* वास्तुशिल्पीय vāstuśīlpīy
architecture *n.* वास्तुकला vāstukalā
archive *n.* अभिलेख abhilekh
arctic *adj.* उत्तरध्रुवीय uttardhruvīy
Arctic Circle *n.* आर्कटिक वृत्त ārkṭik vṛtt
Arctic Ocean *n.* आर्कटिक महासगर ārkṭik mahāsagar
area *n.* इलाक़ा ilāqā
argue *v.t.* बहस करना bahas karnā
argument *n.* बहस bahas
arise *v.i.* उदित होना udit honā
arithmetic *n.* अंकगणित aṅkgaṇit
arm *n.* बाहु bāhu
armchair *n.* बाँहदार कुर्सी bāṁhadār kursī
armpit *n.* बगल bagal
army *n.* सेना senā
aroma *n.* सुगन्ध sugandh
around *adv.* आस-पास ās-pās; *prep.* इधर-उधर idhar-udhar
arrange *v.t.* व्यवस्थित करना vyavasthit karnā

arrangement *n.* इंतज़ाम intazām
arrest *n.* गिरफ्तार giraftār; *v.t.* गिरफ़्तार करना giraftār karnā
arrival *n.* आगमन āgman
arrive *v.i.* पहुँचना pahuṁcnā
arrogance *n.* हेकड़ी hekaṛī
arrogant *adj.* हेकड़ hekaṛ
arrow *n.* तीर tīr, बाण bāṇ
art *n.* कला kalā
artery *n.* धमनी dhamanī
article *n.* लेख lekh, उपपद uppad, अनुच्छेद anucched
artifact *n.* शिल्पकृति śilpakrati
artificial *adj.* नक़ली naqalī
artisan *n.* कारीगर kārīgar
artist *n.* कलाकार kalākār
artistic *adj.* कलात्मक kalātmak
as *adv.* वैसा ही vaisā hī; *conj.* जब कि jab ki
ash *n.* राख rākh
ashamed *adj.* लज्जित lajjit
ashtray *n.* राखदानी rākhdānī
aside *adv.* एक ओर ek aor
ask *v.t.* पूछना pūchnā
asleep *adj./adv.* सोया हुआ soyā huā
aspect *n.* पहलू pahalū
asphalt *n.* डामर ḍāmar
aspirin *n.* ऐस्पिरिन aisprin
assault *n.* आक्रमण ākramaṇ; *v.t.* हमला करना hamlā karnā
assemble *v.t.* जोड़ना joṛnā; *v.i.* एकत्र हो जाना ekatr ho jānā
assembly *n.* सभा sabhā
assert *v.t.* प्रभाव डालना prabhāv ḍālnā
assertion *n.* दावा dāvā
assign *v.t.* निश्चित करना niścit karnā
assimilate *v.t.* सम्मिलित करना sammilit karnā

assist *v.t.* सहायता करना sahāyatā karnā
assistance *n.* सहायता sahāyatā
assistant *n.* सहायक sahāyak
associate *n.* सहयोगी sahayogī; *v.t.* संबंध करना sambandh karnā
association *n.* संस्था saṅsthā, समाज samāj
assume *v.t.* मान लेना mān lenā
assurance *n.* आश्वासन āśvāsan
assure *v.t.* विश्वास दिलाना viśvās dilānā
asthma *n.* दमा damā
asthmatic *adj.* दमा का रोगी damā kā rogī
astonish *v.t.* विस्मित कर देना vismit kar denā
astray *adj.* भूला-भटका bhūlā-baṭakā
astringent *n.* स्तंभक stambhak; *adj.* कटु katu
astrologer *n.* ज्योतिषी jyotiṣī
astrology *n.* फलित-ज्योतिष phalit-jyotiṣ
astronomy *n.* गणित-ज्योतिष gaṇit-jyotiṣ
astute *adj.* चतुर catur
asylum *n* शरण śaraṇ
at *prep.* पर par
atheism *n.* नास्तिकता nāstikatā
atheist *n.* नास्तिक nāstik
athlete *n.* व्यायामी vyāyāmī
athletics *n.pl.* खेलकूद khelkūd
atmosphere *n.* वातावरण vātāvaraṇ
atom *n.* परमाणु parmāṇu
attach *v.t.* लगाना lagānā
attack *n.* हमला hamlā; *v.t.* हमला करना hamlā karnā
attempt *n.* प्रयत्न prayatn; *v.t.* प्रयत्न करना prayatn karnā
attend *v.t.* हाथ में होना hāth meṁ honā; *v.i.* उपस्थित रहना upsthit rehnā
attendance *n.* उपस्थिति upsthiti

attendant *n.* नौकर naukar
attention *n.* ध्यान dhyān; *v.t.* (*to pay attention*) ध्यान देना dhyān denā
attentive *adj.* सावधान sāvdhān
attic *n.* अटारी aṭārī
attitude *n.* मनोवृत्ति manovr̥tti
attorney *n.* न्यायवादी nyāyavādī
attract *v.t.* आकर्षित करना ākarṣit karnā
attraction *n.* आकर्षण ākarṣaṇ
attractive *adj.* आकार्षण ākārṣaṇ
attribute *n.* गुण guṇ
auction *n.* नीलाम nīlām; *v.t.* नीलाम करना nīlām karnā
audience *n.* श्रोतागण śrotāgaṇ
auditory *adj.* श्रवण ṣravaṇ
augment *v.t.* बढ़ाना baṛhānā
August *n.* अगस्त agast
aunt *n.* (*wife of father's brother*) चाची cācī; (*wife of mother's brother*) मामी māmī; (*mother's sister*) मौसी mausī; (*father's sister*) फूफी phūphī
authentic *adj.* प्रमाणिक pramāṇik
author *n.* लेखक lekhak
authority *n.* अधिकार adhikār
authorization *n.* अनुमोदन anumodan
authorize *v.t.* अनुमोदन करना anumodan karnā
automatic *adj.* स्वचालित svacālit
automation *n.* स्वचलन svacalan
automobile *n.* मोटर moṭar
autonomous *adj.* स्वाय svāyatt
autopsy *n.* शव-परीक्षा śav-parīkṣā
autumn *n.* शरद śarad
availability *n.* प्राप्यता prāpyatā
available *adj.* प्राप्य prāpya

avenue *n.* मार्ग mārg
average *n.* औसत ausat
aviation *n.* वायुयान vāyuyān
avoid *v.t.* परिहार करना parihār karnā
awake *v.i.* जागना jāgnā; *adj.* जागत jāgat
award *n.* इनाम inām; *v.t.* निर्णय करना nirṇay karnā
aware *adj.* जानकार jānkār
away *adv.* दूर dūr
awful *adj.* भयानक bhayānak
awkward *adj.* बेढ़गी beṛhagī
ax *n.* कुल्हाड़ी kulhāṛī
axis *n.* अक्ष akṣ
axle *n.* धुरी dhurī

B

baby *n.* बच्चा baccā, शिशु śiśu
baby-sitter *n.m.* बच्चे को देखने वाला bacce ko dekhne vālā; *n.f.* बच्चे को देखने वाली bacce ko dekhne vālī
back *n.* पीठ pīṭh; *adv.* पीछे pīche
backbone *n.* रीढ़ की हड्डी rīṛh kī haḍḍī
backward *adj.* वापसी vāpsī; *adv.* पीछे pīche
bacon *n.* सुअर का मांस sūar kā māṁs
bacteria *n.* जीवाणु jīvāṇu
bacterial *adj.* जीवाण्विक jīvānvik
bad *adj.* बुरा burā, ख़राब qharāb
badge *n.* बिल्ला billā, बैज baij
badly *adv.* बुरी तरह burī tarah
bag *n.* थैला thailā
baggage *n.* सामान sāmān
bail *n.* ज़मानत zamānat
bait *n.* चारा cārā

bake *v.t.* पकाना pakānā
baker *n.* नानबाई nānbāī
balance *n.* तराजू tarājū
balcony *n.* छज्जा chajjā
bald *adj.* गंजा gañjā
ball *n.* गेंद gend
balloon *n.* गुब्बारा gubbārā
banana *n.* केला kelā
band *n.* बैंड baiṁḍ
bandage *n.* पट्टी paṭṭī
banister *n.* जंगला jaṅgala
bank *n.* बैंक baiṅk
banker *n.* महाजन mahājan
banner *n.* फरहरा pharharā
banquet *n.* दावत dāvat
baptism *n.* बपतिस्मा baptismā
baptize *v.t.* बपतिस्मा देना baptismā denā
bar *n.* बार bār
barber *n.* नाई nāī
barbershop *n.* नाई की दुकान nāī kī dukān
bare *adj.* नंगा naṅgā
bargain *n.* सौदा saudā
bark *v.i.* भौंकना bhauṁknā; *n.* (*tree*) छाल chāl
barley *n.* जौ jau
barometer *n.* वायुदाबमापी vāyudābmāphī
barrack *n.* छावनी chāvanī
barrel *n.* पीपा pīpā
barren *adj.* बंजर bañjar
barrier *n.* नाका nākā
base *n.* अड्डा aḍḍā
baseball *n.* बेसबाल besbāl
basement *n.* तहख़ाना tahqhānā

basic *adj.* मूल mūl
basin *n.* चिलमची cilmacī
basis *n.* आधार ādhār
basket *n.* डलिया ḍaliyā
basketball *n.* बास्कट बॉल bāskaṭ bāl
bat *n.* चमगादड़ camgādaṛ
batch *n.* टोली ṭolī
bath *n.* स्नान snān
bathe *v.t.* स्नान करना snān karnā; *v.i.* नहाना nahānā
bathroom *n.* गुसलख़ाना gusalqhānā
bathtub *n.* स्नान टब snān ṭab
batter *n.* लपसी lapsī; *v.t.* कूटना kūṭnā
battery *n.* बैटरी baiṭarī
battle *n./v.t.* लड़ाई laṛāī
bay *n.* खाड़ी khāṛī
B.C. ईसापूर्व īsāpūrv
be *v.i.* होना honā
beach *n.* समुद्र तट samudra taṭ
beak *n.* चोंच coṁc
beam *n.* किरण kiraṇ
bean *n.* सेम sem
bear *n.* भालू bhālū
beard *n.* दाढ़ी dāṛhī
bearing *n.* दिशाकोण diśākoṇ
beast *n.* पशु paśu
beat *n.* (*heart*) धड़कन dhaṛkan; (*music*) ताल tāl; *v.i.* (*heart*) धड़कना dhaṛaknā; *v.t* .(*hit, strike*) मारना mārnā
beautiful *adj.* सुंदर sundar
beauty *n.* सुन्दरता sundartā
because *conj.* क्योंकि kyoṁki
become *v.i.* हो जाना ho jānā
bed *n.* बिस्तर bistar

bedroom *n.* सोने का कमरा sone kā kamrā
bee *n.* मधुमक्खी madhumakkhī
beef *n.* मांस māṁs
beer *n.* बियर biyar
beetle *n.* भृंग bhṛng
beet *n.* चुक़ंदर cuqandar
before *prep.* पहले pahale
beg *v.i.* भीक्षा माँगना bhīkṣā maṁgnā
beggar *n.* भिखारी bhikhārī
begin *v.i.* शुरू करना śurū karnā
beginner *n.* नौसिखिया nausikhiyā
behalf *n.* … की ओर से … kī aor se
behave *v.i.* बरताव करना bartāv karnā
behavior *n.* व्यवहार vyavahār
behind *prep./adv.* पीछे pīche
behold *v.i.* देखना dekhnā
being *n.* अस्तित्व astitva
belief *n.* विश्वास viśvās
believe *v.t.* विश्वास करना viśvās karnā
bell *n.* घंटी ghaṇṭī
belly *n.* पेट peṭ
belong *v.i.* … का होना … kā honā
belongings *n.* सामान sāmān
below *prep./adv.* नीचे nīce
belt *n.* पेटी peṭī
bench *n.* बेंच beñc
bend *v.t.* झुकाना jhukānā
beneath *prep.* … के नीचे … ke nīce
beneficial *adj.* लाभदायक lābhdāyak
benefit *n.* लाभ lābh; *v.t.* लाभ पहुँचाना lābh pahuṁcānā
benign *adj.* सुसाध्य susādhy
bent *adj.* मुड़ा हुआ muṛā huā

berry *n.* बेर ber
beside *prep.* के पास … ke pās
best *adj.* सबसे अच्छा sabse acchā; *adv.* बहुत अच्छी तरह से bahut acchī tarah se
bet *n.* शर्त śart; *v.t.* शर्त लगाना śart lagānā
betray *v.t.* विश्वासघात करना viśvāsghāt karnā
better *adj.* अधिक अच्छा adhik acchā; *adv.* से अधिक se adhik
between *prep.* बीच में bīc meṁ
beverage *n.* पेय pey
beware! *interj.* ख़बरदार qhabardār
beyond *prep.* … के पार … ke pār
bib *n.* बिब bib
bible *n.* बाइबिल bāibil
bicycle *n.* साइकिल sāikil
big *adj.* बड़ा baṛā
bilingual *adj.* व्दिभाषी dvibhāṣī
bill *n.* बिल bil
billiards *n.* बिलियर्ड biliyarḍ
bin *n.* डिब्बा ḍibbā
bind *v.t.* बाँधना bāṁdhnā
biography *n.* जीवनी jīvanī
biological *adj.* जैविक jaivik
biology *n.* जीवविज्ञान jīvavigyān
bird *n.* चिड़िया ciṛiyā
birth *n.* जन्म janam
birthday *n.* जन्मदिन janamdin
biscuit *n.* बिस्कुट biskuṭ
bit *n.* टुकड़ा ṭukaṛā
bite *n.* काटा kāṭā
bitter *adj.* कटु kaṭu
black *adj.* काला kālā

blackberry *n.* काली अंची kālī ancī
blackboard *n.* श्यामपट्ट śyāmapaṭṭ
bladder *n.* मसलाना masalānā
blade *n.* फल phal
blame *n.* दोष doṣ; *v.t.* दोष देना doṣ denā
blanket *n.* कंबल kambal
blast *n.* धमाका dhamākā
blaze *n.* आग की ज्वाला āg kī jvālā
bleak *adj.* निराशापूर्ण nirāśāpūrṇ
bleed *v.i.* ख़ून निकलना qūn nikalnā
bless *v.t.* आशीर्वाद देना aśirvād denā
blessing *n.* आशीर्वाद aśirvād
blind *adj.* अंधा andhā
blindness *n.* अंधापन andhāpan
blink *v.i.* आँख झपकाना āṁkh jhapkānā
block *n.* कण्ड kaṇḍ
blond *adj.* हल्के रंग halke rang
blood *n.* ख़ून khūn
blood pressure *n.* रक्तचाप raktacāp
bloom *v.i.* फूलना phūlnā
blossom *n.* मंजरी mañjarī
blouse *n.* कुरती kurtī
blow *v.t.* उड़ा देना uṛā denā; *v.i.* बहना bahanā
blue *adj.* नीला nīlā
blunt *adj.* भुथरा bhutharā
blush *v.i.* झेंपना jhoṁpnā
board *n.* तख़्ता taqhtā
boarding school *n.* छात्रवास chātravās
boat *n.* नाव nāv
boating *n.* नौकाविहार naukāvihār
body *n.* शरीर śarīr
boil *n.* फोड़ा phoṛā; *v.t.* उबालना ubālnā

boiler *n.* बायलर bāyalar
bold *adj.* दिलेर diler
bolt *n.* चटखनी caṭkhanī
bomb *n.* बम bam; *v.t.* बम गिराना bam girānā
bone *n.* हड्डी haḍḍī
bone marrow *n.* हड्डी की मज्जा haḍḍī kī majjā
book *n.* किताब kitāb, पुस्तक pustak
bookstore *n.* किताब की दुकान kitāb kī dukān
boot *n.* बूट būṭ
border *n.* सीमा sīmā
born *adj.* जन्मजात janamjāt
boss *n.* मालिक mālik
bottle *n.* बोटल boṭal; *v.t.* बोटल में बंद करना boṭal meṁ band karnā
bottom *n.* निचला niclā
bounce *v.t.* उछालना uchālnā; *v.i.* टक्कर मारना takkar māranā
box *n.* सन्दूक sandūk
boxing *n.* मुक्केबाज़ी mukkebāzī
boy *n.* लड़का laṛkā
boyfriend *n.* प्रेमी premī
brake *n.* ब्रेक brek
brave *adj.* बहादुर bahādur
bread *n.* रोटी roṭī
break *n.* ब्रेक brek; *v.i.* टूटना ṭūṭnā
breakfast *n.* नाश्ता nāśtā
breeze *n.* बयार bayār
bribe *n.* घूस ghus; *v.t.* घूस देना ghus denā
brief *adj.* संक्षिप्त saṅkṣipt
briefcase *n.* ब्रीफ़केस brīfkes
bright *adj.* चमकीला camkīlā
brilliant *adj.* चमकीला camkīlā

bring *v.t.* लाना lānā
Britain *n.* ब्रिटेन briṭen
British *n./adj.* अँग्रेज़ aṁgrez; *adj.* अँग्रेज़ी aṁgrezī
broccoli *n.* फूलगोभी phūlgobhī
bronchitis *n.* श्वासनली-शोथ śvāsnalī-śoth
bronze *n.* काँसा kāṁsā; *adj.* काँस्य kāṁsya
broth *n.* शोरवा śoravā
brother *n.* भाई bhāī
brother-in-law *n.* (*wife's brother*) साला sālā; (*husband's older brother*) जेठ jeṭh; (*husband's younger brother*) देवर devar
brush *n.* ब्रश braś
brutal *adj.* क्रूर krūr
bubble *n.* बुलबुला bulbulā
bucket *n.* बाल्टी bālṭī
budget *n.* बजट bajaṭ
bulb *n.* (*light*) बल्ब balb; (*plant*) कंद kand
bullet *n.* गोली golī
bundle *n.* बंडल banḍal
buoy *n.* पीपा pīpā
bureau *n.* कर्यालय karyālay
bureaucrat *n.* दफ़्तरशाह daftarśāh
bureaucratic *adj.* दफ़्तरशाही daftarśāhī
bury *v.t.* गाड़ना gāṛnā
bus *n.* बस bas
business *n.* व्यापार vyāpār
busy *adj.* व्यस्त vyast
but *conj.* लेकिन lekin
butter *n.* मक्खन makkhan
butterfly *n.* तितली titalī
button *n.* बटन baṭan
buttonhole *n.* काख kākh

buy *v.t.* खरीदना kharīdnā
buyer *n.* खरीददार kharīdadār
by *prep.* पास pās
byte *n.* बाइट bāiṭ

C

cabbage *n.* बंदगोभी bandgobhī
cabin *n.* कोठरी koṭharī
cabinet *n.* अलमारी ālmārī
cable *n.* तार tār
café *n.* जलपानगृह jalpāngṛha
cafeteria *n.* कैंटीन kainṭīn
caffeine *n.* कैफ़ीन kaifīn
cage *n.* पिंजरा piñjarā
cake *n.* केक kek
calcium *n.* कैल्सियम kailsiyam
calculate *v.t.* हिसाब लगाना hisāb lagānā
calculation *n.* हिसाब hisāb
calculator *n.* गणक gaṇak
calendar *n.* तिथि-पत्र tithi-patr
calf *n.* (*part of leg*) पिण्ड्ली piṇṛalī; (*animal*) बछड़ा bachṛā
call *n.* बुलावा bulāvā; *v.t.* बुलाना bulānā; (*to telephone*) फ़ोन करना fon karnā
calm *adj.* शान्त śānt; *v.i.* शान्त हो जाना śānt ho jānā; *v.t.* शान्त करना śānt karnā
camel *n.* ऊँट ūṁṭ
camera *n.* कैमरा kaimarā
camp *n.* शिविर śivir; *v.i.* शिविर डालना śivir ḍālnā
campus *n.* मैदान maidān
can *v.aux.* सकना saknā; *n.* कैन kain
canal *n.* नहर nahar

cancel *v.t.* रद्द करना radd karnā
cancellation *n.* मनसूखी mansūkhī
cancer *n.* कैन्सर kainsar
candid *adj.* सरल saral
candidate *n.* उम्मीदवार ummīdvār
candle *n.* बत्ती battī
candy *n.* मिठाई miṭhāī
cane *n.* बेंत beṁt
cannon *n.* तोप top
canoe *n.* डोंगी ḍoṁgī
canteen *n.* कैंटीन kainṭīn
canvas *n.* किरमिच kirmic
cap *n.* (*hat*) टोपी ṭopī; (*cover/lid*) ढक्कन ḍhakkan
capable *adj.* समर्थ samarth
capacity *n.* समाई samāī
cape *n.* ढीला ḍhīlā; (*geographical*) अंतरीप antarīp
capital *n.* (*city*) राजधानी rājdhānī; (*money*) पूँजी pūṁjī
capsule *n.* कैपसूल kaipsūl
captain *n.* कप्तान kaptān
car *n.* गाड़ी gāṛī
cardboard *n.* गत्ता gattā
care *v.i.* परवाह करना parvā karnā; *n.* देख-रेख dekh-rekh
careful *adj.* सावधान sāvdhān
careless *adj.* लापरवाह lāparavāh
carnival *n.* आनंदोत्सव ānandotsav
carry *v.t.* ढोना ḍhonā
cart *n.* ठेला ṭhelā
cartilage *n.* मुरमुरी हड्डी murmurī haḍḍī
carton *n.* गुत्ते का डिब्बा gutte kā ḍibbā
cartoon *n.* कार्टून kārṭūn
cartridge *n.* कारतूस kārtūs
carve *v.t.* उत्कीर्ण करना utkīrṇ karnā

carving *n.* नक़्क़ाशी naqqāśī
case *n.* मुकदमा muqdamā
cash *n.* पैसा paisā
cashier *n.* ख़ज़ानची qhazāncī
cask *n.* पीपा pīpā
cast *n.* साँचा sāṁcā; *v.t.* फेंकना pheṁknā
castle *n.* कोट koṭ
casual *adj.* आकस्मिक ākasmik
casualty *n.* हताहत hatāhat
cat *n.* बिल्ली billī
catalog *n.* सूची-पत्र sūcī-patr
catch *n.* पकड़ pakaṛ; *v.t.* पकड़ना pakaṛnā
cathedral *n.* महामंदिर mahāmandir
Catholic *n.* काथलिक kāthlik
Catholicism *n.* काथलिक धर्म kāthlik dharam
cattle *n.* मवेशी maveśī
cauldron *n.* कड़ाह kaṛāh
cauliflower *n.* गोभी gobhī
cause *n.* कारण kāraṇ
caution *n.* सावधानी sāvdhānī
cautious *adj.* सावधान sāvdhān
cave *n.* गुफ़ा gufā
cease *v.i.* बंद होना band honā
cedar *n.* देवदार devdār
ceiling *n.* छत chat
celebrate *v.t.* मनाना manānā
celebration *n.* समारोह samāroh
cell *n.*(*room*) कोठरी koṭharī; (*biological*) कोशिका kośikā
cellar *n.* तहखाना tahkhānā
cellular *adj.* कोशिकीय kośikīy
cement *n.* सीमेंट sīmeṇṭ
cemetery *n.* क़ब्रिस्तान qabristān

cent *n.* सैकड़ा saikaṛā
center *n.* केंद्र kendra
centimeter *n.* सेनटीमीटर senṭīmīṭar
centipede *n.* शतपद śatpad
central *adj.* केंद्रीय kendrīy
century *n.* शताब्दी śatābdī
ceramic *adj.* मिट्टी का miṭṭī kā
cereal *n.* अनाज anāj
ceremony *n.* संस्कार sanskār
certain *adj.* निश्चित niścit
certificate *n.* प्रमाण-पत्र pramāṇ-patr
certify *v.t.* प्रमाणित करना pramāṇit karnā
chain *n.* चेन cen
chair *n.* कुर्सी kursī
chalk *n.* खड़िया khaṛiyā
challenge *n.* चुनौती cunautī; *v.t.* चुनौती देना cunautī dena
chamber *n.* कमरा kamrā
champion *n.* विजेता vijetā
chance *n.* संयोग sanyog; *v.i.* मौका maukā
change *n.* टुटे पैसे ṭuṭe paise; *v.t.* परिवर्तन parivartan
changeable *adj.* परिवर्तनीय parivartanīy
changing room *n.* कपड़े बदलने का कमरा kapṛc badalne kā kamrā
channel *n.* चैनल cainal
chaotic *adj.* गड़बड़ garbar
chapel *n.* प्रार्थनालय prarthnālay
chapter *n.* अध्याय adhyāy
character *n.* चरित्र caritr
characteristic *n.* लक्षण lakṣaṇ; *adj.* विशेषता viśeṣtā
charge *n.* अभियोग abhiyog; *v.t.* अभियोग लगाना abhiyog lagānā
charity *n.* दान dān

charm *n.* आकर्षण ākarṣaṇ; *v.t.* जादू कर देना jādū kar denā
chart *n.* मानचित्र māncitra; *v.t.* मानचित्र बनाना māncitra banānā
charter *n.* शासनपत्र śāsanpatra; *v.t.* किराये पर लेना kirāye par lenā
chase *n.* पीछा pīchā; *v.t.* पीछा करना pīchā karnā
chassis *n.* चौकी caukī
chat *n.* बातचीत bātcīt; *v.i.* बातचीत करना bātcīt karnā
chatter *n.* चहक cahak; *v.i.* चहचहाना cahcahānā
cheap *adj.* सस्ता sastā
check *v.t.* जाँच करना jāṁc karnā; *n.* (*bank*) चेक cek
checkers *n.* जाँचकर्ता jāṁckartā
checkmate *n.* शह देना śah denā
cheek *n.* गाल gāl
cheese *n.* पनीर panīr
chemical *n.* रासायनिक पदार्थ rāsāynik padārth; *adj.* रासायनिक rāsāynik
chemistry *n.* रसायन विज्ञान rasāyan vigyān
cherish *v.t.* पालना pālnā
cherry *n.* चेरी cerī
chess *n.* शतरंज śatarañj
chest *n.* छाती chātī
chew *v.t.* चबाना cabānā
chick *n.* चूज़ा cūzā
chicken *n.* मुर्गी murgī
chief *n.* मुख्या mukhyā
child *n.* बच्चा baccā
childhood *n.* बचपन bacpan
childish *adj.* बचकाना backānā
chill *n.* ठंड ṭhaṇḍ; *v.t.* ठंडा करना ṭhaṇḍā karnā
chilly *adj.* ठंडा ṭhaṇḍā
chimney *n.* धुआँकश dhuāṁkaś

chin *n.* ठुड्डी ṭhuḍḍī
china, China *n.* चीन cīn
Chinese *n./adj.* चीनी cīnī
chip *n.* चिप cipp; *v.t.* काटना kāṭnā
chisel *n.* छेनी chenī; *v.t.* छेनी से काटना chenī se kāṭnā
chocolate *n.* चाकलेट cākleṭ
choice *n.* चुनाव cunāv
choir *n.* गायक-मण्डल gāyak-maṇḍal
choke *v.t.* गला घोटना galā ghoṭnā
cholesterol *n.* कोलेस्टेरोल kolesṭerol
choose *v.t.* चुनना cunnā
chop *v.t.* काटना kāṭnā
chorus *n.* गायकदल gāyakdal
christen *v.t.* नाम देना nām denā
Christian *n./adj.* ईसाई īsāī
Christianity *n.* ईसाई धर्म īsāī dharm
Christmas *n.* क्रिसमस krismas
chronic *adj.* पुराना purānā
church *n.* गिरजाघर girjāghar
cider *n.* सइडर saiḍar
cigar *n.* सिगार sigār
cigarette *n.* सिगरेट sigareṭ
cinder *n.* सिंडर sinḍar
cinema *n.* सिनेमा sinemā
cinnamon *n.* दालचीनी dālcīnī
circle *n.* गोला golā
circuit *n.* चक्कर cakkar
circulate *v.t.* प्रचारित करना pracārit karnā
circulation *n.* प्रचार pracār
circumference *n.* घेरा परिधि gherā paridhi
circumstance *n.* परिस्थिति paristhiti
circus *n.* सरकस sarkas

cite *v.t.* उद्धरण देना udhdaraṇ denā
citizen *n.* नागरिक nāgarik
city *n.* शहर śahar
civilization *n.* सभ्यता sabhyatā
claim *n.* दावा dāvā; *v.t.* दावा करना dāvā karnā
clam *n.* बडी सीपी baḍī sīpī
clap *v.t.* ताली बजाना tālī bajānā
class *n.* कक्षा kakṣā
classical *adj.* शास्त्रीय śāstrīy
classify *v.t.* वर्गीकरण करना vargīrkaraṇ karnā
classroom *n.* कक्षा kakṣā
claw *n.* पंजा pañjā
clay *n.* मिट्टी miṭṭī
clean *adj.* साफ़ sāf; *v.t.* साफ करना sāf karnā
cleaner *n.* झाडूबरदार jhaṛūbardār
clear *adj.* स्पष्ट spaṣṭ
clergy *n.* पादरी वर्ग pādrī varg
clergyman *n.* पादरी pādrī
clerk *n.* कलर्क klark
clever *adj.* चतुर catur
client *n.* ग्राहक grāhak
cliff *n.* खड़ी चट्टान khāṛī caṭṭān
climate *n.* जलवायु jalvāyu
climax *n.* पराकाष्ठा parākāṣṭā
climb *n.* चढ़ाई caṛhāī; *v.t.* चढ़ना caṛhnā; *v.i.* ऊपर जाना ūpar jānā
cling *v.i.* चिपकना cipkanā
clinic *n.* चिकित्सालय cikitsālay
clip *n.* प्याला pyālā; *v.t.* कतरना katarnā
clock *n.* घड़ी ghaṛī
close *adj.* पास pās; *v.t.* बन्द करना band karnā
closed *adj.* बन्द band

closet *n.* कोठरी koṭharī
cloth *n.* कपड़ा kapṛā
clothe *v.t.* कपड़ा पहनाना kapṛā pehnānā
clothes *n.pl.* कपड़े kapṛe
clothing *n.* कपड़ा kapṛā
cloud *n.* बादल bādal
cloudy *adj.* मेघाच्छन्न meghācchann
clown *n.* मसखरा maskharā
club *n.* कलब kalab; (*group*) सभा sabhā
clue *n.* सूत्र sūtra
cluster *n.* गुच्छा gucchā
clutch *n.* कलच kalac; *v.t.* पकड़ना pakaṛnā
coach *n.* डिब्बा ḍibbā
coal *n.* कोयला koyalā
coarse *adj.* मोटा moṭā
coast *n.* किनारा kināra
coat *n.* कोट koṭ
cobweb *n.* जाला jālā
cock *n.* मुरगा murgā
cocoa *n.* कोको koko
cod *n.* फली phalī
code *n.* गुढ़ संकेत guṛh sanket
coffee *n.* काफ़ी kāfī
coffee shop *n.* काफ़ी-गृहा kāfī gṛhā
coffin *n.* ताबूत tābūt
coil *n.* कुंडली kuṇḍalī
coin *n.* सिक्का sikkā
coincide *v.i.* एक ही समय में होना ek hī samay meṁ honā
coincidence *n.* संयोग sanyog
coincidental *adj.* आकस्मिक ākasmik
cold *n./adj.* ठण्डा ṭhaṇḍā
collaborate *v.i.* साथ काम करना sāth kām karnā

collaboration *n.* सहयोग sahayog
collar *n.* कालर kālar
collect *v.t.* इकट्ठा होना ikṭṭhā honā
collection *n.* संग्रह क्रिया saṅgrah kriyā
collective *n.* बड़ा-बूढ़ा baṛā-būṛhā
college *n.* कालेज kālej
collide *v.i.* टक्कर लगना ṭakkar lagnā
collision *n.* संघर्ष saṅgharṣ
colon *n.* कोलन kolan
colonel *n.* कर्नल karnal
colony *n.* उपनिवेश upniveś
color *n.* रंग rang
column *n.* स्तंभ stambh
comb *n.* कंघी kaṅghī; *v.t.* कंघी करना kaṅghī karnā
combination *n.* संयोग sanyog
combine *v.t.* मिलाना milānā
come *v.i.* आना ānā
comedy *n.* हास्या hāsya
comfort *n.* आराम ārām; *v.t.* दिलासा देना dilāsā denā
comfortable *adj.* आरामदायक ārāmdāyak
comic *n.* हास्यकर hāsyakar
comma *n.* अल्प विराम alp virām
command *n.* आदेश ādeś; *v.t.* आदेश देना ādeś denā
commence *v.i.* शुरू होना śurū honā
comment *n.* टिप्पणी ṭippaṇī; *v.t.* टिप्पणी करना ṭippaṇī karnā
commentary *n.* टीका भाषा ṭīkā bhāṣā
commerce *n.* वाणिज्य vāṇijy
commercial *n.* विज्ञापन vigyāpan; *adj.* व्यापारिक vyāpārik
commission *n.* आयोग āyog
committee *n.* समिति samiti
common *adj.* सामान्य sāmāny
communicate *v.t.* सूचना देना sūcnā denā

communication *n.* सूचना sūcnā
communion *n.* भाईचारा bhāīcārā
communism *n.* साम्यवाद sanyavād
communist *n./adj.* साम्यवादी sāmyavādī
compact *n.* डिब्बा ḍibbā; *adj.* सुसंहत susanhat
compact disc *n.* कोमपैक्ट डिस्क kompaikṭ ḍisk
companion *n.* साथी sāthī
companionship *n.* संगति sangati
company *n.* कंपनी kampanī
compare *v.t.* तुलना करना tulnā karnā
comparison *n.* तुलना tulnā
compartment *n.* उपखंड upkhaṇḍ
compass *n.* दिकसूचक diksūcak
compatible *adj.* संगत sangat
competence *n.* योग्यता yogyatā
competent *adj.* समर्थ samarth
competition *n.* प्रतियोगिता pratiyogitā
competitive *adj.* प्रतियोगी pratiyogī
complain *v.i.* शिकायत करना śikāyat karnā
complaint *n.* शिकायत śikāyat
complete *adj.* पूर्ण pūrṇ; *v.t.* पूरा करना pūrā karnā
complicate *v.t.* जटिल बनाना jaṭil banānā
complicated *adj.* उलझनदार uljhandār
compliment *n.* प्रशंसा praśnsā; *v.t.* अभिनन्दन करना abhinandan karnā
comply *v.i.* पालन करना pālan karnā
compose *v.t.* रचना करना racnā karnā
composition *n.* रचना racnā
compound *n.* अहाता ahātā; *adj.* यौगिक yaugik
comprehensive *adj.* व्यापक vyāpak
comprise *v.t.* समाविष्ट करना samāviṣṭ karnā
compromise *n.* समझौता samjhautā

computer *n.* कंप्यूटर kampyūṭar, पी. सी. pī. sī.
conceal *v.t.* छिपाना chipānā
conceit *n.* अहंकार ahaṅkār
concentrate *v.i.* एकत्र करना ektra karnā
concept *n.* धारणा dhārṇā
concern *n.* चिंता cintā; *v.t.* संबंध रखना sambandh rakhnā
concert *n.* संगीत समारोह sangīt samāroh
concession *n.* रियायत riyāyat
concise *adj.* संक्षिप्त saṅkṣipt
concrete *n.* कंकरीट kankarīṭ
condemn *v.t.* निन्दा करना nindā karnā
condition *n.* शर्त śart
condolence *n.* संवेदना sanvednā
condom *n.* कोण्डोम koṇḍom
condominium *n.* सहराज्य sahrājy
conduct *n.* आचरण ācaraṇ; *v.t.* संचाल्न करना sañcālan karnā
conductor *n.* संचालक sañcālak
cone *n.* शंकु śaṅku
confess *v.t.* मानना manānā
confession *n.* इकबाल ikbāl
confidence *n.* विश्वास viśvās
confirm *v.t.* पक्का करना pakkā karnā
confirmation *n.* पुष्टिकरण puṣṭikaraṇ
conflict *n.* संघर्ष saṅgharṣ
confuse *v.t.* घ्बड़ा जाना ghabaṛā jānā
confusion *n.* घबराहट ghabarāhaṭ
congratulate *v.t.* बधाई देना badhāī denā
congratulation *n.* बधाई हो badhāī ho
congress *n.* महासभा mahāsabhā
conjunction *n.* मेल mel
connect *v.t.* जोड़ना joṛnā
connection *n.* संबंध sambandh

conquer *v.t.* विजय पाना vijay pānā
conscience *n.* विवेक vivek
conscientious *adj.* ईमानदार īmāndār
conscious *adj.* जानकार jānkār
consent *n.* सहमति sahmati; *v.t.* सहमति देना sahmati denā
consequence *n.* परिणाम pariṇām
conservation *n.* संरक्षण sanrakṣaṇ
conserve *v.t.* बनाए रखना banāe rakhnā
consider *v.t.* विचार करना vicār karnā
consideration *n.* विचार vicār
consist *v.i.* ... का होना ... kā honā
consolation *n.* दिलासा dilāsā
console *v.t.* दिलसा देना dilāsā denā
consonant *n.* व्यंजन vyañjan
constant *n.* अचर acar; *adj.* स्थिर sthir
constellation *n.* तारामंडल tārāmaṇḍal
constipation *n.* क़बज़ qabz
constitute *v.t.* नियुक्त करना niyukt karnā
constitution *n.* संविधान sanvihān
consul *n.* कौंसल kauṁsal
consulate *n.* दूतावास dūtāvās
consult *v.i.* सलाह लेना salāh lenā
consultant *n.* परामर्शदाता parāmarśdātā
consume *v.t.* समाप्त करना samāpt karnā
consumer *n.* उपभोक्ता upabhoktā
consumption *n.* उपभोग upabhog
contact *n.* स्पर्श sparś; *v.t.* संपर्क sampark
contagious *adj.* छुतहा chuthā
contain *v.t.* अंतर्विष्ट करना antarviṣṭ karnā
container *n.* आधान adhān
contaminate *v.t.* दूषित करना dūṣit karnā
contend *v.i.* जूझना jūjhnā

content *n.* विषयवस्तु viṣayvastu; *adj.* संतुष्ट santuṣṭ
contest *n.* प्रतियोगिता pratiyogitā; *v.t.* मुकाबला करना mukābalā karnā
continent *n.* महाव्दिप mahādvīp
continue *v.t.* चलता रहना caltā rahnā
continuous *adj.* अविराम avirām
contraceptive *n./adj.* निरोधक nirodhak
contract *n.* अनुबंध anubandh
contrary *adj.* विरुद्ध viruddh
contrast *n.* विषमता viṣamtā
contribute *v.t.* सहयोग देना sahyog denā
contribution *n.* चंदा candā
control *n.* काबू kābū; *v.t.* अंकुश लगाना ankuś lagānā
controller *n.* नियन्त्रक niyantrak
convene *v.t.* आयोजन करना āyojan karnā
convenience *n.* सुविधा suvidhā
convent *n.* मठ maṭh
convention *n.* समझौता samjhautā
conversation *n.* बातचीत bātcīt
convert *v.t.* बदलना badalnā
convey *v.t.* ले जाना le jānā
cook *n.* ख़ानसामा qhānsāmā; *v.t.* पकाना pakānā
cooker *n.* कुकर kukar
cookie *n.* मीठा बिस्कुट mīṭhā biskuṭ
cool *adj.* शीतल śītal; *v.t.* ठण्डा करना ṭhaṇḍā karnā
cooperate *v.i.* सहयोग करना sahyog karnā
coordinate *v.t.* समकक्ष बनाना samkakṣ banānā
cop *n.* पुलिस pulis
copper *n.* ताँबा tāṁbā
copy *n.* प्रतिलिपि pratilipi; *v.t.* प्रतिलिपि करना pratilipi karnā
copyright *n.* रचनास्वत्व racnāsvatva; *v.t.* सुरक्षित रखना surkṣit rakhnā

coral *n.* प्रवाल pravāl
cordially *adv.* हार्दिक रूप से hārdik rūp se
core *n.* सार sār
cork *n.* डाट ḍāṭ
corn *n.* मक्का makkā
corner *n.* कोना konā
corporation *n.* निगम nigam
corpse *n.* लाश lāś
correct *adj.* ठीक ṭīk; *v.t.* ठीक करना ṭīk karnā
correction *n.* संशोधन sanśodhan
correspond *v.i.* पत्र-व्यवहार करना patr-vyavahār karnā
correspondence *n.* पत्र-व्यवहार patr-vyavahār
correspondent *n.* पत्र-लेखक patr-lekhak
corridor *n.* गलियारा galiyārā
corrupt *adj.* भ्रंटष्ट bhrṣṭ; *v.t.* ख़राब करना qharāb karnā
corruption *n.* भ्रष्टाचार bhraṣṭācār
cost *n.* दाम dām; *v.t.* लागत लगाना lāgat lagānā
costume *n.* पोशाक pośāk
cot *n.* खाट khāṭ
cottage *n.* कुटीर kuṭīr
cotton *n.* सूती sūtī
couch *n.* सोफ़ा sofā
cough *n.* खाँसी khāṁsī; *v.i.* खाँसना khāṁsnā
could *v.aux.* सका sakā
council *n.* परिषद pariṣad
count *n.* गणना gaṇnā; *v.t.* गिनना ginnā
counter *n.* काउंटर kāunṭar
counterfeit *adj.* नकली naklī
country *n.* देश deś
county *n.* ज़िला zilā
couple *n.* दंपती dampati
courage *n.* साहस sāhas

courageous *adj.* साहसी sāhasī
course *n.* पाठ्यक्रम pāṭyakram
court *n.* अदालत adālat
courtesy *n.* शिष्टाचार śiṣṭācār
courtyard *n.* आँगन āṁgan
cousin *n.* (*male on father's side*) चचेरा भाई cacerā bhāī; (*male on mother's side*) ममेरा भाई mamerā bhāī; (*female on father's side*) चचेरी बहन cacerī behen; (*female on mother's side*) ममेरी बहन mamerī behen.
cover *n.* ढक्कन ḍhakkan; *v.t.* ढाँपना ḍhāṁpnā
cow *n.* गाय gāy
coward *n.* कायर kāyar
crab *n.* केकड़ा kekaṛā
crack *n.* दरार darār; *v.t.* फोड़ना poṛnā
cracker *n.* कुरकुरा बिस्कुट kurkurā biskuṭ
cradle *n.* पालना pālnā
craft *n.* दस्तकारी dastkārī
craftsman *n.* शिल्पी śilpī
cramp *n.* ऐंठन aiṇṭhan
crane *n.* (*bird*) सारस sāras; (*machine*) क्रेन kren
crash *n.* धमाका dhamākā; *v.t.* धमाके से गिरना dhamāke se girnā
crate *n.* टोका ṭokarā
crawl *v.i.* रेंगना reṅgnā
crazy *adj.* पागल pāgal
cream *n.* मलाई malāī
crease *n.* चुन्नट cunnaṭ
create *v.t.* बनाना banānā
creation *n.* सृष्टि sṛṣṭi
creature *n.* प्राणी prāṇī
credit *n.* क्रेडिट kreḍit; *v.t.* जमा करना jamā karnā
creditor *n.* लेनदार lendār

creep *v.i.* रेंगना rengnā
cremation *n.* दाह संस्कार dāh sanskār
crescent *n.* दूज का चाँद dūj kā cāṁd
crest *n.* शिखा śikhā
crew *n.* कर्मीदल karmīdal
cricket *n.* (*insect*) झींगुर jhīṅgur; (*game*) क्रिकेट kriket̩
crime *n.* अपराध aprādh
criminal *n.* अपराधी aprādhī; *adj.* आपराधिक aprādhika
crisis *n.* संकट sanket̩
criticism *n.* आलोचना ālocanā
criticize *v.t.* अलोचना करना alocanā karnā
crooked *adj.* टेढ़ा t̩er̩ha
crop *n.* फ़सल fasal
cross *n.* सूली sūlī; *v.t.* विरोध करना virodh karnā
crouch *v.i.* झुकना jhuknā, दबकना dabaknā
crow *n.* कौआ kauā
crowd *n.* भीड़ bhīr̩
crowded *adj.* भरा हुआ bharā huā
crown *n.* मुकुट mukut̩
crude *adj.* कच्चा kaccā
cruel *adj.* क्रूर krūr
cruise *n.* समुद्री पर्यटन करना samudrī paryat̩han karnā
crumb *n.* टुकड़ा t̩ukar̩ā
crumble *v.i.* टुकड़े टुकड़े कर देना t̩ukar̩e t̩ukar̩e kar denā
crunch *v.t.* चबाना cabānā
crush *v.t.* कुचलना kucalnā
crust *n.* परत parat
crutch *n.* बैसाखी baisākhī
cry *n.* चीख cīkh; *v.t.* रोना ronā
crystal *n.* स्फटिक spat̩ik
cube *n.* घन ghan
cubicle *n.* कक्षक kakṣak

cuff *n.* थप्पड़ thappaṛ
cultivate *v.t.* जुताई करना jutāī karnā
cultivation *n.* खेती khetī
cultural *adj.* सांस्कृतिक sanskr̥tik
culture *n.* संस्कृति sanskr̥ti
cup *n.* प्याला pyālā
cupboard *n.* आलमारी ālmārī
curb *n.* प्रतिबंध pratibandh; *v.t.* दबाना dabānā
cure *n.* रोगमुक्ति rogmukti; *v.t.* स्वस्थ करना svasth karnā
curious *adj.* उत्सुक utsuk
curl *n.* कुंडल kuṇḍal; *v.t.* घुँघराला बनाना ghuṁgharālā banānā
curly *adj.* घुँघराला ghuṁgharālā
currency *n.* सिक्का sikkā
current *adj* चालू cālū
curse *n.* शाप śāp; *v.t.* शाप देना śāp denā
curtain *n.* परदा pardā
curve *n.* वक्रता vakratā
cushion *n.* गद्दी gaddī
custard *n.* कस्टर्ड kasṭarḍ
custom *n.* रिवाज़ rivāz
customer *n.* ग्राहक grāhak
cut *n.* घाव ghāv; *v.t.* काटना kāṭnā
cycle *n.* साइकिल sāikil; *v.t.* साइकिल चलाना sāikil calānā
cylinder *n.* बेलन belan
cynical *adj.* मानवद्वेषी mānavadveṣī

D

dad(dy) *n.* पिता pita, बाप bāp
daily *adj.* दैनिक dainik
dairy *n.* डेरी ḍerī; *adj.* दूध से बना dūdh de banā

dam *n.* बाँध bāṁdh
damage *n.* क्षति kṣati; *v.t.* बिगड़ा जाना bigaṛā jānā
damn *v.t.* निंदा करना nindā karnā
damp *adj.* नम nam
dampen *v.t.* नम करना nam karnā
dance *n.* नाच nāc; *v.i.* नाचना nācnā
danger *n.* ख़तरा qhatarā
dangerous *adj.* ख़तरनाक qhatarnāk
dare *n.* साहस sāhas; *v.i.* साहस करना sāhas karnā
daring *adj.* साहसी sāhasī
dark *adj.* अँधेरा aṁdherā
darken *v.t.* अँधकारमय बनाना aṁdhkārmay banānā
darkness *n.* अँधेरा aṁdherā
darn *v.t.* रफ़ू करना rafū karnā
dash *n.* टक्कर ṭakkar
data *n.pl.* आधार-सामग्री ādhār-sāmagrī
date *n.* (*calendar*) तारीख़ tārīqh; (*fruit*) खजूर khajūrā
daughter *n.* बेटी beṭī
daughter-in-law *n.* पुत्र वधू putra vadhū
dawn *n.* उषा-काल uṣā-kāl
day *n.* दिन din
dead *adj.* मुर्दा murdā
deaf *adj.* बहरा baharā
deal *n.* सौदा saudā; *v.t.* बाँटना bāṁṭnā
dealer *n.* व्यापारी vyāpārī
dear *adj.* प्रिय priya
death *n.* मृत्यू mṛtyū
debate *n.* बहस bahas; *v.t.* बहस करना bahas karnā
debit *n.* नामे nāme; *v.t.* नामे लिखना nāme likhnā
debt *n.* कर्ज़ karz
decaffeinated *adj.* कैफ़ीन के बिना kaifīn ke binā
decay *n.* सड़न saṛan; *v.i.* सड़ना saṛnā

deceit *n.* धोखा dhokhā
deceive *v.t.* धोखा देना dhokhā denā
December *n.* दिसेम्बर disembar
decent *adj.* उपयुक्त upyukt
deception *n.* धोखा dhokhā
decide *v.t.* फ़ैसला करना faislā karnā; *v.i.* निश्चय कर लेना niścay kar lenā
decimal *adj.* दशमिक daśmik
decision *n.* फ़ैसला faisalā
decisive *adj.* निर्णायक nirnāyak
deck *n.* डेक ḍek
declaration *n.* घोषणा ghoṣṇā
declare *v.t.* घोषित करना ghoṣit karnā
decline *v.i.* झुकना jhuknā
decorate *v.t.* सजाना sajānā
decoration *n.* सजावट sajāvaṭ
decrease *v.t.* घटाना ghaṭānā; *v.i.* घटना ghaṭnā
dedicate *v.t.* समर्पण करना samarpaṇ karnā
dedication *n.* समर्पण samarpaṇ
deduction *n.* घटाव ghaṭāv
deed *n.* दस्तावेज़ sastāvez, कार्य kāry
deem *v.t.* समझना samajhnā
deep *adj.* गहरा gaharā
deer *n.* हिरन hiran
default *n.* चूक cūk
defeat *n.* हार hār; *v.t.* हराना hirānā
defect *n.* त्रुटि truṭi
defend *v.t.* रक्षा करना rakṣā karnā
defendant *n.* प्रतिवादी prativādī
defense *n.* सुरक्षा sukṣā
defer *v.t.* स्थगित करना sthagit karnā
define *v.t.* परि भाषा देना pari bhāṣā denā

definite *adj.* निश्चित niścit
definition *n.* परिभाषा paribhāṣā
definitive *adj.* निश्चायक niścāyak
deflate *v.t.* हवा निकलना havā nikālnā
defy *v.t.* अवज्ञा करना avagyā karnā
degree *n.* उपाधि upīdh
dehydrated *adj.* निर्जलित nirjalit
delay *n.* देर der; *v.t.* देरी करना derī karnā
delete *v.t.* काटना kāṭnā
deliberate *adj.* जानबूझकर jānbūjhkar
delicacy *n.* कोमलता komalā
delicate *adj.* कोमल komal
delight *n.* हर्ष harṣ
deliver *v.t.* पहुँचाना pahuṁcānā
delivery *n.* प्रसव prasav
demand *n.* माँग māṁg; *v.t.* माँगना māṁgnā
democracy *n.* लोकतंत्र loktantra
democratic *adj.* लोकतांत्रिक loktāntrik
demonstrate *v.t.* प्रदर्शन pradarśan
demonstration *n.* प्रदर्शन pradarśan
den *n.* माँद māṁd
dense *adj.* सघन saghan
density *n.* सघनता saghantā
dent *n.* गड्ढा gaḍḍhā; *v.t.* पिचका देना pickā denā
dental *adj.* दाँत का dāṁt kā
dentist *n.* दन्तचिकित्सक dantcikitsak
deny *v.t.* अस्वीकार करना asvīkār karnā
deodorant *n.* डियोडोरैंट ḍiyoḍoraiṇṭ
depart *v.i.* रवाना होना ravānā honā
department *n.* विभाग vibhāg
departure *n.* प्रस्थान prastthān
depend *v.i.* ... पर निर्भर होना ... par nirbhar honā

dependent *n.* आश्रित āśrit; *adj* निर्भर nirbhar
depict *v.t.* चित्रण करना citraṇ karnā
deport *v.t.* निर्वासित करना nirvāsit karnā
depot *n.* डिपो ḍipo
depress *v.t.* (*press*) दबाना dabānā; (*sadden*) उदास करना udās karnā
depressed *adj.* उदास udās, खिन्न khinn
depression *n.* खिन्नता khinntā, उदासी udāsī
deprive *v.t.* वंचित करना vañcit karnā
depth *n.* गहराई gaharāī
deputy *n.* उपायुक्त upāyukt
derive *v.t.* प्राप्त करना prāpt karnā
descend *v.i.* नीचे आना nīce ānā
descent *n.* उतार utār
describe *v.t.* वर्णन करना varṇan karnā
description *n.* वर्णन varṇan
desert *n.* रेगिस्तान registān; *v.t.* त्याग देना tyāg denā
deserve *v.t.* योग्य होना yogya honā
design *n.* परिकल्पना parikalpnā; *v.t.* परिकल्पना करना parikalpnā karnā
designate *v.t.* नमुना बनाना namunā banānā
designer *n.* डिज़ाइन बनाने वाला ḍizāin banāne vālā
desirable *adj.* वांछनीय vāñcnīy
desire *n.* इच्छा icchā; *v.t.* चाहना cāhanā
desk *n.* डेस्क ḍesk
despair *n.* निराशा nirāśā; *v.i.* निराश होना nirāś honā
dessert *n.* डिज़र्ट ḍizarṭ
destiny *n.* नियति niyati
destroy *v.t.* नष्ट करना naṣṭ karnā
destruction *n.* विनाश vināś
detach *v.t.* अलग करना alag karnā
detain *v.t.* बन्दी बनाना bandī banānā

detect *v.t.* पता लगाना patā lagānā
detection *n.* खोज khoj
detective *n.* गुप्तचर guptcar
detergent *n.* प्रक्षालक चूरा prakṣālak cūrā
determination *n.* संकल्प saṅkalp
determine *v.t.* निर्धारित करना nirdhārit karnā
determined *adj.* निश्चित niścit
develop *v.t.* विकसित करना viksit karnā
development *n.* विकास vikās
deviation *n.* विचलन vicalan
device *n.* युक्ति yukti
devil *n.* शैतान śaitān
devise *v.t.* सोच निकालना soc nikālnā
devout *adj.* भक्त bhakt
dew *n.* ओस os
diabetes *n.* मधुमेह madhumeh
diabetic *adj./n.* मधुमेही madhumehī
diagnosis *n.* निदान nidān
diagonal *adj.* विकर्ण vikarṇ
dial *n.* डायल ḍẽyal; *v.t.* टेलीफ़ोन करना ṭelīfon karnā
dialect *n.* बोली bolī
dialogue *n.* संवाद sanvād
diameter *n.* व्यास vyās
diamond *n.* हीरा hīrā
diaper *n.* पोतड़ा कलोट potaṛā kaloṭ
diary *n.* डायरी ḍāyarī
diarrhea *n.* दस्त dast
dictate *v.t.* लिखाना likhānā
dictation *n.* श्रुतलेख śrutlekh
dictator *n.* एकाधिनायक ekādhināyak
dictionary *n.* शब्दकोश śabdkoś
die *n.* पांस pāns; *v.i.* मरना marnā

diesel *n.* डीज़ल ḍizal
diet *n.* आहार āhār
differ *v.i.* अलग होना alag honā
difference *n.* फ़र्क fark
different *adj.* अलग alag
difficult *adj.* मुश्किल muśkil
difficulty *n.* कठिनाई kaṭhināī
dig *v.t.* खोदना khodnā
digest *v.t.* पचाना pacānā
digestion *n.* पाचन pācan
dignified *adj.* प्रतिष्ठित pratiṣṭhit
dignity *n.* प्रतिष्ठा pratiṣṭhā
diligent *adj.* मेहनती mehanatī
dim *adj.* धुँधला dhundhlā; *v.t.* धुँधला करना dhundhlā karnā
dimension *n.* आयाम āyām
diminish *v.t.* कम करना kam karnā
dine *v.i.* भोजन करना bhojan karnā
dining room *n.* भोजन कक्ष bhojan kakṣ
dinner *n.* रात का खाना rāt kā khānā
dip *v.t.* डुबाना ḍubānā
diplomat *n.* राजनयिक rājnayik
diplomatic *adj.* राजनयिक rājnayik
direct *adj.* सीधा sīdhā; *adv.* व्यक्तिगत रूप से vyaktigat rūp se; *v.t.* संबोधित करना sambodhit karnā
direction *n.* दिशा diśā
director *n.* निर्देशक nirdeśak
directory *n.* निदेशिका nideśikā
dirt *n.* धूल dhūl
dirty *adj.* गंदा gandā
disagree *v.i.* असहमत होना asahamat honā
disagreement *n.* असहमति asahamati
disappear *v.i.* गायब हो जाना gāyab ho jānā

disappoint *v.t.* हताश करना hatāś karnā
disappointment *n.* हताशा hatāśā
disaster *n.* विनाश vināś
discipline *n.* अनुशासन anuśāsan
discount *n.* छूट chūṭ
discover *v.t.* खोज करना khoj karnā
discovery *n.* खोज khoj
discreet *adj.* विवेकी vivekī
discriminate *v.i.* भेद करना bhed karnā
discuss *v.t.* विचार करना vicār karnā
discussion *n.* विचार-विमर्श vicār-vimarś
disease *n.* रोग rog
disgrace *n.* बदनामी badnāmī
disguise *n.* वेष veś
disgust *n.* खीझ khījh
disgusting *adj.* घृणा योग्य gṛnā yogya
dish *n.* थाली thālī
dishonest *adj.* बेईमान beīmān
dishonesty *n.* बेईमानी beīmānī
disinfect *v.t.* रोगाणु नष्ट करना rogāṇu naṣṭ karnā
disinfectant *n./adj.* रोगाणुनाशक rogāṇunāśak
disk *n.* डिस्क ḍisk
dislike *v.t.* नापसंद करना nāpasand karnā
dismiss *v.t.* पदच्युत करना padcyut karnā
disobey *v.t.* आज्ञा भंग करना āgyā bhaṅg karnā
display *n.* प्रदर्शन pradarśan; *v.t.* प्रदर्शित करना pradarśit karnā
displease *v.t.* अप्रसन्न करना aprasann karnā
dispose *v.i.* क्रम से रखना kram se rakhnā
dispute *n.* विवाद vivād
disregard *n.* अनादर anādar; *v.t.* उपेक्षा करना upekṣā karnā
distance *n.* दूरी dūrī

distant *adj.* दूर का dūr kā
distill *v.t.* चुआना cuānā
distinct *adj.* भिन्न bhinn
distinction *n.* अंतर antar
distinguish *v.t.* भेद करना bhed karnā
distort *v.t.* विकृत करना vikṛt karnā
distract *v.t.* ध्यान भंग करना dhyān bhaṅg karnā
distress *n.* विपत्ति vipatti
distribute *v.t.* वितरण करना vitaraṇ karnā
distribution *n.* वितरण vitaraṇ
district *n.* इलाका ilākā
distrust *n.* अविश्वास aviśvās; *v.t.* अविश्वास करना aviśvās karnā
disturb *v.t.* अंदोलित करना andolit karnā
ditch *n.* खाई khāī
dive *n.* ग़ोता qgotā; *v.t.* ग़ोता लगाना qgotā lagānā
diverse *adj.* भिन्न-भिन्न bhinn-bhinn
divide *v.t.* भाग देना bhāg denā
diving *n.* ग़ोताख़ोरी qgotāqhārī
division *n.* विभाजन vibhājan
divorce *n.* तलाक़ talāq; *v.t.* तलाक़ देना talāq denā; *v.i.* तलाक़ होना talāq honā
divorced *adj.* तलाकशुदा talākśudā
dizziness *n.* चक्कर cakkar
dizzy *adj.* चक्कर से आक्रांत cakkar se ākrant
do *v.t.* करना karnā
dock *n.* पोतघाट potghāṭ; *v.i.* बंदरगाह में ले आना bandargāh meṁ le ānā
doctor *n.* डॉक्टर ḍākṭar
dog *n.* कुत्ता kuttā
doll *n.* गुड़िया guṛiyā
dollar *n.* डालर ḍēlar

dolphin *n.* सूस sūs
domain *n.* रियासत siyāsat
dome *n.* गुम्बद gumbad
domestic *adj.* घरेलू gharelū; (*animal*) पालतू pāltū; (*geographical*) देशीय deśīy
dominate *v.t.* शासन करना śāsan karnā
domination *n.* शासन śāsan
donate *v.t.* दान में देना dān meṁ denā
donation *n.* दान dān
donkey *n.* गधा gadhā
door *n.* दरवाज़ा darvāzā
dose *n.* मात्रा mātrā
dot *n.* बिन्दु bindu
double *adj.* दुगुना dugunā
doubt *n.* संदेह sandeh; *v.t.* संदेह करना sandeh karnā
doubtful *adj.* संदेहजनक sandehajanak
dough *n.* लोई loī
dove *n.* पड़की paṛkī
down *n.* कोमल रोम komal rom; *adv.* नीचे nīce
dowry *n.* दहेज dahej
dozen *n.* दर्जन darjan
drag *v.t.* खींचना khīṁcnā
dragon *n.* परदार साँप pardār sāṁp
drain *n.* नाली nālī; *v.t.* बहा ले जाना bahā le jānā
drama *n.* नाटक nāṭak
draw *v.t* खींचना khīṁcnā
drawing *n.* आरेखण ārekhaṇ
dread *n.* त्रास trās; *v.t.* डरना ḍarnā
dream *n.* सपना sapnā; *v.i.* सपना देखना sapnā dekhnā
dreary *adj.* निरानन्द nirānand
dress *n.* पहनावा pahnāvā; *v.t.* कपड़े पहनना kapṛe pahnnā
drift *n.* बहाव bahāv; *v.i.* बह जाना bah jānā

drill *n.* बरमा barmā; *v.t.* बरमे से छेद करना barme se ched karnā; (*soldiers*) कवायद करना kavāyad karnā
drink *n.* पेय pey; *v.t.* पीना pīnā
drive *v.t.* चलाना calānā
driver *n.* ड्राईवर drāīvar
drizzle *v.i.* बूँदाबाँदी होना būṁdāvāṁdī honā
drop *v.t.* गिराना girānā
drown *v.t.* डुबाना ḍubānā; *v.i.* डूब मरना ḍūb marnā
drugs *n.* दवाई davāī
drum *n.* ढोल ḍhol
drunk *adj.* नशे में चूर naśe meṁ cūr
dry *v.t.* सूखना sūkhnā; *adj.* सूखा sūkhā
dry cleaner *n.* ड्राई कलीनिंग वाला ḍrāī kalīning vālā
dryer *n.* सुखाने वाला यंत्र sukhāne vālā yantra
duck *n.* बतख़ bataqh
due *adj.* देय dey
dull *adj.* मन्दबुद्धि mandbuddhi
dumb *adj.* गूँगा gūṁgā
dung *n.* गोबर gobar
during *prep.* … के दौरान … ke daurān
dusk *n.* झुटपुटा jhuṭpuṭā
dust *n.* धूल dhūl; *v.t.* साफ़ करना sāf karnā
duster *n.* झाड़न jhāṛān
dusty *adj.* धूल-धूसरित dhūl-dhūsrit
duty *n.* फ़र्ज़ farz
dwell *v.i.* रहना rahnā
dwelling *n.* निवास nivās
dye *n.* रंग rang; *v.t.* रंगना rangnā
dying *adj.* मरण maraṇ
dynamic *adj.* गतिशील gatiśīl

E

each *adj./adv.* हर एक har ek
eager *adj.* उत्सुक utsuk
eagle *n.* गरुड़ garuṛ
ear *n.* कान kān
earache *n.* कान का दर्द kān kā dard
early *adj.* समय से पहले samay se pahale; *adv.* प्रताह कलीन pratāh kalīn
earn *v.i.* कमाना kamānā
earnest *adj.* सच्चा saccā
earnings *n.* कमाई kamāī
earphone *n.* आकर्णक ākarṇak
earring *n.* कर्णफूल karṇphūl
earth *n.* धरती dhartī
earthquake *n.* भूकंप bhūkamp
east *adj.* पूर्व pūrv; *adv.* पूर्वी pūrvi
eastern *adj.* पूर्वी pūrvi
easy *adj.* आसान āsān
eat *v.t.* खाना khānā
eccentric *adj.* उत्केन्द्रक utkendrak
echo *n.* प्रतिध्वनि pratidhvani
economical *adj.* किफ़ायती kifāyatī
economics *n.* अर्थशास्त्र arthśāstra
economist *n.* अर्थशास्त्री arthśāstrī
economy *n.* अर्थव्यवस्था arthvyavasthā
edge *n.* किनारा kinārā
edible *adj.* खाने लायक khāne lāyak
edit *v.t.* संपादन करना sampādan karnā
edition *n.* संस्करण sanskaraṇ
educate *v.t.* शिक्षा देना śikṣā denā
education *n.* शिक्षा śikṣā

educational *adj.* शिक्षा-संबन्ध śikṣā-sambandh
eel *n.* सर्पमीन sarpmīn
effect *n.* परिणाम pariṇām
effective *adj.* प्रभावी prabhāvī
effort *n.* प्रयास prayās
egg *n.* अण्डा aṇḍā
eggplant *n.* बैंगन baingan
Egypt *n.* मिसर misar
Egyptian *n./adj.* मिस्त्री mistrī
eighteen *num.* अठारह aṭhārah
eighteenth *adj.* अठारहवाँ aṭhārahvāṁ
eighth *adj.* आठवाँ āṭhvāṁ
eighty *num.* अस्सी assī
either *conj.* दोनो में से एक dono meṁ se ek
elastic *n.* इलास्टिक ilāsṭik; *adj.* लचीला lacīlā
elbow *n.* कुहनी kuhnī
elderly *adj.* प्रौढ़ prauṛh
elect *v.t.* चुनना cunnā
election *n.* चुनाव cunāv
electric *adj.* बिजली की bijalī kī
electricity *n.* बिजली bijalī
electronic *adj.* इलेक्ट्रॉनिक ilekṭrānik
elegant *adj.* मनोरम manoram
element *n.* तत्त्व tattva
elementary *n.* पहला pahalā; *adj.* प्राथमिक prāthmik
elephant *n.* हाथी hāthī
elevator *n.* लिफ़्ट lifṭ
eleven *num.* ग्यारह gyārah
eleventh *adj.* ग्यारहवाँ gyārahvāṁ
eliminate *v.t.* हटा देना haṭā denā
else *adj.* और aur; *adv.* और क्या aur kyā
embargo *n.* घाटबन्दी ghāṭabandī

embark *v.t.* जहाज़ पर चढ़ना jahāz par caṛhnā
embarrass *v.t.* घबड़ाना ghabaṛānā
embassy *n.* दूतावास dūtāvās
emblem *n.* प्रतीक pratīk
embrace *n.* अलिंगन alingan; *v.t.* गले लगाना gale lagānā
embroider *v.t.* बेलबूटे काढ़ना belbūṭe kāṛhnā
embroidery *n.* कसीदाकारी kasīdākārī
emerge *v.i.* निकल आना nikal ānā
emergency *n.* आपातकाल āpātkāl
emigrant *n.* प्रवासी pravāsī
emigrate *v.i.* परदेस जाना pardes jānā
emigration *n.* प्रवास pravās
emit *v.t.* उत्सर्जन करना utsarjan karnā
emotion *n.* मनोभाव manobhāv
emperor *n.* महाराजधिराजा mahārājādhirājā
emphasis *n.* सम्राट samrāṭ
emphasize *v.t.* बल देना bal denā
empire *n.* साम्राज्य sāmrājya
employ *v.t.* काम पर लगाना kām par lagānā, नियुक्त करना niyukt karnā
employee *n.* कर्मवारी karmvārī
employer *n.* नियोजक niyojak; मालिक mālik
employment *n.* रोज़गार rozgār
empty *adj.* ख़ाली qhālī; *v.t.* ख़ाली करना qhālī karnā
enable *v.t.* योग्य बनाना yogya banānā
enamel *n.* तामचीनी tāmcīnī
enclose *v.t.* बदं करना band karnā
enclosure *n.* घेरा gherā
encounter *n.* भिड़ंत bhīrant; *v.t.* सामना करना sāmnā karnā
encourage *v.t.* बढ़ावा देना baṛāvā denā
encyclopedia *n.* विश्वकोश viśvakoś
end *n.* अंत ant; *v.i.* अंत करना ant karnā

ending *n.* अंत ant
endorse *v.t.* पृष्ठांकन करना pr̥ṣṭhāṅkan karnā
endurance *n.* सहनशीलता sahanśīltā
endure *v.i.* सहना sahnā
enemy *n.* दुश्मन duśman
energetic *adj.* बल bal
energy *n.* शाक्ति śākti
engagement *n.* सगाई sagāī
engagement ring *n.* सगाई की अँगूठी sagāī kī aṁgūṭhī
engine *n.* इंजन injan
engineer *n.* इंजीनियर injīniyar
English *n./adj.* अँग्रेज़ी aṁgrezī
engrave *v.t.* खोदना khodnā
engraving *n.* नक़्क़ाशी naqqāśī
enjoy *v.t.* रस लेना ras lenā
enjoyment *n.* सुख sukh
enlarge *v.t.* बड़ा करना baṛā karnā
enormous *adj.* विशाल viśāl
enough *adj./adv.* काफ़ी kāfī
enquire *v.t.* जाँच करना jāṁc karnā
ensure *v.t.* सुरक्षित कर देना surakṣit kar denā
enter *v.i.* प्रवेश करना praveś karnā
enterprise *n.* उद्यम udyam
entertain *v.t.* मनोरंजन करना manoranjan karnā
entertainer *n.* नर्तक nartak
entertaining *adj.* मनोरंजक manorañjak
entertainment *n.* मनोरंजन manorañjan
enthusiasm *n.* उत्साह utsāh
entire *adj.* संपूर्ण sampūrṇ
entrance *n.* प्रवेश praveś
entrust *v.t.* सौंपना saumpnā
entry *n.* प्रवेश praveś

envelop *v.t.* ढक लेना ḍhak lenā
envelope *n.* लिफ़ाफ़ा lifāfā
envious *adj.* ईर्ष्यालू īṣyaryālū
environment *n.* वातावरण vātāvaraṇ
environs *n.* पास-पड़ोस pās-paros
envy *n.* ईर्ष्या īṣyaryā; *v.t.* ईर्ष्या करना īṣyaryā karnā
epidemic *n.* महामारी mahāmārī; *adj.* सक्रामक sakrāmak
epilepsy *n.* मिरगी miragī
equal *adj.* समान samān; *v.t.* समान बनाना samān banānā
equality *n.* बराबरी barābarī
equator *n.* विषुक्त रेखा viṣukt rekhā
equip *v.t.* लैस करना lais karnā
equipment *n.* साज़-सामान sāz-sāmān
equity *n.* निष्पक्षता niṣpakṣatā
equivalent *adj.* बराबर barābar
era *n.* युग yug
erase *v.t.* मिटाना miṭānā
eraser *n.* रबर rabar
erect *adj.* सीधा sīdhā; *v.t.* निर्माण करना nirmāṇ karnā
errand *n.* सदेश sandeś
error *n.* गलती galtī
escalator *n.* स्वचालित svacālit
escape *n.* पलायन palāpan; *v.t.* पलायन करना palāpan karnā
escort *n.* रक्षक rakṣak; *v.t.* रक्षार्थ साथ जाना rakṣārth sāth jānā
especially *adv.* ख़ास तौर से qhās taur se
essay *n.* निबंध nibandh
essence *n.* सार sār
essential *adj.* आवश्यक āvaśyak
establish *v.t.* स्थापित करना sthāpit karnā
estate *n.* जायदाद jāydād
estimate *n.* अंदाज़ andāz; *v.t.* अनुमान करना anumān karnā; *v.i.* अनुमान लगाना anumān lagānā

etcetera *n.* वग़ैरह vaqgairah
eternal *adj.* नित्य nitya
ethical *adj.* नीतिपरक nītiparak
Europe *n.* यूरोप yūrop
European *n.* यूरोपियन yūropiyan; *adj.* यूरोपीय yūropiy
evacuate *v.t.* खाली कराना khālī karānā
evacuation *n.* निकास nikās
evaluation *n.* मूल्यांकन mūlyāṅkan
eve *n.* पूर्व दिन pūrv din
even *adj.* बराबर barābar; *v.t.* बराबर करना barābar karnā; *adv.* भी bhī
evening *n.* शाम śām
event *n.* घटना ghaṭnā
ever *adv.* कभी kabhī
every *adj.* हर har
everybody *pron.* हर कोई har koī
everyone *pron.* हर एक har ek
everything *pron.* सब कुछ sab kuch
everywhere *adv.* सब जगह sab jagah
evidence *n.* गवाही gavāhī
evident *adj.* स्पष्ट spaṣṭ
evil *n.* बुराई burāī; *adj.* बुरी नज़र burī nazar
exact *adj.* ठीक ṭhīk
exaggerate *v.t.* अतिरंजना करना atiranjanā karnā
exaggeration *n.* अतिश्योक्ति atiśyokti
examination *n.* परीक्षा parīkṣā
examine *v.t.* जाँच करना jāṁc karnā
example *n.* उदाहरण udāharaṇ
excavation *n.* खोदाई khodāī
exceed *v.t.* बढ़ जाना baṛh jānā
excellent *adj.* बढ़िया baṛhiyā
except *prep.* ... को छोड़कर ... ko choṛkar

exception *n.* अपवाद apvād
excess *n.* अधिकता adhiktā
exchange *n.* विनिमय vinimay; *v.t.* विनिमय करना vinimay karnā
excite *v.t.* उत्तेजित करना uttejit karnā
excitement *n.* उत्तेजना uttejnā
exclaim *v.t.* चिल्ला उठना cillā uṭhnā
exclude *v.t.* निकालना nikālnā
excuse *n.* माफ़ी māfī; *v.t.* माफ़ करना māf karnā
execute *v.t.* पूरा करना pūrā karnā
executive *n.* निष्पादक niṣpādak
exempt *v.t.* छूट देना chūṭ denā
exemption *n.* छूट chūṭ
exhale *v.i.* श्वास निकालना śvās nikālnā
exhaust *n.* निकासनली nikāsnalī; *v.t.* थका देना thakā denā
exhibit *n.* प्रदर्शन pradarśan; *v.t.* प्रदर्शित करना pradarśiṭ karnā
exile *n.* निर्वासन nivarsan; *v.t.* निर्वासित करना nivarsit karnā
exist *v.i.* अस्तित्व रखना astitva rakhnā
existence *n.* अस्तितव astitva
expand *v.t.* फैलाना phailānā
expansion *n.* फैलाव phailāv
expect *v.t.* आशा करना āśā karnā
expectation *n.* आशा āśā
expel *v.t.* निकाल देना nikāl denā
expense *n.* ख़र्च qharc
expensive *adj.* महंगा mahangā
experience *n.* अनुभव anubhav; *v.t.* अनुभव करना anubhav karnā
expert *n.* विशेषज्ञ viśeṣagya
explain *v.t.* स्पष्ट करना spaṣṭ karnā
explanation *n.* व्याख्या vyākhyā
explode *v.t.* उठा देना uṭhā denā; *v.i.* फूटना phūṭnā

explore *v.t.* छान-बीन करना chān-bīn karnā
explosion *n.* धड़ाका dhaṛākā
export *n.* निर्यात niryāt; *v.t.* निर्यात करना niryāt karnā
expose *v.t.* खोलना kholnā
exposure *n.* दिखावा dikhāvā
express *adj.* तेज़ tez; *v.t.* प्रकट करना prakaṭ karnā
extend *v.t.* तानना tānnā
extension *n.* विस्तार vistār
external *adj.* बाहरी bāharī
extinguish *v.t.* बुझाना bujhānā
extra *n.* अतिरिक्त atirikt; *adj.* अति ati
extract *n.* निचोड़ nicoṛ; *v.t.* निचोड़ना nicoṛnā
extradite *v.t.* प्रत्यर्पित करना pratyarptit karnā
extraordinary *adj.* निराला nirālā
extreme *adj.* परम param
eye *n.* आँख āṁkh
eyeball *n.* कोया koyā
eyebrow *n.* भौंह bhauṁh
eyelash *n.* बरौनी baraunī
eyelid *n.* पलक palak

F

fabric *n.* कपड़ा kapṛā
facade *n.* मुहरा muharā
face *n.* मुँह muṁh
facial *adj.* चेहरे का … cehare kā …
facilitate *v.t.* सरल बनाना saral banānā
facility *n.* सुविधा suvidhā
fact *n.* सच्चाई saccāī
factory *n.* फैक्टरी faikṭarī

faculty *n.* गुण guṇ
fad *n.* सनक sanak
fade *v.* फीका पड़ना phīkā paṛnā
fail *v.i.* कम होना kam honā; *v.t.* चूकना cūknā
failure *n.* असफलता asphaltā
faint *v.i.* बेहोश हो जाना behoś ho jānā; *adj.* बेहोश behoś
fair *n.* मेला melā; *adj.* उचित ucit
fairy *n.* परी parī
faith *n.* विश्वास viśvās
faithful *adj.* विश्वसनीय viśvāsnīy
fall *n.* (*season*) पतझड़ patjhaṛ; *v.i.* गिरना girnā
false *adj.* झूठा jhūṭhā
falsify *v.t.* जाल करना jāl karnā
fame *n.* नाम nām
familiar *adj.* परिचित paricit
family *n.* परिवार parivār
famous *adj.* प्रसिद्ध prasiddh
fan *n.* पंखा paṅkhā
fancy *adj.* रंग-विरंगा rang-virangā
far *adj.* दूर dūr; *adv.* अधिक adhik
faraway *adj.* दूर dūr
fare *n.* किराया kirāyā
farm *n.* खेत khet
farmer *n.* किसान kisān
farsighted *adj.* दूरदर्शी dūrdarśī
fascinate *v.t.* मोह लेना moh lenā
fascination *n.* सम्मोहन sammohan
fashion *n.* फैशन phaiśan
fashionable *adj.* शौकीन śaukīn
fast *n.* व्रत vrat; *adj.* तेज़ tez
fasten *v.t.* बाँधना bāṁdhnā
fat *adj.* मोटा moṭā

fatal *adj.* घातक ghātak
father *n.* पिताजी pitājī
father-in-law *n.* ससुर sasur
fatty *adj.* चर्बीदार carbīdār
faucet *n.* टोंटी ṭoṁṭī
fault *n.* ग़लती qgaltī
faulty *adj.* ख़राब qharāb
favor *n.* अनुग्रह anugrah
favorite *adj.* मनपंसद manpasand
fear *n.* डर ḍar; *v.t.* डरना ḍarnā
feasible *adj.* सहज sahaj
feast *n.* भोज bhoj
feather *n.* पंख paṅkha
February *n.* फ़रवरी farvarī
fee *n.* शुल्क śulk
feed *n.* चारा cārā; *v.t.* खिलाना khilānā
feel *n.* स्पर्श sparś; *v.t.* स्पर्श करना sparś karnā; *v.i.* स्पर्श लगना sparś lagnā
feeling *n.* भावना bhāvnā
fellow *n.* साथी sāthī
female *n.* मादा mādā; *adj.* स्त्री का strī kā
feminine *adj.* ज़नाना zanānā
fence *n.* बाड़ bāṛ
ferment *v.t.* खमीर उठना khamīr uṭhnā
ferry *n.* नाव nāv
fertile *adj.* उपजाऊ upjāū
festival *n.* उत्सव utsav
fever *n.* बुख़ार buqhār
few *n.* कुछ kuch
fiber *n.* तंतु tantu
fiction *n.* कल्पना kalpnā
fiddle *n.* बेला belā

field *n.* खेत khet
fierce *adj.* खूँखार khūṁkhār
fifteen *num.* पंद्रह pandrah
fifteenth *adj.* पंद्रहवाँ pandrahvāṁ
fifth *adj.* पंचम pañcam
fiftieth *adj.* पचासवाँ pacāsvāṁ
fifty *num.* पचास pacās
fig *n.* अंजीर añjīr
fight *v.t.* लड़ना laṛnā
figure *n.* आकार ākār; चित्र citra; *v.t.* हिसाब लगाना hisāb lagānā; *v.i.* सामने आना sāmne ānā
file *n.* रेती retī; *v.t.* रेती से रेतकर काटना retī se retkar kāṭnā
fill *v.t.* भरना bharnā
filling *n.* भराई bharāī
film *n.* फ़िल्म film
filter *n.* फ़िल्टर filṭar
filthy *adj.* मैला mailā
final *adj.* अंतिम antim
finally *adj.* अंत में ant meṁ
finance *n.* वित्त vitt
financial *adj.* आर्थिक ārthik
find *n.* खोज khoj; *v.t.* पाना pānā
fine *n.* जुर्माना jurmānā; *adj* बढ़िया baṛhiyā
finger *n.* अँगुली aṁgulī
fingerprint *n.* अँगुली की छाप aṁgulī kī chāp
finish *n.* अंत ant; परिष्कार pariṣkār; *v.t.* परिष्कार करना pariṣkār karnā
fire *n.* आग āg; *v.t.* दागना dāgnā
firm *n.* फ़र्म farm; *adj.* निश्चल niścal; पक्का pakkā
first *adj.* पहला pahalā; *adv.* पहले से pahale se
fish *n.* मछली machlī; *v.t.* मछली पकड़ना machlī pakaṛnā
fisherman *n.* मछुआ machuā

fishing *n.* मछली पकड़ना machlī pakaṛnā
fist *n.* मुक्का mukkā
fit *n.* (*cut, style*) काट kāṭ; (*attack, illness*) दौरा daurā; *adj.* उपयुक्त upyuktt; *v.t.* ठीक आना ṭhīk ānā; *v.i.* ठीक होना ṭhīk honā
fitness *n.* अनुकूलता anukūltā
five *num.* पाँच pāṁc (pānch)
fix *v.t.* जमाना jamānā, ठीक करना ṭhīk karnā
flag *n.* झण्डा jhaṇḍā
flame *n.* ज्वाला jvālā
flannel *n.* फ़लालेन falālen
flap *n.* लटकन laṭkan; (*flapping of birds*) फ़ड़फ़ड़ाहट faṛfaṛāhaṭ; *v.t.* फड़फड़ाना faṛfaṛānā
flash *n.* दमक damak; *v.i.* चमकना camaknā
flat *adj.* समतल samtal
flatter *v.t.* चापलूसी करना cāplūsī karnā
flavor *n.* स्वाद svād; *v.t.* स्वाद मिलाना svād milānā
flaw *n.* दोष doṣ
flea *n.* पिस्सू pissū
flee *v.i.* भागना bhāgnā
fleet *n.* बेड़ा beṛā
flesh *n.* मांस māṁs
flight *n.* उड़ान uṛān
flirt *n.* चुलबुली culbulī; *v.t* फड़फड़ाना faṛfaṛānā, हाव-भाव दिखलाना hāv bhāv dikhlānā
float *v.i.* तैरना tairnā
flock *n.* दल dal
flood *n.* बाढ़ bāṛh
floor *n.* फ़र्श farś
florist *n.* फूल-वाला phūl-vālā
flour *n.* आटा āṭā
flow *n.* बहाव bahāv; *v.i.* बहना bahanā

flower *n.* फूल phūl
fluent *adj.* धाराप्रवाह dhārāpravāh
fluid *n./adj.* तरल taral
fly *n.* मक्खी makkhī; *v.i.* उड़ना uṛnā
foam *n.* झाग jhāg
focus *n.* केन्द्र kendra; *v.t.* केन्द्रित करना kendrit karnā
fog *n.* खुश khuś
foggy *adj.* कोहरेवाला koharevālā
fold *n.* तह tah; *v.t.* तहाना tahānā
folder *n.* पुस्तिका pustikā
follow *v.i.* पीछे-पीछे चलना pīche-pīche calnā
following *adj.* अगला aglā
fond *adj.* स्नेही snehī
food *n.* खाना khānā
fool *n.* मूर्ख mūrkh
foolish *adj.* बेवकूफ़ bevkūf
foot *n.* पैर pair; (*a measure*) फुट phuṭ
football *n.* फुटबाल phuṭbāl
for *prep.* के लिए ke liye
forbid *v.t.* मना करना manā karnā
forbidden *adj.* वर्जित varjit
force *n.* बल bal; *v.t.* ज़बरदस्ती करना zabardastī karnā
forearm *n.* भुजाग्र bhujāgr
forecast *n.* पूर्वानुमान pūrvājumān
forehead *n* माथा māthā
foreign *adj.* विदेशी videśī
foreigner *n.* विदेशी videśī
foresight *n.* दूरदर्शिता dūrdarśitā
forest *n.* वन van
forever *adv.* सदा के लिये sadā de liye
foreword *n.* प्रस्तावना prastāvnā
forget *v.t.,v.i.* भूल जाना bhūl jānā

forgive *v.t.* क्षमा करना kṣamā karnā
fork *n.* काँटा kāṁṭā
form *n.* रूप rūp
formal *adj.* औपचारिक aupcārik
format *n.* ग्रन्थाकार granthākār
former *adj.* पहला pahalā
formula *n.* सूत्र sūtra
fort *n.* किला kilā
fortieth *adj.* चालीसवाँ cālīsvāṁ
fortnight *n.* पक्ष pakṣ
fortress *n.* गढ़ baṛh
fortunate *adj.* सौभाग्यशाली saubhāgyaśālī
fortunately *adv.* सौभाग्यवश saubhāgyavaś
fortune *n.* किस्मत kismat
forty *num.* चालीस cālīs
forward *adv.* आगे āge
fossil *n.* जीवाश्म jīvāśam
foster *v.t.* पोषण करना poṣaṇ karnā
found *v.t.* स्थापित करना sthāpit karnā
foundation *n.* बुनियाद buniyād
founder *n.* संस्थापक sansthāpak
fountain *n.* स्रोता srotā
four *num.* चार cār
fourteen *num.* चौदह caudah
fourteenth *adj.* चौदहवाँ caudahvāṁ
fourth *adj.* चौथा cauthā
fowl *n.* मुर्गा murgā
fox *n.* लोमड़ी lomṛī
fraction *n.* टुकड़ा tukṛā; (*math*) भिन्न अंक bhinn ank
fragile *adj.* भंगुर bhungur
frame *n.* चौखटा caukhṭā; *v.t.* चौखटा लगाना caukhṭā lagānā
frantic *adj.* उत्तेजित uttejit

fraud *n.* छल chal
free *adj.* मुफ़्त muft
freedom *n.* स्वतंत्रता svatantratā
freeze *v.t.* जमाना jamānā; *v.i.* जमना jamnā
freight *n.* भाड़ा bhāṛā
French *n./adj.* फ्रांसीसी frānsīsī
frequency *n.* आवृत्ति āvrtti
frequent *adj.* अकसर aksar
frequently *adv.* बारंबार bārambār
fresh *adj.* ताज़ा tāzā
Friday *n.* शुक्रवार śukravār
fried *adj.* तला हुआ talā huā
friend *n.* दोस्त dost
friendly *adj.* दोस्ताना dostānā
friendship *n.* दोस्ती dostī
fright *n.* भय bhay
frighten *v.t.* डराना ḍarānā
frightening *adj.* भयंकर bhayankar
frog *n.* मेंढक meṇḍhak
from *prep.* से se
front *adj.* सामने का sāmne kā
frontier *n.* सीमा sīmā
frost *n.* तुषार tuṣār
frostbite *n.* शीतदंश śītadanś
frown *n.* त्योरी tyorī; *v.i.* त्योरी चढ़ाना tyorī caṛhānā
frozen *adj.* जमा हुआ jamā huā
fruit *n.* फल phal
frustrate *v.t.* निराश करना nirāś karnā
frustrated *adj.* हतोत्साहित होना hatotsāhit honā
frustration *n.* निराशा nirāśā
fry *v.t.* तलना talnā
frying pan *n.* कड़ाही kaṛāhī

fuel *n.* पेट्रोल peṭrol
fugitive *adj.* फ़रारी farārī
full *adj.* पूर्ण pūrṇ
fun *n.* मज़ा mazā
function *n.* समारोह samāroh; *v.i.* काम करना kām karnā
fund *n.* निधि nidhi; *v.t.* निधि में रखना nidhi meṁ rakhnā
fundamental *adj.* मूल mūl
funeral *n.* दाह संस्कार dāh sanskār
fungus *n.* फफूंदी phaphūndī
funny *adj.* हास्यकर hāsyakar
fur *n.* रोवा rovā
furious *adj.* अतिक्रूद्ध atikūddh
furnace *n.* भट्ठी bhaṭṭhī
furnish *v.t.* जुटाना juṭānā
furniture *n.* फ़र्नीचर farnīcar
further *adv.* और आगे aur āge
fuselage *n.* धड़ dhaṛ
future *n./adj.* भविष्य bhaviṣya

G

gain *n.* लाभ lābh; *v.t.* प्राप्त करना prāpt karnā
gall *n.* पित्त pitt
gallery *n.* गैलरी gailarī
gallon *n.* गैल्न gailan
gallop *n.* छलाँग chalāṁg; *v.i.* छलाँग लगाना chalāṁg lagānā
gallstone *n.* पित्ताश्मरी phittāśmarī
game *n.* खेल khel
gang *n.* टोली ṭolī
gap *n.* छेद ched
garage *n.* गैरज gairaj

garbage *n.* रद्दी raddī
garden *n.* बाग़ bāqg
gardener *n.* बाग़बान bāqgbān
gargle *v.i.* कुल्ली करना kullī karnā
garland *n.* माला mālā
garlic *n.* लहसुन tahsun
garment *n.* कपड़ा kapṛā
gas *n.* गैस gais
gasoline *n.* पेट्रोल peṭrol
gassy *adj.* गैसीय gaisīy
gate *n.* फाटक phāṭak
gather *v.i.* जमा होना jamā honā; *v.t.* जमा करना jamā karnā
gauge *n.* माप māp; *v.t.* मापना māpnā
gay *adj.* खुश khuś; समलैंगिक samalaiṅgik
gear *n.* साज़-सामान sāz-sāmān
gem *n.* रत्न ratn
gender *n.* लिंग ling
general *n.* जनरल janaral; *adj.* आम ām
generally *adv.* सामान्यता sāmānyatā
generate *v.t.* उत्पन्न करना utpann karnā
generation *n.* उत्पादन utpādan
generous *adj.* उदार udār
genetic *adj.* उत्पत्ति से समबन्धित utpatti se sambandhit
genital *adj.* जनान संबंधी janān sambandhī
genitals *n.pl.* जननांग jananāṅg
genius *n.* प्रतिभाशाली pratibhāśālī
gentle *adj.* भला bhalā
gentleman *n.* सज्जन sajjan
geography *n.* भूगोल bhūgol
geology *n.* भूविज्ञान bhūvigyān
germ *n.* जीवाणु jīvāṇu
German *n./adj.* जर्मन jarman

Germany *n.* जर्मनी jarmanī
gesture *n.* चेष्टा coṣṭā
get *v.t.* प्राप्त करना prāpt karnā
ghost *n.* भूत bhūt
giant *n.* भीमकाय bhīmakāy; *adj.* बड़ा baṛā
gift *n.* तोहफ़ा tohfā
gild *v.t.* सोना चढ़ाना sonā caṛhānā
gill *n.* गिल gil
gilt *n.* मुलम्मा mulammā; *adj* सुनहला sunhalā
gin *n.* जिन jin
girl *n.* लड़की laṛkī
girlfriend *n.* प्रेमिका premikā
give *v.t.* देना denā
glad *adj.* प्रसन्न prasann
glamour *n.* मोहकता mohktā
glance *n.* सरसरी नज़र sarsarī nazar; *v.i.* झलकाना jhalkānā
gland *n.* गिल्टी gilṭī
glare *n.* चमक camak; *v.i.* चमकना camaknā
glass *n.* शीशा śīśā
glasses (eyeglasses) *n.* चश्मा caśmā
glimpse *n.* झलक jhalak; *v.t.* झलकाना jhalakānā
global *adj.* विश्व-संबंधी viśv-sambandhī
globe *n.* ग्लोब glob
gloom *n.* धुधलापन dhudhlāpan
gloomy *adj.* धुंधला dhundhalā
glory *n.* महिमा mahimā
glove *n.* दस्ताना dastānā
glow *n.* लाली lālī; *v.i.* उल्लसित होना ullasit honā
glue *n.* सरेशा sareśā; *v.t.* सरेशा लगाना sareśā lagānā
go *v.i.* जाना jānā
goal *n.* लक्ष्य lakṣya
goat *n.* बकरा bakrā

God *n.* भगवान bhagavān
godchild *n.* धर्मपुत्र dharmputra
goddaughter *n.* धर्मपुत्री dharamputrī
goddess *n.* देवी devī
godfather *n.* धर्मपिता dharampitā
godmother *n.* धर्ममाता dharammātā
godson *n.* धर्मपुत्र dharamputra
gold *n.* सोना sonā
golden *adj.* सोने का sone kā
golf *n.* गोल्फ़ golf
good *adj.* अच्छा acchā
good-bye! *interj.* नमस्ते namaste
goods *n.* माल māl
goose *n.* कलहंसी kalhansī
gospel *n.* हिदायत hidāyat
gossip *n.* गपशप gapśap; *v.i.* गपशप करना gapśap karnā
govern *v.t.* शासन करना śāsan karnā
government *n.* सरकार sarkār
governor *n.* राज्यपाल rājypāl
grace *n.* मनोहरता manohartā
graceful *adj.* मनोहर manohar
gracious *adj.* कृपालु kṛpālu
grade *n.* श्रेणी sṛeṇī; *v.t.* क्रमानुसार रखना kramānusār rākhnā
gradual *adj.* क्रामिक krāmik
graduate *n.* स्नातक snātak; *v.i.* स्नातक होना snātak honā
graft *n.* कलम kalam; *v.t.* कलम बाँधना kalam bāṁdhnā
grain *n.* अनाज anāj
gram *n.* चना canā
grammar *n.* व्याकरण vyākaraṇ
grand *adj.* मुख्य mukhya
grandchild *n.* नाती nātī

granddaughter *n.* (*son's daughter*) पोती potī; (*daughter's daughter*) दुहती duhtī
grandfather *n.* (*paternal*) दादा dādā; (*maternal*) नाना nānā
grandmother *n.* (*paternal*) दादी dādī; (*maternal*) नानी nānī
grandson *n.* (*son's son*) पोता potā; (*daughter's son*) दुहता duhtā
granite *n.* ग्रेनाइट grenāiṭ
grant *n.* अनुदान anudān; *v.t.* प्रदान करना pradān karnā
grape *n.* अंगूर angūr
grapefruit *n.* छोटा चकोतरा choṭā cakotrā
graph *n.* रेखाचित्र rekhācitra
graphic *adj.* आलेखी ālekhī
grasp *v.t.* कसकर पकड़ना kaskar pakaṛnā
grass *n.* घास ghās
grasshopper *n.* टिड्डा ṭiḍḍā
grateful *adj.* आभारी abhārī
gratitude *n.* आभार ābhār
grave *n.* कब्र kabr; *adj.* गंभीर gambhīr
gravity *n.* भार bhār
gray *adj.* धूसर dhūsar
grease *n.* चरबी carbī; *v.t.* ग्रीस लगाना grīs lagānā
great *adj.* महान mahān
greatness *n.* बड़ाई baṛāī
Greece *n.* यूनान yūnān
Greek *n./adj.* यूनानी yūnānī
green *n./adj.* हरा harā
greenhouse *n.* पौधा घर paudhā ghar
greet *v.t.* नमस्कार करना namaskār karnā
greeting *n.* नमस्कार namaskār
grief *n.* दुख dukh
grievance *n.* शिकायत śikāyat
grieve *v.t.* दुख देना dukh denā

grill *v.t.* ग्रिल में पकाना gril meṁ pakānā
grind *v.t.* पीसना pīsnā
grip *n.* पकड़ pakaṛ; *v.t.* पकडना pakaṛnā
groan *n.* कराह karāh; *v.i.* कराहना karāhnā
grocer *n.* पंसारी pansārī
grocery *n.* पंसारी की दुकान pansārī kī dukān
groin *n.* ऊरू मूल ūrū mūl
ground *n.* ज़मीन zamīn; *adj.* पिसा pisā
groundwork *n.* आधार कर्म ādhār karm
group *n.* समूह samūh
grow *v.t.* उगाना ugānā; *v.i.* उगना ugnā
growl *n.* गुरहिट gurahiṭ; *v.i.* गुराना gurānā
grown-up *n.* बालिग़ bālinqg
growth *n.* बढ़ती baṛhtī
guarantee *n.* गारंटी gāranṭī; *v.t.* गारंटी gāranṭī
guard *n.* रक्षा rakṣā; *v.t.* रक्षा करना rakṣā karnā
guerilla *n./adj.* छापामार chāpāmār
guess *n.* अनुमान anumān; *v.i.* अनुमान करना anumān karnā
guest *n.* अतिथि atithi
guide *n.* गाइड gāiḍ; *v.t.* संचाल्न करना sancālan karnā
guidebook *n.* संदर्शिका sandarśikā
guilt *n.* दोष doṣ
guilty *adj.* दोषी doṣī
guitar *n.* गिटार giṭār
gulf *n.* खाड़ी khāṛī
gun *n.* बंदूक bandūk
gust *n.* झोंका jhoṅkā
gutter *n.* गंदी नाली gandī nālī
guy *n.* जवान javān
gymnasium *n.* व्यायामशाला vyāyāmśālā
gynecologist *n.* औरतों का डाकटर auratoṁ kā ḍākṭar
Gypsy *n.* जिप्सी jipsī

H

habit *n.* आदत ādat
hair *n.* (*of body*) बाल bāl; (*of head*) रोम rom
hairdresser *n.* नाई nāī
half *adj.* आधा ādhā
hall *n.* हाल hāl
ham *n.* पुट्ठा puṭṭhā
hammer *n.* हथौड़ा hathaurā
hamper *n.* डलिया ḍaliyā
hand *n.* हाथ hāth
handbag *n.* हैंडबैग haindḍbaig
handbook *n.* पुस्तिका purstikā
handicap *n.* अड़चन arcan
handicapped *adj.* विकलांग viklāng
handicraft *n.* शिल्प śilp
handkerchief *n.* रुमाल rumāl
handle *n.* मूठ mūṭh
handrail *n.* जंगला jangalā
handsome *adj.* मनोहार manohār
handy *adj.* दक्ष dakṣ
hang *v.t.* टागना ṭāṇgnā
hangar *n.* विमानशाला vimānśālā
hanger *n.* हैंगर haingar
hangover *n.* शराब पीने से सरदर्द śarāb pīne se sardard
happen *v.i.* हो जाना ho jānā
happiness *n.* ख़ुशी khuśī
happy *adj.* ख़ुश khuś
harass *v.t.* तंग करना taṅg karnā
harassment *n.* परेशानी pareśānī
harbor *n.* बंदरगाह bandargāh
hard *adj.* कड़ा kaṛā

harden *v.i.* कड़ा बनाना kaṛā banānā
hardly *adv.* मुश्किल से muśkil se
hardness *n.* कड़ापन kaṛāpan
hardship *n.* कष्ट kaṣṭ
hardware *n.* लोहे का सामान lohe kā sāmān
hardy *adj.* लगड़ा lagṛā
hare *n.* खरगोश khargoś
harm *n.* हानि hāni; *v.t.* कष्ट देना kaṣṭ denā
harmful *adj.* हानिकर hānikar
harmless *adj.* अहानिकर ahānikar
harness *n.* साज़ sāz; *v.t.* पढ़ाना paṛānā
harp *n.* वीणा vīṇā
harsh *adj.* रूखा rūkhā
harvest *n.* फ़सल fasal
haste *n.* जल्दी jaldī
hasty *adj.* चिड़चिड़ी ciṛciṛī
hat *n.* टोपी ṭopī
hatch *n.* निचला झरोखा niclā jharokhā
hate *n.* नफ़रत nafrat; *v.t.* नफ़रत करना nafrat karnā
haul *n.* कर्षण karṣaṇ; *v.t.* घसीटना ghasīṭnā
haunt *v.t.* आवाजाही लगाना āvājāhī lagānā
have *v.t.* पास होना pās honā
hawk *n.* बाज़ bāz
hay *n.* सूखी घास sūkhī ghās
hazard *n.* दाँव dāṁv
haze *n.* धुंध dhuṁdh
hazy *adj.* धुँधला dhuṁdhlā
he *pron.* वह vaha
head *n.* सिर sir
heading *n.* शीर्षक śīrṣak
headlight *n.* अग्रदीप agradīp
headline *n.* शीर्षक śīrṣak

headquarters *n.pl.* मुख्यालय mukhyālay
heal *v.t.* ठीक करना ṭhīk karnā; *v.i.* ठीक होना ṭhīk honā
health *n.* तबीयत tabīyat
healthy *adj.* स्वस्थ svasth
heap *n.* ढ़ेर ṛher
hear *v.t.* सुनना sunanā
hearing *n.* श्रवण śravaṇ; (*court*) सुनवाई sunvāī
heart *n.* दिल dil
hearth *n.* चूल्हा cūlhā
hearty *adj.* हार्दिक hārdik
heat *n.* गरमी garmī
heater *n.* हीटर hīṭar
heating *n.* तापन tāpan
heaven *n.* स्वर्ग svarg
heavy *adj.* भारी bhārī
hedge *n.* बाड़ bāṛ
heel *n.* एड़ी eṛī
height *n.* ऊँचाई ūṁcāī
heir *n.* वारिस vāris
helicopter *n.* हेलिकॉप्टर helikāpṭar
hell *n.* नरक narak
hello *n.* नमस्कार namaskār
helm *n.* पतवार patvār
helmet *n.* हेलमिट helmiṭ
help *n.* मदद madad; *v.t.* मदद करना madad karnā
helper *n.* सहायक shāyak
helpful *adj.* उपयोगी upyogī
hem *n.* गोट goṭ
hen *n.* मुर्गी murgī
hepatitis *n.* यकृत-शोथ yakṛt-śoth
herd *n.* गल्ला gallā
here *adv.* यहाँ yahāṁ

hernia *n.* हर्निया harniyā
hero *n.* वीर vīr
heroic *adj.* वीरताका vīratākā
heron *n.* बगुला bagulā
herring *n.* हिलसा hilsā
hers *pron.* उसका uskā
herself *pron.* अपने-आप apne-āp
hesitate *v.t.* हिचकिचाना hickicānā
hesitation *n.* हिचकिचाहट hickicāhaṭ
heterosexual *adj.* इतरलिंगी itarliṅgī
hiccup *n.* हिचकी hickī; *v.i.* हिचकी लेना hickī lenā
hidden *adj.* गुप्त gupt
hide *v.t.* छिपाना chipānā
high *adj.* ऊँचा ūṁcā
highway *n.* राजपथ rājpath
hike *n* सैर sair; *v.i.* पैदल सैर करना paidal sair karnā
hiker *n.* पैदल सैर करने वाला paidal sair karne vāl
hiking *n.* पदयात्रा करना padyātrā karnā
hill *n.* पहाड़ी pahāṛī
hilly *adj.* पहाड़ी pahāṛī
him *pron.* उसे use
himself *pron.* अपने-आप apne-āp
hinder *v.t.* विध्न-डालना vidhn-ḍālnā
Hindi *n.* हिन्दी hindī
Hindu *n./adj.* हिन्दू hindū
Hinduism *n.* हिन्दू धर्म hindū dharam
hinge *n.* कब्ज़ा kabzā; *v.t.* कब्ज़ा लगाना kabzā lagānā
hint *n.* संकेत sanket; *v.i.* संकेत करना sanket karnā
hip *n.* कुल्हा kulhā
hire *v.t.* किराए पर होना kirāe par honā
his *pron.* उसका uskā
historical *adj.* ऐतिहासिक etihāsik

history *n.* इतिहास itihās
hit *v.i.* मारना mārnā
hitchhike *v.i.* अनुरोध anurodh
hive *n.* छत्ताधानी chattādhānī
hoarse *adj.* भारी bhārī
hobby *n.* शौक śauk
hockey *n.* हाकी hākī
hoe *n.* खुरपा khurpā
hoist *v.t.* उठाना uṭhānā
hold *n.* पकड़ pakaṛ; *v.t.* पकड़ना pakaṛnā
hole *n.* छिद्र chidr
holiday *n.* छुट्टी chuṭṭī
hollow *adj.* खोखला khokhalā
holy *adj.* पवित्र pavitra
holy day *n.* पुण्य दिवस puṇya divas
home *n.* घर ghar
homeland *n.* जन्म-भूमि janam-bhūmi
homesick *adj.* गृह-वियोगी gṛha-viyogī
homesickness *n.* गृह-वियोग gṛha-viyog
hometown *n.* गृह जनपद gṛha-janpad
homework *n.* गृह-कार्य gṛha-kārya
homosexual *n./adj.* समलैंगी samlaingī
honest *adj.* ईमानदार īmāndār
honesty *n.* ईमानदारी īmāndārī
honey *n.* मधु madhu
honeymoon *n.* मधुमास madhumās
honor *n.* सम्मान sammān; *v.t.* सम्मानित करना sammānit karnā
hood *n.* छत्र chatr
hook *n.* काँटा kāṁṭā
hoop *n.* छल्ला challā
hope *n.* आशा āśā; *v.t.* आशा करना āśā karnā
hopeful *adj.* आशाजनक āśājanak

hopeless *adj.* निराशाजनक nirāśājanak
horizon *n.* क्षितिज kṣitij
horizontal *adj.* पड़ा paṛā
horn *n.* सींग siṅg
horrible *adj.* भयंकर bhayaṅkar
horror *n.* संत्रास santrās
hors-d'oeuvre *n.* हल्का नाश्ता halkā nāśtā
horse *n.* घोड़ा ghoṛā
hose *n.* होज़ hoz
hospitable *adj.* सत्कारशील satkārśīl
hospital *n.* अस्पताल aspatāl
host *n.* मेज़बान mezbān
hostel *n.* छात्रावास chātrāvās
hostess *n.* मेहमानशरिन mehmānśarin
hostile *adj.* विरोधी virodhī
hot *adj.* गरम garam
hotel *n.* होटल hoṭal
hour *n.* घंटा ghaṇṭā
house *n.* घर ghar
household *n.* गृहस्थी gṛhasthī
housekeeper *n.* नौकरानी naukrānī
housewife *n.* गृहस्वामिनी gṛhasvāminī
how *adv.* कैसे kaise
however *adv.* फिर भी phir bhī
hug *n.* गले gale; *v.t.* गले लगाना gale lagānā
huge *adj.* विशाल viśāl
human *adj.* मानवीय mānvīy; *n.* मानव अधिकार mānav adhikār
humane *adj.* मानवोचित mānvocit
humanity *n.* मानवता mānvatā
humble *adj.* विनीत vinīt
humid *adj.* नम nam

humidity *n.* नमी namī
humor *n.* हास्य hāsya
hump *n.* कोहान kohān
hundred *num.* सौ sau
hundredth *adj.* सौवां sauvāṁ
hunger *n.* भूख bhūkh
hungry *adj.* भूखा bhūkhā
hunt *n.* शिकार śikār
hunter *n.* शिकारी śikārī
hurray! *interj.* हुरे hure!
hurry *n.* जल्दी jaldī; *v.t.* जल्दी करना jaldī karnā
hurt *n.* चोट coṭ; *v.t.* चोट खाना coṭ khānā
husband *n.* पति pati
hut *n.* झोपड़ा jhopaṛā
hymn *n.* भजन bhajan
hyphen *n.* योजक चिन्ह yojak cinh

I

I *pron.* मैं maiṁ
ice *n.* बरफ़ barf
ice cream *n.* आइसक्रीम āiskrīm
icon *n.* प्रतिमा pratimā
icy *adj.* बरफ़ीला barfīlā
idea *n.* विचार vicār
ideal *n./adj.* आदर्श ādarś
identical *adj.* समरूप samarūp
identification *n.* पहिचान pahicān
identify *v.t.* पहचानना pahacānnā
idiom *n.* मुहावरा muhāvarā
idiot *n.* मूर्ख mūrkh
idle *adj.* बेकार bekār
if *conj.* यदि yadi; अगर agar

ignition *n.* ज्वलन jvalan
ignorance *n.* अज्ञान agyān
ignorant *adj.* अनजान anjān
ignore *v.t.* उपेक्षा करना upekṣā karnā
ill *adj.* बीमार bīmār
illegal *adj.* ग़ैर-कानूनी qgair-kānūnī
illegible *adj.* अस्पष्ट aspaṣt
illiterate *adj.* अनपढ़ anpaṛh
illness *n.* बीमारी bīmārī
illumination *n.* प्रदीप्त pradīpt
illusion *n.* भ्रांति bhrānti
illustrate *v.t.* सचित्र करना sacitra karnā
illustration *n.* चित्र citra
image *n.* मुर्ति murtī
imagination *n.* कल्पना kalpanā
imagine *v.t.* कल्पना करना kalpanā karnā
imitate *v.t.* नकल करना nakal karna
imitation *n.* अनुकरण anukaraṇ
immense *adj.* विशाल viśāl
immoral *adj.* अनैतिक anaitik
immortal *adj.* अमर amar
impasse *n.* गतिरोध gātirodh
impatient *adj.* बेचैन becain
imperfect *adj.* अपूर्ण apūrṇ
implement *n.* औज़ार auzār; *v.t.* लागू करना lāgū karnā
imply *v.t.* अर्थ रखना arth rakhnā
impolite *adj.* अशिष्ट aśiṣṭ
import *n.* आयात āyāt; *v.t.* आयात करना āyāt karnā
importance *n.* महत्व mahatva
important *adj.* महत्वपूर्ण mahatvapūrṇ
impose *v.t.* लगाना lagānā
impossible *adj.* असंभव asambhav

impotent *adj.* नपुंसक napunsak
impress *v.t.* छाप लगाना chāp lagānā
impressive *adj.* प्रभावशाली prabhāśālī
imprint *v.t.* अंकित करना ankit karnā
imprison *v.t.* कैद करना kaid karnā
improper *adj.* अशुद्ध aśuddh
improve *v.t.* सुधारना sudhārnā; *v.i.* सुधार होना sudhār honā
improvement *n.* सुधार sudhār
improvise *v.t.* तत्काल भाषण देना tatkāl bhāṣaṇ denā
impulse *n.* अंतप्रेरणा antprerṇā
inability *n.* असमर्थता asamarthatā
inaccessible *adj.* अगम्य agamy
inactive *adj.* निष्क्रिय niṣkriya
inaugurate *v.t.* उदघाटन करना udghāṭan karnā
inauguration *n.* उदघाटन udghāṭan
incentive *n.* प्रेरणा prerṇā
inch *n.* इंच iñc
inclination *n.* झुकाव jhukāv
incline *n.* ढाल ḍhāl; *v.i.* झुकना jhuknā
include *v.t.* शामिल करना śāmil karnā
income *n.* आय āy
incompetent *adj.* अक्षम akṣam
incorrect *adj.* गलत galat
increase *n.* बढ़ती baṛhtī; *v.i.* बढ़ना baṛhnā
indeed *adv.* वास्तव में vāstav meṁ
independence *n.* स्वतंत्रता svatantratā
independent *adj.* स्वतंत्र svatantra
index *n.* अनुक्रमिका anukramikā; *v.t.* अनुक्रमिका करना anukramikā karnā
indicate *v.t.* सूचित करना sūcit karnā
indicator *n.* संकेतक sanketak
indifferent *adj.* उदासीन udāsīn

indignation *n.* रोष roṣ
indirect *adj.* अप्रत्यक्ष apratyakṣ
individual *n.* व्यक्ति vyakti; *adj.* व्यक्तिगत vyaktigat
indoor *adj.* भीतर bhītar
industrial *adj.* औद्योमिक audyomik
industrious *adj.* अध्यवसायी adhyavasāyī
industry *n.* उद्योग udyog
inefficient *adj.* अयोग्य ayogy
inexpensive *adj.* सस्ता sastā
infant *n.* बच्चा baccā; *adj.* प्रारंभिक prarambhik
infect *v.t.* संक्रमित करना sankramit karnā
infection *n.* संदूषण sandūṣaṇ
infectious *adj.* छुतहा chuthā
inferior *adj.* निम्न nimn
inflammable *adj.* ज्वलनशील jvalanśīl
inflammation *n.* सूजन sūjan
inflamed *adj.* लाल lāl, प्रदाही pradāhī
inflation *n.* मुद्रा-स्फीति mudrā-sphīti
influence *n.* प्रभाव prabhāv
inform *v.t.* बता देना batā denā, सूचित करना sūcit karnā
information *n.* सूचना sūcnā
infringe *v.t.* उल्लंघन करना ullaṅghan karnā
ingenious *adj.* चतुर catur
ingredient *n.* घटक ghaṭak
inhabit *v.t.* निवास करना nivās karnā
inhabitant *n.* रहने वाला rahene vālā
inhale *v.t.* साँस खींचना sāṁs khīncnā
inhaler *n.* श्वासयंत्र śavāsyantra
inherit *v.t.* दाय पाना dāy pānā
inheritance *n.* दाय dāy
initial *n.* आधाक्षरित ādhākṣarit; *adj.* प्रारंभिक prarambhik; *v.t.* आधाक्षरित करना ādhākṣarit karnā

initiative *n.* नेतृत्व netṛatva
inject *v.t.* सूई लगाना sūī lagānā
injection *n.* सूई sūī
injure *v.t.* घायल करना ghāyal karnā
injured *adj.* घायल ghāyal
injury *n.* चोट coṭ
ink *n.* स्याही syāhī
inn *n.* सराय sarāy
inner *adj.* भीतरी bhītarī
innocent *adj.* निर्दोष nirdoṣ
inoculate *v.t.* टीका लगाना ṭīkā lagānā
inoculation *n.* टीका ṭīkā
inquire *v.i.* पूछना pūchnā
inquiry *n.* जाँच jāṁc
insane *adj.* पागल pāgal
insect *n.* कीट kīṭ
insert *n.* सन्निवेश sanniveś; *v.t.* घुसेड़ना ghuseṛnā
inside *adj* अन्दर andar; *prep.* में meṁ
insight *n.* अन्तर्दृष्टि antardṛṣṭi
insist *v.i.* आग्रह करना āgrah karnā
insistence *n.* आग्रह āgrah
insomnia *n.* अनिद्रारोग anidrārog
inspect *v.t.* जाँच-पड़ताल करना jāṁc-paṛtāl karnā
inspection *n.* निरीक्षण nirīkṣaṇ
inspector *n.* निरीक्षक nirīkṣak
inspiration *n.* प्रेरणा prerṇā
inspire *v.t.* प्रेरणा देना prerṇā denā
install *v.t.* लगाना lagānā
installation *n.* अधिष्ठापन adhiṣṭhāpan
instance *n.* उदाहरण udāharaṇ
instant *n.* पल pal; *adj.* तुरंत turant
instead *adv.* के स्थान पर ke sthān par

instep *n.* पिचिण्डिका piciṇḍikā
instinct *n.* नैसार्गिक nausārgik
institute *n.* संस्थान sansthān
instruct *v.t.* शिक्षा देना śikṣā denā
instruction *n.* अनुदेश anudeś
instrument *n.* यंत्र yantra
insufficient *adj.* अपर्याप्त aparyāpt
insulate *v.t.* पृथक करना pr̥thak karnā
insulation *n.* पृथक्करण pṛathakkaraṇ
insult *n.* अपमान apmān; *v.t.* अपमान करना apmān karnā
insurance *n.* बीमा bīmā
insure *v.t.* बीमा कराना bīmā karānā
intelligence *n.* बुद्धि buddhi
intelligent *adj.* बुद्धिमान budhhimān
intend *v.t.* इरादा करना irādā karnā
intense *adj.* तेज़ tez
intention *n.* इरादा irādā; अभिप्राय abhipray
interest *n.* दिलचस्पी dilcaspī; *v.t.* दिलचस्पी लेना dilcaspī lenā
interesting *adj.* दिलचस्प dilcasp
interior *n.* अंदर andar; *adj.* भीतरी bhītarī
internal *adj.* भीतरी bhītarī
international *adj.* अंतरराष्ट्रीय antarrāṣṭrīy
interpreter *n.* दुभाषिया dubhāṣiyā
interrupt *v.t./v.i.* टोकना ṭoknā
interruption *n.* बाधा bādhā
interval *n.* मध्यांतर madhyāntar
intervene *v.i.* बीच में पड़ना bīc meṁ paṛnā
interview *n.* मुलाकात mulākāt
intestines *n.* अँतड़ी aṁtaṛī
intimate *adj.* घनिष्ठ ghaniṣṭh
into *prep.* में meṁ
introduce *v.t.* परिचय देना paricay denā

introduction *n.* (*personal*) परिचय paricay; (*book*) भूमिका bhūmikā
invade *v.t.* चढ़ाई करना cāṛhāī karnā
invasion *n.* चढ़ाई caṛhāī
invent *v.t.* आविष्कार करना āviṣkār karnā
invention *n.* अविष्कार aviṣkār
inventory *n.* तालिका tālikā
investigate *v.t.* पता लगाना patā lagānā
investigation *n.* जाँच-पड़ताल jāṁc-paṛtāl
invisible *adj.* अदृश्य adṛśya
invitation *n.* निमंत्रण nimantraṇ
invite *v.t.* निमंत्रण देना nimntraṇ denā
invoice *n.* बीजक bījak; *v.t.* बीजक बनाना bījak banānā
involve *v.t.* उलझाना uljhānā
iron *n.* इस्तरी istarī; *v.t.* इस्तरी करना istarī karnā
ironic *adj.* व्यंग्यात्मक vyangyātmak
irony *n.* व्यग्य vyagy
irrigate *v.t.* सींचना sīñcnā
irrigation *n.* सिंचाई siñcāī
Islam *n.* इस्लाम islām
Islamic *adj.* इस्लामी islāmī
island *n.* टापू ṭāpū
isolate *v.t.* अलग करना alag karnā
Israel *n.* इज़राइल izrāil
Israeli *adj.* इज़राइली izrāilī
issue *n.* निकास nikās; *v.t.* निकलना nikalnā
it *pron.* यह yah; वह voh
italics *n.* तिरछा tirchā
itch *n.* खुजली khujlī; *v.i.* खुजली होना khujlī honā
item *n.* विषय viṣay
its *adj.* उसका uskā
itself *pron.* स्वयं svayam

ivory *n.* हाथी दाँत hāthī dāṁt
ivy *n.* लबालब labālab

J

jack *n.* गुलाम gulām
jacket *n.* जाकेट jākeṭ
jail *n.* जेल jel
jam *n.* मुरब्बा murabbā
janitor *n.* द्वारपाल dvārpāl
January *n.* जनवरी janvarī
Japan *n.* जापान jāpān
Japanese *n./adj* जापानी jāpānī
jar *n.* मर्तबान martabān
jasmine *n.* चमेली camelī
jaw *n.* जबड़ा jabṛā
jealous *adj.* ईर्ष्यालु īṣyaryalu
jealousy *n.* जलन jalan
jelly *n.* जेली jelī
jellyfish *n.* शत्रिक śāstrik
jersey *n.* जर्सी jarsī
jet *n.* जेट jeṭ; विमान vimān
Jew *n.* यहूदी yahūdī
jewel *n.* मणि maṇi
jewelry *n.* जवाहरात javāharāt
Jewish *adj.* यहूदी yahūdī
jigsaw puzzle *n.* टुकड़े-टुकड़े ṭukaṛe-ṭukaṛe
job *n.* नौकरी naukarī
jog *n.* धक्का dhakkā; *v.i.* धीमे चलना dhīme calnā
join *v.t.* मिलाना milānā
joint *n.* जोड़ joṛ
joke *n.* मज़ाक mazāk; *v.t.* मज़ाक करना mazāk karnā

joker *n.* जोकर jokar
journal *n.* पत्रिका patrikā
journalist *n.* पत्रकार patrakār
journey *n.* यात्रा yātrā; *v.i.* यात्रा करना yātrā karnā
joy *n.* आनंद ānand
judge *n.* जज jaj; *v.t.* फ़ैसला करना faisalā karnā
judgment *n.* फ़ैसला faisalā
jug *n.* जग jag
juggle *v.t.* बाज़ीगरी करना bāzīgarī karnā
juice *n.* रस ras
July *n.* जुलाई julāī
jumble *n.* गड्डमड्ड gaḍḍmaḍḍ; *v.t.* गड्डमड्ड करना gaḍḍmaḍḍ karnā
jump *v.t* कूदना kūdnā
junction *n.* संगम sangam
June *n.* जून jūn
jungle *n.* जंगल jangal
junior *adj.* छोटा choṭā
junk *n.* कबाड़ kabāṛ
jury *n.* पंच समिति panc samiti
just *adv.* केवल keval; सिर्फ़ sirf
justice *n.* न्याय nyāy
justification *n.* औचित्य aucity
justify *v.t.* न्यायसंगत सिद्ध करना nyāyasangat siddh karnā
juvenile *n.* किशोर kiśor; *adj.* बाल bāl

K

kangaroo *n.* कंगारू kaṅgārū
keel *n.* मौतल mautal
keen *adj.* उत्साही utsāhī
keep *v.t.* रखना rakhnā

keeper *n.* रक्षक rakṣak
kennel *n.* काठघर kāṭhaghar
kernel *n.* गरी garī
kerosene *n.* मिट्टी का तेल miṭṭī kā tel
kettle *n.* केतली ketalī
key *n.* चाबी cābī
khaki *n./adj.* खाकी khākī
kick *n.* ठोकर ṭhokar; *v.t.* ठोकर मारना ṭhokar mārnā
kid *n.* बच्चा baccā; *v.t.* बहकाना bahkānā
kidnap *v.t.* अपहरण करना apharaṇ karnā
kidney *n.* गुर्दा gurdā
kill *v.t.* मार डाल्ना mār ḍālnā
kilo(gram) *n.* किलोग्राम kilogrām
kilometer *n.* किलोमीटर kilomīṭar
kind *adj.* कृपालु kṛpālu; *n.* प्रकार prakār
kindergarten *n.* बाल-बाड़ी bāl-bāṛī
kindle *v.t.* जलाना jalānā
kindness *n.* कृपा kṛpā
king *n.* राजा rājā
kingdom *n.* राज्य rājya
kiosk *n.* गुमटी gumṭī
kiss *n.* चुम्मा cumma; *v.t.* चुमना cummā
kit *n.* किट kiṭ
kitchen *n.* रसोईघर rasoīghar
kite *n.* चील cīl
kitten *n.* बिल्ली का बच्चा billī kā baccā
knapsack *n.* झोला jholā
knead *v.t.* गुँधना guṁdhnā
knee *n.* घुटना ghuṭnā
kneel *v.i.* घुटने टेकना ghuṭne ṭeknā
knife *n.* चाकू cākū
knight *n.* सामंत sāmant

knit *v.t.* बुनना bunnā
knock *n.* खटखटाना khaṭkhaṭānā
knot *n.* गाँठ gāṁṭh; *v.t.* गाँठ बाँधना gāṁth bāṁdhnā
know *v.t.* (*recognize, identify*) पहचानना pahcānnā; जानना jānnā
knowledge *n.* ज्ञान gyān
knuckle *n.* उंगली की गाँठ uṅgalī kī gāṁṭh
kosher *adj.* कोषेर koṣer

L

label *n.* नामपत्र nāmpatra; *v.t.* लेबल लगाना lebal lagānā
labor *n.* मज़दूर mazdūr
laboratory *n.* प्रयोगशाला prayogśālā
labyrinth *n.* भूलभुलैया bhūlbhulaiyā
lace *n.* फ़ीता fītā
lack *n.* कमी kamī; *v.t.* कमी होना kamī honā
ladder *n.* सीढ़ी sīṛhī
ladle *n.* कलछी kalchī
lady *n.* औरत aurat
lag *v.i.* पीछे रह जाना pīche rah jānā
lake *n.* झील jhīl
lamb *n.* मेमना memanā
lame *adj.* लगड़ा lagaṛā
lamp *n.* बत्ती battī
lamppost *n.* बत्ती का खंभा battī kā khambhā
land *n.* भूमि bhūmi
landing *n.* अवतरण avtaraṇ
landlord *n.* मकानमालिक makānmālik
landmark *n.* सीमाचिह्न sīmācihn
landscape *n.* भू-दृश्य bhū-dṛśya
lane *n.* गली galī

language *n.* भाषा bhāṣā
lantern *n.* लालटेन lālṭen
lap *n.* गोद god
lapel *n.* लौट lauṭ
lapse *n.* भूल bhūl; *v.i.* फिर गिर जाना phir gir jānā
lard *n.* सुअर की चरबी suar kī carbī
large *adj.* बड़ा baṛā
laryngitis *n.* खरयंत्रशोथ kharyantraśoth
laser *n.* लेज़र lezar
last *adj.* अन्तिम antim
latch *n.* सिटकिनी siṭkinī
late *adj.* देर der; *adv.* देर से der se
lately *adv.* हाल में hāl meṁ
lathe *n.* खराद kharād
lather *n.* झाग jhāg
Latin *n./adj.* लैटिन laiṭin
latitude *n.* अक्षांश akṣanś
latrine *n.* शौचालय saucālay
latter *adj.* परवर्ती parvartī
laugh *n.* हँसी haṁsī; *v.i.* हँसना haṁsnā
laughter *n.* हँसी haṁsī
launch *n.* लांच lānc; *v.t.* छोड़ना choṛnā, चलाना calānā
laundry *n.* धोबीख़ाना dhobīqhānā
lavatory *n.* पैख़ाना paiqhānā
lavish *adj.* उदार udār
law *n.* क़ानून qānūn
lawful *adj.* विधिसम्मत vidhisammat
lawn *n.* मैदान maidān
lawsuit *n.* वाद vād
lawyer *n.* वकील vakīl
laxative *n.* दस्तावर dastāvar
lay *v.t.* बिछाना bichānā

layer *n.* रखनेवाला rakhnevālā
lazy *adj.* आलसी ālsī
lead *n.* सीसा sīsā; *v.t.* ले चलना le calnā; *v.i.* ले जाना le jānā
leader *n.* नेता netā
leadership *n.* नेतागिरी netāgirī
leaf *n.* पत्ता pattā
leak *n.* दरार darār; *v.t.* चूना cūnā; *v.i.* टपकना ṭapaknā
lean *adj.* दुबला dubalā; *v.i.* झुकना jhuknā
leap *n.* उछाल uchāl; *v.i.* कूदना kūdnā
leap year *n.* अधिवर्ष adhivarṣ
learn *v.t.* सीखना sīkhnā
learner *n.* नौसिखिया nausikhiyā
lease *n.* पट्टा paṭṭā; *v.t.* पट्टे पर देना paṭṭe par denā
leash *n.* पट्टा paṭṭā
least *adj.* तनिक tanik; *adv.* कम-से कम kam-se kam
leather *n.* चमड़ा camṛā
leave *v.t.* छोड़ना choṛnā
lecture *n.* व्याख्यान vyākhyān
ledge *n.* कगार kagār
left *adj.* बायाँ bāyāṁ
left-handed *adj.* बायें हाथ से काम करने वाला bāyāṁ hāth se kām karne wālā
leg *n.* टाँग tāṁg
legal *adj.* क़ानूनी qānūnī
legality *n.* वैधता vaidhtā
legation *n.* दूतप्रेषण dūtpreṣaṇ
legend *n.* उपाख्यान upākhyān
legible *adj.* सुवाच्य suvācy
legislation *n.* कानून kānūn
legitimate *adj.* वैध vaidh
leisure *n.* अवकाश avkāś
lemon *n.* नीबू nībū

lend *v.t.* उधार देना udhār denā
length *n.* लंबाई lambāī
lengthen *v.t.* लंबा करना lambā karnā
lens *n.* लेन्स lens
Lent *n.* चालीसा cālīsā
lentil *n.* मसूर masūr
lesion *n.* क्षत kṣt
less *adj.* और कम aur kam; *adv.* कम kam, लघु laghu
lesson *n.* पाठ pāṭh
let *v.t.* होने देना hone denā
letter *n.* चिट्ठी ciṭṭhī
lettuce *n.* सलाद पत्ता salād pattā
level *adj.* समतल samtal
lever *n.* टेकन ṭekan
liability *n.* देनदारी dendārī
liable *adj.* ज़िम्मेवार zimmevār
liaison *n.* संपर्क sampark
liar *n.* झूठा jhūṭhā
libel *n.* अपमान-लेख apmān-lekh; *v.t.* अपमान-लेख लिखना apmān-lekh likhnā
liberal *adj.* उदार udār
liberation *n.* मुक्ति mukti
liberty *n.* स्वतंत्रता svatantratā
librarian *n.* पुस्ताकालयाध्यक्ष pustākālayādhyakṣ
library *n.* पुस्तकालय pustakālay
license *n.* आज्ञा āgyā
lid *n.* ढक्कन ḍhakkan
lie *n.* झूठ jhūṭh; *v.i.* झूठ बोलना jhūṭh bolnā
lieutenant *n.* सहायक sahāyak
life *n.* जीवन jīvan, ज़िन्दगी zindagī
lifeboat *n.* रक्षा-नौका rakṣā-naukā
lifeless *adj.* निर्जीव nirjīv

lifetime *n.* जीवन काल jīvan kāl
lift *n.* लिफ़्ट lifṭ; *v.t.* उठाना uṭhānā
light *n.* प्रकाश prakāś; (*lamp, car, etc.*) बत्ती battī; *v.t.* जलाना jalānā; *adj.* रोशन rośan
lighten *v.t.* जलाना jalānā
lighthouse *n.* प्रकाश गृह prakāś gṛha
lighting *n.* प्रदीपन pradīpan
lightning *n.* बिजली bijalī
like *adj./adv.* समान samān; *v.t.* पसंद करना pasand karnā
likely *adv.* संभावित sambhāvit
likewise *adv.* और भी aur bhī
limb *n.* अंग aṅg
lime *n.* (*fruit*) नीबू nībū; चूना cūnā
limit *n.* सीमा sīmā
limp *n.* लँगड़ी laṁgaṛī; *v.i.* लँगड़ना laṁgaṛnā
line *n.* लाइन lāin; *v.t.* पंक्तिबद्ध करना paṅktibaddh karnā
linen *n.* सन san
liner *n.* लाइनर lāinar
lining *n.* अस्तर astar
link *n.* (*of chain*) कड़ी kaṛī; (*relation*) संबंध sambandh; *v.t.* संबंध होना sambandh honā
lion *n.* सिंह sinha; शेर śer
lip *n.* होंठ hoṁṭh
liqueur *n.* मदिरा madirā
liquid *n.* द्रव drav; *adj.* द्रवीय dravīy
liquor *n.* शराब śarāb
list *n.* सूची sūcī; *v.t.* सूची बनाना sūcī banānā
listener *n.* श्रोता śrotā
literary *adj.* साहित्यिक sāhityik
literature *n.* साहित्य sāhity
litter *n.* कूड़ा-कचरा kūṛā-kacarā
little *adj.* छोटा choṭā; *adv.* थोड़ा सा thoṛā sā

live *adj.* ज़िन्दा zindā; *v.i.* (*to be alive*) जीना jīnā; (*exist, stay in*) रहना rahenā
lively *adj.* क्रियाशील kriyāśīl
liver *n.* कलेजा kalejā
living room *n.* रहने का कमरा rehne kā kamrā
lizard *n.* छिपकली chipkalī
load *n.* भार bhār; *v.t.* लादना lādnā
loaf *n.* पावरोटी pāvroṭī
loan *n.* उधार udhār; *v.t.* उधार देना udhār denā
lobby *n.* बरामदा barāmdā
lobster *n.* समुद्री झींगा samudrī jhīngā
lock *n.* ताला tālā; *v.t.* ताला लगाना tālā lagānā
locker *n.* लाकर lākar
locomotive *n.* इंजन iñjan
locust *n.* टिड्डा ṭiḍḍā
lodge *n.* झोपड़ी jhopaṛī
lodging *n.* आवास āvās
loft *n.* अटारी aṭārī
log *n.* लट्ठा laṭṭā; *v.t.* लकड़ी के लिए पेड़ काटना lakaṛī ke lie peṛ kāṭnā
logic *adj.* तर्कशास्त्र tarkśāstra
logical *adj.* तर्कसंगत tarksangat
lone *adj.* अकेला akelā
lonely *adj.* अकेला akelā
long *adj.* लम्बा lambā
longitude *n.* देशांतर deśāntar
look *n.* दृश्य dṛśya; *v.i.* देखना dekhnā
loom *n.* करघा karghā
loop *n.* फन्दा phandā
loose *adj.* खुला khulā
loosen *v.t.* ढीला करना ḍhīlā karnā
lord *n.* स्वामी svāmī, प्रभू prabhū

lose *v.t.* खोना khonā
loss *n.* अप्राप्ति aprāpti
lost *adj.* खोया khoyā
lot *n.*भूखंड bhūkaṇḍ
loud *adj.* तेज़ tez
loudspeaker *n.* लाउडस्पीकर lāuḍspīkar
lounge *n.* विश्राम-कक्ष viśrām-kakṣa, प्रतीकषालय pratīkṣālāy
love *n.* प्रेम prem, प्यार pyār, मुहाब्बत muhābbat; *v.t.* प्यार करना pyār karnā
lovely *adj.* मनोहर manohar
lover *n.* प्रेमी premī, प्रेमिका premikā
low *adj.* नीचे nīce
loyal *adj.* वफ़ादार vafādār
luck *n.* भाग्य bhāgya
lucky *adj.* सौभाग्यशाली saubhāgyaśālī
luggage *n.* सामान sāmān
lump *n.* ढेला ḍhelā
lunar *adj.* चांद्र cāndra
lunatic *adj.* पागल pāgal
lunch *n.* दिन का खाना din kā khānā
lungs *n.* फेफड़ा phepharạ̄
luxurious *adj.* विलासी vilāsī
luxury *n.* ऐश aiś
lye *n.* लज्जीदार lajjīdār

M

machine *n.* मशीन maśīn
machinery *n.* यंत्र yantra
mad *adj.* पागल pāgal, गुस्सा gussā
madam *n.* मैडम maiḍam
magazine *n.* पत्रिका patrikā

magic *n.* जादू jādū
magical *adj.* जादुई jāduī
magician *n.* जादूगर jādūgar
magistrate *n.* मजिस्ट्रेट majisṭreṭ
magnet *n.* चुंबक cumbak
magnetic *adj.* चुम्बकीय cumbakīy
magnificent *adj.* शानदार śāndār
magnify *v.t.* बढ़ाना baṛhānā
maid *n.* कुमारी kumārī
mail *n.* डाक ḍāk
mailman *n.* डाकिया ḍākiyā
main *adj.* मुख्य mukhya
mainland *n.* मुख्य भू-भाग mukhya bhū-bhāg
maintain *v.t.* बनाए रखना banāe rakhnā
maintenance *n.* पालन pālan
majestic *adj.* राजसी rājsī
majesty *n.* प्रताप pratāp
major *n.* मेजर mejar; *adj.* मुख्य mukhya, बड़ा baṛā
majority *n.* बहुमत bahumat
make *n.* निर्माण nirmāṇ; *v.t.* बनाना banānā
maker *n.* बनाने वाला banāne vālā
make-up *n.* बनावट banāvaṭ
male *adj.* नर nar
malignant *adj.* अहितकर ahitkar
mammal *n.* स्तनपायी stanpāyī
man *n.* आदमी ādmī
manage *v.t.* प्रबंध करना prabandh karnā
management *n.* प्रबंध prabandh
manager *n.* मैनेजर mainejar
manhood *n.* पुरुषत्व puruṣtv
manifold *n.* विविध vividh
manipulate *v.t.* चलाना calānā

mankind *n.* मानव जाति mānav jāti
mannequin *n.* पुतला putlā
manner *n.* ढंग ḍhang
mansion *n.* हवेली havelī
manufacture *n.* निर्माण nirmāṇ; *v.t.* निर्माण करना nirmāṇ karnā
manure *n.* खाद khād
manuscript *n.* हस्तलिपि hastlipi
many *adj.* बहुत bahut
map *n.* नक्शा nakśā
marathon *n.* लम्बी दौड़ lambī dauṛ
marble *n.* संगमरमर saṅgmarmar
March *n.* मार्च mārc
mare *n.* घोड़ी ghoṛī
margarine *n.* मारगरीन mārgarīn
margin *n.* हशिया haśiyā, किनारा kinārā
marine *n.* जहाज़ी बेड़ा jahāzī beṛā; *adj.* समुद्री samudrī
mark *n.* चिह्न cihn
market *n.* बाज़ार bāzār
marketing *n.* विपणन vipṇan
marmalade *n.* मुरब्बा murbbā
maroon *adj.* चाकलेट रंग का … cākleṭ rang kā …
marriage *n.* शादी śādī
married *adj.* विवाहित vivāhit
marrow *n.* मज्जा majjā
marry *v.t.* शादी करना śādī karnā
marsh *n.* कच्छ kacch
marshal *n.* मार्शल mārśal
marvelous *adj.* आश्चर्यजनक āścaryajanak
masculine *adj.* (*manly, brave*) मरदाना mardānā; (*gender*) पुल्लिंग pulling
mash *v.t.* मरगजा करना maragjā karnā
mask *n.* नक़ाब naqāb; *v.t.* नक़ाब लगाना naqāb lagānā

mass *n.* राशिक rāśik; *adj.* सामूहिक sāmūhik
massage *n.* मालिश māliś
massive *adj.* भारी bhārī
mast *n.* मस्तूल mastūl
master *n.* स्वामी svāmī
mastery *n.* आधिपत्य ādhipaty
mat *n.* चटाई catāī
match *n.* जोड़ joṛ; (*for fire*) दियासलाई diyāsalāī
mate *n.* साथी sāthī
material *n.* सामान sāmān
mathematics *n.* गणित gaṇit
matter *n.* बात bāt
mattress *n.* गद्दा gaddā
mature *adj.* प्रौढ़ prauṛh
maturity *n.* परिपक्वता paripakvatā
maximum *adj.* अधिकतम adhikatam
may *v.aux.* हो सकना ho saknā; **May** *n.* (*month*) मई maı
maybe *adv.* शायद śāyad
mayonnaise *n.* सलाद का मसाला salād kā masālā
mayor *n.* मेयर meyar
maze *n.* भूल-भूलैया bhūl-bhūlaiyā
me *pron.* मुझे mujhe
meadow *n.* घास-स्थली ghās-sthalī
meager *adj.* अल्प
meal *n.* भोजन bhojan
mean *n.* बीच का रास्ता bīc kā rāstā; *adj.* कंजूस kanjūs
meaning *n.* अर्थ arth
means *n.* उपाय upāy, साधन sādhan
meantime *n.* इतने में itne meṁ; *adv.* इसी बीच isī bīc
measure *n.* नाप nāp
meat *n.* मांस māṁs
mechanic *n.* मैकेनिक maikenik

medal *n.* पदक padak
medical *adj.* डाक्टरी ḍākṭarī
medicine *n.* दवा davā
medium *n.* माध्यम mādhyam; *adj.* माझोला mājholā
meet *v.t.* मिलाना milānā; *v.i.* मिलना milnā
meeting *n.* सभा sabhā
mellow *adj.* रसीला rasīlā
melon *n.* खरबूज़ा kharbūzā
melt *v.i.* पिघलना pighalnā
member *n.* सदस्य sadsya
membrane *n.* झिल्ली jhillī
memoir *n.* संस्मरण sansmaraṇ
memorize *v.t.* याद करना yād karnā
memory *n.* याद yād
menace *n.* ख़तरा qhatarā
mend *v.t.* मरम्मत करना marammat karnā
mental *adj.* मानसिक mānsik
mention *n.* उल्लेख ullekh; *v.t.* उल्लेख करना ullekh karnā
menu *n.* मेन्यू menyū
merchandise *n.* व्यापारी माल vyāpārī māl
merchant *n.* व्यापारी vyāpārī
merciful *adj.* दयालु dyālu
merciless *adj.* निर्दय niarday
mercy *n.* दया dayā
merely *adv.* केवल keval
merit *n.* पुण्य puṇya
merry *adj.* विनोदी vinodī
mesh *n.* छिद्र chidr
mess *n.* खुराक khurāk
message *n.* संदेश sandeś
messenger *n.* दूल dūl, संदेहहर sandehahar
metal *n.* धातु dhātu

method *n.* ढंग ḍhang
methodical *adj.* सुव्यवस्थित suvyavsthit
microphone *n.* माइक māik
microscope *n.* सूक्ष्मदर्शी sūkśamdarśī
midday *n.* दोपहर dopahar
middle *adj.* मध्यम madhyam
middle-aged *adj.* अधेड़ adheṛ
midnight *n.* मध्यरात्रि madhyarātri
midwife *n.* दाई dāī
might *v.aux.* सकना saknā
migrate *v.i.* प्रवास करना pravās karnā
mild *adj.* मृदुल mr̥dul
mile *n.* माइल māil
milestone *n.* मील-पत्थर mīl-patthar
militant *adj.* लड़ाका laṛākā
military *n.* सेना senā
milk *n.* दूध dūdh
mill *n.* चक्की cakkī
miller *n.* चक्कीवाला cakkīvālā
millimeter *n.* मिलीमीटर milīmīṭar
million *n.* दस लाख das lākh
mind *n.* मन man
mindful *adj.* सावधान sāvdhān
mindless *adj.* तर्कहीन tarkhīn
mine *n.* खान khan; *pron.* मेरा merā
mingle *v.i.* ... से मिल जाना ... se mil jānā
minimum *n.* अल्पतम alpatam
mining *n.* खनन khanan
minister *n.* मंत्री mantrī
ministry *n.* मंत्रालय mantrālay
minor *n.* नाबालिग़ nābāliq; *adj.* थोड़ा thoṛā
minority *n.* अल्पसंख्यक alpsankhyak

mint *n.* तकसाल taksāl
minus *prep.* (*math*) बिना binā, कम kam
minute *n.* मिनट minaṭ; *adj.* हल्का सा halkā sā
miracle *n.* चमत्कार camatkār
miraculous *adj.* चमत्कारी camatkārī
mirage *n.* मृगतृष्ण mr̥gatr̥ṣṇ
mire *n.* कीचड़ kīcaṛ
mirror *n.* दर्पण darpaṇ
misadventure *n.* अनिष्ठ aniṣṭ
mischief *n.* नटखटी naṭkhaṭī
misdeed *n.* दुष्कर्म duṣkarm
misery *n.* तंगहाली tanghālī
misfortune *n.* दुर्भागय durbhāgy
mislay *v.t.* रखकर भूल जाना rakhakar bhūl jānā
misplace *v.t.* गलत जगह पर रखना galat jagah par rakhnā
Miss *n.* कुमारी kumārī; **miss** *n.* गलती galtī; *v.t.* खाली जाना khālī jānā
missile *n.* प्रक्षेपास्त्र prakṣepāstra
mission *n.* शिष्टमंडल śiṣṭmaṇḍal
mist *n.* कुहासा kuhāsā
mistake *n.* भूल bhūl; *v.t.* भूल होना bhūl honā
mistaken *adj.* गलत galat
mister *n.* (*Mr.*) श्रीमान śrīmān
mistress *n.* स्वामिनी svāminī
mistrust *v.t.* अविश्वास करना aviśvās karnā
misunderstanding *n.* ग़लतफ़हमी qgalatfahamī
mix *n.* मिश्रण miśraṇ; *v.t.* मिलाना milānā
mixture *n.* मिश्रण miśraṇ
moan *n.* कराह karāh
mode *n.* ढंग ḍhaṇg
model *n.* माडल mādal
modem *n.* मोडेम moḍem

modification *n.* परिवर्तन parivartan
modify *v.t.* परिवर्तन करना parivartan karnā
modular *adj.* प्रमापीय pramāpīy
module *n.* मापांक māpānk
moist *adj.* नम nam
moisten *v.t.* तर करना tar karnā
moisture *n.* नमी namī
mold *n.* फफूँदी phaphūṁdī; *v.t.* फफूँदी लगना phaphūṁdī lagnā
mom(my) *n.* माँ māṁ
moment *n.* पल pal
monarch *n.* राजा rājā
monarchy *n.* राजशाही rājśāhī
monastery *n.* मठ maṭh
Monday *n.* सोमवार somvār
money *n.* पैसा paisā
monitor *n.* मानीटर manıṭar
monk *n.* तपस्वी tapasvī
monkey *n.* बंदर bandar
monopoly *n.* एकाधिकार ekādhikār
monotonous *adj.* एकसुरा eksurā
monster *n.* राक्षस rakṣas
monstrous *adj.* भीमाकार bhīmākār
month *n.* महीना mahīnā
mood *n.* मिजाज़ mijāz
moon *n.* चन्द्र candra
moonlight *n.* चांदनी cāndanī
mop *n.* झाड़ू jhāṛū; *v.t.* पुचारे से साफ़ करना pucāre se sāf karnā
moral *n.* अभिप्राय abhiprāy; *adj.* नैतिक naitik
morale *n.* हौसला hausalā
more *adj./adv.* ज़्यादा zyādā

moreover *adv.* इसके अलावा iske alāvā
morning *n.* सवेरा saverā
mortar *n.* (*mud*) गारा gārā; (*gun*) मार्टर mārṭar
mortgage *n.* बंधक bandhak
mosque *n.* मस्जिद masjid
mosquito *n.* मच्छर macchar
most *adj.* अधिकतम adhikatam; *adv.* सबसे अधिक sabse adhik; *n.* ज़्यादा से ज़्यादा zyādā se zyādā
motel *n.* सराय sarāy
moth *n.* पतंगा pataṅgā
mother *n.* माता-जी mātā-jī
mother-in-law *n.* सास sās
motion *n.* गति gati
motivate *v.t.* प्रेरित करना prerit karnā
motivation *n.* प्रेरणा prerṇā
motive *n.* प्रेरणा prerṇā
motor *n.* मोटर moṭar
motorbike *n.* स्कूटर skūṭar
motorcycle *n.* मोटर साइकिल moṭar sāikil
mount *v.t.* चढ़ाना caṛhānā; *v.i.* चढ़ना caṛhnā
mountain *n.* पहाड़ pahāṛ
mourn *v.t.* शोक मनाना śok manānā
mourning *n.* मातम mātam
mouse *n.* चूहा cūhā
mouth *n.* मुँह muṁh
mouthpiece *n.* लगाम lagām
move *n.* चेष्टा ceṣṭā; *v.t.* हटाना haṭānā; *v.i.* चलना calnā
movie *n.* फ़िल्म film
moving *adj.* चलता caltā
Mrs. *n.* श्रीमती śrīmatī
much *adj.* बहुत bahut; *adv.* ज़्यादा zyādā
mud *n.* कीचड़ kīcaṛ

muffle *v.t.* ढक लेना ḍhak lenā
muffler *n.* मफ़लर maflar
mug *n.* प्याला pyālā; *v.t.* लूटना lūṭnā
multiplication *n.* गुणा guṇā
multiply *v.t.* गुणा करना guṇā karnā
municipality *n.* नगरपालिका nagarpālikā
murder *n.* हत्या hatyā; *v.t.* हत्या करना hatyā karnā
murderer *n.* हत्यारा hatyyārā
muscle *n.* मांसपेशी mānspeśī
muscular *adj.* पेशीय peśīy
museum *n.* संग्राहलय saṅgrāhalay
mushroom *n.* छत्रक chatrak
music *n.* संगीत sangīt
musician *n.* संगीतकार sangītkār
Muslim *n.* मुसलमान musalmān; *adj.* मुसलमानी musalmānī
mussel *n.* मसल masal
must *v.aux.* पड़ना paṛnā
mustache *n.* मूँछ mūṁh
mustard *n.* सरसों sarsoṁ
mute *adj.* गूँगा gūṁgā
mutiny *n.* बग़ावत baqgāvat
mutton *n.* भेड़ का मांस bheṛ kā māṁs
mutual *adj.* आपसी āpsī
muzzle *n.* थूथन thūthan
my *pron. m.s.* मेरा merā; *m.pl.* मेरे mere; *f.s./f.pl.* मेरी merī
myself *pron.* स्वयं svayam, खुद khud
mystery *n.* रहस्य rahasya
myth *n.* पौराणिक paurāṇik
mythology *n.* पुराणावधा purāṇāvadhā

N

nail *n.* (*metal*) कील kīl; (*finger*) नख nakh
naive *adj.* भोला-भाला bholā-bhālā
naked *adj.* नंगा nangā
name *n.* नाम nām
namely *adv.* अर्थात arthāt
nanny *n.* मादा mādā
nap *n.* झपकी jhapkī; *v.i.* झपकी लेना jhapakī lenā
napkin *n.* नैपकिन naipkin
narcotic *n./adj.* संवेदनमन्दक sanvedanmandak, स्वापक svāpak
narrate *v.t.* वर्णन करना varṇan karnā
narrator *n.* कथावाचक kathāvācak
narrow *adj.* तंग taṅg
nasty *adj.* गंदा gandā
nation *n.* राष्ट्र rāṣṭra
national *n./adj.* राष्ट्रीय rāṣṭrīy
nationality *n.* राष्ट्रीयता rāṣṭrīyatā
native *n.* मूलवासी mūlvāsī; *adj.* देशीय deśīy, जन्म भूमि janam bhūmi
natural *adj.* प्राकृतिक prākṛtik
naturally *adv.* स्वाभाव से svābhāv se
nature *n.* प्रकृति prakṛti; (*character*) स्वभाव svabhāv
naughty *adj.* नटखट naṭkhaṭ
nausea *n.* मिचली micalī
nauseous *adj.* मिचली आ रही है micalī ā rahī hai
naval *adj.* नौसैनिक nausainik
navel *n.* नाभि nābhi
navigate *v.t.* समुद्री यात्रा करना samudrī yātrā karnā
navigation *n.* साचालन sācālan
navy *n.* नौ-सेना nau-senā
near *adj.* पास pās; *adv.* पास से pās se

nearby *adj.* निकट nikaṭ; *adv.* निकट से nikaṭ se
nearly *adv.* लगभग lagbhag
nearsighted *adj.* निकटदर्शी nikaṭdarśī
neat *adj.* विशुध्द viśudhd
necessarily *adv.* अवश्यमेव avaśyamev
necessary *adj.* आवश्यक āvaśyak
necessity *n.* आवश्यकता āvaśyaktā
neck *n.* गर्दन gardan
necklace *n.* कण्ठी kaṇṭhī
necktie *n.* टाई ṭāī
need *n.* आवश्यकता āvaśyaktā; *v.t.* चाहना cāhanā
needle *n.* सूई sūī
needless *adj.* अनावश्यक anāvaśyak
negation *n.* इनकार inkār
negative *n.* नकार nakār; *adj.* नकारात्मक nakārātmak
neglect *v.t.* उपेक्षा करना upekṣā karnā
negotiate *v.i.* बातचीत करना bātcīt karnā, वार्ता करना vārtā karnā
negotiation *n.* वार्ता vārtā
neighbor *n.* पड़ोसी paṛosī
neighborhood *n.* पड़ोस paṛos
nephew *n.* (*sister's son*) भांजा bhāñjā; (*brother's son*) भत्रिका bhatrikā
nerve *n.* तंत्रिका tantrikā
nervous *adj.* उत्तेजित uttejit
nest *n.* घोंसला ghonsalā; *v.i.* घोंसला बनाना ghonsalā banānā
net *n.* जाल jāl
network *n.* जाल तंत्र jāl tantra; *v.t.* जाल तंत्र बनाना jāl tantra banānā
neural *adj.* तंत्रिकीय tantrikīy
neuralgia *n.* तंत्रिकाति tantrikāti
neurologist *n.* तंत्रका-विज्ञानी tantrakā-vigyānī

neuter *adj.* नपुंसक napunsak
neutral *adj.* तटस्थ taṭstha
neutrality *n.* तटस्थता taṭsthatā
never *adv.* कभी नहीं kabhī nahīṁ
nevertheless *adv.* फिर भी phir bhī
new *adj.* नया nayā
newborn *n./adj.* नवजात navjāt
news *n.* समाचार samāchār, सूचना sūcnā
newspaper *n.* समाचारपत्र samācārpatr
New Year *n.* नया साल nayā sāl, नववर्ष navvarṣ
next *adj./adv./prep.* अगला aglā; **next door** *adj./adv.* बगल का bagal kā
nice *adj.* अच्छा acchā
niche *n.* ताक़ tāq
nickel *n.* गिलट gilaṭ
nickname *n.* उपनाम upnām
niece *n.* (*brother's daughter*) भतीजी bhatījī; (*sister's daughter*) भानजी bhānjī
night *n.* रात rāt
nightmare *n.* कुस्वप्न kusvapn
nimble *adj.* फुर्तीला phurtīlā
nine *num.* नौ nau
nineteen *num.* उन्नीस unnīs
nineteenth *adj.* उन्नीसवाँ unnīsvāṁ
ninety *num.* नब्बे nabbe
ninth *adj.* नौवाँ nauvāṁ
nitrogen *n.* नाइट्रजन nāiṭrajan
no *adj./adv.* नहीं nahīṁ
noble *adj.* उदार udār
nobody *pron.* कोई नहीं koī nahīṁ
noise *n.* शोर śor
noisy *adj.* बहुत शोर bahut śor

nomadic *adj.* यायावरी yāyāvarī
nominate *v.t.* नामजद करना nāmajad karnā
nomination *n.* नामज़दगी nāmzadagī
none *pron.* कोई भी नहीं koī bhī nahīṁ
nonsense *n.* बेहूदगी behūdagī
noodle *n.* नूडल nūḍal
noon *n.* दोपहर dopahar
no one *pron.* कोई नहीं koī nahīṁ
nor *conj.* और न aur na
normal *adj.* सामान्य sāmānya
normality *n.* प्रसामान्यता prasāmānyatā
normally *adv.* अकसर aksar
north *n.* उत्तर uttar
northeast *n./adj.* उत्तरी-पूर्व uttar-pūrv
northern *adj.* उत्तरी uttarī
northwest *n./adj.* उत्तर-पश्चिम utar-paścim
nose *n.* नाक nāk
nostril *n.* नथुना nathunā
not *adv.* न na
notary public *n.* लेखय प्रमाणक lekhya pramāṇak
note *n.* नोट noṭ; *v.t.* उल्लेख करना ullekh karnā
notebook *n.* कॉपी kāpī
nothing *pron.* कुछ नहीं kuch nahīṁ
notice *n.* नोटिस noṭis; *v.t.* देखना dekhnā
noticeable *adj.* सुस्पष्ट suspaṣṭ
notification *n.* अधिसूचना adhisūcnā
notify *v.t.* सूचना देना sūcnā denā
notion *n.* धारणा dhārṇā
noun *n.* संज्ञा sañgyā
nourish *v.t.* खिलाना-पिलाना khilānā-pilānā
nourishing *adj.* पुष्टिकर puṣṭikar
nourishment *n.* आहार āhār

novel *n.* उपन्यास upanyās
novelty *n.* नवीनता navīntā
November *n.* नवंबर navambar
now *adv.* अब ab
nowadays *adv.* आजकल ājkal
nowhere *adv.* कहीं नहीं kahīṁ nahīṁ
noxious *adj.* हानिकर hānikar
nozzle *n.* टोंटी ṭoṁṭī
nuance *n.* सूक्ष्म भेद sūkṣam bhed
nuclear *adj.* परमाण्विक parmāṇvik
nucleus *n.* नाभिक nābhik
nude *adj.* नंगा nangā
nudity *n.* नग्नता nagantā
nuisance *n.* कण्टक kaṇṭak
null *adj.* रद्द radd
nullify *v.t.* रद्द करना radd karnā
numb *adj.* सुन्न sunn
number *n.* संख्या sankhyā
numerous *adj.* बहुत ज़्यादा bahut zyādā
nun *n.* मठवासिनी maṭhvāsinī
nurse *n.* नर्स nars; *v.t.* दूध पिलाना dūdh pilānā
nursery *n.* नर्सरी narsarī
nursing *n.* उपचर्या upcaryā
nut *n.* गिरीदार फल girīdār phal
nutrition *n.* पोषण poṣaṇ
nutritious *adj.* पोषक poṣak

O

oak *n.* बाँज bāṁj
oar *n.* चप्पू cappū
oat *n.* जी jī
oath *n.* शपथ śapath
oatmeal *n.* जी का दलिया jī kā daliyā
obedience *n.* आज्ञापालन āgyāpālan
obedient *adj.* आज्ञाकारी āgyākārī
obey *v.t.* आज्ञा का पालन करना āgyā kā pālan karnā
object *n.* वस्तु vastu; *v.t.* विरोध करना virodh karnā
objection *n.* आपत्ति āpatti
objective *adj.* वस्तुगत vastugat
obligation *n.* बाध्यता bādhyatā
oblige *v.t.* बाध्य करना bādhya karnā
oblong *n.* आयत āyat, *adj.* आयताकार āyatākār
obscene *adj.* अश्लील aślīl
obscure *adj.* धुँधला dhuṁlā; *v.t.* धुँधला कर देना dhuṁdhlā kar denā
observation *n.* पर्यवेक्षण paryavekṣaṇ
observatory *n.* वेधशाला vedhśālā
observe *v.t.* अनुसार चलना anusār calnā
obstacle *n.* बाधा bādhā
obstetrician *n.* प्रसूति-विशेषज्ञ prasūti-viśeṣagya
obstinate *adj.* दुराग्रही durāgrahī
obstruct *v.t.* बाधा डालना bādhā ḍālnā
obstruction *n.* बाधा bādhā
obtain *v.t.* पाना pānā
obtainable *adj.* प्राप्य prapy
obvious *adj.* स्पष्ट spaṣṭ
occasion *n.* अवसर avsar

occasional *adj.* कभी कभी kabhī kabhī
occult *adj.* गुप्त gupt
occupancy *n.* दख़ल daqhal
occupation *n.* पेशा peśā
occupy *v.t.* अधिकार में करना adhikār meṁ karnā
occur *v.i.* घटित होना ghaṭit honā
occurrence *n.* घटना ghaṭnā
ocean *n.* महासागर mahāsāgar
o'clock *adv.* बेज bej
October *n.* अकटूबर akṭūbar
octopus *n.* अष्टभुज aṣṭbhuj
odd *adj.* अनोखा anokhā
oddity *n.* अनोखापन anokhāpan
odor *n.* गंध gandh
odorless *adj.* गन्धहीन gandhhīn
offend *v.t.* अपराध करना aprādh karnā
offense *n.* अपराध aprādh
offensive *adj.* अपमानजनक apmānjanak
offer *n.* मोल mol; *v.t.* चढ़ाना caṛhānā
office *n.* दफ़्तर daftar
officer *n.* पदाधिकारी padādhikārī
official *n.* अधिकारी adhikārī; *adj.* अधिकारिक adhikārik
offset *v.t.* क्षतिपूर्ति करना kṣatipūrti karnā
often *adv.* अक्सर avsar
oil *n.* तेल tel; *v.t.* तेल निकालना tel nikālnā
oily *adj.* तेल सा tel sā
ointment *n.* लेप lep
OK! *interj.* ठीक है ṭhīk hai
old *adj.* (*people*) बूढ़ा būṛhā; (*things*) पुराना purānā
old-fashioned *adj.* पुरानी चाल का purānī cāl kā
olive *n.* ज़ैतून zaitūn
Olympic *adj.* ऑलम्पिक ālampik

Olympics *n.* ऑलम्पिक खेल ālampik khel
omelet(te) *n.* आम्लेट āmleṭ
omission *n.* छूट chūṭ
omit *v.t.* छोड़ देना choṛ denā
on *prep.* पर par
once *adv.* एक बार तुरंत ek bār turant
one *num.* एक ek
onion *n.* प्याज़ pyāz
only *adj.* अकेला akelā; *adv.* सिर्फ़ sirf
opaque *adj.* अपारदर्शी apārdarśī
open *adj.* खुला khulā; *v.t.* खोलना kholnā; *v.i.* खुलना khulnā
opening *n.* प्रारंभ prārambh
opera *n.* गीति-नाट्य gīti-nāṭya
operate *v.t.* चलाना calānā
operation *n.* चीर-फाड़ cīr-phāṛ
opinion *n.* राय rāy
opponent *n.* प्रार्तपक्षी prārtpakṣī
opportunity *n.* अवसर avsar
oppose *v.t.* विरोध करना virodh karnā
opposite *n.* सामने का sāmne kā; *adj.* विपरीत viparit
opposition *n.* विरोध virodh
oppress *v.t.* दमन करना daman karnā
oppression *n.* दमन daman
oppressive *adj.* अत्याचारी atyācārī
optical *adj.* दृष्टि dṛṣṭi
optician *n.* चश्मा बनानेवाला caśmā banānvālā
optimist *n.* अशावादी āśāvādi
optimistic *adj.* अशान्वित aśānvit
option *n.* विकल्प vikalp
optional *adj.* वैकल्पिक vaikalpik
or *conj.* या yā
oral *adj.* मौखिक maukhik

orange *n.* सन्तरा santarā; *adj.* नरंगी narangī
orchard *n.* फलोद्यान phalodyān
orchestra *n.* वाद्य-वृत vādyā-vṛt
order *n.* आर्डर ārḍar; *v.t.* आदेश देना ādeś denā
orderly *adj.* सुव्यवस्थित suvyavasthit
ordinary *adj.* मामूली māmūlī
ore *n.* कच्ची धातु kaccī dhātu
organ *n.* अवयव avyav
organic *adj.* जैव jaiv
organization *n.* संगठन saṅgaṭhan
organize *v.t.* संघटित करना saṅghaṭit karnā
origin *n.* उदभव udbhav
original *n./adj.* मूल mūl
originally *adv.* प्रारंभ-से prārambh-se
ornament *n.* गहना gahanā
orphan *n.* अनाथ anāth
oscillate *v.i.* डोलना ḍolnā
ostracism *n.* निर्वासन nivarsan
other *adj.* दूसरा dūsrā
otherwise *adv.* अन्यथा anyathā
ounce *n.* तेन्दुआ tenduā
our *adj.* हमारा hamārā
ours *pron.* हमारा hamārā
ourselves *pron.* खुद khud
out *adv.* बाहर bāhar
outcast *n.* बहिष्कृता bahiṣkṛtā
outcome *n.* परिणाम pariṇām
outdoors *n.* बाहरी bāharī
outer *adj.* बाहरी bāharī
outline *n.* रूपरेखा rūprekhā; *v.t.* रूपरेखा बनाना rūprekhā banānā
outside *n.* बाहर bāhar; *adj.* बाहरी bāharī; *adv./prep.* बाहर bāhar

outskirts *n.* किनारे kināre
outstanding *adj.* विशिष्ट viśiṣṭ
oval *n.* अंडाकार aṇḍākār; *adj.* अंडाकार aṇḍākār
oven *n.* चूल्हा cūlhā
over *adv.* ऊपर ūpar, पार pār
overall *adj./adv.* कुल मिलाकर kul milākar
overcast *adj.* आच्छन्न ācchann
overdue *adj.* अतिदेय atidey
overlook *v.t.* अनदेखी करना anadekhī karnā; *v.i.* अनदेखी होना anadekhī honā
overnight *adv.* रात भर rāt bhar
overseas *adj.* विदेश videś; *adv.* समुद्र पार samudra pār
overtake *v.t.* आगे निकल जाना āge nikal jānā
overtime *n.* अधिसमय adhisamay
overweight *adj.* अतिभार atibhār
owe *v.t.* देनदार होना dendār honā
owl *n.* उल्लू ullū
own *adj.* अपना apnā; *v.i.* स्वामी होना svāmī honā
owner *n.* मालिक mālik
ox *n.* बैल bail
oxygen *n.* आक्सीजन āksījan
oyster *n.* शुक्ति śukti
ozone *n.* ओज़ोन ozon

P

pace *n.* गति gati; *v.t.* कदम-कदम जाना kadam-kadam jānā
pack *v.t.* पैक करना paik karnā; *v.i.* पैक होना paik honā
package *n.* पैकेज paikej
packing *n.* संकुलन sankulan
pad *n.* गद्दी gaddī; *v.t.* गद्दी लगाना gaddī lagānā
pagan *n.* ग़ैर-ईसाई qgair-īsāī

page *n.* पन्ना pannā
pail *n.* डोल ḍol
pain *n.* दर्द dard; *v.t.* दर्द होना dard honā
painful *adj.* दर्दनाक dardnāk
painless *adj.* पीड़ाहीन pīṛāhīn
paint *n.* पेंट peṇṭ; *v.t.* (*a picture*) तस्वीर बनाना tasvīr banānā; *v.i.* रंगना rangnā
painter *n.* चित्रकार citrakār
painting *n.* चित्र citra
pair *n.* जोड़ा joṛā
pajamas *n.pl.* पाजामा pājāmā
pal *n.* साथी sāthī
palace *n.* राजभवन rājbhavan, महल mahal
pale *adj.* हल्का halkā
palette *n.* रंगपट्टिका rangpaṭṭikā
pall *n.* आवरण āvaraṇ
pallet *n.* रंगपट्टिका raṅg-paṭṭikā
palm *n.* हथेली hathelī
palm tree *n.* ताड़ tāṛ
palpitation *n.* धड़कन dhaṛkan
pamphlet *n.* छोटी पत्रिका choṭī patrikā
pan *n.* तवा tavā
panel *n.* दिलहा dilahā
panic *n.* आकस्मिक भय ākasmik bhay
pant *v.i.* छटपटाना chaṭpaṭānā
panties *n.pl.* औरतों की जाघिया auratoṁ kī jāghiyā
pantry *n.* रसोई-भंडार rasoī-bhaṇḍār
pants *n.* पतलून patlūn
paper *n.* काग़ज़ kāqgaz
paperback *n.* काग़ज़-चढ़ी kāqgaz-caṛhī
parachute *n.* हवाई छतरी havāī chatarī
parade *n.* परेड pareḍ; *v.t.* परेड करना pareḍ karnā

paradise *n.* स्वर्ग svarg
paragraph *n.* अनुच्छेद anucched
parallel *adj.* समांतर samāntar
paralysis *n.* लकवा lakvā
paralyze *v.i.* लकवा मारना lakvā mārnā
parasite *n.* परजीवी parjīvī
parasitic *adj.* परजीवी parjīvī
parcel *n.* पारसल pārsal
parchment *n.* चर्मपत्र carampatr
pardon *n.* क्षमा kṣamā; *v.t.* क्षमा करना kṣamā karnā
parents *n.* माता-पिता mātā-pitā
parish *n.* पैरिश pairiś
park *n.* उपवन upvan; *v.t.* पार्क करना pārk karnā
parking lot *n.* गाड़ी-स्थान gāṛī-sthān
parliament *n.* संसद sansad
parliamentary *adj.* संसदीय sansadīy
parrot *n.* तोता totā
parsley *n.* अजमोद ajmod
part *n.* पुरज़ा purzā
partial *adj.* आंशिक ānśik
participate *v.i.* भाग लेना bhāg lenā
particle *n.* कण kaṇ
particular *adj.* विशेष viśeṣ
partition *n.* विभाजन vibhājan
partner *n.* हिस्सेदार hissedār
party *n.* पार्टी pārṭī
pass *n.* घाटी ghāṭī; *v.t.* गुजरना gujarnā
passage *n.* गमन gaman
passenger *n.* यात्री yātrī
passerby *n.* पथिक pathik
passion *n.* मनोभाव manobhāv
passionate *adj.* भावुक bhāvuk

passive *adj.* कर्मवाच्य karamvācy
passport *n.* पासपोर्ट pāsporṭ
password *n.* गुप्त शब्द gupt śabd
past *n.* अतीत atīt; *adj.* गत gat
paste *n.* लेई leī; *v.t.* चिपकाना cipkānā
pasteurize *v.t.* गरम करके जीवाणु रति करना garam karke jīvāṇuu rati karnā
pastime *n.* मनोरंजन manorañjan
pastry *n.* पेस्ट्री pesṭrī
patch *n.* पैबंद paiband; *v.t.* पैबंद लगाना paiband lagānā
patent *n.* एकसव eksav
path *n.* पथ path, रास्ता rāstā
pathetic *adj.* कारुणिक kāruṇik
patience *n.* धीरज dhīraj
patient *n.* रोगी rogī; *adj.* सहनशील sahanśīl
patriot *n.* देशभक्त deśbhakt
patriotic *adj.* देशभक्तिपूर्ण deśbhaktipūrṇ
patrol *n.* गश्त gaśt; *v.i.* गश्त करना gaśt karnā
patron *n.* संरक्षक sanrakṣak
pattern *n.* पैटर्न paiṭarn, नमूना namūnā
paunch *n.* तोंद tond
pause *n.* विराम virām; *v.t.* रूकना rūknā; *v.i.* ठहर जाना ṭhahar jānā
pave *v.t.* सड़क डालना saṛak ḍālnā
pavement *n.* रास्ते का फर्श raste kā pharś
pavilion *n.* मण्डप maṇḍap
paw *n.* पंजा pañjā
pawn *n.* कठपुतली kaṭhputlī, प्यादा pyādā
pay *v.t.* पैसे देना paise denā; *v.t.* (*pay attention*) ध्यान देना dhyān denā
payment *n.* भुगतान bhugtān
pea *n.* मटर maṭar

peace *n.* शान्ति śānti
peaceful *adj.* शान्तिपूर्ण śāntipūrṇ
peach *n.* आड़ू āḍū
peacock *n.* मोर mor
peak *n.* चोटी coṭī
peanut *n.* मूँगफ़ली mūṁgfalī
pear *n.* नाशपाती nāśpātī
pearl *n.* मोती motī
peasant *n.* देहाती dehātī, किसान kisān
pebble *n.* बटिया baṭiyā
pedal *n.* पैडल paiḍal
pedestrian *n.* पादचारी pādcārī
peel *n.* छिलका chilkā; *v.t.* छीलना chīlnā
peg *n.* खूँटी khūṁṭī
pelvis *n.* श्रोणी śroṇi
pen *n.* क़लम qalam
penalty *n.* दण्ड daṇḍ
pencil *n.* पेंसिल pensil
penetrate *v.t.* छेदना chednā; *v.i.* फैल जाना phel jānā
penis *n.* लिंग liṅg
penny *n.* पेनी penī
people *n.* लोग log
pepper *n.* मिर्च mirc
peppermint *n.* पेपरमिंट peparmiṇṭ
perceive *v.t.* महसूस करना mehsūs karnā
perception *n.* प्रत्यक्ष ज्ञान pratyakṣ gyān
perch *n.* छतरी chatarī
perfect *adj.* संपूर्ण sanpūrṇ
perform *v.i.* पूरा करना pūrā karnā
performance *n.* पालन pālan
perfume *n.* सुगन्ध sugandh
perhaps *adv.* शायद śāyad

peril *n.* जोखिम jokhim
period *n.* पूर्ण-विराम pūrṇ-virām
periodic *adj.* आवर्ती āvartī
periodical *n.* पत्रिका patrikā
perishable *adj.* बिगड़ने वाला bigaḍarne vālā
permanence *n.* स्थायित्व sthāyitva
permanent *adj.* स्थायी sthāyī
permission *n.* अनुमति anumati, इजाज़त ijāzat
permit *n.* अनुमति पत्र anumati patr; *v.t.* अनुमति देना anumati denā
perpendicular *adj.* लम्ब lamb
persist *v.i.* लगा रहना lagā rahenā
person *n.* व्यक्ति vyakti
personal *adj.* व्यक्तिगत vyaktigat, निजी nijī
personality *n.* व्यक्तित्व vyaktigat
personnel *n.* कर्मचारीगण karamcārīgaṇ
perspective *n.* संदर्श sandarś
perspiration *n.* पसीना pasīnā
perspire *v.i.* पसीना निकलना pasīnā nikalnā
persuade *v.t.* मनाना manānā
persuasion *n.* प्रत्यायन pratyāyan
pessimistic *adj.* निराशावादी nirāśāvādī
pester *v.t.* सताना satānā
pet *n.* पालतू जीव pāltū jīv; *v.t.* दुलारना dulārnā
petal *n.* पंखुड़ी paṅkhuḍī
petrol *n.* पेट्रोल peṭrol
petroleum *n.* पेट्रोलियम peṭroliyam
petty *adj.* छोटा-मोटा choṭā-moṭā
phantom *n.* साया sāyā
pharmaceutical *adj.* औषधीय auṣadhīy
pharmacist *n.* दवासाज davāsāj
pharmacology *n.* औषध auṣadh

pharmacy *n.* दवा-ख़ाना davā-qhānā
phase *n.* अवस्था avasthā
pheasant *n.* तीतर tītar
phenomenon *n.* तथ्य tathya
philosophy *n.* दर्शन शास्त्र darśan śāstra
phlegm *n.* कफ kap
phone. *See* **telephone**
phonetic *adj.* ध्वन्यात्मक dhvanyātmak
phonetics *n.pl.* ध्वनिविज्ञान dhvanivigyān
photo(graph) *n.* फ़ोटो foṭo; *v.t.* फ़ोटो खींचना foṭo khīṁcnā
photographer *n.* फ़ोटोग्राफ़र foṭogrāfar
photography *n.* फ़ोटोग्राफ़ी foṭogrāfī
phrase *n.* (*grammar*) वाक्यांश vākyānś; (*saying*) मुहावरा muhāvarā
physical *adj* शारीरिक śārīrik
physician *n.* चिकित्सक cikitsak, वैद्य vaidya
physicist *n.* भौतिक bhautik
physics *n.* भौतिकी bhautikī
piano *n.* पियानो piyāno
pick *n.* गैती gaitī; *v.t.* चुनना cunnā
picket *n.* खूँटा khūṁṭā
pickle *n.* अचार acār; *v.t.* अचार डालना acār ḍālnā
pickpocket *n.* जेबकट jebkaṭ
picnic *n.* वनभोज vanbhoj
picture *n.* चित्र citra; *v.t.* का चित्र बनाना kā citra banānā
picturesque *adj.* चित्र सा citra sā
pie *n.* कचौड़ी kacauṛī
piece *n.* टुकड़ा ṭukaṛā
pierce *v.t.* छेदित करना chedit karnā
pig *n.* सूअर sūar
pigeon *n.* कबूतर kabūtar

pile *n.* ढेर ḍher; *v.t.* ढेर लगाना ḍher lagānā; *v.i.* जमा हो जाना jamā ho jānā
pilgrim *n.* तीर्थयात्री tīrthyātrī
pilgrimage *n.* तीर्थयात्रा tīrthyātrā
pill *n.* गोली golī
pillar *n.* खंभा khambā
pillow *n.* तकिया takiyā
pillowcase *n.* तकिये का गिलाफ़ takiye kā gilāf
pilot *n.* पायलट pāylaṭ
pimple *n.* फुंसी phunsī
pin *n.* आलपिन ālpin; **PIN** *abbrev. of "personal identification number"* पिन कोड pin koḍ
pincers *n.pl.* चिमटा cimṭā
pinch *n.* चिकोटी cikoṭī; *v.t.* काटना kāṭnā
pine (tree) *n.* चीड़ cīṛ
pineapple *n.* अनन्नास anannās
pink *adj.* गुलाबी gulābī
pioneer *n.* अगुआ aguā
pious *adj.* धर्मनिष्ठ dharmniṣṭh
pipe *n.* चिलम cilam
piper *n.* मुरली बजानेवाला murlī bajānevālā
pirate *n.* समुद्री डाकू samudrī ḍākū; *v.t.* डाका डालना ḍākā ḍālnā
pistol *n.* पिस्तौल pistaul
piston *n.* पिस्टन pisṭan
pit *n.* गड्ढा gaḍḍhā
pitcher *n.* घड़ा ghaṛā
pity *n.* दया dayā; *v.i.* दया करना dayā karnā
place *n.* स्थान sthān; *v.t.* रखना rakhnā
plague *n.* ताऊन tāun; *v.t.* सताना satānā
plain *n.* मैदान maidān; *adj.* सादा sādā
plan *n.* योजना yojnā; *v.t.* योजना बनाना yojnā banānā
plane. *See* **airplane**

planet *n.* ग्रह grah
plank *n.* तख़्ता taqhtā
plant *n.* पौधा paudhā; *v.t.* बोना bonā
plasma *n.* प्लाविका plāvikā
plaster *n.* पलस्तर palstar
plastic *n.* प्लास्टिक plāsṭik; *adj.* प्लास्टिक plāsṭik
plate *n.* प्लेट pleṭ, थाली thālī
platform *n.* प्लेटफ़ार्म pleṭfārm
platinum *n.* प्लैटिनम plaiṭinam
play *n.* नाटक nāṭak; *v.t.* (*a game*) खेलना khelnā; (*a musical instrument*) बजाना bajānā
player *n.* खिलाड़ी khilāṛī, वादक vādak
playground *n.* क्रीड़ास्थल krīṛāsthal
plea *n.* सफ़ाई safāī, निवेदन nivedan
plead *v.i.* अभिवचन करना abhivacan karnā
pleasant *adj* सुखकर sukhkar
please *v.t.* कृपया kṛpyā
pleasure *n.* विलास vilās
plenty *n.* प्रचुरता pracurtā
plot *n.* (*story*) कथानक kathānak; षड्यंत्र ṣaḍyantra; *v.t.* षड्यंत्र रचना ṣaḍyantra racanā
plow *n.* हल hal; *v.t.* हल चलाना hal calānā
plug *n.* गुल्ली gullī
plum *n.* बेर ber
plumber *n.* नलसाज़ nalsāz
plume *n.* पंख pankha
plump *adj.* गोल-मटोल hol-maṭol
plunge *v.i.* गोता लगाना gotā lagānā
plural *n.* बहुवचन bahuvacan, एकाधिक ekādhik
p.m. *adj. abbrev. for "post meridiem"* बाद दोपहर bād dopahar
pneumonia *n.* शीत ज्वर śīt jvar

pocket *n.* जेब jeb
pod *n.* फली phalī
poem *n.* कविता kavitā
poet *n.* कवि kavi
poetry *n.* काव्य kāvya
point *n.* नोक nok; (*conversation*) विचार बिंदु vicār bindū
poison *n.* ज़हर zahar
poisonous *adj.* ज़हरदार zahardār
pole *n.* खंभा khambhā; **Pole** *n.* ध्रुव dhruv
police *n.* पुलिस pulis
policy *n.* नीति nīti
polish *n.* पालिश pāliś; *v.t.* पालिश करना pāliś karnā; **Polish** *adj.* पोलिश poliś;
polite *adj.* शिष्ट śiṣṭ
political *adj.* राजनीतिक rājnītik
politician *n.* राजनीतिज्ञ rājnītigya
politics *n.pl.* राजनीति rājnīti
poll *n.* मतदान matdān
pollute *v.t.* प्रदूषित करना pradūṣit karnā; *v.i.* प्रदूषित होना pradūṣit honā
polluted *adj.* प्रदूषित pradūṣit
pollution *n.* प्रदूषण pradūṣaṇ
pond *n.* तालाब tālāb
pony *n.* टट्टू ṭaṭṭū
pool *n.* तालाब tālāb
poor *adj.* ग़रीब qgarīb
popcorn *n.* लावा lāvā
pope *n.* सन्त पिता sant pitā
pop music *n.* पॉप संगीत pāp sangīt
population *n.* जनसंख्या janamsaṅkhyā
porcelain *n.* पोर्सिलेन porsilen
porch *n.* डयोढ़ी ḍayoṛhī

pore *n.* रोम-कूप rom-kūp
pork *n.* सुअर का गोश्त suar kā gośt
port *n.* पत्तन pattan
portable *adj.* उठाऊ uṭhāū
porter *n.* पल्लेदार palledār
portfolio *n.* पत्राधान patrādhān
portrait *n.* चित्र citra
position *n.* स्थिति sthiti
positive *adj.* सकारात्मक sakārātmak
possess *v.t.* ... का मालिक होना ... kā mālik honā
possession *n.* कब्जा kabjā
possessive *adj.* स्वत्व बोधक svatva bodhak
possible *adj.* संभव sambhav
post *n.* (*location*) स्थान sthān; (*pole*) खंभा khambhā
post office *n.* डाकघर ḍākghar
postage *n.* महसूल mahsūl
postcard *n.* पोस्ट-कार्ड posṭ-kārḍ
posterity *n.* सन्तान santān
postmark *n.* डाक मोहर ḍāk mohar; *v.t.* मोहर लगाना mohar lagānā
postpone *v.t.* स्थगित करना sthagit karnā
pot *n.* बर्तन bartan
potato *n.* आलू ālū
pottery *n.* कुम्हारी kumhārī
pouch *n.* थैली thailī
poultry *n.* पालतू मुर्गी pāltū murgī
pound *n.* पाउन्ड pāunḍ; *v.t.* पीसना pīsnā; *v.i.* कूटना kūṭnā
pour *v.t.* उड़ेलना uṛelnā; *v.i.* बहना bahanā
powder *n.* चूर्ण cūrṇ
power *n.* शक्ति śakti
powerful *adj.* शक्तिशाली śaktiśālī
practical *adj.* व्यावहारिक vyāvahārik

practically *adv.* व्यावहारिक vyāvahārik
practice *n.* व्यवहार vyavahār; *v.t.* प्रयोग करना prayog karnā; *v.i.* अभ्यास करना abhyās karnā
praise *n.* प्रशंसा praśansā; *v.t.* सराहना करना sarāhanā
praiseworthy *adj.* प्रशंसनीय praśansanīy
pram *n.* प्रैम praim
prawn *n.* झींगा jhīṅgā
pray *v.i.* प्रार्थना करना prārthanā karnā
prayer *n.* प्रार्थना prārthanā
preach *v.t.* प्रवचन देना pravacan denā; *v.i.* प्रवचन करना pravacan karnā
precarious *adj.* अनिश्चित anikścit
precede *v.t.* घटित होना ghaṭit honā
precise *adj.* सही sahī
predict *v.t.* भविष्यवाणी bhaviṣyavāṇī
prefer *v.t.* ज़्यादा पसंद करना zyādā pasand karnā
preference *n.* अधिमान्यता adhimānyatā
prefix *n.* उपसर्ग upsarg
pregnant *adj.* गर्भवती garabhvatī
prejudice *n.* पूर्वाग्रह pūrvāgrah
preparation *n.* तैयारी taiyārī
prepare *v.t.* तैयार करना taiyār karnā; *v.i.* तैयार होना taiyār honā
preposition *n.* पूर्वसर्ग pūrvasarg
prescribe *v.t.* निर्धारित करना nirdhārit karnā
prescription *n.* नुसख़ा nusqhā
present *n./adj.* तोहफ़ा tohfā; *v.t.* उपस्थित करना upsthit karnā
presently *adv.* अभी अभी abhī abhī
preserve *n.* परिरक्षण parikṣaṇ; *v.t.* सुरक्षित रखना surkṣit rakhnā
president *n.* राष्ट्रपति rāṣṭrapati
press *n.* प्रेस pres; *v.t.* दबाना dabānā
pressure *n.* दाब dāb; *v.t.* दबाव डालना dabāb ḍālnā
prestige *n.* प्रतिष्ठा pratiṣthā

pretty *adj./adv.* सुन्दर sundar
prevailing *adj.* प्रबल prabal
prevent *v.t.* रोकना roknā
prevention *n.* रोकथाम rokthām
preventive *adj.* निवारक nivārak
previous *adj.* पूर्ववर्ती pūrvavartī
price *n.* दाम dām
priceless *adj.* अनमोल anmol
pride *n.* गर्व garv
priest *n.* पुजारी pujārī, पादरी pādrī, मौलवी maulvī
primary *adj.* प्राथमिक prāthmik
prime *adj.* आदिम ādim
prince *n.* राजकुमार rājkumār
princess *n.* राजकुमारी rājkumārī
principal *n.* प्राचार्य pracārya; *adj.* मुख्य mukhya
principle *n.* सिद्धांत siddhānt
print *v.t.* छापना chāpnā
printer *n.* मुद्रक mudrak
printing *n.* छपाई chapāī
priority *n.* प्राथमिकता prāthmiktā
prison *n.* जेलख़ाना jelqhānā
prisoner *n.* बन्दी bandī
privacy *n.* एकांत ekānt
private *adj.* व्याक्तिगत vyāktigat
privilege *n.* विशेषाधिकार viśeṣādhikār
prize *n.* पुरस्कार purskār
probable *adj.* संभावित sambhāvit
problem *n.* समस्या samasyā
procedure *n.* क्रिया-विधि kriyā vidhi
proceed *v.i.* आगे बढ़ना āge baṛhānā
process *n.* प्राक्रिया prākriyā; *v.t.* मुकदमा चलाना mukadamā calānā

produce *v.t.* उत्पन्न करना utpann karnā
product *n.* उत्पाद utpād
profession *n.* व्यवसाय vyavasāy, पेशा peśā
professional *adj.* व्यावसायिक vyāvasāyik
professor *n.* आचार्य ācārya
profile *n.* बाहरी रेखा bāharī rekhā
profit *n.* लाभ lābh; *v.i.* लाभ लेना lābh denā
profound *adj.* गहरी gehrī
program *n.* कार्यक्रम kāryakram
programmer *n.* प्रोग्रैमर prograimar
progress *n.* प्रगति pragati; *v.i.* प्रगति करना pragati karnā
progressive *adj.* प्रगतिशील pragatiśīl
prohibit *v.t.* रोकना roknā
prohibition *n.* मनाही manāhī
project *n.* परियोजना pariyojnā
projector *n.* प्रोजेक्टर projekṭar
promenade *n.* विहार स्थान vihār sthān
promise *n.* वादा vādā; *v.t.* वादा करना vādā karnā
pronoun *n.* सर्वनाम sarvanām
pronounce *v.t.* उच्चारित करना uccārit karnā
pronunciation *n.* उच्चारण uccāraṇ
proof *n.* सबूत sabūt
propaganda *n.* प्रचार pracār
propel *v.t.* ठेलना ṭhelnā
propeller *n.* नोदक nodak
proper *adj.* उपयुक्त upyukt
property *n.* संपत्ति sampatti
prophecy *n.* भविष्यवाणी bhaviṣyavāṇī
proposal *n.* प्रस्ताव prastāv
propose *v.t.* प्रस्ताव करना prastāv karnā
proprietor *n.* मालिक mālik
prose *n.* गद्य gadya

prospective *adj.* अग्रदर्शी agradarśī
prosper *v.i.* फूलना phūlnā
prosperity *n.* समृद्धि samṛddhi
prosperous *adj.* समृद्ध samṛaddh
prostate *n.* प्रस्टैट ग्रन्थि prasṭait granthi
prostitute *n.* रण्डी raṇḍī
protect *v.t.* रक्षा करना rakṣā karnā
protection *n.* रक्षा rakṣā
protein *n.* प्रोटीन proṭīn
protest *n.* विरोध virodh; *v.t.* विरोध करना virodh karnā; *v.i.* विरोध होना virodh honā
proud *adj.* गर्वित garvit
prove *v.t.* प्रमाणित करना pramāṇti karnā
proverb *n.* कहावत kahāvat
provide *v.t.* देना denā
province *n.* प्रदेश prades
prudent *adj.* बुद्धिमान buddhimān
prune *n.* आलूबुखारा ālūbukhārā
psychiatrist *n.* मनश्चिकित्सक manśicakitsak
psychological *adj.* मनोवैज्ञानिक manovaigyānik
psychologist *n.* मनोवैज्ञानी manovaigyānī
psychology *n.* मनोविज्ञान manovigyān
public *adj.* सार्वजनिक sārvjanik
publication *n.* प्रकाशन prakāśan
publicity *n.* प्रचार pracār
publish *v.t.* प्रकाशित करना prakāśit karnā
publisher *n.* प्रकाशक prakāśak
puff *n.* फूँक phūṁk
pull *v.t./v.i.* खींचना khīncnā
pulley *n.* घिरनी ghiranī
pulse *n.* दाल dāl
pump *n.* पम्प pamp; *v.t.* पम्प करना pamp karnā

pumpkin *n.* कद्दू kaddū
punch *n.* मूक्का mūkkā; *v.t.* मुक्का मारना mukkā mārnā
punctuate *v.t.* विरामचिन्ह लगाना virāmcinh lagānā
punctuation *n.* विराम-चिह्न virām-cihn
puncture *n.* पंकचर paṅkcar; *v.t.* पंकचर करना pankcar karnā
punish *v.t.* दंड देना daṇḍ denā
punishment *n.* सज़ा sazā
pupil *n.* छात्र chātra
puppet *n.* गुड़िया guṛiyā
puppy *n.* पिल्ला pillā
purchase *n.* ख़रीद qharīd; *v.t.* ख़रीदना qharīdnā
pure *adj.* शुद्ध śuddh
purification *n.* शुद्धिकरण śuddhikaraṇ
purify *v.t.* शुद्ध करना śuddh karnā
purple *adj.* बैंगनी baiganī
purpose *n.* प्रयोजन prayojan
purse *n.* पर्स pars
pursue *v.t.* पीछा करना pīchā karnā
pus *n.* पीव pīv
push *v.t.* धकेलना dhakelnā; *n.* फुंसी phunsī
puzzle *n.* पहेली pahelī; *v.t.* उलझन में डालना uljhan meṁ ḍālnā
pyramid *n.* पिरैमिड piraimiḍ

Q

quack *n.* कठवैद्य kaṭhvaidya
quail *n.* बटेर baṭer
quaint *adj.* अनोखा anokhā
qualified *adj.* योग्य yogya
qualify *v.i.* योग्य होना yogya honā

quality *n.* गुण guṇ
qualm *n.* अशंका aśankā
quantity *n.* परिमाण parimāṇ
quarantine *n.* संगरोध sangrodh
quarrel *n.* झगड़ा jhagṛā; *v.i.* झगड़ा करना jhagṛā karnā
quarry *n.* खुली khulī
quart *n.* क्वार्ट kvyārṭ
quarter *n.* चतुर्थांश catuthāṁś
quarterly *adj.* त्रैमासिक traimāsik; *adv.* प्रति त्रिमास prati trimās
quartz *n.* स्फटिक sphaṭik
queasy *adj.* रोगी rogī
queen *n.* रानी rānī
queer *adj.* अजीब ajīb
query *n.* प्रश्न praśan; *v.t.* प्रश्न करना praśan karnā
question *n.* सवाल savāl; *v.t.* सवाल करना savāl karnā
queue *n.* चोटी coṭī
quick *adj.* तेज़ tez
quickly *adv.* तेज़ी से tezī se
quiet *n./adj.* शान्त śānt
quilt *n.* रजाई rajāī
quit *v.t.* छोड़ देना choṛ denā
quite *adv.* बिलकुल bilkul
quiz *n.* प्रश्नोत्तरी praśanottarī; *v.t.* प्रश्नोत्तरी करना praśanot-tarī karnā
quota *n.* कोटा koṭā
quotation *n.* अवतरण avtaraṇ
quote *v.t.* उदधरण देना uddharaṇ denā

R

rabbit *n.* खरगोश khargoś
rabies *n.* अलर्क रोग alark rog
race *n.* दौड़ daur̥; (*human*) मानव जाति mānav jāti
racial *adj.* जातीय jātīy
rack *n.* ताँड़ tāṁr̥
racket *n.* हल्ला hallā
radiator *n.* विकिरक vikirak
radical *adj.* उग्र ugra
radio *n.* रेडियो reḍiyo
radioactive *adj.* विघटनाभिक vighaṭnābhik
radius *n.* त्रिज्या trijyā
raffle *n.* लाटरी lāṭarī
raft *n.* बेड़ा ber̥ā
rag *n.* चिथड़ा cithar̥ā
rage *n.* रोष roṣ
ragged *adj.* फटा-पुराना phatā-purānā
raid *n.* छापा chāpā; *v.t.* धावा मारना dhāvā mārnā
rail *n.* पटरी paṭarī
railing *n.* रेलिंग reliṇg
railroad *n.* रेलवे relve
railway *n.* रेल पटरी rel paṭarī
rain *n.* बारिश bāriś; *v.i.* बारिश होना bāriś honā
rainbow *n.* इन्द्रधनुष indradhanuṣ
rainy *adj.* बारिशी bāriśī
raise *v.t.* उठाना uṭhānā; (*a child, etc.*) पालन-पोषण करना pālan-poṣaṇ karnā
raisin *n.* किशमिश kiśmiś
rake *n.* पाँचा pāṁcā; *v.t.* कुरेदना kurednā
rally *n.* रैली railī
ramble *v.i.* भ्रमण करना bhramaṇ karnā

ramification *n.* प्रशाखन praśākhan
ramp *n.* फलांग phalāng
rancid *adj.* बासी bāsī
random *adj.* छिटपुट chiṭpuṭ
range *n.* माला mālā
rank *n.* दर्जा darjā
ransack *v.t.* छान डालना chān ḍālnā
ransom *n.* फ़िरौती firautī; *v.t.* छुड़ाना chuṛānā
rape *n.* बलात्कार balātkār; *v.t.* बलात्कार करना balātkār karnā
rapid *adj.* तेज़ tez
rare *adj.* विरल viral
rash *n.* ददोरा dadorā
rat *n.* चूहा cūhā
rate *n.* दर dar
rather *adv.* बल्कि balki
ratification *n.* अनुसमर्थन anusamarthan
ratify *v.t.* अनुसमर्थन करना anusamarthan karnā
ration *n.* राशन rāśan; *v.t.* राशन से देना rāśan se denā
rational *adj.* विवेकशील vivekśīl
rattan *n.* बेंत beṇt
ravine *n.* तंगघाटी tangghāṭī
raw *adj.* कच्चा kaccā
ray *n.* किरण kiraṇ
razor *n.* उस्तरा ustarā
reach *n.* पहुँच pahuṁc; *v.t.* पहुँचना pahuṁcnā
react *v.i.* प्रतिक्रिया लाना pratikriyā lānā
reaction *n.* प्रतिक्रिया pratikriyā
read *v.t.* पढ़ना paṛhnā
reader *n.* पाठक pāṭhak
reading *n.* पठन paṭhan
ready *adj.* तैयार taiyār
real *adj.* असली aslī

reality *n.* वास्तविकता vāstaviktā
realize *v.t.* पूरा होना pūrā honā
ream *n.* रीम rīm
reap *v.t.* काटना kāṭnā
reappear *v.i.* फिर से दिखाई पड़ना phir se dikhāī paṛnā
rear *n./adj.* पिछाड़ी pichāṛī
reason *n.* कारण kāraṇ; *v.i.* तर्क करना tark karnā
reasonable *adj.* विवेकी vivekī
reassure *v.t.* आश्वासन देना āśvāsan denā
rebate *n.* बट्टा baṭṭā, छूट chūt
rebel *n.* विद्रोही vidrohī; *v.i.* विद्रोह करना vidrohī karnā
rebellion *n.* विद्रोह vidroh
rebuff *v.t.* नकार देना nakār denā
recall *v.t.* वापस बुलाना vāpas bulānā
receipt *n.* रसीद rasīd
receive *v.t.* प्राप्त करना prāpt karnā
receiver *n.* चोरहटिया corahṭiyā
recent *adj.* हाल का hāl kā
reception *n.* स्वागत svāgat
receptionist *n.* स्वागतक svāgatak
recipe *n.* नुसख़ा nusaqhā
reciprocity *n.* आदान-प्रदान ādān-pradān
recite *v.t.* पढ़ना paṛhnā
reckon *v.t.* गिनती करना gintī karnā
reclamation *n.* सुधार sudhār
recognition *n. (acceptance, validity)* मान्यता mānyatā; *(distinction)* पहचान pehcān
recognize *v.t.* पहचानना pehcānnā
recommend *v.t.* सिफ़ारिश करना sifāriś karnā
recommendation *n.* सिफ़ारिश sifāriś
recompense *n.* इनाम inām; *v.t.* पुरस्कार देना purskār denā
reconcile *v.t.* मेल-मिलाप करना mel-milāp karnā

reconciliation *n.* मेल-मिलाप mel-milāp
record *n.* अभिलेख abhilekh, रेकार्ड rekārḍ; *v.t.* लिखना likhnā
recover *v.i.* (*recuperate*) चंगा हो जाना caṅgā ho jānā; (*reclaim*) उबर जाना ubar jānā
recreation *n.* मन-बहलाव man-behlāv
recruit *n.* रंगरूट rangrūṭ; *v.t.* भरती करना bharatī karnā
rectangle *n.* आयत āyat
rectangular *adj.* आयाताकार āyātākār
recuperate *v.i.* चंगा कर देना caṅgā kar denā
recurrence *n.* आवर्तन āvartan
recurring *adj.* आवर्तक āvartak
red *adj.* लाल lāl
reddish *adj.* कुछ लाल kuch lāl
redness *n.* लालपन lālpan
reduce *v.t.* घटाना ghaṭānā
reduction *n.* घटाव ghaṭāv
reed *n.* नरकुल narkul
reef *n.* समुद्री चट्टान samudrī caṭṭān
reel *n.* फिरकी phirkī
refer *v.t.* … के पास भेजना … ke pās bhejnā
reference *n.* संबंध sambandh
refill *v.t.* फिर से भरना phir se bharnā
refine *v.t.* शुद्ध करना śuddh karnā
refinery *n.* परिष्करण-शाला pariṣkaraṇ-śālā
refit *v.t.* दुरुस्त करना durūst karnā
reflect *v.t.* चिंतन करना cintan karnā
reflector *n.* परावर्तक prāvartak
reform *v.i.* फिर से बनाना phir se banānā
refresh *v.t.* ताज़ा करना tāzā karnā
refreshment *n.* जलपान jalpān
refrigerate *v.t.* प्रशीतित करना praśītit karnā
refrigerator *n.* फ़्रिज frij

refuge *n.* शरण śaraṇ
refugee *n.* शरणार्थी śarṇārthī
refund *v.t.* लौटाना lauṭānā
refusal *n.* इंकार inkār
refuse *n.* कचरा kacrā; *v.t.* इंकार करना inkār karnā
regard *n.* सम्मान sammān; *v.t.* मानना mānnā
regarding *prep.* ... के बारे में ... ke bāre meṁ
regime *n.* शासन śāsan
region *n.* इलाक़ा ilāqā
regional *adj.* प्रादेशिक pradeśik
register *n.* रजिस्टर rajisṭar
regret *n.* अफ़सोस afsos; *v.t.* पछताना pachtānā
regular *adj.* (*of occurrence*) नियमित niyamit; (*common, ordinary*) आम ām, साधारण sādhāraṇ
regulation *n.* नियमन niyaman
rehabilitation *n.* पुनर्वास purvārs
rehearsal *n.* पूर्वाभ्यास purvābhyās
rehearse *v.t.* रिहर्सल करना riharsal karnā
reimburse *v.t.* वापस लेना vāpas lenā
rein *n.* बागडोर bāgḍor
reinforce *v.t.* मज़बूत करना mazbūt karnā, बढ़ाना baṛhānā
reject *v.t.* नामंज़ूर करना nāmanzūr karnā
rejection *n.* अस्वीकरण asvīkaraṇ
relapse *n.* पुनरावर्तन punrāvartan
relate *v.t.* संबंध होना sambandh honā, सुनाना sunānā
relation *n.* संबंध sambandh, रिश्ता riśtā
relationship *n.* संबंध sambandh
relative *n.* रिश्तेदार riśtedār; *adj.* प्रासंगिक prāsangik
relax *v.i.* आराम करना ārām karnā
relaxation *n.* आराम ārām
release *n.* मोचन mocan; *v.t.* मुक्त करना mukt karnā
reliable *adj.* विश्वसनीय viśvasnīy

relief *n.* आराम ārām
relieve *v.t.* (*from duty*) आराम देना ārām denā; (*from worry*) चिंता से मुक्त करना cintā se mukt karnā
religion *n.* धर्म dharam
religious *adj.* धार्मिक dhārmik
rely *v.i.* … पर भरोसा रखना … par bharosā rakhnā
remain *v.i.* शेष रह जाना śeṣ reh jānā
remaining *adj.* बचा-कुचा bacā-kucā
remark *n.* टिप्पणी ṭippanī; *v.i.* कहना kahenā
remedy *n.* दवा davā; *v.t.* प्रतिकार करना pratikār karnā
remember *v.t* याद करना yād karnā; *v.i.* याद होना yād honā
remind *v.t.* याद दिलाना yād dilānā
reminder *n.* अनुस्मारक anusmārak
remit *v.t.* प्रेषित करना preṣit karnā
remittance *n.* प्रेषित रुपया preṣit rupayā
remorse *n.* अनुताप anutāp
remote *adj.* दूरवर्ती dūravarti
remove *v.t.* हटा देना haṭā denā
renew *v.t.* नया करना nayā karnā
renewal *n.* नवीकरण navīkaraṇ
renounce *v.t.* त्याग देना tyāg denā
renovate *v.t.* नया कर देना nayā kar denā
renovation *n.* नवीनीकरण navīkaraṇ
rent *n.* किराया kirāyā; *v.t.* किराये पर लेना kirāye par lenā
reorganize *v.t.* फिर से रखना phir se rakhnā
repair *n.* मरम्मत marammat; *v.t.* मरम्मत करना marammat karnā
repeat *n.* दोहराई doharāī; *v.t.* दोहराना dohrānā
repel *v.t.* मार भगाना mār bhagānā
repetition *n.* पुनरावृत्ति punarāvṛtti
replace *v.t.* वापस रख देना vāpas rakh denā
reply *n.* जवाब javāb; *v.i.* जवाब देना javāb denā

report *n.* रिपोर्ट riporṭ; *v.t.* प्रस्तुत करना prastut karnā
reporter *n.* संवाददाता saṁvāddātā
represent *v.t.* दोबारा देना dobārā denā
representative *n.* प्रतिनिधि pratinidhi; *adj.* प्रतिनिधिक pratinidhik
repression *n.* दमन daman
reprimand *n.* फटकार phaṭkār; *v.t.* फटकारना phaṭkārnā
reprisal *n.* प्रत्यपकार pratyapkār
reproduce *v.t.* उत्पन्न करना utpann karnā
reproduction *n.* पुनरुत्पादन punrutpādan
reptile *n.* रेंगनेवाला reṅganevālā
republic *n.* गणतंत्र gaṇtantra
republican *n./adj.* गणतंत्रवादी gaṇtantravādī
reputation *n.* नाम nām
request *n.* निवेदन nivedan; *v.t.* निवेदन करना nivedan karnā
require *v.t.* माँगना māṁgnā
requirement *n.* आवश्यकता āvaśyaktā
rescue *n.* बचाव bacāv; *v.t.* बचाना bacānā
research *n.* शोध śodh; *v.t.* शोध करना śodh karnā
resemblance *n.* सादृश्य sādṛaśya
resemble *v.t.* ... पर पड़ा होना ... par paṛā honā
resent *v.t.* बुरा मानना burā mānnā
reservation *n.* बुकिंग bukiṇg
reserve *n.* आरक्षित ārkṣit; *v.t.* आरक्षित करना ārkṣit karnā
reservoir *n.* टंकी ṭankī
reside *v.i.* रहना rahenā
residence *n.* निवास nivās
resident *n.* निवासी nivāsī
residue *n.* अवशेष avśeṣ
resign *v.i.* इस्तीफ़ा देना istīfā denā
resignation *n.* इस्तीफ़ा istīfā
resin *n.* राल rāl

resist *v.t.* विरोध करना virodh karnā
resistance *n.* रोध rodh
resistant *adj.* विरोधी virodhī
resort *n.* आश्रया āśrayā; (*a last resort*) अंतिम उपाय antim upāy
respect *n.* आदर ādar; *v.t.* आदर करना ādar karnā
respirator *n.* श्वासयंत्र śvasyantra
respond *v.i.* उत्तर देना uttar denā, जवाब देना javāb denā
response *n.* जवाब javāb
responsible *adj.* ज़िम्मेदार zimmedār
rest *n.* आराम ārām; *v.i.* आराम करना ārām karnā
restaurant *n.* रेस्तराँ restarāṁ
restless *adj.* बेचैन becain
restore *v.t.* मरम्त करना maramat karnā
restrain *v.t.* रोकना roknā
restrict *v.t.* सीमित करना sīmit karnā
restriction *n.* रोक rok
result *n.* परिणाम pariṇām; *v.i.* परिणाम होना pariṇām honā
résumé *n.* संक्षेप saṅkṣep
resume *v.t.* पुन आंरभ होना pun ārambh honā
retail *n.* परचूनी parcūnī; *v.t.* फुटकर बेचना phuṭkar becnā
retailer *n.* परचूनिया parcūniyā
retain *v.t.* अधिकार में रखना adhikār meṁ rakhnā
retina *n.* दृष्टिपटल dr̥ṣṭpaṭal
retire *v.i.* चला जाना calā jānā
retired *adj.* सेवानिवृत्ति sevānivr̥tti
retribution *n.* प्रतिफल pratiphal
return *n.* वापसी vāpsī; *v.t.* लौटना lauṭnā
reunite *v.t.* एक हो जाना ek ho jānā, जोड़ना joṛnā
reveal *v.t.* प्रकट करना prakaṭ karnā
revelation *n.* प्रकटन prakaṭan
revenge *n.* बदला badlā

revenue *n.* आय āy
reverse *n./adj.* उलटा ulṭā; *v.t.* उलटा करना ulṭā karnā
review *n.* समीक्षा samīkṣā; *v.t.* परखना parakhnā
revise *v.t.* दुहराना duhrānā
revive *v.t.* जी उठाना jī uṭhānā; *v.i.* जी उठना jī uṭhnā
revocation *n.* प्रतिसंहरण pratisanharaṇ
revoke *v.t.* प्रतिसंहरण करना pratisanharaṇ karnā
revolt *n.* विद्रोह vidroh; *v.i.* विद्रोह करना vidroh karnā
revolution *n.* क्रांति krānti; (*rotation*) परिक्रमा parikramā
revolve *v.t.* परिक्रम करना parikram karnā
reward *n.* इनाम inām; *v.t.* इनाम देना inām denā
rhyme *n.* तुक tuk
rhythm *n.* ताल tāl
rib *n.* पसली paslī
ribbon *n.* फ़ीता fītā
rice *n.* भात bhāt, चावल cāval
rich *adj.* अमीर amīr
rickety *adj.* सुखारोगी sukhārogī
riddle *n.* पहेली pahelī
ride *n.* सवारी करने की सैर savārī karnē kī sair; *v.t.* चढ़ना caṛhnā
rider *n.* सवार savār
ridge *n.* चोटी coṭī
ridiculous *adj.* हास्यपद hāsyapad
rifle *n.* राइफ़ल rāifal
right *adj.* (*direction*) दाहिना dāhinā; (*correct*) ठीक ṭhīk
right now *adv.* अभी-अभी abhī-abhī
right-handed *adj.* दक्षिणहस्त dakṣiṇhast
rigid *adj.* कठोर kaṭhor
rim *n.* किनारा kinārā
rind *n.* छिलका chilkā
ring *n.* (*jewelry*) अँगूठी aṁgūṭhī; *v.t.* बजाना bajānā
rinse *v.t.* खँगालना khaṁgālnā

riot *n.* हो-हल्ला ho-hallā; *v.t.* हो-हल्ला करना ho-hallā karnā
rip *n.* चीर cīr, फाड़ phāṛ; *v.t.* फाड़ना phāṛnā
ripe *adj.* पका pakā
rise *n.* उठान uṭhān; *v.t.* उठना uṭhnā
risk *n.* जोखिम jokhim; *v.t.* जोखिम उठाना jokhim uṭhānā
rival *n./adj.* प्रतिद्वन्द्वी pratidvandvī
rivalry *n.* प्रतिद्वन्द्विता pratidvanddvitā
river *n.* नदी nadi
road *n.* सड़क saṛak
roar *n.* गरज garaj; *v.i.* गरजना garajnā
roast *n.* भुना हुआ मांस bhunā huā māṁs; *adj.* भुना हुआ bhunā huā
rob *v.t.* लूटना lūṭnā
robber *n.* लुटेरा luṭerā
robbery *n.* लूट lūṭ
robe *n.* पद की पोशाक pad kī pośāk
robot *n.* यंत्रमानव yantramānav
rock *n.* चट्टान caṭṭān
rocket *n.* रोकेट roket
rocky *adj.* चट्टानी caṭṭāni
rod *n.* छड़ chaṛ
role *n.* भूमिका bhūmikā
roll *n.* मुट्ठा muṭṭhā; *v.t.* लपेटना lapeṭnā
romance *n.* प्रेम-लीला prem-līlā
romantic *adj.* रोमानी romānī
roof *n.* छत chat
room *n.* कमरा kamrā
rooster *n.* मुरगा murgā
root *n.* जड़ jaṛ
rope *n.* रस्सी rassī
rosary *n.* माला mālā
rose *n.* गुलाब gulāb

rosebush *n.* गुलाब का पौधा gulāb kā paudhā
rot *v.i.* सड़ना saṛnā
rotten *adj.* सड़ा saṛā
rouge *n.* रूज़ rūz
rough *adj.* खुरदरी khurdarī
round *adj.* गोल gol
routine *n.* नित्यक्रम nityakram; *adj.* नेमी nemī
row *n.* पंक्ति paṅkti; *v.t.* खेना khelnā
royal *adj.* शाही śāhī
rub *v.t.* मलना malnā
rubber *n.* रबर rabar
ruby *n.* माणिकय māṇikay
rucksack *n.* रकसैक raksaik
rudder *n.* पतवार patvār
rude *adj.* अपमानिक apmānik
rug *n.* गलीचा galīcā
ruin *n.* बिनाष bināṣ; *v.t.* नष्ट करना naṣṭ karnā
rule *n.* नियम niyam; *v.t.* शासन करना śāsan karnā
ruler *n.* रूलर rūlar; (*person*) शासक śāsak
rum *n.* रम ram
rumble *n.* गड़गड़ाहट gaṛgaṛāhaṭ
rumor *n.* किंवदंती kinvadantī
run *n.* दौड़ dauṛ; *v.i.* दौड़ना daūṛnā, भाग जाना bhāg jānā
runner *n.* दौड़ाक dauṛāk
rush *n.* हड़बड़ी haṛbaṛī; *v.t.* झपटना jhapṭanā
Russia *n.* रूस rūs
Russian *n./adj.* रूसी rūsī
rust *n.* ज़ंग zaṅg; *v.t.* ज़ंग लगना zaṅg lagnā
rustic *adj.* देहाती dehātī
rusty *adj.* ज़ंग लगा हुआ zaṅg lagā huā
rye *n.* राई rāī

S

saccharin *n.* सैकरिन saikarin
sack *n.* बोरा borā
sacred *adj.* पवित्र pavitra
sacrifice *n.* कुरबानी kurbānī; *v.t.* हानि सहना hāni sahanā
sad *adj.* उदास udās
sadden *v.i.* उदास होना udās honā
saddle *n.* ज़ीव zīv; *v.t.* ज़ीव कसना zīv kasnā
sadness *n.* उदासी udāsī
safe *n.* तिजौरी tijaurī; *adj.* सुरक्षित surakṣit
safety *n.* सुरक्षा surakṣā
sail *n.* पाल pāl; *v.t.* जलयात्रा करना jalyātrā karnā; *v.i.* जलयात्रा होना jalyātrā honā
sailboat *n.* पाल-नाव pāl-nāv
sailor *n.* मल्लाह mallāh
saint *n.* संत sant, पीर pīr
sake *n.* ख़ातिर qhātir
salable *adj.* बिकाऊ bikāū
salad *n.* सलाद salād
salary *n.* तनखव़्वाह tankhqhvāh
sale *n.* बिक्री bikrī
salesman *n.* बेचने वाला कार्यकर्ता becne vālā kāryakartā
salt *n.* नमक namak; *v.t.* नमक लगाना namak lagānā
salty *adj.* नमकीन namkīn
salute *v.t.* प्रणाम करना praṇām karnā, सलाम करना salām karnā
salvation *n.* मुक्ति mukti
salve *n.* मरहम marham
same *adj.* वैसा ही vaisā hī
sample *n.* नमूना namūnā; *v.t.* नमुना लेना namunā lenā

sanctuary *n.* शरण-स्थान śaraṇ-sthān
sand *n.* बालू bālū
sandal *n.* चप्पल cappal
sandalwood *n.* चंदन की लकड़ी candan kī lakaṛī
sandpaper *n.* रेगमार regamār
sandwich *n.* सैंडविच saiṅḍvic
sane *adj.* स्वस्थचित svasthcit
sanitary *adj.* स्वास्थ्य svāsthy, सफ़ाई का safāī kā
sanitary napkin *n.* टैम्पान ṭaimpān
sanity *n.* मानसिक सन्तुलन mānsik santulan
sap *n.* रस ras, सार sār
sapphire *n.* नीलम nīlam
sardine *n.* सार्डीन sārḍīn
satellite *n.* उपग्रह upgrah
satisfaction *n.* संतोष santoṣ
satisfactory *adj.* संतोषजनक santoṣjanak
satisfied *adj.* संतुष्ट santuṣṭ
satisfy *v.t.* पूरा करना pūrā karnā
Saturday *n.* शनिवार śanivār
sauce *n.* चटनी caṭnī
saucepan *n.* डेगची ḍegcī
saucer *n.* तश्तरी taśtarī
sausage *n.* गुल्मा gulmā
savage *adj.* जंगली jangalī
save *v.t.* (*keep*) रखना rakhnā; जान बचाना jān bacānā
saving *n.* बचत bacat
savior *n.* परित्राता paritrātā
savor *n.* स्वाद सुगंध svād sugandh; *v.t.* स्वाद लेना svād lenā
savory *adj.* स्वादिष्ट svādiṣṭ
saw *n.* आरा ārā; *v.t.* आरे से काटना āre se kāṭnā
sawdust *n.* लकड़ी का बुरादा lakaṛī kā burādā
say *v.t.* बोलना bolnā; *v.i.* कहना kahenā

saying *n.* कथन kathan
scab *n.* स्कैब skaib
scaffold *n.* मचान macān
scald *n.* द्रवदाह dravdāh; *v.t.* गरम पानी से जलाना garam pānī se jalānā
scale *n.* मापक māpak
scallop *n.* शम्बूक śambūk
scan *v.t.* अवलोकन करना avlokan karnā
scandal *n.* बदनामी badnāmī
scandalous *adj.* बदनामी का badnāmī kā
scar *n.* पपड़ी papaṛī
scarce *adj.* दुर्लभ durlabh
scare *v.t.* डराना ḍarānā
scarf *n.* दुपट्टा dupaṭṭā
scarlet *adj.* सिंदूरी sindūrī
scatter *v.t.* छितराना chitrānā; *v.i.* तितर-बितर होना titar-bitar honā
scene *n.* दृश्य dr̥śya
scenery *n.* प्रकृतिक दृश्य prakr̥tik dr̥̈śya
scent *n.* सुगंध sugandh
schedule *n.* अधिसूची adhisūcī; *v.t.* अधिसूची में रखना adhisūcī meṁ rakhnā
scheme *n.* योजना yojnā
scholar *n.* पंडित paṇḍit
scholarship *n.* छात्रवृत्ति chātravr̥tti
school *n.* विद्यालय vidyālay
schoolchild *n.m.* स्कूली लड़का skūlī laṛkā; *n.f.* स्कूली लड़की skūlī laṛkī
schoolmate *n.* सहपाठी sahpāṭhī
schoolteacher *n.* शिक्षक śikṣak
science *n.* विज्ञान vigyān
scientific *adj.* वैज्ञानिक vaigyānik

scientist *n.* विज्ञानी vigyānī
scissors *n.pl.* कतरनी katarnī
scold *v.t.* डाँटना ḍāṁṭnā
scope *n.* विषयक्षेत्र viṣaykṣetra
score *n.* प्राप्तांक prāptāṅk; *v.t.* अंक बनाना aṅk banānā
scorn *n.* घृणा ghṛṇā; *v.t.* घृणा करना ghṛṇā karnā
scorpion *n.* बिच्छू bicchū
scour *v.t.* माँजना māṁjnā
scout *n.* गुप्तचर guptcar; *v.t.* गुप्तचर्या करना guptcaryā karnā
scrap *n.* टुकड़ा ṭukaṛā
scrape *v.t.* खुरचना khurcnā
scratch *v.t.* खरोचना kharocnā
scream *v.t./v.i.* चीख़ना cīqhnā
screen *n.* परदा pardā
screw *n.* पेच pec; *v.t.* कसना kasnā
screwdriver *n.* पेचकस peckas
scribble *v.t.* घसीटना ghasīṭnā
scrub *v.t.* माँजना māṁjnā
scruple *n.* नैति संकोच naiti saṅkoc
scrupulous *adj.* विवेकी vivekī
scrutiny *n.* जाँच jāṁc
sculpt *v.i.* मूर्ति बनाना mūrti banānā
sculptor *n.* मूर्तिकार mūrtikār
sculpture *n.* मूर्ति mūrti
scum *n.* झाग jhāg
scythe *n.* दरांती darāntī
sea *n.* समुद्र samudra
seacoast *n.* समुद्रत्र तट samudra taṭ
seafood *n.* समुद्री मछली samudrī machlī
seagull *n.* समुद्रिक samudrik
seal *n.* सील मछली sīl machlī; *v.t.* मोहर लगाना mohar lagānā
seam *n.* सीवन sīvan

seaport *n.* समुद्र-पत्तन samudra-pattan
search *n.* तलाशी talāśī; *v.i.* तलाशी देना talāśī denā; *v.t.* खोजना khojnā
seasick *adj.* जहाज़ी मतली से बीमार jahāzī matlī se bīmār
seasickness *n.* जहाज़ी मतली jahāzī matlī
season *n.* ऋतु ṛtu
seasonal *adj.* मौसमी mausamī
seat *n.* कुर्सी kursī
seatbelt *n.* कुर्सी की पेटी kursī kī peṭī
seawater *n.* समुद्र जल samudra jal
seaweed *n.* समुद्री शैवाल samudrī śaivāl
seclusion *n.* एकांत ekānt
second *n./adj.* दूसरा dūsarā
secret *n.* भेद bhed; *adj.* गुप्त gupt
secretary *n.* मंत्री mantrī, सेक्रटरी sekraṭarī
section *n.* भाग bhāg
secular *adj.* लौकिक laukik
secure *adj.* सुरक्षित surakṣit; *v.t.* सुरक्षित करना surakṣit karnā
security *n.* सुरक्षा surakṣā
sedate *v.t.* नींद की गोली देना nīnd kī golī denā
sedated *adj.* शान्त śānt
sedative *n.* उपशामक upśāmak
seduce *v.t.* बहकाना bahkānā
seduction *n.* प्रलोभन pralobhan
see *v.t.* देखना dekhnā; *v.i.* दिखाना dikhānā
seed *n.* बीज bīj
seek *v.t.* खोजना khojnā
seem *v.i.* प्रतीत होना pratīt honā
seesaw *n.* झूला jhūlā
segment *n.* भाग bhāg
seize *v.t.* पकड़ना pakaṛnā
seizure *n.* गिरफ़्तारी giraftārī

seldom *adv.* विरले ही virale hī
select *v.t.* चुन लेना cun lenā
selection *n.* चयन cayan
self *adj.* स्वयं svayam
self-service *n./adj.* स्वयं-सेवा svayam-sevā
sell *v.t.* बेचना becnā
seller *n.* बेचने वाला becne vālā
semicolon *n.* अर्ध-विराम ardh-virām
senate *n.* राज्यसभा rājyasabhā
senator *n.* सीनेटर sīneṭar
send *v.t.* भेजना bhejnā
sender *n.* भेजने वाला bhejne vālā
senior *n./adj.* बड़ा baṛā
sensation *n.* अनुभूति anubhūti
sense *n.* इंद्रिय indriya
senseless *adj.* बेहोश behoś
sensitive *adj.* संवेदनशील sanvedanaśīl
sentence *n.* (*conviction*) दंड का आदेश daṇḍ kā ādeś; (*grammar*) वाक्य vākya; *v.t.* दंड का आदेश देना daṇḍ kā ādeś denā
separate *adj.* अलग alag; *v.i./v.t.* अलग होना alag honā
separation *n.* विच्छेद vicched
September *n.* सितंबर sitambar
septic *adj.* विषाक्त viśākt; *n.* (*septic tank*) मल टैंक mal ṭaiṅk; *v.t.* विषाक्त हो जाना viṣākt ho jānā
sequel *n.* नतीजा natījā
sergeant *n.* सारजेंट sārjenṭ
series *n.pl.* सिलसिला silsilā
serious *adj.* गंभीर gambhīr
sermon *n.* प्रवचन pravacan
serum *n.* सीरम sīram
servant *n.* नौकर naukar

serve *v.t.* सेवा करना sevā karnā
service *n.* सेवा sevā
session *n.* सत्र satra
set *n.* सेट seṭ; *adj.* (*ready*) तैयार taiyār; *v.t.* कड़ा हो जाना kaṛā ho jānā; *v.t.* रखना rakhnā
settle *v.t.* बसाना basānā; *v.i.* बस जाना bas jānā
settlement *n.* समझौता samjhautā; निपटारा nipṭārā
seven *num.* सात sāt
seventeen *num.* सत्रह satrah
seventeenth *num.* सत्रहवाँ satrahvāṁ
seventh *num.* सातवाँ sātvāṁ
seventy *num.* सत्तर sattar
several *adj.* कई kaī
severe *adj.* कठोर kaṭhor
sew *v.t./v.i.* सिलाई करना silāi karnā
sewer *n.* सीने वाला sīne vālā
sewing *n.* सिलाई silāī
sewing machine *n.* सिलाई की मशीन silāi kī maśīn
sex *n.* लिंग liṅg
sexual *adj.* लैंगिक laiṅgik
sexuality *n.* लैंगिकता laiṅgiktā
shabby *adj.* फटा-पुराना phaṭā-purānā
shade *n.* (*shadow*) छाया chāyā; (*of color*) रगं की मात्रा rang kī mātrā
shadow *n.* छाया chāyā
shady *adj.* छायादार chāyādar
shaggy *adj.* झबरा jhabarā
shake *v.t.* हिलाना hilānā; *v.i.* हिलना hilnā
shallow *adj.* छिछला chichalā
sham *n.* बनावट banāvaṭ
shame *n.* लज्जा lajjā
shampoo *n.* शैंपू śaiṁpū

shape *n.* रूप rūp; *v.t.* रूप देना rūp denā
share *n.* हिस्सा hissā; *v.t.* बाँट देना bāṁṭ denā
shareholder *n.* हिस्सेदार hissedār
shark *n.* हाँगर hāṁgar
sharp *adj.* पैना तेज़ painā tez
sharpen *v.t.* धार रखना dhār rakhnā
shave *v.t./v.i.* मूँड़ना mūṁṛnā
shaving brush *n.* हजामत का ब्रश hajāmat kā braś
shaving cream *n.* हजामत क्रीम hajāmat krīm
shawl *n.* शाल śāl
she *pron.* वह vah
sheaf *n.* पुलिन्दा pulindā
shear *n.* कतरनी katarnī; *v.t.* कतरना katarnā
shed *n.* छप्पर chappar; *v.t.* झाड़ना jhāṛnā
sheep *n.* भेड़ bheṛ
sheer *adj.* एकदम ekdam
sheet *n.* चादर cādar
shelf *n.* टाँड़ ṭāṁṛ
shell *n.* छिलका chilkā
shellfish *n.* घोंघा ghoṅghā
shelter *n.* शरण śaraṇ
shepherd *n.* गड़रिया gaṛriyā
shield *n.* ढाल ḍhāl
shift *n.* पाली pālī; *v.t.* हटाना haṭānā; *v.i.* हटना haṭnā
shine *v.t.* चमकना camaknā
ship *n.* जहाज़ jahāz; *v.t.* भेजना bhejnā
shirt *n.* कमीज़ kamīz
shiver *v.i.* ठिठुरना ṭhiṭhurnā
shock *n.* धक्का dhakkā; *v.t.* बिजली के धक्के bijalī ke dhakke
shoe *n.* जूता jūtā
shoehorn *n.* सीगड़ा sīgṛā
shoelace *n.* जूते का फ़ीता jūte kā fītā

shoot *v.t.* गोली मारना golī mārnā
shop *n.* दुकान dukān; *v.i.* खरीदारी करना kharīdārī karnā
shopkeeper *n.* दुकानदार dukāndār
shopping *n.* खरीदारी kharīdārī
shore *n.* समुद्र-तट samudra-taṭ
short *adj.* छोटा choṭā
shortage *n.* कमी kamī
short circuit *n.* लघुपथ laghupath
shorten *v.t.* छोटा करना choṭā karnā
shortening *n.* घटाई ghaṭāī
shortly *adv.* अविलंब avilamb
shorts *n.pl.* हाफ़पैंट hāfpainṭ
should *v.i.* चाहिए cāhiye
shoulder *n.* कंधा kandhā
shove *v.t.* खिसकाना khiskānā
shovel *n.* बेलचा belcā
show *n.* तमाशा tamāśā; *v.t.* दिखाना dikhānā
shower *n.* शावर śāvar; *v.i.* फुहारा स्नान करना phuhārā snan karnā
shrewd *adj.* चतुर catur
shrimp *n.* झींगी jhīṅgī
shrine *n.* तीर्थ मंदिर tīrth mandir
shrink *v.t.* सिकुड़ाना sikuṛānā; *v.i.* सिकुड़ना sikuṛnā
shuffle *v.t.* फेंटना fenṭnā
shut *v.t.* बंद करना band karnā
shutter *n.* झिलमिली jhilmilī
shuttle *n.* शटल गाड़ी śaṭal gāṛī
shy *adj.* संकोची saṅkocī
sick *adj.* बीमार bīmār
sickness *n.* बीमारी bīmārī
side *n.* बगल bagal
sidewalk *n.* किनारे की पगडंडी kināre kī pagḍaṇḍī

sideways *adj./adv.* तिरछा tirchā
sieve *n.* छलनी chalnī
sift *v.t.* छानना chānnā
sigh *n.* आह āh; *v.i.* आह भरना āh bharnā
sight *n.* दृष्टि dr̥ṣṭi
sign *n.* संकेत saṅket; *v.t.* हस्ताक्षर करना hastākṣar
signal *n.* संकेत saṅket
signature *n.* दस्तखत dastkhat
significance *n.* अर्थ arth
signify *v.t.* सूचित करना sūcit karnā
sign language *n.* इंगित भाषा ingit bhāṣā
silence *n.* चुप्पी cuppī; *v.t.* चूप करना cūp karnā
silent *adj.* चुप cup
silk *n.* रेशम reśam
sill *n.* देहली dehalī
silly *adj.* मूर्ख mūrkh
silver *n.* चाँदी cāṁdī
silverware *n.* चाँदी के बरतन-भाँड़े cāṁdī ke bartan-bhāṁr̥e
similar *adj.* समान samān
similarity *n.* समानता samāntā
simmer *v.i.* सिमसिमाना simsimānā
simple *adj.* सरल saral
simplify *v.t.* सरल बना देना saral banā denā
simply *adv.* सादगी से sādgī se
simulate *v.t.* अनुकरण करना anukaraṇ karnā
simulation *n.* अनुरूपण anurūpaṇ
sin *n.* पाप pāp; *v.i.* पाप करना pāp karnā
since *adv.* … के बाद से … ke bād se; *conj.* चूँकि cūṁki
sincere *adj.* सच्चा saccā
sincerity *n.* सच्चाई saccāī
sinew *n.* नस nas
sing *v.t./v.i.* गाना gānā

singer *n.* गायक gāyak
singing *n.* गायन gāyan
single *adj.* अकेला akelā
sinister *adj.* दुष्ट duṣṭ
sink *n.* नाली nālī
sip *n.* चुस्की cuskī; *v.t.* चुस्की लेना cuskī lenā
sir *n.* श्रीमान śrīmān
sister *n.* बहन behen
sister-in-law *n.* (*brother's wife*) भाभी bhābhī; (*wife's sister*) साली sālī; (*husband's sister*) ननद nanad
sit *v.i.* बैठना baiṭhnā
site *n.* स्थल sthal
situation *n.* स्थिति sthiti
six *num.* छह chah
sixteen *num.* सोलह solah
sixteenth *adj.* सोलहवाँ solahvāṁ
sixth *adj.* छठा chaṭhā
sixty *num.* साठ sāṭh
size *n.* आकार ākār
skate *n.* स्केट sket़; *v.i.* स्केट पर चलना skeṭ par calnā
skeleton *n.* ठठरी ṭhaṭharī
sketch *n.* रूपरेखा rūprekhā; *v.t.* रूपरेखा बनाना rūprekhā banānā
ski *n.* स्की skī
skid *v.i.* फिसलना phisalnā
skill *n.* कुशल kuśal
skillful *adj.* कुशलता kuśaltā
skim *v.t.* मलाई उतारना malāī utārnā
skin *n.* चमड़ी camṛī
skinny *adj.* दुबला-पतला dublā-patlā
skip *v.i.* उछलकूद करते चलना uchalkūd karte calnā
skirt *n.* घाघरा ghāgharā

skull *n.* खोपड़ी khopaṛī
sky *n.* आसमान āsmān
slack *adj.* ढीली ḍhīlī
slam *v.t.* ज़ोर से बंद करना zor se band karnā
slang *n.* वर्ग-बोली varg-bolī
slant *n.* तिरछा tirchā; *v.i.* तिरछा होना tirchā honā
slap *n.* थप्पड़ thappaṛ
slash *v.t.* काट मारना kāṭ mārnā
slate *n.* स्लेटी पत्थर sleṭī patthar
slave *n.* दास dās
slavery *n.* दासप्रथा dāsprathā
sleep *n.* नींद nīnd; *v.i.* सोना sonā
sleeping bag *n.* सोने का थैला sone kā thailā
sleeping car *n.* शायिता śāyitā
sleeping pill *n.* नींद की गोली nīnd kī golī
sleepy *adj.* निद्रालू nidrālū
sleeve *n.* आस्तीन āstīn
slender *adj.* पतला patlā
slice *n.* फाँक phāṁk; *v.t.* फाँक काटना phāṁk kāṭnā
slide *n.* सरकन sarkan, स्लाइड slāiḍ; *v.i.* सलसरकना salsaraknā
slight *adj.* छरहरा charharā
slim *adj.* पतला patlā
sling *n.* ढेलवार ḍhelvār
slip *n.* फिसलना phisalnā; *v.i.* फिसल जाना phisal jānā
slipper *n.* स्लीपर slīpar
slippery *adj.* फिसलनी phisalnī
slogan *n.* नारा nārā
slope *n.* ढाल ḍhāl
sloppy *adj.* कीचड़दार kīcaṛdār
slot *n.* छिद chid
slow *adj.* धीमा dhīmā
slowly *adv.* धीरे-धीरे dhīre-dhīre

slug *n.* घोंघा ghoṅghā
sluggish *adj.* मंद mand
sluice *n.* नहर nahar
slum *n.* गंदी-बस्ती gandī-bastī
small *adj.* छोटा choṭā
smart *adj.* बुद्धिमान buddhimān
smash *v.t.* टुकड़े-टुकड़े कर देना ṭukaṛe-ṭukaṛe kar denā
smell *n.* (*bad*) बदबू badbū; (*good*) खुशबू khuśbū; *v.t.* सूँघना sūṁghnā
smile *n.* मुस्कराहट muskarāhaṭ; *v.i.* मुस्कराना muskarānā
smith *n.* धातुकर्मी dhātukarmī
smog *n.* धुम-कोहरा dhum-koharā
smoke *n.* धुआँ dhuāṁ; *v.t.* सिग्रेट पीना sigreṭ pīnā
smoky *adj.* धुँधुआता dhuṁdhuātā
smooth *adj.* समतल samtal
smuggle *v.t.* तस्करी मारना taskarī mārnā
smuggler *n.* तस्कर taskar
smuggling *n.* तस्करी taskarī
snack *n.* नाश्ता nāśtā
snail *n.* घोंघा ghoṅghā
snake *n.* साँप sāṁp
snapshot *n.* स्नैपशाट snaipśāṭ
snarl *v.i.* गुर्राना gurānā
sneeze *n.* छींक chīṅk; *v.i.* छींकना chīṅknā
snob *n.* दंभी dambhī
snobbish *adj.* दंभ-भरा dambh-bharā
snore *v.i.* खर्राटा लेना kharrāṭā lenā
snorkel *n.* साँस लेने की नली sāṁs lene kī nalī
snort *v.i.* फुफकारना phuphkārnā
snout *n.* थूथन thūthan
snow *n.* बर्फ़ barf; *v.i.* बर्फ़ पड़ना barf paṛnā
snowflake *n.* हिमलव himlav

snowstorm *n.* हिम झंझावात him jhamjhāvāt
snub *v.t.* डाँटना ḍāṁṭnā
so *adv.* इतना itanā
soak *v.t.* भिगोना bhigonā; *v.i.* भीगना bhīgnā
soaking *n.* तर-बतर tar-batar
soap *n.* साबुन sābun; *v.t.* साबुन लगाना sābun lagānā
soar *v.i.* चढ़ना caṛhnā
sob *v.i.* सिसकना sisaknā
social *adj.* सामाजिक sāmājik
socialism *n.* समाजवाद samājvād
socialist *n.* समाजवादी samājvādī; *adj.* समाजवादी samājvādī
sock *n.* मोज़ा mozā
socket *n.* साकेट sākeṭ
soda *n.* सोडा soḍā
sodium *n.* सोडियम soḍiyam
sofa *n.* सोफ़ा sofā
soft *adj.* मुलायम mulāyam
soil *n.* मिट्टी miṭṭī
solar *adj.* सौर saur
soldier *n.* सिपाही sipāhī
sole *n.* (*of foot*) तलवा talvā; (*of shoe*) तला talā; *adj.* कुकुरजीभी kukurjībhī
solid *n.* पिंड piṇḍ; *adj.* ठोस ṭhos
solution *n.* हल hal; (*mixture*) घोल ghol
solve *v.t.* हल करना hal karnā
solvent *n.* विलायक vilāyak
somber *adj.* उदास udās, निराशजनक nirāśjanak
some *adj.* कुछ kuch
somebody *pron.* कोई koī
somehow *adv.* किसी तरह kisī tarah
someone *pron.* कोई koī
someplace *adv.* कहीं kahīṁ

something *pron.* कुछ kuch
sometimes *adv.* कभी-कभी kabhī-kabhī
somewhat *adv.* कुछ-कुछ kuch-kuch
somewhere *adv.* कहीं kahīṁ
son *n.* बेटा beṭā
song *n.* गाना gānā
son-in-law *n.* दामाद dāmād
soon *adv.* जल्दी jaldī
sore *n.* फोड़ा phoṛā; *adj.* नाराज़ nārāz
sorrow *n.* दुख dukh
sorry *interj.* माफ़ कीजिये māf kījiye
sort *n.* प्रकार prakār; *v.t.* छाँटना chāṁṭnā
soul *n.* आत्मा ātmā
sound *n.* आवाज़ āvāz; *v.i.* आवाज़ करना āvāz karnā; *adj.* ठीक ṭhīk
soup *n.* शोरबा śorbā
sour *adj.* खट्टा khaṭṭa
source *n.* स्त्रोत strot
south *n.* दक्षिण dakṣiṇ; *adj.* दक्षिणी dakṣiṇī
southeast *n.* दक्षिण-पूर्व dakṣiṇ-pūrv
southeastern *adj.* दक्षिण-पूर्वी dakṣiṇ-pūrvī
southern *adj.* दक्षिणी dakṣiṇī
southwest *n.* दक्षिण-पश्चिम dakṣiṇ-paścim
southwestern *adj.* दक्षिण-पश्चिमी dakṣiṇ-paścimī
souvenir *n.* निशानी niśānī
sovereign *adj.* प्रधान pradhān
sow *n.* सूअरी sūarī
soy *n.* सोया soyā
soybean *n.* सोया बीन soyā bīn
space *n.* जगह jagah; (*outerspace*) अन्तरिक्ष antarikṣ
spade *n.* फावड़ा phāvṛā
spare part *n.* अतिरिक्त पुरज़ा atirikt purzā

spark *n.* चिनगारी cingārī; *v.t.* चिनगारी निकलना cingārī nikalnā
sparkle *v.i.* चिनगारियाँ निकलना cingāriyāṁ nikalnā
sparrow *n.* गौरैया gauraiyā
spatial *adj.* अवकाशिक avakāśik
speak *v.t.* बोलना bolnā; *v.i.* कहना kahenā
speaker *n.* बोलने वाला bolne vālā
special *adj.* खास khās, विशेष viśeṣ
specialist *n.* विशेषज्ञ viseṣagy
specify *v.t.* स्पष्ट उल्लेख करना spaṣṭ ullekh karnā
specimen *n.* नमूना namūnā
spectator *n.* दर्शक darśak
speech *n.* (*lecture*) भाषण bhāṣaṇ; (*language*) बोली bolī
speed *n.* चाल cāl; *v.i.* जल्दी करना jaldī karnā
speed limit *n.* गति सीमा gati sīmā
speedometer *n.* गतिमापी gati māpī
spell *v.t.* हिज्जे करना hijje karnā
spend *v.t.* ख़र्च करना qharc karnā
sphere *n.* आकाशीय पिंड ākāśīy pinḍ
spice *n.* मसाला masālā
spicy *adj.* मसालेदार masāledār; (*hot*) तीता tītā
spider *n.* मकड़ी makaṛī
spider web *n.* मक्ड़ी के जाल makṛī ke jāl
spill *n.* छल chal; *v.t.* छलकाना chalkānā
spin *v.i.* घूमना ghūmnā
spinach *n.* पालक pālak
spine *n.* रीढ़ rīṛh
spiral *adj.* सर्पिलाकार sarpilākār
spire *n.* मीनार का शिखर mīnār kā śikhar
spirit *n.* आत्मा ātmā
spiritual *adj.* आत्मिक ātmik
spit *v.t.* थूकना thūknā
spite *n.* द्वेष dveṣ

splash *n.* छपछप chapchap; *v.i.* छिड़कना chiṛaknā
splint *n.* खपच्ची khapccī
splinter *n.* चैली cailī
spoil *v.t.* सिर चढ़ाना sir caṛhānā; *v.i.* बरबाद करवा देना barbād karvā denā
spoke *n.* आरा ārā
sponge *n.* स्पंज spañj
spontaneous *adj.* स्वत svat
spool *n.* फिरकी phirkī
spoon *n.* चम्मच cammac
sport *n.* मनोरंजन manoranjan
sportsman *n.* खिलाड़ी khillāṛī
spot *n.* चिट्ठी cittī; *v.t.* पहचान लेना pahacān lenā
spout *n.* धारा dhārā
sprain *n.* मोच moc; *v.i.* मोच आना moc ānā
spray *n.* फुहार phuhār; *v.t.* फुहार देना phuhār denā
spread *n.* फैलाव phallav; *v.t.* फैलाना phailānā, लगाना lagānā
spring *n.* वसंत vasant; *v.i.* उछलना uchalnā
sprinkle *v.t.* छिड़कना chiṛaknā
sprint *v.i.* बड़ी तेज़ी से दौड़ना baṛī tezī se dauṛnā
sprout *n.* अंकुर aṅkur; *v.i.* अंकुरित होना aṅkurit honā
spur *n.* एड़ eṛ
spy *n.* गुप्तचर guuptcar; *v.i.* गुप्तचरी करना guptcarī karnā
square *n.* वर्ग varg; *adj.* वर्गाकार vargākār
squash *n.* कुम्हड़ा kumhaṛā; *v.t.* दबाना dabānā
squint *v.i.* तिरछा देखना tirchā dekhna
squirrel *n.* गिलहरी gilharī
stable *n.* अस्तबल astabal; *adj.* स्थिर sthir
stadium *n.* खेलकूद का मैदान khelkūd kā maidān
staff *n.* सोंटा soṇṭā; (*employee*) कर्मचारी karamcārī
stage *n.* (*platform*) मंच mañc; (*of life, etc.*) अवस्था avasthā
stain *n.* धब्बा dhabbā; *v.t.* दाग़ डालना dāq ḍālnā

stainless *n.* बेदाग़ bedāqg
stainless steel *n.* ज़गरोधी इस्पात zagrodhī ispāt
stair *n.* सीढ़ी sīṛhī
staircase *n.* सीढ़ियाँ sīṛhiyāṁ
stake *n.* खूँटा khūṁṭā
stale *adj.* बासी bāsī
stalk *n.* डंठल ḍaṇṭhal; *v.t.* चोरी से जाना corī se jānā
stall *n.* थान thān; *v.t.* टालना ṭālnā
stammer *n.* हकलाहट haklāhaṭ; *v.i.* हकलाना haklānā
stamp *n.* (*ink*) छाप chāp; (*postage*) टिकट ṭikaṭ; *v.t.* छापना chāpnā
stand *n.* चबूतरा cabūtarā; *v.t.* रखना rakhnā; *v.i.* खड़ा होना kharạ̄ honā
standard *n.* मानक mānak; *adj.* स्तर star
standing *adj.* स्थायी sthāyī
staple *n.* स्टेपल sepal; *adj.* (*chief*) मुखय mukhya; *v.t.* स्टेपल से बाँधना sṭepal se bāṁdhnā
star *n.* तारा tārā
starboard *n.* जहाज़ का दायाँ भाग jahāz kā dāyāṁ bhāg
starch *n.* स्टार्च sṭārc; *v.t.* कलफ़ लगाना kalaf lagānā
stare *v.i.* आँखें पाड़कर देखना āṁkheṁ pāṛkar dekhnā
starfish *n.* तारमीन tārmīn
start *n.* आरंभ ārambh; *v.t.* शुरू करना śurū karnā; *v.i* शुरू होना śurū honā
starter *n.* प्रतियोगी pratiyogī
starvation *n.* भुखमरी bhukhmarī
state *n.* (*governmental*) प्रदेश pradeś; (*condition*) हालत hālat; *v.i.* बताना batānā
statement *n.* कथन kathan
statesman *n.* राजनेता rājnetā
station *n.* स्टेशन sṭeśan; *v.t.* तैनात करना taināt karnā
stationary *adj.* अचल acal

stationery *n.* लेखन सामग्री lekhan sāmagrī
statistic *n.* आँकड़े āṁkaṛe
statistical *adj.* आंख्यिकीय āṇkhyikīy
statue *n.* मूर्ति mūrti
status *n.* स्थिति sthiti
status quo *n.* यथावत स्थिति yathāvat sthiti
statutory *adj.* संवैधनिक sānvaidhanik
stay *n.* निवास nivās; *v.i.* रहना rahenā
steady *adj.* स्थिर sthir
steak *n.* माँस का टुकड़ा māṁs kā ṭukaṛā
steal *v.t.* चोरी करना corī karnā
steam *n.* भाप bhāp
steamship *n.* स्टीमर sṭīmar
steel *n.* इस्पात ispāt
steer *v.t.* चलाना calānā; *v.i* चल पड़ना cal paṛnā
steering wheel *n.* चाल्न चक्का cālan cakkā
stem *n.* तना tanā
step *n.* क़दम qadam; *v.i.* क़दम करना qadam karnā
stepbrother *n.* सौतेला भाई sautelā bhāī
stepdaughter *n.* सौतेली बेटी sautelī beṭī
stepfather *n.* कठबाप kaṭhbāp, सौतेला बाप sautelā bāp
stepmother *n.* सौतेली माँ sautelī māṁ
stepsister *n.* सौतेली बहन sautelī behen
stepson *n.* सौतेला बेटा sautela beṭā
stereo *n.* स्टीरियो sṭīriyo
stereotype *n.* रूढ़िबद्ध ruṛhibaddh
sterile *adj.* बाँझ bāṁjh
sterilize *v.t.* जीवाणुहीन बना देना jīvāṇuhīn banā denā
stern *n.* दुम्बाल dumbāl; *adj.* कड़ा kaṛā
stethoscope *n.* स्टेथास्कोप sṭethāskop
stew *n.* दमपुख़्त dampukht
steward *n.* खिदमतगार khidamtagār

stewardess *n.* परिचारिका paricārikā
stick *n.* डण्डा ḍaṇḍā; *v.t.* चिपकाना cipakānā
sticky *adj.* चिपचिपा cipcipā
stiff *adj.* कड़ा kaṛā
stiffen *v.t.* कड़ा बनाना kaṛā banānā; *v.i.* कड़ा होना kaṛā honā
still *adj.* निश्चल niścal; *adv.* अभी तक abhī tak
stimulant *n.* उत्तेजक uttejak, उद्दीपक uddīpak
stimulate *v.t.* प्रेरित करना prerit karnā
sting *n.* डंक ḍaṅk; *v.t.* डंक मारना ḍaṅk mārnā; *v.i.* दुखना dukhnā
stir *v.t.* चलाना calānā
stirrup *n.* रक़ाब raqāb
stitch *n.* टाँका ṭāṁkā
stock *n.* (*financial*) शेयर śeyar; (*goods*) भंडार में माल bhanḍār meṁ māl; *v.t.* सामान रखना sāmān rakhnā
stockbroker *n.* शेयर दलाल śeyar dalāl
stocking *n.* लंबा मोज़ा lambā mozā
stomach *n.* पेट peṭ
stomachache *n.* पेट का दर्द peṭ ā dard
stone *n.* पत्थर patthar
stool *n.* स्टूल sṭūl
stop *n.* रोक rok; *v.t.* रोकना roknā; *v.i.* रुकना ruknā, ठहरना ṭhaharnā
storage *n.* संग्रहण saṅgrahaṇ
store *n.* दुकान dukān; *v.t.* संग्रह करना saṅgrah karnā
storeroom *n.* भंडार गृह bhaṇḍār gṛh
stork *n.* लकलक laklak
storm *n.* तूफ़ान tūfān
stormy *adj.* तूफ़ानी tūfānī
story *n.* कहानी kahānī
stout *n.* तेज़ बियर tez biyar; *adj.* तगड़ा tagṛā
stove *n.* चूल्हा cūlhā

straight *adj.* सीधा sīdhā
strain *v.t.* कसकर तानना kaskar tānnā
strainer *n.* चलनी calnī
strand *n.* लट laṭ
strange *adj.* अजीब ajīb
stranger *n.* अजनबी ajnabī
strangle *v.t.* गला घोंटना galā ghonṭnā
strap *n.* पट्टा paṭṭā
straw *n.* पुआल puāl
strawberry *n.* शतावरी śatāvarī
streak *n.* धारी dhārī; *v.i.* दौड़ लगाना dauṛ lagānā
stream *n.* धारा dhārā
street *n.* सड़क saṛak
strength *n.* बल bal
strengthen *v.t.* ताकत मज़बूत करना tākat mazbūt karnā
stress *n.* (*pressure*) दबाव dabāv; (*mental*) मानसिक तनाव mānsik tanāv; *v.t.* बल देना bal denā
stretch *v.t.* तानना tānnā
stretcher *n.* स्ट्रेचर sṭrecar
strict *adj.* कठोर kaṭhor
strike *n.* हड़ताल haṛtāl
striking *adj.* हड़ताली haṛtālī
string *n.* धागा dhāgā
strip *n.* पट्टी paṭṭī
stripe *n.* धारी dhārī
striped *adj.* धारीदार dhārīdār
stroke *n.* लू लगना lū lagnā; *v.t.* सहलाना sahlānā
strong *adj.* बली balī
structure *n.* संरचना sanracanā
struggle *n.* संघर्ष saṅgharṣ; *v.i.* हाथ-पैर मारना hāth-pair mārnā
stubborn *adj.* हठीला haṭhīlā

student *n.* विद्यार्थी vidyārthī
study *n.* पढ़ाई paṛhāī; *v.t.* पढ़ना paṛhnā
stuff *n.* सामग्री sāmgrī; *v.t.* ठूसकर भरना ṭhūskar bharnā
stumble *v.i.* ठोकर खाना ṭhokar khānā
stun *v.t.* अचेत कर देना accet kar denā
stupid *adj.* मूर्ख mūrkh
style *n.* शैली śailī
stylish *adj.* फ़ैशनेबल faiśanebal
subdue *v.t.* वश में लाना vaś meṁ lānā
subject *n.* विषय viṣay
subjective *adj.* आत्मगत ātmagat
submarine *n.* पनडुब्बी panḍubbī
submit *v.t.* ... की अधीनता स्वीकार करना ... kī adhīntā svīkār karnā; *v.i.* झुक जाना jhuk jānā
subscribe *v.i.* हस्ताक्षर करना hastākṣar karnā
subscription *n.* चंदा candā
subsidy *n.* आर्थिक सहायता ārthik sahāyatā
substance *n.* तत्व tatva
substantial *adj.* महत्वपूर्ण mahatvapūrṇ
substitute *adj.* एवज़ी evazī; *n.* एवज़ evaz; *v.t.* प्रतिस्थापित करना pratisthāpit karnā
substitution *n.* प्रतिस्थापन pratisthāpan
subtitle *n.* उपशीर्षक upśīrṣak
subtle *adj.* सूक्ष्म sūkṣam
subtract *v.t.* घटाना ghaṭānā
suburb *n.* उपनगर upnagar
subway *n.* सुरंगपथ suraṅgpath
succeed *v.i.* कामयाब होना kāmyāb honā
success *n.* सफलता saphaltā
such *adj.* ऐसा aisā, जैसा jaisā
suck *v.t.* चूसना cūsnā
sudden *adj.* एकाएक ekāek, अचानक acānak

suede *n.* सिझाया हुआ चमड़ा sijhāyā huā camaṛā
suffer *v.i.* सहना sahanā
suffice *v.i.* काफ़ी होना kāfī honā
sufficient *adj.* पर्याप्त puryāpt
suffix *n.* प्रत्यय pratyay
sugar *n.* चीनी cīnī
suggest *v.t.* सुझाव देना sujhāu denā
suggestion *n.* सुझाव sujhāu
suicide *n.* आत्महत्या ātamhatyā; *v.t.* आत्महत्या करना ātamhatyā karnā
suit *n.* सूट sūṭ; *v.t.* अनुकूल होना anukūl honā
suitable *adj.* उपयुक्त upyukt
suitcase *n.* सूटकेस sūṭkes
suite *n.* परिचर paricar
sullen *adj.* रूखा rūkhā
sum *n.* जोड़ joṛ; *v.t.* जोड़ना joṛnā
summary *n.* संक्षेप saṅkṣep
summer *n.* गरमी garmī
summit *n.* चोटी coṭī
sun *n.* सूर्य sūrya
sunbathe *v.i.* धूप खाना dhūp khānā
sunburned *v.i.* धूप से जलना dhūp se jalnā
Sunday *n.* रविवार ravivār
sunflower *n.* सूरजमुखी sūrajmukhī
sunglasses *n.pl.* धूप का चश्मा dhūp kā caśmā
sunny *adj.* उजला ujlā
sunrise *n.* सूर्योदय sūryoday
sunset *n.* सूर्यास्त sūryast
sunshine *n.* धूप dhūp
sunstroke *n.* लू लगने का रोग lū lagne kā rog
suntan *n.* धूपताम्रता dhūptāgratā
superficial *adj.* सतही sathī

superior *adj.* उच्च ucca
supermarket *n.* सुपरबाज़ार suparbāzār
superstitious *adj.* अंधविश्वासी andhaviśvāsī
supervise *v.t.* पर्यवेक्षण करना paryavekṣaṇ karnā
supervisor *n.* पर्यवेक्षक paryavekṣak
supper *n.* रात का खाना rāt kā khānā
supplement *n.* परिशिष्ट pariśiṣṭ; *v.t.* पूरा करना pūrā karnā
supply *n.* सप्लाई saplāī; *v.t.* सप्लाई करना saplāi karnā
support *n.* सहारा sahāra; *v.t.* सहारा देना sahārā denā
supporter *n.* समर्थक samarthak
suppose *v.i.* मान लेना mān lenā
suppository *n.* वर्तिका vartikā
suppress *v.t.* दमन करना daman karnā
surcharge *n.* अधिमूल्य adhimūly
sure *adj.* निश्चित niścit; *v.t.* निश्चित करना niścit karnā
surety *n.* ज़मानतदार zamānatdār
surf *n.* समुद्री लहरें samudri laharem̐; *v.i.* पटरे पर लहरों पर खेलना paṭare par laharoṁ par khelnā
surface *n.* सतह satah
surgeon *n.* सर्जन sarjan
surgery *n.* शल्यचिकित्सा śalycikitsā
surly *adj.* रूखा rūkhā
surname *n.* परिवार का नाम parivār kā nām
surpass *v.t.* बढ़कर होना baṛhkar honā
surplus *n.* अतिरिक्त atirikt
surprise *n.* आश्चर्य āścarya; *v.t.* आश्चर्य करना āścarya karnā
surrender *v.t.* आत्म-समर्पण करना ātm-samarpaṇ karnā; *v.i.* वश में हो जाना vaś meṁ ho jānā
surround *v.t.* घेरना ghernā
surrounding *adj.* आस-पास का … ās-pās kā …
surroundings *n.pl.* पास-पड़ोस pās-paṛos
survive *v.i.* जीवित रहना jīvit rehnā

survivor *n.* उत्तरजीवी uttarjīvī
suspend *v.t.* लटकाना laṭkānā
suspenders *n.pl.* होटिस hoṭis
suspense *n.* अनिश्चय aniścay
suspicion *n.* संदेह sandeh
suspicious *adj.* संदेहजनक sandehjanak
sustain *v.t.* थाम रखना thām rakhnā
swallow *n.* अबाबील abābīl; *v.t.* निगलना nigalnā
swamp *n.* दलदल daldal
swan *n.* राजहंस rājhans
swarm *n.* झुण्ड jhuṇḍ
swear *v.t.* गाली बकना gālī baknā; *v.i.* कसम खाना kasam khānā
sweat *n.* पसीना pasīnā; *v.i.* पसीना बहाना pasīnā bahānā
sweater *n.* स्वेटर sveṭar
sweep *v.t.* झाड़ू देना jhāḍū denā
sweet *n.* मिठाई miṭhāī; *adj* मीठा mīṭhā
sweeten *v.t.* मीठा बनाना mīṭhā banānā
swell *n.* महातरंग mahātrang; *v.i.* बढ़ना baṛhnā
swelling *n.* फुलाव phulāv
swift *adj.* तेज़ tez
swim *v.i.* तैरना tairnā
swimmer *n.* तैराक tairāk
swimming *n.* तैराई tairāī
swindle *v.t.* धोखा देना dhokhā denā
swindler *n.* झाँसिया jhāṁsiyā
swing *n.* झूला jhūlā; *v.t.* झुलना jhulnā; *v.i.* डोलना ḍolnā
switch *n.* स्विच svic; *v.t.* स्विच खोलना svic kholnā
sword *n.* तलवार talvār
syllable *n.* अक्षर akṣar
symbol *n.* प्रतीक pratīk
symbolic *adj.* प्रतीकार्थ pratīkārth

sympathetic *adj.* हमदर्द hamdard
sympathize *v.i.* सहानुभूति जताना sahānubhūti jatānā
sympathy *n.* हमदर्दी hamdardī
symphony *n.* स्वर मेल svar mel
symptom *n.* लक्षण lakṣaṇ
synagogue *n.* यहूदियों का मंदिर yahūdiyoṁ kā mandir
synonym *n.* पर्याय paryāy
syntax *n.* वाक्यविन्यास vākyavinyās
synthetic *adj.* संश्लिष्ट sanśliṣṭ
syringe *n.* पिचकारी pickārī
syrup *n.* शीरा śīrā
system *n.* प्रणाली praṇālī
systematic *adj.* व्यवस्थित vyavasthit

T

table *n.* मेज़ mez
tablecloth *n.* मेज़पोश mezpoś
tablet *n.* टिकिया ṭikiyā
tack *n.* चपटी कील capṭī kīl
tact *n.* व्यवहार कुशलता vyavahār kuśaltā
tactful *adj.* व्यवहारकुशल vyavahārkuśal
tactic *n.* रणनीति raṇnīti
tag *n.* टगनी ṭagnī, लेबल lebal
tail *n.* लंबा lambā
tailor *n.* दर्ज़ी darzī; *v.t.* सिलाई करना silāī karnā
take *v.t.* ले जाना le jānā
talc *n.* टैल्क ṭailk
talent *n.* योग्यता yogyatā
talented *adj.* प्रतिभाशाली pratibhāśālī
talk *n.* बातचीत bātcīt; *v.i.* बातचीत करना bātcīt karnā
talkative *adj.* बातूनी bātūnī

tall *adj.* लंबा lambā
tame *adj.* पालतू pāltū; *v.t.* पालतू बनाना pāltū banānā
tamper *v.t.* गड़बड़ करना gaṛbaṛ karnā
tampon *n.* टैम्पान ṭaimpān
tan *adj.* भूरा रंग bhūrā rang; *v.t.* ताम्रवर्ण बनाना tāmrvarṇ banānā
tangerine *n.* सन्तरा santarā
tangle *v.t.* उलझाना uljhānā
tank *n.* टंकी ṭankī
tanker *n.* टंकी जहाज़ ṭankī jahāz
tap *n.* टोंटी ṭomṭī; *v.t.* टोंटी लगाना tomṭī lagānā
tape *n.* फीता phītā; *v.t* फीते से बाँधना pīte se bāṁdhnā
tape recorder *n.* टेपरेकार्डर ṭeprekārḍar
tapered *adj.* कम हो गया है kam ho gayā hai
tapestry *n.* चित्रपट citrapaṭ
tar *n.* डामर ḍāmar
target *n.* लक्ष्य lakṣy; *v.t.* लक्ष्य साधना lakṣy sādhunā
tariff *n.* सामा शुल्क sāmā śulk
tart *adj.* चरपरा carparā
task *n.* काम kām
taste *n.* स्वाद svād; *v.t.* स्वाद लेना svād lenā
tasty *adj.* स्वादिष्ट svādiṣṭ
tavern *n.* मदिरा गृह madirā grah
tax *n.* कर kar
taxi *n.* टैक्सी ṭaiksī
tea *n.* चाय cay
teach *v.t.* पढ़ाना paṛhānā, सिखाना sikhānā
teacher *n.* अध्यापक adhyāpak
teakettle *n.* चायदान cāydān
team *n.* टीम ṭīm
teapot *n.* चायदानी cāydānī
tear *n.* आँसू āṁsū; *v.t.* फाड़ना phāṛnā

tease *n.* चिढ़ानेवाला ciṛhānevālā; *v.t.* चिढ़ाना ciṛhānā
teaspoon *n.* छोटा चम्मच choṭā cammac
technical *adj.* तकनीकी taknīkī
teenager *n.* किशोर kiśor
telegram *n.* तार tār
telephone *n.* फ़ोन fon
telescope *n.* दूरबीन dūrbīn
television *n.* टी. वी. ṭī. vī.
tell *v.t.* बताना batānā
temper *n.* मिज़ाज mizāj
temperate *adj.* संयमी sanyamī
temperature *n.* (*fever*) बुख़ार buqhār; (*climate measure*) तापमान tāpmān
temple *n.* मंदिर mandir
temporary *adj.* अस्थायी asthāyī
tempt *v.t.* लुभाना lubhānā
temptation *n.* प्रलोभन pralobhan
ten *num.* दस das
tenacious *adj.* दृढ़ dṛṛh
tenant *n.* काश्तकार kāśtkār
tend *v.i.* चलना calnā
tendency *n.* झुकाव jhukāv
tender *adj.* दयालु dayālu
tendon *n.* शिरा śirā
tennis *n.* टेनिस ṭenis
tenor *n.* पुरूषस्वर purūṣsvar
tense *n.* काल kāl; *adj.* कसी हुई kasī huī
tension *n.* तनाव tanāv
tent *n.* तंबू tambū
tentacle *n.* स्पर्शक sparśak
tentative *adj.* प्रयोगात्मक prayogātmak
tenth *adj.* दसवाँ dasvāṁ

tenuous *adj.* दुबला dubalā
tepid *adj.* कुनकुना kunkunā
term *n.* अवधि avadhi
terminate *v.t* समाप्त करना samāpt karnā; *v.i.* समाप्त हो जाना samāpt ho jāna
termite *n.* दीमक dīmak
terrace *n.* छज्जा chajjā
terrestrial *adj.* पार्थिव pārthiv
terrible *adj.* भयंकर bhayankar
terribly *adv.* भयंकर रूप से bhayankar rūp se
terrific *adj.* भयानक bhayānak
territory *n.* क्षेत्र kṣetra
terror *n.* डर ḍar
test *n.* परीक्षा pārīkṣā; *v.t.* परीक्षा देना pārīkṣā denā
testify *v.i.* गवाही देना gavāhī denā
testimony *n.* साक्ष्य sākṣy
text *n.* पाठ pāṭh
textbook *n.* पाठ्यपुस्तक pāṭhyapustak
textile *n.* कपड़ा kapṛā
than *conj.* … से … se
thank *v.t.* धन्यवाद देना dhanyavād denā
thankful *adj.* आभारी ābhārī
thankfulness *n.* आभार ābhār
thank you *interj.* धन्यवाद dhanyavād, शुक्रिया śukriyā
that *adj./pron.* वह voh
thaw *v.t.* गलाना galānā; *v.i.* गलना galnā
theater *n.* थिएटर thieṭar
their *pron.* उनका unkā
them *pron.* उनको unko
theme *n.* विषय viṣay
themselves *pron.* अपने से apne se
then *adv.* तब tab

theology *n.* धर्मविज्ञान sharmvigyān
theoretical *adj.* सिद्धांतसंबंधी siddhāntsambandhī
theory *n.* सिद्धांत saddhānt
therapeutic *adj.* चिकित्सीय cikitsīy, रोगहर roghar
therapist *n.* चिकित्सक cikitsak
therapy *n.* चिकित्सा cikitsā
there *adv.* वहाँ vahāṁ
therefore *adv.* इसलिये isliye
thermometer *n.* तापमापी tāpmāpī
thermos *n.* थर्मस tharmas
thermostat *n.* तापस्थायी tāpsthāyī
these *pron.* ये ye
thesis *n.* शोध-प्रबन्ध śodh-prabandh
they *pron.* वे ve
thick *adj.* मोटा moṭā
thicken *v.t.* गाढ़ा बनाना gāṛhā banānā; *v.i.* गाढ़ा बनना gāṛhā bannā
thickness *n.* मोटाई moṭāī
thief *n.* चोर cor
thigh *n.* जाँघ jāṁgh
thimble *n.* अंगुश्ताना aṅguśtānā
thin *adj.* पतला patlā
thing *n.* चीज़ cīz
think *v.i.* सोचना socnā
third *adj.* तीसरा tīsrā
thirst *n.* प्यास pyās
thirsty *adj.* प्यासा pyāsā
thirteen *num.* तेरह terah
thirteenth *adj.* तेरहवाँ terahvāṁ
thirty *num.* तीस tīs
this *adj./pron.* यह yeh
thorn *n.* काँटा kāṁṭā

thorough *adj.* पूरा pūrā
thoroughfare *n.* आम रास्ता ām rāstā
those *pron.* वे ve
though *conj.* हालाँकि hālāṁki
thought *n.* विचार vicār
thoughtful *adj.* ख्याल करने वाला khyāl karne vālā
thousand *num.* हज़ार hazār
thousandth *adj.* हज़ारवाँ hazārvāṁ
thread *n.* धागा dhāgā
threat *n.* धमकी dhamkī
threaten *v.t.* धमकी देना dhamkī denā
three *num.* तीन tīn
threshold *n.* देहली dehalī
thrift *n.* मितव्यय mitvyay
thrifty *adj.* मितव्ययी mitvyayī
thrive *v.i.* फलना-फूलना phalnā-phūlnā
throat *n.* गला gala
throb *v.i.* काँपना kāṁpnā
throne *n.* सिहासन sihāsan
throttle *n.* गला galā
through *adv.* पार pār
throughout *adv.* पूरा pūrā
throw *n.* फ़ेक fenk; *v.t.* फ़ेकना fenknā; *v.i.* उल्टी हो जाना ulṭī ho jānā
thumb *n.* अंगूठा aṅgūṭhī
thunder *n.* गरज garaj
thunderstorm *n.* गरज के साथ तूफ़ान garaj ke sāth tūfān
Thursday *n.* गुरुवार guruvār
thyme *n.* अवाइन avāin
ticket *n.* टिकट ṭikaṭ
tickle *v.t.* गुदगुदाना gudgudānā; *v.i.* झुनझुनी होना jhunjhunī honā

tide *n.* ज्वार-थाटा jvār-thāṭā
tidy *adj.* ठीक-ठीक ṭhīk-ṭhīk
tie *n.* बंधन bandhan; *v.t.* टाई बाधना ṭāī bādhnā
tiger *n.* शेर śer
tight *adj.* तंग taṅg
tighten *v.t.* कसना kasnā
tile *n.* थपुआ thapuā
tilt *v.i.* झुकना jhuknā
timber *n.* इमारती लकड़ी imārtī lakaṛī
time *n.* समय samay, वक्त vakt; (*occurrence*) बार bār
timetable *n.* समय सारिणी samay sāriṇī
tin *n.*(*metal*) टिन ṭin; (*can*) डिब्बा ḍibbā
tingle *v.i.* झुनझुनी चढ़ना jhunjhunī caṛhnā
tint *n.* रंगत raṅgat; *v.t.* रंगत देना raṅgat denā
tiny *adj.* छोटा-सा choṭā-sā
tip *n.* (*for services*) बख़्शीश baqhśīs; *v.t.* उल्ट देना ulṭ denā
tiptoe *n.* पंजा pañjā; *v.i.* पंजों के बल चलना pañjoṁ ke bal calnā
tire *n.* टायर tāyar; *v.t.* थक जाना thak jānā
tired *adj.* थका thakā; *v.i.* थका हुआ thakā huā
tiredness *n.* थकावट thakāvaṭ
tireless *n.* अथक athak
tiresome *adj.* थकाऊ thakāū
tissue *n.* टिशू ṭiśū, ऊतक ūtak
title *n.* शीर्षक śīrṣak
to *prep.* को ko
toad *n.* थेक thek
tobacco *n.* तंबाकू tambākū
today *adv.* आज āj
toe *n.* पैर की उँगली pair kī uṁgalī
together *adv.* साथ साथ sāth sāth
toil *n.* मेहनत mehanat; *v.t.* मेहनत करना mehanat karnā

toilet *n.* शौचालय śaicālay
token *n.* प्रतीक pratīk
tolerance *n.* सहनशीलता sahanśīltā
tolerate *v.t.* सहना sahanā
toll *n.* राहदारी rāhdārī
tomato *n.* टमाटर ṭamāṭar
tomb *n.* क़ब्र qabr
tomorrow *adv.* कल kal
ton *n.* टन ṭan
tone *n.* स्वर svar
tongs *n.pl.* चिमटा cimṭā
tongue *n.* ज़बान zabān
tonnage *n.* टनथार ṭanthār
tonsils *n.pl.* टान्सिल ṭẽnsil
too *adv.* भी bhī
tool *n.* औज़ार auzār
tooth *n.* दाँत dāṁt
toothache *n.* दाँत का दर्द dāṁt kā dard
toothbrush *n.* दाँत का ब्रश dāṁt kā braś
toothpaste *n.* टूथपेस्ट ṭūthpesṭ
top *adj.* सब्से उपरला sabse uparlā, सबसे अधिक sabse adhik
topic *n.* विषय viṣay
topical *adj.* प्रासंगिक prasaṅgik
torch *n.* टार्च ṭārc
torment *n.* पीड़ा pīṛā; *v.t.* यातना देना yātnā denā
torrent *n.* प्रचण्ड धारा pracaṇḍ dhārā
torture *n.* उत्पीड़न utpīṛan; *v.t.* उत्पीड़न करना utpīṛan karnā
toss *v.t.* उछालना uchālnā
total *n.* जोड़ joṛ; *adj.* पूरा pūrā; *v.t.* जोड़ निकालना joṛ nikālnā
totalitarian *adj.* सर्वसम्मत sarvasammat
totally *adv.* बिलकुल bilkul
touch *n.* स्पर्श sparś; *v.t.* छूना chūnā

touching *adj.* मर्मस्पर्शी maramsparśī

touchy *adj.* चिड़चिड़ा ciṛciṛā

tough *adj.* कड़ा kaṛā

toughen *v.t.* कड़ा करना kaṛā karnā

toughness *n.* चीमड़पन cīmaṛpan

tour *n.* सैर sair; *v.t.* सैर करना sair karnā

tourism *n.* पर्यटन paryaṭan

tourist *n.* पर्यटक paryaṭak

tournament *n.* खेल-प्रतियोगिता khel-pratiyogitā

tow *v.t.* खींचना khīṁcnā

towards *adv.* ... की तरफ़ ... kī taraf

tower *n.* मीनार mīnār

town *n.* नगर nagar

toy *n.* खिलौना khilaunā

trace *n.* चिह्न cihn; *v.t.* खाका उतारना khākā utārnā

trachea *n.* श्वासनली śvāsnalī

track *n.* मार्ग mārg, पटरी paṭarī; *v.t.* पटा लगाना paṭā lagānā

traction *n.* कैर्षण kairṣaṇ

tractor *n.* ट्रैकटरप ṭraikṭar

trade *n.* व्यापार vyāpār; *v.t.* व्यापार करना vyāpār karnā

trader *n.* सौदागर saudāgar

tradition *n.* परम्परा paramparā

traditional *adj.* पारम्परिक pāramparik

traffic *n.* यातायात yātāyāt

tragedy *n.* त्रासदी trāsadī

tragic *adj.* कारूणिक kārūṇik

trail *n.* पगडंडी pagḍandī; *v.i.* घिसट्टे चलना ghisṭate calnā

trailer *n.* घसीटनेवाला ghasīṭnevālā

train *n.* रेलगाड़ी relgāṛī; *v.t.* प्रशिक्षित करना praśikṣit karnā

trainer *n.* प्रशिक्षक praśikṣak

training *n.* प्रशिक्षण praśikṣaṇ

trait *n.* विशेषता viśeṣtā
traitor *n.* विश्वासघाती viśvāsghātī
tram *n.* ट्राम ṭrām
tramp *n.* आवारा āvārā
trance *n.* भाव-समाधि bhāv-samādhi
transaction *n.* कारोबार kārobār
transfer *n.* अन्तरण antaraṇ; *v.t.* अन्तरण करना antaraṇ karnā
transit *n.* परिवहन parivahan
translate *v.t.* अनुवाद करना anuvād karnā
translation *n.* अनुवाद anuvād
translator *n.* अनुवादक anuvādak
transmission *n.* प्रसारण prasāraṇ
transmit *v.t.* पहुँचाना pahuṁcānā
transport *n.* परिवहन parivahan; *v.t.* वहन करना vahan karnā
transporter *n.* वाहक vāhak
trap *n.* फंदा phandā; *v.t.* फँसाना phaṁsānā
trash *n.* कचरा kacarā
travel *n.* यात्रा yātrā; *v.i.* यात्रा करना yātrā karnā
traveler *n.* यात्री yātrī
tray *n.* किश्ती kiśtī
treason *n.* देशद्रोह deśdroh
treasure *n.* ख़ज़ाना qhazānā
treasurer *n.* ख़ज़ांची qhazāñcī
treasury *n.* राजकोष rājkoṣ
treat *n.* आनंद ānand; *v.t.* बरताव करना bartāv karnā
treatise *n.* प्रबन्ध prabandh
treatment *n.* व्यवहार vyavyahār
treaty *n.* संधि sandhi, समझौता samjhautā
tree *n.* पेड़ peṛ
tremble *v.i.* काँपना kāṁpnā
trench *n.* खाई khāī
trend *n.* झुकाव jhukāv

trespass *v.i.* अनाधिकार प्रवेश करना anādhikār praveś karnā
trial *n.* परीक्षण parīkṣaṇ; (*legal*) मुकदमा mukdamā
triangle *n.* त्रिकोण trikoṇ
triangular *adj.* तिकोना tikonā
tribe *n.* जनजाति janjāti
tribute *n.* श्रद्धांजलि śraddhānjali
trick *n.* चाल cāl; *v.t.* धोका देना dhokā denā
trickle *n.* बूँद-बूँद būṁd-būṁd; *v.i.* बूँद-बूँद गिरना būṁd-būṁd girnā
tricycle *n.* तीन पहिए की साइकिल tīn pahie kī sāikil
trifle *n.* तुच्छ वस्तु tucch vastu
trigger *n.* लिबलिबी liblibī; *v.t.* उत्पन्न करना utpann karnā
trimester *n.* त्रिमास trimās
triumph *n.* विजय vijay; *v.i.* जीतना jītnā
trivia *n.* तुच्छ बातें tucch bāteṁ
trivial *adj.* तुच्छ tucch, मामूली māmūlī
troops *n.* सेना senā
tropical *adj.* उष्णकटिबन्धी uṣṇakaṭibandhī
tropics *n.pl.* उष्णकटिबन्ध uṣṇakaṭibandh
trouble *n./adj.* गड़बड़ gaṛbaṛ; *v.t.* गड़बड़ करना gaṛbaṛ karnā
troublesome *adj.* दुखदायी dukhdāyī
trowel *n.* करनी karnī, पाटा pāṭā
truant *n./adj.* नाग़ा करने वाला nāqgā karne vālā
truck *n.* ट्रक ṭrak
true *adj.* सही sahī
truffle *n.* कवक kavak
truly *adv.* सचमुच sacmuch
trump *n.* तुरूप का प ा turūp kā pattā; *v.t.* तुरूप चलना turūp calnā
trunk *n.* तना tanā
trust *n.* विश्वास viśvās; *v.t.* विश्वास करना viśvās karnā
trustworthy *adj.* विश्वसनीय viśvasnīy

truth *n.* सच्चाई saccāī
truthful *adj.* सत्यवादी satyavādī
try *n.* कोशिश kośiś; *v.t.* कोशिश करना kośiś karnā; (*legal*) मुकदमा चलाना mukdamā calānā
tube *n.* नली nalī, ट्यूब ṭūyūb
Tuesday *n.* मंगलवार mangalvār
tug *n.* झटका jhaṭkā; *v.i.* घसीटना ghasīṭnā
tugboat *n.* कर्षनाव karṣnāv
tulip *n.* कन्दपुष्प kandpuṣp
tumor *n.* रसौली rasaulī
tune *n.* सुर sur; *v.t.* सुर मिलाना sur milānā
tunnel *n.* सुरंग suraṅg
turkey *n.* पीरू pirū; **Turkey** *n.* तुर्की turkī
Turkish *n./adj.* तुर्की turkī
turmoil *n.* खलबली khalbalī
turn *n.* (*bend, twist*) घुमाव ghumāv; (*in games, line, etc.*) बारी bārī; *v.t.* मुड़ना muṛna
turtle *n.* कछुआ kachuā
tweezers *n.* चिमटी cimṭī
twelfth *adj.* बारहवाँ bārhavāṁ
twelve *num.* बारह bārah
twentieth *adj.* बीसवाँ bīsvāṁ
twenty *num.* बीस bīs
twice *adv.* दो बार do bār
twig *n.* छोटी टहनी choṭī ṭahnī
twilight *n.* झुटपुटा jhuṭpuṭā
twin *n.* जुड़वाँ juṛvāṁ
twinge *n.* टीस ṭīs
twinkle *v.i.* टिमटिमाना ṭimṭimānā
twist *n.* मरोड़ maroṛ; *v.t.* मरोड़ना maroṛnā
two *num.* दो do
type *n.* प्रकार prakār; *v.t.* टाइप करना ṭāip karnā

typewriter *n.* टाइप मशीन tāip maśīn
typical *adj.* आम ām
typist *n.* टाइपिस्ट ṭāipisṭ

U

ugly *adj.* कुरूप kurūp
ulcer *n.* फोड़ा phoṛā
ultraviolet *adj.* पराबैंगनी parābaiṅganī
umbrella *n.* छाता chātā
unable *adj.* अशक्त aśakt
unacceptable *adj.* अस्वीकार्य asvīkārya
unaccountable *adj.* अनुत्तरदायी anuttardāyī
unanimous *adj.* एकमत ekmat
unarmed *adj.* निरस्त्र nirastra
unauthorized *adj.* अप्राधिकृत aprādhikr̥t
unavoidable *adj.* अवश्यंभावी avśambhāvī
unaware *adj.* अनजान anjān
unbearable *adj.* असहनीय asahanīy
uncertain *adj.* अनिश्चित aniścit
uncle *n.* (*father's younger brother*) चाचा cācā; (*father's older brother*) ताऊ tāū; (*mother's brother*) मामा māmā; (*husband of father's sister*) फूफा phūphā; (*husband of mother's sister*) मौसा mausā
uncomfortable *adj.* बेआराम beārām
unconscious *adj.* बेहोश behoś
uncover *v.t.* नंगा करना nangā karnā
undamaged *adj.* अक्षत akṣat
undecided *adj.* अनिर्णीत anirṇāt
under *prep.* नीचे nīce
undergo *v.i.* सहना sahanā
underground *adj.* भूमिगत bhūmigat

underline *v.t.* रेखांकित करना rekhānkit karnā
underneath *prep.* ... के नीचे ... ke nīce
underpants *n.pl.* अन्दर के कपड़े andar ke kapṛe
undersign *v.t.* हस्ताक्षर करना hastākṣar karnā
understand *v.t.* समझना samajhnā
understanding *n.* समझने की शक्ति samajhne kī śakti
undertake *v.t.* वचन देना vacan denā
underwater *adj.* अन्तर्जलीय antarjalī
underwear *n.* नीचे पहनने के कपड़े nīce pahenne ke kapṛe
undo *v.i.* अन्यथा कर देना anyathā kar denā
uneasiness *n.* बेचैनी becainī
uneasy *adj.* बेचैन becain
uneducated *adj.* अनपढ़ anpaṛh
unemployed *adj.* बेरोज़गार berozgār
unemployment *n.* बेरोज़गारी berozgārī
unending *adj.* अनन्त anant
unequal *adj.* असमान asmān
unfair *adj.* अनुचित anucit
unfamiliar *adj.* अनजान anjān
unfasten *v.t.* खोलना kholnā
unfortunate *adj.* अभाग्य abhāgya, दुर्भाग्य durbhāgya
unfriendly *adj.* अस्नेही asnehī
unhappy *adj.* दुखी dukhī
unhealthy *adj.* अस्वास्थ्यकर asvāsthyakar
uniform *n..* वरदी vardī; *adj.* एक समान ek smān
unimportant *adj.* महत्वहीन mahatvahın
unintentional *adj.* अनभिप्रेत anabhipret
union *n.* संघ saṅgha
unique *adj.* बेजोड़ bejoṛ
unisex *adj.* एकलिंगी ek liṅgī
unit *n.* इकाई ikāī
unite *v.t.* जोड़ना joṛnā

United Nations *n.* संयुक्त राष्ट्र sanyukt rāṣṭra
unity *n.* एकता ektā
universal *adj.* सर्वसम्मति sarvsammati
universe *n.* विश्व viśva
university *n.* विश्वविद्यालय viśvavidyālay
unknown *adj.* अंजान anjān
unless *conj.* जब तक न … jab tak na …
unlike *adj.* असमान asamān
unlikely *adj.* असंभाव्य asambhāvy
unload *v.t.* माल उतारना māl utārnā
unlucky *adj.* बदकिस्मत badkismat
unnecessary *adj.* अनावश्यक anāvśyak
unofficial *adj.* अशासकीय aśāsakīy
unpack *v.t.* सामान निकालना sāmān nikālnā
unpleasant *adj.* गंदा gandā
unpopular *adj.* अलोकप्रिय alokpriyā
unrest *n.* गड़बड़ gaṛbaṛ
unsafe *adj.* असुरक्षित asurakṣit
unsatisfactory *adj.* असन्तोषजनक asantoṣjanak
unskilled *adj.* अकुशल akuśal
unstable *adj.* अस्थिर asthir
unsuccessful *adj.* असफल asaphal
untie *v.t.* खोलना kholnā
until *prep.* जब तक … jab tak …
untrue *adj.* झूठा jhūṭhā
unwell *adj.* अस्वस्थ asvasth
unwrap *v.t.* खोलना kholnā
up *adj./adv./prep.* ऊपर ūpar
upkeep *n.* देखभाल dekhbhāl
upon *prep.* पर par
upper *adj.* ऊपरी ūparī
uproar *n.* हो-हल्ला ho-hallā

upset *n.* गिरावट girārvaṭ; *v.t.* गड़बड़ कर देना gaṛbaṛ kar denā
upsetting *adj.* घबरा देनेवाला ghabarā denevālā
upside down *adv./adj.* उलटा पुलटा ulṭā pulṭā
upstairs *adj.* ऊपरी ūparī; *adv.* ऊपर ūpar
upstream *adj.* उजान का ujān ka; *adv.* उजान ujān
up-to-date *adj.* आज तक āj tak
upward *adv.* ऊपर की ओर ūpar kī or
urban *adj.* नगरीय nagrīy
urge *n.* ललक lalak; *v.t.* उकसाना uksānā
urgency *n.* अत्यावश्यकता atyāvaśyaktā
urgent *adj.* बहुत ज़रूरी bahut zarūrī
urinary *adj.* मूत्रीय mūtrīy
urinate *v.* पेशाब करना peśāb karnā
urine *n.* पेशाब peśāb
urn *n.* कलश kalaś
urologist *n.* मूत्र-विज्ञानी mūtr-vigyānī
us *pron.* हमको hamko
usage *n.* प्रयोग prayog
use *n.* प्रयोग prayog; *v.t.* इस्तेमाल करना istemāl karnā
used *adj.* प्रयुक्त prayukt
useful *adj.* उपयोगी upyogī
useless *adj.* बेकार bekār
user *n.* उपयोगकर्ता upyogkartā
usher *n.* प्रवेशक praveśak
usual *adj.* साधारण sādhāraṇ
usually *adv.* अकसर aksar
utensil *n.* बरतन bartan
uterus *n.* गर्भाशय garbhāśy
utility *n.* उपयोगिता upyogitā
utilize *v.t.* प्रयोग में लाना prayog meṁ lānā
utmost *adj.* अधिक से अधिक adhik se adhik
utter *adj.* बिल्कुल bilkul; *v.t.* कहना kahenā

V

vacancy *n.* रिक्कता rikkatā
vacant *adj.* ख़ाली qhālī
vacation *n.* छुट्टी chuṭṭī
vaccinate *v.t.* टीका लगाना ṭīkā lagānā
vaccination *n.* टीकाकरण ṭīkākāraṇ
vaccine *n.* टीका ṭīkā
vacuum *n.* शुन्य स्थान śunya sthān, निर्वातक मशीन nirvātak maśīn
vague *adj.* अस्पष्ट aspaṣṭ
vain *adj.* घमंडी ghamaṇḍī; (*worthless*) बेकार bekār
valet *n.* टहलुआ ṭahluā
valiant *adj.* शूरवीर śūrvīr
valid *adj.* मान्य mānya
validity *n.* मान्यता mānyatā
valley *n.* घाटी ghāṭī
valuable *n./adj.* मूल्यवान mūlyavān
value *n.* मूल्य mūly; *v.t.* मूल्यांकन करना mūlyānkan karnā
valve *n.* कपाट kapāt
vanilla *n.* वैनिला vainilā
vanish *v.i.* ओझल हो जाना ojhal ho jānā
vapor *n.* वाष्पकण vāṣpkaṇ
variable *n.* चर car; *adj.* परिवर्ती parivartī
variation *n.* विभिन्न रूप vibhinn rūp
variety *n.* विविधता vividhtā
various *adj.* तरह तरह tarah tarah
varnish *n.* वारनिश vārniś; *v.t.* वारनिश लगाना vārniś lagānā
vary *v.t.* बदलना badalnā; *v.i.* बदल जाना badal jānā
vase *n.* पात्र pātra
vault *n.* छलांग chalāng, शव-कक्ष śav-kakṣ

veal *n.* बछड़े का मांस bachaṛe kā māṁs
vegetable *n.* सब्ज़ी sabzī
vegetarian *n.* शाकाहारी śākākārī; *adj.* शाकाहारी śākākārī
vegetation *n.* हरियाली hariyālī
vehement *adj.* प्रचंड pracaṇḍ
vehicle *n.* गाड़ी gāṛī
veil *n.* परदा pardā
vein *n.* शिरा śirā
velvet *n.* मख़मल maqhmal
venerate *v.t.* ... का आदर करना ... kā ādar karnā
venereal disease *n.* गुप्त रोग gupt rog
vengeance *n.* बदला badlā
venom *n.* ज़हर zahar
vent *n.* निकास nikās; *v.t.* छेद बनाना ched banānā
ventilate *v.t.* हवादार बनाना havādār banānā
ventilation *n.* हवादारी havādārī
ventilator *n.* झरोखा jharokhā
ventricle *n.* निलय nily
venture *n.* जोखिम jokhim
verb *n.* क्रिया kriyā
verbal *adj.* शाब्दिक śābdik
verdict *n.* फ़ैसला faisalā, अभिनिर्णय abhinirṇy
verge *n.* किनारा kinārā, छोर chor
verification *n.* सत्यापन satyāpan
verify *v.t.* प्रमाणित करना pramāṇit karnā
versatile *adj.* अस्थिर asthir
verse *n.* पद pad
version *n.* अनुवाद anuvād
versus *prep.* बनाम banām
vertebra *n.* रीढ़ की हड्डी rīṛh kī haḍḍī
vertical *adj.* खड़ा khaṛā
very *adv.* बहुत bahut

vessel *n.* (*ship*) जहाज़ jahāz; (*blood-vessel*) शिरा śirā; (*container*) बरतन bartan
vest *n.* बनियान baniyān
veteran *n.* अनुभवी व्यक्ति anubhavī vyakti; *adj.* अनुभवी anubhavī
veterinarian *n.* पशुचिकित्सक paśucikitsak
veterinary *adj.* पशुचिकित्सा paśucikitsā
via *prep.* के रास्ते ke rāste
vial *n.* शीशी śīsī
vibrate *v.i.* कम्पायमान होना kampāymān honā
vibration *n.* कम्पन kampan
vice *n.* दुर्गुण durguṇ
vice president *n.* उपराष्ट्रपति uparāṣṭrapati
vicinity *n.* अड़ोस-पड़ोस aṛos-paṛos
vicious *adj.* बुरा burā
victim *n.* शिकार śikār
victory *n.* जीत jīt
video *n.* वीडियो vīḍiyo
view *n.* दृश्य dṛśya; *v.t.* जाँचना jāṁcnā
viewfinder *n.* दृश्यदर्शी dṛśyadarśī
vigor *n.* बल bal
villa *n.* देहाती बंगला dehātī bangalā
village *n.* गाँव gāṁv
vine *n.* बेल bel
vinegar *n.* सिरका sirkā
vineyard *n.* अंगूर का बाग़ angūr kā bāqg
vintage *n.* अंगूरी angūrī
violate *v.t.* भंग करना bhaṅg karnā
violation *n.* भंग bhaṅg
violence *n.* हिंसा himsā
violent *adj.* हिंसापूर्ण himsāpūrṇ
violet *n.* नीलपुष्प nīlpuṣp; *adj.* बैंगनी baiṁganī

violin *n.* वायलिन vāyalin
violoncello *n.* मन्द्र वायलिन mandra vāyalin
viral *adj.* विषाणु viṣāṇu
virgin *n.* कुंआरी kumārī
virtual *adj.* यथार्थ yathārth, वस्तुत vastu
virtue *n.* गुण guṇ
virus *n.* वाइरस vāiras
visa *n.* वीज़ा vīzā
visibility *n.* दशयता daśyatā
visible *adj.* दिखाई देने वाला dikhāī dene vālā
vision *n.* नज़र nazar
visit *n.* भेंट bheṇṭ; *v.t.* से मिलने जाना se milne jānā
visitor *n.* अतिथि atithi
visor *n.* अग्र भाग agra bhāg
visual *adj.* आँख का āṁkh kā
vital *adj.* महत्वपूर्ण mahatvapūrṇ, आवश्यक āvaśyak
vitality *n.* तेज tej
vitamin *n.* विटामिन viṭāmin
vivid *adj.* विशद viśad
vocabulary *n.* शब्दावली śabdāvalī
vocal *adj.* स्वर का svar kā
voice *n.* आवाज़ āvāz; *v.t.* आवाज़ करना āvāz karnā
void *adj.* शून्य śūnya
volcano *n.* ज्वालामुखी पहाड़ jvālāmukhī pahāṛ
volt *n.* वोल्ट volt
voltage *n.* वोल्टता volṭtā
volume *n.* पुस्तक pustak
voluntary *adj.* ऐच्छिक aicchik
volunteer *n.* स्वयं सेवक svayaṁ sevak
vomit *v.i.* उलटी करना ulṭī karnā
vote *n.* वोट voṭ; *v.i.* वोट देना voṭ denā
voter *n.* मतदाता matdātā

voucher *n.* वाउचर vāucar
vow *n.* व्रत vrat; *v.t.* व्रत लेना vrat lenā
vowel *n.* स्वर svar
voyage *n.* यात्रा yātrā; *v.t.* यात्रा करना yātrā karnā
vulgar *adj.* अशिष्ट aśiṣṭ

W

wad *n.* गद्दी gaddī
wade *v.i.* पैदल पर करना paidal par karnā
wag *v.i.* हिलना hilnā; *v.t.* हिलाना hilānā
wage *n.* तन्ख़्वाह tanqhvāh
wagon *n.* माल ढोने की गाड़ी māl ḍhone kī gāṛī
waist *n.* कमर kamar
wait *n.* विलाप vilāp; *v.i.* इतज़ार करना itazār karnā
waiter *n.* बैरा bairā
waiting room *n.* प्रतीक्षालय pratīkṣālay
waitress *n.* पारोसनेवाली parosanevālī
waiver *n.* बाज़दावा bāzdāvā
wake *n.* जागरण jāgaraṇ; *v.t.* जगाना jagānā; *v.i.* नींद से जागना nīnd se jāgnā
walk *n.* चाल cāl; *v.t.* पैदल जाना paidal jānā
walker *n.* चलनेवाला calnevālā
wall *n.* दीवार dīvār
wallet *n.* बटुआ baṭuā
walnut *n.* अख़रोट aqhroṭ
wand *n.* छड़ी chaṛī
wander *v.i.* घूमते फिरना ghūmte phirnā
want *n.* इच्छा icchā; *v.t.* चाहना cāhnā
war *n.* युद्ध yuddh
wardrobe *n.* अलमारी almārī

ware *n.* माल māl
warehouse *n.* गोदाम godām
warm *adj.* गरम garam
warmth *n.* गरमी garmī
warn *v.t.* चेतावनी देना cetāvanī denā
warning *n.* चेतावनी cetāvanī
warrant *n.* वारंट vāranṭ
warranty *n.* आक्षासन ākṣāsan
wart *n.* मस्सा massā
wary *adj.* चौकन्ना cauknnā
wash *v.t.* धोना dhonā
washable *adj.* धुलाई-सह dhulāī-sah
washing machine *n.* धुलाई की मशीन dhulāī kī maśīn
wasp *n.* थिड़ thiṛ
waste *n.* कूड़ा kūṛā; *v.t.* उजाड़ना ujāṛnā
wasteful *adj.* अपव्ययी apavyayī
wastepaper basket *n.* कूड़ादान kūṛādān
watch *n.* घड़ी ghaṛī; *v.t.* देखना dekhnā
watchful *adj.* सतर्क satark
watchman *n.* चौकीदार caukīdār
water *n.* पानी pānī; *v.t.* पानी देना pānī denā
watercolor *n.* जलरंग jalrang; *adj.* जलरंग का jalrang kā
waterfall *n.* झरना jharnā
waterfront *n.* तटीय नगरभाग taṭīy nagarbhāg
watermelon *n.* तरबूज़ tarbūz
waterproof *adj.* जलरूद्ध jalrūddh
watery *adj.* जलीय jalīy
watt *n.* वाट vāṭ
wattage *n.* वाट-संख्या vāṭ-saṅkyā
wave *n.* लहर lahar; *v.t.* लहराना lahrānā
wavelength *n.* तरंग-दैर्ध्य taraṅg-dairdhya
waver *v.i.* हिचकना hicknā

wax *n.* मोम mom; *v.t.* मोम लगाना mom lagānā
way *n.* रास्ता rāstā
wayward *adj.* ज़िद्दी ziddī
we *pron.* हम ham
weak *adj.* कमज़ोर kamzor
weaken *v.t.* कमज़ोर कर देना kamzor kar denā
weakness *n.* कमज़ोरी kamzorī
wealth *n.* धन dhan
wealthy *adj.* अमीर amīr
weapon *n.* शस्त्र śāstra
wear *v.t./v.i* पहनना pahennā
weary *adj.* थका-माँदा thakā-māṁdā
weather *n.* मौसम mausam
weave *v.t.* बुनना bunnā
weaver *n.* जुलाहा julāhā
web *n.* जाला jālā
website *n.* वेबसाईट vebsāīṭ
wedding *n.* शादी śādī
wedge *n.* पच्चर paccar
Wednesday *n.* बुधवार budhvār
weed *n.* खर-पतवार khar-patvār; *v.t.* खर-पतवार साफ करना khar-patvār sāf karnā
week *n.* हफ़्ता haftā
weekday *n.* काम के दिन kām ke din
weekend *n.* सप्ताहांत saptāhānt
weep *v.i.* रोना ronā
weigh *v.t.* तोलना tolnā
weight *n.* वज़न vazan; *v.t.* भार उठाना bhār uṭhānā; *v.i.* वज़न बढ़ जाना vazan baṛh jānā
weird *adj.* अजीब ajīb
welcome *n.* स्वागतम svāgatam; *v.t.* स्वागत करना svāgat karnā

weld *v.t.* टाँका लगाना ṭāṁkā lagānā
welfare *n.* भला bhalā
well *n.* तंदुरुस्त tandurust; *adj.* ठीक ṭhīk; *interj.* अच्छी तरह से acchī tarah se
west *n.* पश्चिम paścim; *adv.* पश्चिमी paścimī
western *adj.* पश्चिमी paścimī
wet *v.t.* गीला gīlā
whale *n.* ह्वेल hvel
wharf *n.* जहाज़-घाट jahāz-ghāṭ
what *adj.* क्या kyā; *pron.* जो jo
whatever *adv./pron.* जो भी jo bhī
wheat *n.* गेहूँ gehūṁ
wheel *n* चक्र cakr
wheelbarrow *n.* ठेला ṭhelā
wheeze *n.* घेरघराहट ghergharāhaṭ; *v.i.* घरघर करते हुए सांस लेना gharghar karte hue sāns lenā
when *adv.* कब kab; *conj.* जब ... तब jab ... tab
where *conj.* जहाँ jahāṁ; *interr.* कहाँ kahāṁ
wherever *adv./conj.* कहीं भी kahīṁ bhī
which *adj.* कौन kaun; *pron.* जो jo
whichever *pron., adj.* जो कोई jo koī
while *n.* समय samay; *conj.* जब तक jab tak
whirl *v.i.* तेज़ी-से घूमना tezī-se ghūmnā
whirlpool *n.* भंवर bhanvar
whisk *n.* फ़ेटनी feṭnī; *v.t.* झाड़ना jhāṛnā
whisker *n.* मूँछ mūṁch
whiskey, whisky *n.* ह्विस्की hviskī
whisper *n.* खुसुर-फुसुर khusur-phusur; *v.i.* कानाफूसी करना kānāphūsī karnā
whistle *n.* सीटी sīṭī; *v.i.* सीटी बजाना sīṭī bajānā
white *adj.* सफ़ेद safed
whiten *v.t.* सफ़ेद करना safed karnā

who *pron./interr.* कौन kaun
whoever *pron./adj.* जो कोई jo koī
whole *adj.* पूरा pūrā
wholesale *adj.* थोक thok
wholesome *adj.* हितकर hitkar
whom *pron.* किसे kise
whose *interr. pron.* किसका kiskā
why *adv./interr./conj.* क्यों kyoṁ
wick *n.* बत्ती battī
wicked *adj.* दुष्ट duṣṭ
wicker *n.* लचीनी टहनी lacīnī ṭahnī, टोकरा ṭokarā
wide *adj.* चौड़ा cauṛā
widen *v.t.* चौड़ा करना cauṛā karnā
widespread *adj.* व्यापक vyāpak
widow *n.* विधवा vidhvā
widower *n.* विधुर vidhur
width *n.* चौड़ाई cauṛāī
wield *v.t.* चलाना calānā
wife *n.* पत्नी patnī
wig *n.* बालों की टोपी bāloṁ kī ṭopī
wild *adj.* जंगली jangalī
wilderness *n.* उजाड़ ujāṛ
wildlife *n.* जंगली जानवर jangalī jānvar
will *n.* (*desire*) इच्छा icchā; (*legal document*) वसीयत vasīyat
willing *adj.* रज़ामंद razāmand, खुशी से khuśī se
willow *n.* भिसा bhisā
win *n.* विजय vijay; *v.t.* जीतना jītnā
wind *n.* हवा havā; *v.t.* चाबी भरना cābī bharnā
windmill *n.* पवन-चक्की pavan-cakkī
window *n.* खिड़की khiṛkī
windy *adj.* हवादार havādār
wine *n.* वाइन vāin

wing *n.* पंख paṅkha
wink *n.* झपकी jhapkī; *v.i.* झपकाना jhapkānā
winner *n.* विजेता vijetā
winter *n.* जाड़ा jāṛā
wipe *v.t.* पोछना pochnā
wire *n.* तार tār; *v.t.* तार लगाना tār lagānā
wireless *adj.* बेतार का तार betār kā tār
wisdom *n.* विवेक vivek
wise *adj.* बुद्धिमान buddhimān
wish *n.* इच्छा icchā; *v.i.* इच्छा होना icchā honā
wit *n.* होश hoś
witch *n.* डाइन ḍāin
with *prep.* ... के साथ ... ke sāth
withdraw *v.t.* हटाना haṭānā; *v.i.* हट जाना haṭ jānā
withdrawal *n.* निकासी nikāsī
withhold *v.t.* रोक रखना rok rakhnā
within *adv.* अन्दर andar; *prep.* ... के अन्दर ... ke andar
without *adv./prep.* ... के बिना ... ke binā
withstand *v.t.* सामना करना sāmnā karnā
witness *n.* गवाह gavāh; *v.t.* गवाही देना gavāhī denā
witty *adj.* विनोदी vinodī
wolf *n.* भेड़िया bheṛiya
woman *n.* औरत aurat
womb *n.* गर्भाशय garbhāśya
wonder *v.i.* आश्चर्यचाकित होना āścaryacākit honā
wonderful *adj.* आश्चर्यजनक āścaryajanak
wood *n.* लकड़ी lakaṛī
woods *n.* जंगल jangal
wool *n.* ऊन ūn
woolen *adj.* ऊनी ūnī
word *n.* शब्द śabd
work *n.* काम kām

worker *n.* मज़दूर mazdūr
workshop *n.* कारखाना kārkhānā
world *n.* संसार sansār, दुनिया duniyā
worldwide *adj.* विश्वव्यापी viśvavyāpī
worm *n.* कीड़ा kīṛā
worn out *adj.* थका-माँदा thakā-māṁdā
worried *adj.* चिन्तित cintit
worry *n.* चिन्ता cintā, परेशान pareśān; *v.i.* चिन्ता करना cintā karnā, परेशान करना pareśan karnā
worse *adj.* और बुरा aur burā; *adv.* और बुरी तरह से aur burī tarah se
worship *n.* भक्त bhakt; *v.t.* पूजा करना pūjā karnā
worst *adj.* सबसे बुरा sabse burā; *adv.* सबसे ख़राब sabse qharāb
worthless *adj.* बेकार bekār
worthwhile *adj.* उचित ucit
wound *n.* घाव ghāv; *v.t.* घायल करना ghāyal karnā
wrap *n.* लपेटन lapeṭan; *v.t.* लपेटना lapeṭnā
wrath *n.* रोष roṣ
wreck *n.* सत्यानाश satyānāś; *v.t.* नष्ट करना naṣṭ karnā
wrench *n.* रिन्च rinc
wrestle *v.t.* कुश्ती लड़ना kuśtī laṛnā
wrestler *n.* कुश्तीबाज़ kuśtībāz
wrinkle *n.* झुरी jhurī; *v.i.* झुरी होना jhurī honā
wrist *n.* कलाई kalāī
wristwatch *n.* घड़ी ghaṛī
write *v.t.* लिखना likhnā
writer *n.* लेखक lekhak
writing *n.* लेखन lekhan
wrong *adj.* ग़लत qgalat

X

xenophobia *n.* विदेशी भीति vedeśī bhīti
Xmas *n. abbreviation of* **Christmas** क्रिसमस krismas
X-ray *n.* एक्स-किरण eks-kiraṇ; *v.t.* एकस-किरण करना eks-kiraṇ karnā
xylophone *n.* काष्ठतरंग kāṣṭhtarang

Y

yacht *n.* याट yāṭ
yank *v.t.* झटके से खींचना jhaṭke se khīṁcnā
Yankee *n.* अमरीकन amrīkan
yard *n.* गज़ gaz
yarn *n.* सूत sūt
yawn *n.* जंभाई jambhāī; *v.i.* जंभाई लेना jambhāī lenā
year *n.* साल sāl
yearly *adj.* वार्षिक varṣik
yearn *v.i.* लालसा होना lālsā honā
yeast *n.* ख़मीर qhamīr
yell *v.t.* चिल्लाना cillānā
yellow *adj.* पीला pīlā
yes *adv.* हाँ hāṁ
yesterday *n.* कल kal
yet *adv.* अभी तक abhī tak
yield *n.* उपज upaj; *v.t.* उत्पन्न करना utpann karnā
yoga *n.* योग yog
yogurt *n.* दही dahī
yoke *n.* जुआ juā
yolk *n.* ज़र्दी zardī
yonder *adv.* वहाँ vahāṁ

you *pron.* तुम tum, आप āp (*formal*)
young *n./adj.* जवान javān
your *pron.* तुम्हारा tumhāra, आपका āpkā
yourself *pron.* आप स्वयं āp svayaṁ
youth *n.* जवानी javānī
youthful *adj.* जवान javān

Z

zany *adj.* भँडेहरी bhaṁḍeharī
zeal *n.* उत्साह utsāh
zealous *adj.* उत्साही utsāhī
zebra *n.* ज़ेबरा zebarā
zenith *n.* शिरोबिन्दु śirobindu
zero *num.* शून्य śūnya
zest *n.* मज़ा mazā
zigzag *n.* टेढ़ी-मेढ़ी रखा ṭeṛhī-meṛhī rakha; *v.t.* टेढ़ी-मेढ़ी रीति से चलना ṭeṛhī-meṛhī rīti se calnā
zinc *n.* जस्ता jastā
zip *v.t.* ज़िप बंद करना zip band karnā
zip code *n.* पिन कोड pin koḍ
zipper *n.* ज़िप zip
zodiac *n.* राशी चक्र rāśī cakr
zone *n.* क्षेत्र kṣetra
zoo *n.* चिड़ियाघर ciṛiyāghar
zoological *adj.* प्राणी-विज्ञान संबंधी prāṇī-vigyān sambandhī
zoology *n.* प्राणी-विज्ञान prāṇī-vigyān
zoom *v.t.* अचानक तेज़ी से गुज़रना acānak tezī se guzarnā

Hindi–English Dictionary

अ

अंकगणित **aṅkgaṇit** *n.m.* arithmetic
अंकित करना **aṅkit karnā** *v.t.* imprint
अंकुर **aṅkur** *n.m.* sprout
अंकुरित होना **aṅkurit honā** *v.i.* sprout
अंग **aṅg** *n.m.* limb
अंगुश्ताना **aṅguśtānā** *n.m.* thimble
अंगूठा **aṅgūṭhī** *n.m.* thumb
अंगूर **angūr** *n.m.* grape
अंगूरी **angūrī** *n.f.* vintage
अंगूर का बाग़ **angūr kā bāqg** *n.m.* vineyard
अंजान **anjān** *adj.* unknown
अंजीर **añjīr** *n.f.* fig
अंडाकार **aṇḍākār** *n.m.* oval
अंत **ant** *n.m.* finish
अंत में **ant meṁ** *adv.* finally
अंत: प्रेरणा **antahprerṇā** *n.f.* impulse
अंतर **antar** *n.m.* distinction
अंतर्राष्ट्रीय **antarrāṣṭrīy** *adj.* international
अंतरीप **antarīp** *n.m.* cape
अंतयोष्टि **antyoṣṭi** *n.f.* funeral
अंतर्विष्ट करना **antarviṣṭ karnā** *v.t.* contain
अंतिम **antim** *adj.* extreme
अंदाज़ **andāz** *n.m.* estimate
अंदर **andar** *n.m.* interior
अंदोलित करना **andolit karnā** *v.t.* disturb
अंधविश्वासी **andhaviśvāsī** *adj.* superstitious
अंधा **andhā** *adj.* blind
अंधापन **andhāpan** *n.m.* blindness
अँगुली **aṁgulī** *n.f.* finger

अँगुली की छाप **aṁgulī kī chāp** *n.f.* fingerprint
अँगूठी **aṁgūṭhī** *n.f.* ring
अँग्रेज़ **aṁgrez** *n.m.* Englishman
अँग्रेज़ी **aṁgrezī** *n.f./adj.* English
अँतड़ी **aṁtaṛī** *n.f.* intestines
अँधेरा **aṁdherā** *n.m.* darkness
अँधकारमय बनाना **aṁdhkārmay banānā** *v.t.* darken
अकादमी **akādamī** *n.f.* academy
अकुशल **akuśal** *adj.* unskilled
अकेला **akelā** *adj.* only
अक्टूबर **akṭūbar** *n.m.* October
अक्सर **aksar** *adv.* usually
अख़रोट **aqhroṭ** *n.m.* walnut
अगम्य **agamy** *adj.* inaccessible
अगला **aglā** *adj.* next
अगर **agar** *conj.* if
अगस्त **agast** *n.m.* August
अगुआ **aguā** *n.m.* pioneer
अग्रदीप **agradīp** *n.m.* headlight
अग्रदर्शी **agradarśī** *adj.* prospective
अग्र भाग **agra bhāg** *n.m.* visor
अचर **acar** *n.m.* constant
अचल **acal** *adj.* stationary
अचानक **acānak** *adj.* sudden
अचानक तेज़ी से गुज़रना **acānak tezī se guzarnā** *n.m.* zoom
अचार **acār** *n.m.* pickle
अचार डालना **acār ḍālnā** *v.t.* pickle
अचेत कर देना **accet kar denā** *v.i.* stun
अच्छा **acchā** *adj.* nice
अच्छी तरह से **acchī tarah se** *adj.* well
अजमोद **ajmod** *n.f.* parsley
अजनबी **ajnabī** *n.m.* stranger

अजीब **ajīb** *adj.* weird
अटारी **aṭārī** *n.f.* loft
अठारह **aṭhārah** *num.* eighteen
अठारहवाँ **aṭhārahvāṁ** *adj.* eighteenth
अड़चन **aṛcan** *n.f.* handicap
अड़ोस-पड़ोस **aṛos-paṛos** *n.m.* vicinity
अति **ati** *adj.* extra
अतिक्रुद्ध **atikuddh** *adj.* furious
अतिथि **atithi** *n.m.* guest
अतिदेय **atidey** *adj.* overdue
अतिभार **atibhār** *adj.* overweight
अतिरंजना करना **atiranjanā karnā** *v.t.* exaggerate
अतिरिक्त **atirikt** *n.m.* extra
अतिरिक्त पुरज़ा **atirikt purzā** *n.m.* spare part
अतीत **atīt** *adj.* past
अत्याचारी **atyācārī** *adj.* oppressive
अत्यावश्यकता **atyāvaśyaktā** *n.f.* urgency
अथक **athak** *n.m.* tireless
अर्थ **arth** *n.m.* significance
अर्थ रखना **arth rakhnā** *v.t.* imply
अर्थव्यवस्था **arthvyavasthā** *n.m.* economy
अर्थशास्त्री **arthśāstrī** *n.m.* economist
अर्थात **arthāt** *adj.* namely
अदालत **adālat** *n.f.* court
अदृश्य **adṛśya** *adj.* invisible
अधिक **adhik** *adj./adv.* more
अधिक अच्छा **adhik acchā** *adj.* better
अधिक से अधिक **adhik se adhik** *adj.* utmost
अधिकतम **adhikatam** *adj.* most
अधिकता **adhiktā** *n.f.* excess
अधिकार **adhikār** *n.m.* authority
अधिकार में करना **adhikār meṁ karnā** *v.t.* occupy

अधिकार में रखना **adhikār meṁ rakhnā** *v.t.* retain
अधिकारिक **adhikārik** *adj.* official
अधिकारी **adhikārī** *n.m.* officer
अधिकृत **adhikṛat** *adj.* occupied
अधिमान्यता **adhimānyatā** *n.m.* preference
अधिमूल्य **adhimūly** *n.m.* surcharge
अधिवर्ष **adhivarṣ** *n.m.* leap year
अधिसमय **adhisamay** *n.m.* overtime
अधिसूचना **adhisūcanā** *n.f.* notification
अधिसूची **adhisūcī** *n.f.* schedule
अधिसूची में रखना **adhisūcī meṁ rakhnā** *v.t.* schedule
अधिष्ठापन **adhiṣṭhāpan** *n.m.* installation
अधेड़ **adheṛ** *adj.* middle-aged
अर्ध-विराम **ardh-virām** *n.m.* semicolon
अध्यवसायी **adhyavasāyī** *adj.* industrious
अध्यापक **adhyāpak** *n.m.* teacher
अध्याय **adhyāy** *n.m.* chapter
अन्तरिक्ष **antarikṣ** *n.m.* space
अन्यलोकवासी **anyalokavāsī** *adj.* alien
अनधिकार प्रवेश करना **andhikār praveś karnā** *v.i.* trespass
अनभिप्रेत **anbhipret** *adj.* unintentional
अनाज **anāj** *n.m.* corn
अनाथ **anāth** *n.m.* orphan
अनादर **anādar** *n.m.* disregard
अनावश्यक **anāvaśyak** *adj.* unnecessary
अनावश्यकता **anāvaśyaktā** *adv.* needlessly
अनिर्णीत **anirṇīt** *adj.* undecided
अनिश्चित **aniścit** *adj.* uncertain, doubtful
अनिश्चय **aniścay** *n.m.* suspense
अनिष्ठ **aniṣṭ** *adj.* undesired, harmful
अनुकरण **anukaraṇ** *n.m.* imitation
अनुकूल करना **anukūl karnā** *v.t.* adapt

अनुकूलक **anukūlak** *n.m.* adapter
अनुक्रमिका **anukramikā** *n.m.* index
अनुचित **anucit** *adj.* unfair
अनुच्छेद **anucched** *n.m.* paragraph
अनुताप **anutāp** *n.m.* remorse
अनुत्तरदायी **anuttardāyī** *adj.* unaccountable
अनुदान **anudān** *n.m.* grant
अनुदेश **anudeś** *n.m.* instruction
अनुपस्थिति **anupsthiti** *n.f.* absence
अनुभव **anubhav** *n.m.* experience
अनुभवी व्यक्ति **anubhavī vyakti** *n.m.* veteran
अनुभूति **anubhūti** *n.f.* sensation
अनुमति **anumati** *n.f.* permission
अनुमति देना **anumati denā** *v.t.* allow
अनुमति पत्र **anumati patr** *n.m.* permit
अनुमान **anumān** *n.m.* guess
अनुमान करना **anumān karnā** *v.t.* estimate, guess
अनुमोदन **anumodan** *n.m.* authorization
अनुमोदन करना **anumodan karnā** *v.t.* authorize
अनुराग **anurāg** *n.m.* affection
अनुरोध **anurodh** *v.i.* request
अनुवाद **anuvād** *n.m.* version
अनुवाद करना **anuvād karnā** *v.t.* translate
अनुवादक **anuvādak** *n.m.* translator
अनुशासन **anuśāsan** *n.m.* discipline
अनुसमर्थन **anusamarthan** *n.m.* ratification
अनुसमर्थन करना **anusamarthan karnā** *v.t.* ratify
अनुस्मारक **anusmārak** *n.m.* reminder
अन्दर **andar** *prep.* within, inside
अन्दर के कपड़े **andar ke kapṛe** *n.m.* underpants
अन्यथा **anyathā** *adv.* otherwise
अन्यथा कर देना **anyathā kar denā** *v.i.* undo

अन्तिम **antim** *adj.* last
अपना **apnā** *adj.* own
अपने-आप **apne-āp** *pron.* herself, himself
अपने से **apne se** *pron.* themselves
अपमान **apmān** *n.m.* insult
अपमान करना **apmān karnā** *v.t.* insult
अपमानजनक **apmānjanak** *adj.* offensive
अपमान-लेख **apmān-lekh** *n.m.* libel
अपमानिक **apmānik** *adj.* rude
अपराध **aprādh** *n.m.* offense
अपराधी **aprādhī** *n.m.* criminal
अपराध करना **aprādh karnā** *v.t.* offend
अपर्याप्त **aparyāpt** *adj.* insufficient
अपवाद **apvād** *n.m.* exception
अपर्साप्त **apsārpt** *adj.* meager
अप्रत्पक्ष **apratpakṣ** *adj.* indirect
अप्रसन्न करना **aprasann karnā** *v.t.* displease
अप्रसम **aprasam** *adj.* abnormal
अपारदर्शी **apārdarśī** *adj.* opaque
अप्राधिकृत **aprādhikṛt** *adj.* unauthorized
अप्राप्ति **aprāpti** *n.f.* loss
अपूर्ण विराम **apūrṇ virām** *n.m.* colon
अफ़सोस **afsos** *n.m.* regret
अब **ab** *adv.* now
अब तक **ab tak** *adv.* up to now
अबाबील **abābīl** *v.t.* swallow
अबाधित **abādhit** *adj.* absolute
अभाग्य **abhāgya** *adj.* unfortunate
अभिकथन **abhikathan** *n.m.* affirmation
अभिनेता **abhinetā** *n.m.* actor
अभियोग **abhiyog** *n.m.* accusation
अभिलेख **abhilekh** *n.m.* record

अभिवचन करना **abhivacan karnā** *v.i.* plead
अभी-अभी **abhī-abhī** *adv.* right now, presently
अभी तक **abhī tak** *adv.* still, yet
अभ्यस्त बनना **abhyast bananā** *v.i.* accustom
अमर **amar** *adj.* immortal
अमरीकी **amrīkī** *n.m./adj.* American
अमीर **amīr** *adj.* wealthy
अमोनिया **amoniyā** *n.m.* ammonia
अम्ल **amal** *n.m.* acid
अम्लीय **amlīy** *n.f.* acidity
अयोग्य **ayogy** *adj.* inefficient
अरबी **arabī** *n.f.* Arabic; *n.f./adj.* Arab
अराजकता **arājaktā** *n.f.* anarchy
अफ़्रीकी **afrīkī** *n.m./adj.* African
अलर्क रोग **alark rog** *n.m.* rabies
अलग **alag** *adj.* separate
अलग करना **alag karnā** *v.t.* isolate, separate
अलग होना **alag honā** *v.i.* differ, separate
अलमारी **almārī** *n.m.* wardrobe
अलारम घड़ी **alāram ghaṛī** *n.f.* alarm
अलावा **alāvā** *adv.* moreover
अलिंगन **alingan** *n.m.* embrace
अलोकप्रिय **alokpriya** *adj.* unpopular
अलोचना करना **alocanā karnā** *v.t.* criticize
अल्प **alp** *adj.* meager
अल्पमत **alpmat** *n.m.* minority
अल्प मात्रा **alp mātrā** *n.m.* trace
अल्प विराम **alp virām** *n.m.* comma
अल्पसंख्यक **alpsankhyak** *n.m.* minority
अल्लाह **allāh** *n.m.* God
अवकाश **avkāś** *n.m.* leisure
अवतरण **avtaraṇ** *n.m.* landing

अवधि **avadhi** *n.f.* term, period
अवयव **avyav** *n.m.* organ
अवर **avar** *adj.* inferior
अवलोकन करना **avlokan karnā** *v.t.* scan
अवशेष **avśeṣ** *n.m.* residue
अवश्यंभावी **avśambhāvī** *adj.* unavoidable
अवश्यमेव **avaśyamev** *adv.* necessarily
अवसर **avsar** *n.m.* opportunity
अवस्था **avasthā** *n.f.* stage, phase
अवज्ञा करना **avgyā karnā** *v.t.* defy
अव्यवसायी **avyavasāyī** *n.m.* amateur
अविराम **avirām** *adj.* continuous
अविलंब **avilamb** *adv.* shortly
अविश्वास **aviśvās** *n.m./v.t.* distrust
अविश्वास करना **aviśvās karnā** *v.t.* mistrust
अविष्कार **aviṣkār** *n.m.* invention
अशक्त **aśakt** *adj.* unable
अश्लील **aślīl** *adj.* obscene
अशुद्ध **aśuddh** *adj.* impure
अशासकीय **aśāsakīy** *adj.* unofficial
अशावादी **āśāvādī** *n.* optimist
अशान्वित **aśānvit** *adj.* optimistic
अशिष्ठ **aśiṣṭh** *adj.* impolite
असन्तोषजनक **asantoṣjanak** *adj.* unsatisfactory
असंभव **asambhav** *adj.* impossible
असंभाव्य **asambhāvy** *adj.* unlikely
असफल **asaphal** *adj.* unsuccessful
असफलता **asphaltā** *n.f.* failure
असमर्थता **asamarthatā** *n.f.* inability
असमान **asmān** *adj.* unequal
असली **aslī** *adj.* real

असहनीय **ashanīy** *adj.* unbearable
असहमत होना **asahamat honā** *v.i.* disagree
असहमति **asahamati** *n.f.* disagreement
असुरक्षित **asurakṣit** *adj.* unsafe
अस्नेही **asnehī** *adj.* unfriendly
अस्तबल **astabal** *n.m.* stable
अस्तर **astar** *n.m.* lining
अस्थायी **asthāyī** *adj.* temporary
अस्थिर **asthir** *adj.* versatile
अस्पताल **aspatāl** *n.m.* hospital
अस्पताल गाड़ी **aspatāl gāṛī** *n.f.* ambulance
अस्पष्ट **aspaṣṭ** *adj.* vague, illegible
अस्वस्थ **asvasth** *adj.* unwell
अस्वीकरण **asvīkaraṇ** *n.m.* rejection
अस्वीकार्य **asvīkārya** *adj.* unacceptable
अस्वीकार करना **asvīkār karnā** *v.t.* deny
अस्सी **assī** *num.* eighty
अहंकार **ahaṅkār** *n.m.* conceit
अहाता **ahātā** *n.m.* compound
अहानिकर **ahānikar** *adj.* harmless
अहितकर **ahitkar** *adj.* malignant
अक्ष **akṣ** *n.m.* axis
अक्षत **akṣat** *adj.* undamaged
अक्षम **akṣam** *adj.* incompetent
अक्षर **akṣar** *n.m.* syllable
अक्षांश **akṣāṅś** *n.m.* latitude
अज्ञान **agyān** *n.m.* ignorance

आ

ऑप्रशन **āpraśan** *n.m.* operation
ऑलम्पिक **ālampik** *adj.* Olympic
आँकड़े **āṁkaṛe** *n.m.* statistic
आँख **āṁkh** *n.f.* eye
आँख का **āṁkh kā** *adj.* visual
आँख झपकाना **āṁkh jhapkānā** *v.i.* blink
आँखें पाड़कर देखना **āṁkheṁ pāṛkar dekhnā** *v.i.* stare
आँसू **āṁsū** *n.m.* tear
आँगन **āṁgan** *n.m.* courtyard
आंशिक **ānśik** *adj.* partial
आकार **ākār** *n.m.* figure
आकर्षण **ākarṣaṇ** *adj.* attractive
आकर्षित करना **ākarṣit karnā** *v.t.* attract
आक्सीजन **āksījan** *n.m.* oxygen
आख्यान **ākhyān** *n.m.* legend
आगमन **āgman** *n.m.* arrival
आगे **āge** *adj.* ahead
आगे निकल जाना **āge nikal jānā** *v.t.* overtake
आगे बढ़ना **āge baṛhānā** *v.i.* proceed
आग्रह करना **āgrah karnā** *v.i.* insist
आचरण **ācaraṇ** *n.m.* conduct
आचार्य **ācārya** *n.m.* professor
आच्छन्न **ācchann** *adj.* overcast
आज **āj** *adv.* today
आजकल **ājkal** *adv.* nowadays
आज तक **āj tak** *adj.* up-to-date
आटा **āṭā** *n.m.* flour
आठ **āṭh** *num.* eight
आठवाँ **āṭhvāṁ** *adj.* eighth

आड़ू **āḍū** *n.m.* peach
आत्मा **ātmā** *n.f.* spirit
आत्मगत **ātmagat** *adj.* subjective
आत्महत्या **ātamhatyā** *n.f.* suicide
आत्महत्या करना **ātamhatyā karnā** *v.t.* to commit suicide
आत्म-समर्पण करना **ātm-samarpaṇ karnā** *v.t.* surrender
आर्थिक **ārthik** *adj.* financial
आर्थिक सहायता **ārthik sahāyatā** *n.m.* subsidy
आदत **ādat** *n.f.* habit
आदमी **ādmī** *n.m.* man
आदर **ādar** *n.m.* respect
आदर करना **ādar karnā** *v.t.* respect, venerate
आदर्श **ādarś** *n.m./adj.* ideal
आदान-प्रदान **ādān-pradān** *n.m.* reciprocity
आदेश **ādeś** *n.m.* command
आदेश देना **ādeś denā** *v.t.* command
आधा **ādhā** *adj.* half
आधाक्षर **ādhākṣar** *n.m.* initial
आधाक्षर करना **ādhākṣar karnā** *v.t.* initial
आधान **adhān** *n.m.* pledge
आधार **adhāsr** *n.m.* basis
आधार कर्म **ādhār karm** *n.m.* groundwork
आधार-सामग्री **ādhār-sāmagrī** *n.m.pl.* data
आनंद **ānand** *n.m.* joy, bliss
आनंदोत्सव **ānandotsav** *n.m.* carnival
आपका **āpkā** *pron.* your
आप स्वयं **āp svayaṁ** *pron.* yourself
आपत्ति **āptti** *n.f.* objection
आपसी **āpsī** *adj.* mutual
आपातकाल **āpātkāl** *n.m.* emergency
आशंका **āśankā** *n.f.* doubt, apprehension
औपचारिक **aupcārik** *adj.* formal

आम **ām** *adj.* typical, regular
आम रास्ता **ām rāstā** *n.m.* thoroughfare
आम्लेट **āmleṭ** *n.m.* omelet(te)
आय **āy** *n.f.* income
आयाम **āyām** *n.m.* dimension
आयात **āyāt** *n.m.* import
आयात करना **āyāt karnā** *v.t.* import
आयात कर **āyāt kar** *n.m.* import tax
आयाताकार **āyātākār** *adj.* rectangular
आयोग **āyog** *n.m.* commission
आयोजन करना **āyojan karnā** *v.t.* convene
आयत **āyat** *n.f.* rectangle
आयताकार **āyatākār** *adj.* oblong
आज्ञा भंग करना **āgyā bhaṅg karnā** *v.t.* disobey
आज्ञा का पालन करना **āgyā kā pālan karnā** *v.t.* obey
आज्ञाकारी **āgyākārī** *adj.* obedient
आज्ञापालन **āgyāpālan** *n.m.* obedience
आविष्कार करना **āviṣkār karnā** *v.t.* invent
आवरण **āvaraṇ** *n.m.* pall
आवर्ती **āvartī** *adj.* periodic
आवर्तक **āvartak** *adj.* recurring
आवर्तन **āvartan** *n.m.* recurrence
आवश्यकता **āvaśyakitā** *n.m.* necessity
आवाजाही लगाना **āvājāhī lagānā** *v.t.* haunt
आवाज़ **āvāz** *n.f.* voice, sound
आवाज़ करना **āvāz karnā** *v.t.* voice
आवारा **āvārā** *n.m.* tramp
आवास **āvās** *n.m.* lodging
आवेदन करना **āvedan karnā** *v.t.* apply
आवेदन पत्र **āvedan patr** *n.m.* application
आशा **āśā** *n.f.* expectation
आशाजनक **āśājanak** *adj.* hopeful

आशा **āśā** *n.f.* hope
आशा करना **āśā karnā** *v.t.* hope
आशीर्वाद **aśirvād** *n.m.* blessing
आशीर्वाद देना **aśirvād denā** *v.t.* bless
आश्चर्य **āścarya** *n.m./v.t.* surprise
आश्चर्यचाकित होना **āścaryacākit honā** *v.i.* wonder
आश्चर्यजनक **āścaryajanak** *adj.* wonderful
आश्वासन **āśvāsan** *n.m.* assurance
आश्वासन देना **āśvāsan denā** *v.t.* reassure
आसंजक **āsanjak** *adj.* adhesive
आस्तीन **āstīn** *n.f.* sleeve

इ

इंकार **inkār** *n.m.* refusal
इंकार करना **inkār karnā** *v.t.* refuse
इंगित भाषा **ingit bhāṣā** *n.m.* sign
इंजन **iñjan** *n.m.* locomotive
इंजीनियर **injīniyar** *n.m.* engineer
इंतज़ाम **intazām** *n.m.* arrangement
इतज़ार करना **itazār karnā** *v.t.* wait
इंद्रिय **indriya** *n.m.* sense
इंसान **insān** *n.m.* human
इकाई **ikāī** *n.f.* unit
इकबाल **ikbāl** *n.m.* confession
इकट्ठा होना **ikṭṭhā honā** *v.t.* cluster
इजाज़त **ijāzat** *n.f.* permission
इतना **itanā** *adv.* so
इतरलिंगी **itarliṅgī** *adj.* heterosexual
इतिहास **itihās** *n.m.* history
इधर-उधर **idhar-udhar** *prep.* around
इनाम **inām** *v.t.* award; *n.m.* reward

इनाम देना **inām denā** *v.t.* reward
इनाम **inām** *n.m.* recompense
इन्द्रधदनुष **indradhanuṣ** *n.m.* rainbow
इस्तीफ़ा **istīfā** *n.m.* resignation
इस्तीफ़ा देना **istīfā denā** *v.i.* resign
इस्तरी करना **istarī karnā** *v.t.* iron
इस्पात **ispāt** *n.f.* steel
इस्लाम **islām** *n.m.* Islam
इस्लामी **islāmī** *adj.* Islamic

ई

ईर्ष्या **īṣyaryā** *n.f.* envy
ईर्ष्यालु **īṣyaryālu** *adj.* jealous
ईमानदार **īmāndār** *adj.* honest
ईमानदारी **īmāndārī** *n.f.* honesty
ईसाई **īsāī** *n.m./adj.* Christian
ईसाई धर्म **īsāī dharm** *n.m.* Christianity
ईसापूर्व **īsāpūrv** B.C.
ईसवी सन **īsavī** A.D.

उ

उकसाना **uksānā** *v.t.* urge
उछलना **uchalnā** *v.i.* spring
उचित **ucit** *adj.* fair
उच्चारण **uccāraṇ** *n.m.* pronunciation
उठाना **uṭhānā** *v.t.* lift
उदास **udās** *n.m.* depressed, sad
उदास करना **udās karnā** *v.t.* depress
उपयुक्त **upyukt** *adj.* appropriate

उपयोग **upyog** *n.m.* application, use, usefulness
उपयोगी **upyogī** *adj.* useful
उपस्थित रहना **upsthit rehnā** *v.t.* attend
उपेक्षा करना **upekṣā karnā** *v.t.* disregard
उबर जानु **ubar jānā** *v.i.* recover
उड़ना **uṛnā** *v.i.* fly
उत्कृष्ट **utkṛṣṭ** *adj.* noble
उत्कीर्ण **utkīrṇ** *n.m.* carving
उत्तेजित करना **uttejit karnā** *v.t.* alarm
उल्लंघन करना **ullaṅghan karnā** *v.t.* infringe
उल्लेख करना **ullekh karnā** *v.t.* specify

ऊ

ऊँट **ūṁṭ** *n.m.* camel
ऊँचा **ūṁcā** *adj.* high
ऊँचा पढ़ना **ūṁcā paṛhnā** *v.i.* soar
ऊँचाई **ūṁcāī** *n.m.* height
ऊँचे पर **ūṁce par** *adj.* aloft
ऊन **ūn** *n.m.* wool
ऊनी **ūnī** *adj.* woolen
ऊपर **ūpar** *adj.* aloft; *adj./adv./prep.* up; *adv.* upstairs; over
ऊपर की ओर **ūpar kī or** *adv.* upward
ऊपर जाना **ūpar jānā** *v.t.* climb
ऊपरी **ūparī** *adj.* upper, upstairs

ए

एड्ज़ **eḍz** *n.m.* AIDS
एड़ **eṛ** *n.f.* spur
एड़ी **eṛī** *n.f.* heel
ए.टी.एम. **e.ṭī.em.** *n.m.* ATM

ए. सी. **e. sī.** *n.f.* air-conditioning
एक **ek** *num.* one
एक बार **ek bār** *adv.* once
एक ही समय में होना **ek hī samay meṁ honā** *v.i.* coincide
एक हो जाना **ek ho jānā** *v.t.* unite
एकड़ **ekaṛ** *n.f.* acre
एकत्र करना **ektra karnā** *v.i.* concentrate
एकदम **ekdam** *adj.* sheer
एकलिंगी **ekliṅgī** *adj.* unisex
एकमत **ekmat** *adj.* unanimous
एक्स-किरण **eks-kiraṇ** *n.m.* X-ray
एकस-किरण करना **eks-kiraṇ karnā** *v.t.* X-ray
एकसुरा **eksurā** *adj.* monotonous
एकस्व **ekasav** *n.m.* patent
एकता **ektā** *n.f.* unity
एकत्र हो जाना **ekatr ho jānā** *v.t.* assemble
एका **ekā** *n.m.* alliance
एकाएक **ekāek** *adj.* sudden
एकाधिक **ekādhik** *adj.* plural
एकाधिकार **ekādhikār** *n.m.* monopoly
एकाधिनायक **ekādhināyak** *n.m.* dictator
एकांत **ekānt** *n.m.* seclusion
एजेंट **ejenṭ** *n.m.* agent
एरियल **eriyal** *n.m.* aerial
एलर्जी संबन्धी **elarjī sambandhī** *adj.* allergic
एलर्जी होना **elarjī honā** *v.i.* to be allergic
एलरर्जी **elarjī** *n.m.* allergy
एप्रन **epran** *n.m.* apron
एवज़ी **evazī** *adj.* substitute

ऐ

ऐंठन **ainṭhan** *n.f.* cramp
ऐच्छिक **aicchik** *adj.* voluntary
ऐडमिरल **aiḍmiral** *n.m.* admiral
ऐतिहासिक **etihāsik** *adj.* historical
ऐन्टेना **ainṭenā** *n.m.* antenna
ऐलुमिनियम **ailuminiyam** *n.m.* aluminum
ऐश **aiś** *n.m.* luxury
ऐसा **aisā** *adj.* such
ऐस्परिन **aisprin** *n.m.* aspirin

औ

औचित्य **aucity** *n.m.* justification
औज़ार **auzār** *n.m.* tool, implement
औद्योमिक **audyomik** *adj.* industrial
औपचारिक **aupcārik** *adj.* formal
और **aur** *conj.* and; *adv.* else
और आगे **aur āge** *adv.* further
और कम **aur kam** *adv.* less
और क्या **aur kyā** *adv.* what else
और कोई **aur koī** *adv.* who else
और बुरा **aur burā** *adv.* worse
और बुरी तरह से **aur burī tarah se** *adj.* worse
और न **aur na** *conj.* nor
और भी **aur bhī** *adv.* likewise
औरत **aurat** *n.f.* woman
औरतों का डाकटर **auratoṁ kā ḍākṭar** *n.m.* gynecologist
औरतों की जाघिया **auratoṁ kī jāghiyā** *n.m.* panties
औषध **auṣadh** *n.* pharmacology

औषधीय auṣadhīy *adj.* pharmaceutical
औसत ausat *n.m./adj.* average

क

कंकरीट kankarīṭ *n.m.* concrete
कंघी kaṅghī *n.f.* comb
कंघी करना kaṅghī karnā *v.t.* comb
कंद kand *n.m.* bulb
कंधा kandhā *n.m.* shoulder
कंपनी kampanī *n.f.* company
कंबल kambal *n.m.* blanket
कंगारू kaṅgārū *n.m.* kangaroo
कगार kagār *n.f.* ledge
कचरा kacrā *n.m.* refuse
कचौड़ी kacauṛī *n.f.* pie
कच्चा kaccā *adj.* raw
कच्ची धातु kaccī dhātu *n.f.* ore
कच्छ kacch *n.m.* marsh
कटु kaṭu *adj.* bitter
कठपुतली kaṭhputlī *n.f.* pawn
कठबाप kaṭhbāp *n.m.* stepfather
कठवैद्य kaṭhvaidya *n.m.* quack
कठिनाई kaṭhināī *n.f.* difficulty
कठोर kaṭhor *adj.* strict, rigid
कड़ा kaṛā *adj.* stiff, stern
कड़ा करना karā karnā *v.t.* toughen
कड़ा बनाना kaṛā banānā *v.t.* stiffen, harden
कड़ा हो जाना kaṛā ho jānā *v.t.* set
कड़ा होना kaṛā honā *v.i.* stiffen
कड़ापन kaṛāpan *n.m.* hardness
कड़ाह kaṛāh *n.m.* cauldron

कड़ाही **kaṛāhī** *n.m.* frying
कड़ी **kaṛī** *n.f.* link
कण्ठी **kaṇṭhī** *n.f.* necklace
कण्टक **kaṇṭak** *n.m.* nuisance
कण्ड **kaṇḍ** *n.m.* block
कण **kaṇ** *n.m.* particle
कर्णफूल **karṇphūl** *n.m.* earring
कतरनी **katarnī** *n.m.* scissors, shears
कथन **kathan** *n.m.* statement
कथानक **kathānak** *n.m.* plot
कथावाचक **kathāvācak** *n.m.* narrator
क़दम **qadam** *n.m.* step
क़दम-क़दम जाना **qadam-qadam jānā** *v.t.* pace
क़दम करना **qadam karnā** *v.i.* step
कद्दू **kaddū** *n.m.* pumpkin
कपड़ा **kapṛā** *n.m.* textile
कपड़ा पहनाना **kapṛā pehnānā** *v.t.* clothe
कपड़े **kapṛe** *n.m.* clothes
कपड़े बदलने का कमरा **kapṛe badalne kā kamrā** *n.m.* dressing room
कप्तान **kaptān** *n.m.* captain
कंप्यूटर **kampyūṭar** *n.m.* computer
कफ **kap** *n.m.* phlegm
कब **kab** *n.m.* cub; *adv.* when
कबाड़ **kabāṛ** *n.f.* junk
कबूतर **kabūtar** *n.m.* pigeon
क़ब्र **qab** *n.f.* tomb
क़बज़ **qabz** *n.m.* constipation
क़ब्रिस्तान **qabristān** *n.m.* cemetery
कभी-कभी **kabhī-kabhī** *adv.* sometimes
कभी नहीं **kabhī nahīṁ** *adv.* never
कम **kam** *adj.* less

कम करना **kam karnā** *v.t.* diminish
कम से कम **kam se kam** *adj.* at least
कम हो गया है **kam ho gayā hai** *adj.* tapered
कम होना **kam honā** *v.i.* reduce, fade
कमज़ोर **kamzor** *adj.* weak
कमज़ोर कर देना **kamzor kar denā** *v.t.* weaken
कमज़ोरी **kamzorī** *n.f.* weakness
कमर **kamar** *n.f.* waist
कमाई **kamāī** *n.m.* earnings
कमरा **kamrā** *n.m.* room
कमाना **kamānā** *v.i.* earn
कमी **kamī** *n.f.* shortage
कमीज़ **kamīz** *n.f.* shirt
कम्पन **kampan** *n.m.* vibration
कम्पायमान होना **kampāymān honā** *v.i.* vibrate
कर **kar** *n.m.* tax
करघा **karghā** *n.m.* loom
करना **karnā** *v.i.* do
करनी **karnī** *n.f.* trowel
कराह **karāh** *n.f.* moan, groan
कराहना **karāhnā** *v.i.* groan
कर्ज़ **karz** *n.m.* debt
कर्मचारीगण **karamcārīgaṇ** *n.m.* personnel
कर्मवाच्य **karamvācy** *adj.* passive
कर्मवारी **karmvārī** *n.f.* employee
कर्मीदल **karmīdal** *n.m.* crew
कर्षण **karṣaṇ** *n.m.* haul
कर्षनाव **karṣnāv** *n.f.* tugboat
कल **kal** *n.m.* yesterday; tomorrow
कलछी **kalchī** *n.m.* ladle
कलफ़ लगाना **kalaf lagānā** *v.t.* starch
कलवरिया **kalvariyā** *n.m.* tavern

कलम **kalam** *n.f.* pen
कलम बाँधना **kalam bāṁdhnā** *v.t.* graft
कलश **kalaś** *n.m.* urn
कलहंसी **kalhansī** *n.f.* goose
कला **kalā** *n.f.* art
कलाई **kalāī** *n.m.* wrist
कलाकार **kalākār** *n.m.* artist
कलात्मक **kalātmak** *adj.* artistic
कलेजा **kalejā** *n.m.* liver
कल्पना **kalpnā** *n.f.* fiction
कल्पना करना **kalpanā karnā** *v.t.* imagine
कवि **kavi** *n.m.* poet
कविता **kavitā** *n.f.* poem
कसना **kasnā** *v.t.* screw
कसम खाना **kasam khānā** *v.t.* swear
कसी हुई **kasī huī** *adj.* tense
कहाँ **kahāṁ** *conj./interr.* where
कहानी **kahānī** *n.f.* story
कहावत **kahāvat** *n.f.* proverb
कहीं **kahīṁ** *adv.* somewhere
कहीं भी **kahīṁ bhī** *adv.* anywhere
कहीं नहीं **kahīṁ nahīṁ** *adv.* nowhere
कक्षक **kakṣak** *n.m.* cubicle
कक्षा **kakṣā** *n.f.* classroom
काँटा **kāṁṭā** *n.m.* thorn
काँपना **kāṁpnā** *v.i.* tremble
काँसा **kāṁsā** *n.m.* bronze
काउंटर **kāunṭar** *n.f.* counter
काग़ज़ **kāqgaz** *n.m.* paper
काग़ज़-चढ़ी **kāqgaz-caṛhī** *n.f.* paperback
काट **kāṭ** *v.t.* cut
काट डालना¨ **kāṭ ḍālnā** *v.t.* amputate

काटना **kāṭnā** *v.t.* chip
काट मारना **kāṭ mārnā** *v.t.* slash
काटना **kāṭnā** *v.t.* delete
काटा **kāṭā** *n.m.* bite
कार्टून **kārṭūn** *n.m.* cartoon
काथलिक **kāthlik** *adj.* Catholic
काथलिक धर्म **kāthlik dharam** *n.m.* Catholicism
कान **kān** *n.* ear
काख **kākh** *n.m.* buttonhole
कान का दर्द **kān kā dard** *n.m.* earache
कानाफूसी करना **kānāphūsī karnā** *v.i.* whisper
कानून **kānūn** *n.m.* legislation
काष्ठतरंग **kāṣṭhtarang** *n.f.* xylophone
कॉपी **kāpī** *n.f.* notebook
काफ़ी **kāfī** *adj./adv.* enough
काफ़ी होना **kāfī honā** *v.i.* suffice
काफ़ी-गृहा **kāfī gr̥hā** *n.m.* coffee
काबू **kābū** *n.m.* control
काम **kām** *n.m.* work
काम करना **kām karnā** *v.i.* function
काम के दिन **kām ke din** *n.m.* weekday
काम पर लगाना **kām par lagānā** *v.t.* employ
कामयाब होना **kāmyāb honā** *v.i.* succeed
कायर **kāyar** *n.m.* coward
कारखाना **kārkhānā** *n.m.* workshop
कारण **kāraṇ** *n.m.* cause, reason
कारतूस **kārtūs** *n.m.* cartridge
कारीगर **karīgar** *n.m.* artisan
कारोबार **kārobār** *n.m.* transaction
कार्यालय **kāyārlay** *n.m.* bureau
कार्य **kārya** *n.m.* act, deed
कार्य करना **kārya karnā** *v.i.* act

कार्यक्रम **kāryakram** *n.m.* program
कार्यसम्पादन **kāryasampādan** *n.m.* achievement
कार्यसूची **kāryasūcī** *n.f.* agenda
क्रांति **krānti** *n.f.* revolution
काल **kāl** *n.m.* tense
कालर **kālar** *n.m.* collar
काला **kālā** *adj.* black
काली अंची **kālī ancī** *n.m.* blackberry
काली मिर्च **kālī mirc** *n.m.* pepper
कालेज **kālej** *n.m.* college
काव्य **kāvya** *n.m.* poetry
काश्तकार **kāśtkār** *n.m.* tenant
किंवदंती **kinvadantī** *n.m.* rumor
किताब **kitāb** *n.f.* book
किताब की दुकान **kitāb kī dukān** *n.m.* bookstore
किनारा **kinārā** *n.m.* edge, margin
किनारे **kinare** *n.m.* outskirts
किनारे की पगडंडी **kināre kī pagḍaṇḍī** *n.f.* sidewalk
किरण **kiraṇ** *n.f.* ray
किरमिच **kirmic** *n.m.* canvas
किराए पर होना **kirāe par honā** *v.t.* hire
किराया **kirāyā** *n.m.* rent
किराये पर लेना **kirāye par lenā** *v.t.* rent
किरासन **kirāsan** *n.m.* kerosene
क़िला **qilā** *n.m.* fort
किलोग्राम **kilogrām** *n.m.* kilo(gram)
किलोमीटर **kilomīṭar** *n.m.* kilometer
किशमिश **kiśmiś** *n.f.* raisin
किशोर **kiśor** *n.m.* teenager, juvenile
किश्ती **kiśtī** *n.m.* tray
किसका **kiskā** *adj.* whose
किसान **kisān** *n.m.* farmer; peasant

किसी तरह **kisī tarah** *adv*. somehow
किसे **kise** *pron*. whom
किस्मत **kismat** *n.f.* fortune
किस्सा **kissā** *n.m.* anecdote
कीट **kīṭ** *n.m.* insect
कीड़ा **kīṛā** *n.m.* worm
कीचड़ **kīcaṛ** *n.m.* mud
कीचड़दार **kīcaṛdār** *n.m.* sloppy
क्रीड़ास्थल **krīṛāsthal** *n.m.* playground
कील **kīl** *n.m.* nail
कुंआरी **kumārī** *n.m.* virgin
कुंडली **kuṇḍalī** *n.f.* coil
कुकर **kukar** *n.m.* cooker
कुचलना **kucalnā** *v.t.* crush
कुछ **kuch** *pron*. something
कुछ भी **kuch bhī** *pron*. anything
कुछ नहीं **kuch nahīṁ** *pron*. nothing
कुछ-कुछ **kuch-kuch** *adv*. somewhat
कुडल **kuḍal** *n.m.* curl
कुत्ता **kuttā** *n.m.* dog
कुनकुना **kunkunā** *adj*. tepid
कुमारी **kumārī** *n.f.* Miss
कुम्हारी **kumhārī** *n.f.* pottery
कुम्हड़ा **kumhaṛā** *n.m.* squash
कुरकुरा बिस्कुट **kurkurā biskuṭ** *n.m.* cracker
कुरती **kurtī** *n.f.* blouse
कुरबानी **kurbānī** *n.m.* sacrifice
कुरूप **kurūp** *adj*. ugly
कुरेदना **kurednā** *v.t.* rake
कुर्सी **kursī** *n.f.* seat
कुर्सियों की पंकित **kursiyoṁ kī paṅkti** *n.f.* row

कुर्सी की पेटी **kursī kī peṭī** *n.f.* seatbelt
कुल मिलाकर **kul milākar** *adj./adv.* overall
कुल्ली करना **kullī karnā** *v.i.* gargle
कुल्हाड़ी **kulhāṛī** *n.f.* axe
कुशल **kuśal** *n.m.* skill
कुशलता **kuśaltā** *adj.* skillful
कुश्ती लड़ना **kuśtī laṛnā** *v.t.* wrestle
कुश्तीबाज़ **kuśtībāz** *n.m.* wrestler
कुस्वप्न **kusvapn** *n.m.* nightmare
कुहनी **kuhnī** *n.f.* elbow
कुहासा **kuhāsā** *n.m.* mist
कूटना **kūṭnā** *v.i.* pound; *n.f.* batter
कूल्हा **kūlhā** *n.m.* hip
कृपा **kṛpā** *n.m.* grace
कृपालु **kṛpālu** *adj.* gracious
कृपया **kṛpyā** *interj.* please
केंद्र **kendra** *n.m.* center
केंद्रीय **kendrīy** *adj.* central
केक **kek** *n.m.* cake
केकड़ा **kekaṛā** *n.m.* crab
केतली **ketalī** *n.f.* kettle
केला **kelā** *n.m.* banana
केवल **keval** *adv.* just, only
कैंटीन **kainṭīn** *n.m.* cafeteria
कैन **kain** *n.m.* can
कैन्सर **kainsar** *n.m.* cancer
कैपसूल **kaipsūl** *n.m.* capsule
कैफ़ीन **kaifīn** *n.m.* caffeine
कैफ़ीन के बिना **kaifīn ke binā** *adj.* decaffeinated
कैमरा **kaimarā** *n.m.* camera
कैल्सियम **kailsiyam** *n.m.* calcium

कैसे **kaise** *adv.* how
को **ko** *prep.* to
को छोड़कर **ko choṛkar** *adv.* aside
कष्ठ **kaṣṭh** *n.m.* hardship
कोई **koī** *pron.* someone
कोई भी **koī bhī** *pron.* anyone
कोई भी नहीं **koī bhī nahīṁ** *pron.* none
कोई नहीं **koī nahīṁ** *pron.* nobody
कोको **koko** *n.m.* cocoa
कोट **koṭ** *n.m.* coat
कोटा **koṭā** *n.m.* quota
कोठरी **koṭharī** *n.f.* closet; cell
कोड **koḍ** *n.f.* code
कोण **koṇ** *n.m.* angle
कोणडोम **koṇḍom** *n.m.* condom
कोना **konā** *n.m.* corner
कोमपैक्ट डिस्क **kompaikṭ ḍisk** *n.m.* compact disc
कोमल **komal** *adj.* sensitive
कोमल रोम **komal rom** *n.m.* down
कोमलता **komalā** *n.f.* delicacy
कोमलास्थि **komlāsthi** *n.m.* carton
कोयला **koyalā** *n.m.* coal
कोया **koyā** *n.m.* eyeball
कोलन **kkālej** *n.m.* kolan
कोलेस्टेरोल **kolesṭerol** *n.m.* cholesterol
कोशिकीय **kośikīy** *adj.* cellular
कोशिश **kośiś** *n.f.* try
कोशिश करना **kośiś karnā** *v.t.* try
कोहरेवाला **koharevālā** *adj.* foggy
कौंसल **kauṁsal** *n.m.* consul
कौआ **kauā** *n.m.* crow

कौन **kaun** *pron.* who; *adj.* which
क्रम से रखना **kram se rakhnā** *v.i.* dispose
क्रमानुसार राखना **kramānusār rākhnā** *v.t.* grade
क्रमिक **krāmik** *adj.* gradual
क्रिकेट **kriket̤** *n.m.* cricket
क्रिया **kriyā** *n.f.* verb
क्रिया करना **kriyā karnā** *v.t.* action
क्रियाविधि **kriyāvidhi** *n.f.* procedure
क्रियाविशेषण **kriyāviśeṣaṇ** *n.m.* adverb
क्रियाशील **kriyāśīl** *adj.* lively
क्रिसमस **krismas** *n.m.* Christmas
क्रेन **kren** *n.m.* crane
क्लच **kalac** *n.m.* clutch
क्लब **kalab** *n.m.* club
क्लीनर **klīnar** *n.m.* cleaner
क्लर्क **klark** *n.m.* clerk
कवक **kavak** *n.m.* truffle
क्वार्ट **kvyārṭ** *n.m.* quart
क्षत **kṣat** *n.m.* lesion
क्षति **kṣati** *n.f.* damage
क्षतिपूर्ति करना **kṣatipūrti karnā** *v.t.* offset
क्षमता **kṣamatā** *n.m.* aptitude
क्षमा करना **kṣamā karnā** *v.t.* forgive
क्षमा माँगना **kṣamā māṁgnā** *v.i.* apologize
क्षमा-याचना **kṣakmā-yācnā** *n.m.* apology
क्षेत्र **kṣetra** *n.m.* zone

ख

खँगालना **khaṁgālnā** *v.t.* rinse
खंभा **khambhā** *n.m.* pillar, post, pole
ख़ज़ाना **qhazānā** *n.m.* treasure
ख़ज़ानची **qhazāncī** *n.m.* cashier
खजूरा **khajūrā** *n.m.* date
खटखटाना **khaṭkhaṭānā** *v.i.* knock
खट्टा **khaṭṭā** *adj.* sour
खण्ड **khaṇḍ** *n.m.* fraction
खड़ा **khaṛā** *adj.* vertical
खड़ा होना **khaṛā honā** *v.t.* stand
खड़ी चट्टान **khāṛī caṭṭān** *n.f.* cliff
खड़जा डालना **khaṛjā ḍālnā** *v.t.* pave
खड़िया **khaṛiyā** *n.f.* chalk
ख़तरनाक **qhatarnāk** *adj.* dangerous
ख़तरा **qhatarā** *n.m.* menace
खनन **khanan** *n.m.* mining
खपची **khacī** *n.f.* splint
ख़बरदार **qhabardār** *interj.* beware!
ख़मीर **qhamīr** *n.m.* yeast
खरगोश **khargoś** *n.m.* rabbit
खर-पतवार **khar-patvār** *n.m.* weed
खरबूज़ा **kharbūzā** *n.m.* melon
खरयंत्रशोथ **kharyantraśoth** *n.m.* laryngitis
ख़राब करना **qharāb karnā** *v.t.* corrupt
ख़राब होना **qharāb honā** *v.i.* decay
खलबली **khalbalī** *n.f.* turmoil
ख़राब **qharāb** *adj.* faulty
ख़रीद **qharīd** *n.m.* purchase
खरीदना **kharīdnā** *v.t.* buy

खरीदार **kharīdār** *n.m.* buyer
खरीदारी **kharīdārī** *v.t.* shopping
खरोचना **kharocnā** *v.t.* scratch
ख़र्च **qharc** *n.m.* expense
ख़र्च कर सकना **qharc kar saknā** *v.t.* afford
ख़र्च करना **qharc karnā** *v.t.* spend
खर्राटा लेना **kharrāṭā lenā** *v.i.* snore
खाँसना **khāṁsnā** *v.i.* cough
खाँसी **khāṁsī** *n.f.* cough
खाई **khāī** *n.f.* trench
खाका उतारना **khākā utārnā** *v.t.* trace
खाकी **khākī** *n./adj.* khaki
खाट **khāṭ** *n.f.* cot
खाड़ी **khāṛī** *n.f.* gulf, bay
खाता **qhātā** *n.m.* account
ख़ातिर **qhātir** *n.* sake
खाद **khād** *n.f.* manure
खान **khān** *n.f./pron.* mine
ख़ानसामा **qhānsāmā** *n.m.* cook
खाना **khānā** *n.* food
खाने लायक **khāne lāyak** *adj.* edible
ख़ाली **qhālī** *adj.* vacant, empty
ख़ाली करना **qhālī karnā** *v.t.* empty
खाली जाना **khālī jānā** *v.t.* miss
खास **khās** *adj.* special
ख़ास तौर से **qhās taur se** *adv.* especially
खिड़की **khiṛkī** *n.f.* window
खिदमतगार **khidamtagār** *n.* steward
खिन्न **khinn** *adj.* depressed
खिलाड़ी **khilāṛī** *n.m.* player, sportsman
खिलाना **khilānā** *v.t.* feed
खिलाना-पिलाना **khilānā-pilānā** *v.t.* nourish

खिलाफ़ **khilāf** *v.t.* against
खिलौना **khilaunā** *n.* toy
खिसकाना **khiskānā** *v.t.* shove
खींचना **khīṁcnā** *v.t.* tow
खीज **khīj** *n.m.* annoyance
खीझ **khījh** *n.m.* disgust
खुजली **khujlī** *n.f.* itch
खुद **khud** *pron.* ourselves, myself
खुदाई **khudāī** *n.f.* excavation
खुरचना **khurcnā** *v.t.* scrape
खुरदरी **khurdarī** *adj.* rough
खुरपा **khurpā** *n.m.* hoe
खुला **khulā** *adj./v.t.* open
खुली **khulī** *n.m.* quarry
खुश **khuś** *adj.* gay, happy
खुशबू **khuśbū** *n.m.* smell
खुशी **khuśī** *n.m.* happiness
खुशी से **khuśī se** *adj.* willing
खुसुर-फुसुर **khusur-phusur** *n.f.* whisper
खूंखार **khūṁkhār** *adj.* fierce
खूंटा **khūṁṭā** *n.m.* stake
खूंटी **khūṁṭī** *n.f.* peg
खूबानी **khūbānī** *n.f.* apricot
खेत **khet** *n.m.* field
खेत का **khet kā** *adj.* agricultural
खेती **khetī** *n.f.* cultivation
खेतीबारी **khetībārī** *n.f.* agriculture
खेना **khenā** *v.t.* row
खेल **khel** *n.* game
खेलना **khelnā** *v.t.* play
खेलकूद **khelkūd** *n.m.* athletics
खेलना **khelnā** *v.t.* play

खेल-प्रतियोगिता **khel-pratiyogitā** *n.* tournament
खोखला **khokhalā** *adj.* hollow
खोज **khoj** *n.f.* discovery, find
खोज करना **khoj karnā** *v.t.* discover
खोजना **khojnā** *v.t.* seek
खोदना **khodnā** *v.t.* engrave
खोना **khonā** *v.t.* lose
खोपड़ी **khopaṛī** *n.* skull
खोया **khoyā** *adj.* lost
खोलना **kholnā** *v.t.* unwrap

ग

गंजा **gañjā** *adj.* bald
गाँठ **gāṁṭh** *n.f.* knot
गाँठ बाँधना **gāṁth bāṁdhnā** *v.t.* knot
गंदा **gandā** *adj.* unpleasant
गंदी नाली **gandī nālī** *n.f.* gutter
गंदी-बस्ती **gandī-bastī** *n.f.* slum
गंध **gandh** *n.f.* odor
गंभीर **gambhīr** *adj.* serious
गाँव **gāṁv** *n.m.* village
गड्डमड्ड **gaḍḍmaḍḍ** *n.m.* jumble
गड्डमड्ड कर देना **gaḍḍmaḍḍ kar denā** *v.i.* jump
गज़ **gaz** *n.m.* yard
गड़बड़ **gaṛbaṛ** *n.f.* unrest
गड़बड़ जाना **gaṛbaṛ jānā** *v.t.* confuse
गड़बड़ करना **gaṛbaṛ karnā** *v.t.* tamper
गड़गड़ाहट **gaṛgaṛāhaṭ** *n.f.* rumble
गड़बड़ कर देना **gaṛbaṛ kar denā** *v.t.* upset
गड़रिया **gaṛriyā** *n.m.* shepherd
गड्ढा **gaḍḍhā** *n.m.* dent, pit

गढ़ **garh** *n.m.* fortress
गणक **gaṇak** *n.m.* calculator
गणना **gaṇnā** *v.t.* count
गणतंत्र **gaṇtantra** *n.m.* republic
गणतंत्री **gaṇtantrī** *n.m./adj.* republican
गत **gat** *n.m.* past
गति **gati** *n.f.* motion, pace
गतिमापी **gati māpī** *n.m.* speedometer
गति सीमा **gati sīmā** *n.f.* speed
गतिरोध **gātirodh** *n.f.* impasse
गतिशील **gatiśīl** *adj.* dynamic
गत्ता **gattā** *n.m.* cardboard
गद्दी **gaddī** *n.f.* wad
गद्य **gadya** *n.m.* prose
गधा **gadhā** *n.m.* donkey
गन्धहीन **gandhhīn** *adj.* odorless
गपशप **gapśap** *n.m.* gossip
गपशप करना **gapśap karnā** *v.i.* gossip
गरज **garaj** *n.f.* thunder, roar
गरजना **garajnā** *v.i.* roar
गरज के साथ तूफ़ान **garaj ke sāth tūfān** *n.m.* thunderstorm
गरम **garam** *adj.* warm
गरम करके जीवाणु रहित करना **garam karke jīvāṇuu rahit karnā** *v.t.* pasteurize
गरम पानी से जलाना **garam pānī se jalānā** *v.t.* scald
गरमी **garmī** *n.f.* warmth
गरी **garī** *n.f.* kernel
ग़रीब **qarīb** *adj.* poor
गरुड़ **garuṛ** *n.m.* eagle
गर्दन **gardan** *n.f.* neck
गर्भपात **garabhpāt** *n.m.* abortion
गर्भवती **garabhvatī** *adj.* pregnant

गर्भाशय **garbhāśy** *n.m.* uterus, womb
ग़लत **qgalat** *adj.* mistaken, wrong
ग़लतफ़हमी **qgalatfahamī** *n.f.* misunderstanding
ग़लती **qgaltī (guilt)** *n.* fault, error
ग़लत जगह पर रखना **qgalat jagah par rakhnā** *v.t.* misplace
गलना **galnā** *v.i.* thaw
गला **galā** *n.m.* throat
गला घोटना **galā ghoṭnā** *v.t.* choke, strangle
गलाना **galānā** *v.t.* thaw
गले **gale** *n.m.* hug
गले लगाना **gale lagānā** *v.t.* embrace, hug
गली **galī** *n.f.* lane
गलीचा **galīcā** *n.m.* rug
गल्ला **gallā** *n.m.* herd
गवाह **gavāh** *n.m.* witness
गवाही **gavāhī** *n.f.* evidence
गवाही देना **gavāhī denā** *v.i.* testify, witness
गर्व **garv** *n.m.* pride
गश्त **gaśt** *n.f.* patrol
गहना **gahanā** *n.m.* ornament
गहरा **gaharā** *adj.* deep
गहराई **gaharāī** *n.f.* depth
गहरी **gehrī** *adj.* profound
गाँठ **gāṁṭh** *n.f.* knot
गाँठ बाँधना **gāṁth bāṁdhnā** *v.t.* knot
गाँव **gāṁv** *n.m.* village
गाड़ी **gāṛī** *n.f.* vehicle
गाड़ी-स्थान **gāṛī-sthān** *n.m.* parking
गाड़ना **gāṛnā** *v.t.* bury
गाढ़ा बनाना **gāṛhā banānā** *v.i.* thicken
गाइड **gāiḍ** *n.m.* guide
गाढ़ा बनना **gāṛhā bannā** *v.i.* thicken

गाढ़ा बनाना **gāṛhā banānā** *v.t.* thicken
गाना **gānā** *n.m.* song
गाय **gāy** *n.f.* cow
गायक **gāyak** *n.m.* singer
गायकदल **gāyakdal** *n.m.* chorus
गायक-मण्डल **gāyak-maṇḍal** *n.m.* choir
गायन **gāyan** *n.m.* singing
गायब हो जाना **gāyab ho jānā** *v.i.* disappear
गाय-बैल **gāy-bail** *n.m.* ox
गायिका **gāyikā** *n.f.* singer
गारा **gārā** *n.m.* mortar
गाल **gāl** *n.m.* cheek
गाली बकना **gālī baknā** *v.t.* swear
गिटार **giṭār** *n.m.* guitar
गिनती करना **gintī karnā** *v.t.* reckon
गिनन **ginn** *v.t.* count
गिरजाघर **girjāghar** *n.m.* church
गिर जाना **gir jānā** *v.i.* lapse
गिरना **girnā** *v.t.* fall
गिराना **girānā** *v.t.* drop
गिरावट **girāvaṭ** *v.t.* fall
गिरफ़्तार **giraftār** *n.m.* arrest
गिरफ़्तार करना **giraftār karnā** *v.t.* arrest
गिरफ़्तारी **giraftārī** *n.f.* seizure
गिरीदार **girīdār** *n.m.* nut
गिल **gil** *n.m.* gill
गिलहरी **gilharī** *n.f.* squirrel
गिल्टी **gilṭī** *n.f.* gland
गीति-नाट्य **gīti-nāṭya** *n.m.* opera
गीला **gīlā** *adj.* wet
गुँधना **guṁdhnā** *v.t.* knead
गुच्छा **gucchā** *n.m.* cluster

गुण **guṇ** *n.m.* virtue
गुणा **guṇā** *n.m.* multiplication
गुणा करना **guṇā karnā** *v.t.* multiply
गुदगुदाना **gudgudānā** *v.t.* tickle
गुर्दा **gurdā** *n.m.* kidney
गुप्त **gupt** *adj.* secret, occult
गुप्त रोग **gupt rog** *n.m.* venereal disease
गुप्तचर **guptcar** *n.m.* detective, scout
गुप्तचर्या करना **guptcaryā karnā** *v.t.* scout
गुप्त शब्द **gupt śabd** *n.m.* password
गुफ़ा **gufā** *n.m.* cave
गुब्बारा **gubbārā** *n.m.* balloon
गुमटी **gumṭī** *n.f.* kiosk
गुमनाम **gumnām** *adj.* anonymous
गुम्बद **gumbad** *n.m.* dome
गुरुवार **guruvār** *n.m.* Thursday
गुराना **gurānā** *v.i.* growl, snarl
गुराहिट **gurāhiṭ** *n.f.* growl
गुलाब **gulāb** *n.m.* rose
गुलाब का पौधा **gulāb kā paudhā** *n.m.* rosebush
गुलाबी **gulābī** *adj.* pink
गुलमा **gulmā** *n.m.* sausage
गुसलख़ाना **gusalqhānā** *n.m.* bathroom
गुस्सा **gussā** *n.m.* anger; *adj.* angry, mad
गुस्सा दिलाना **gussā dilānā** *v.i.* anger
गेहूँ **gehūṁ** *n.m.* wheat
गृह **gṛh** *n.m.* home
ग्रेनाइट **grenāiṭ** *n.m.* granite
गैती **gaitī** *n.m.* pick
गैरज **gairaj** *n.m.* garage
ग़ैर-ईसाई **qgair-īsāī** *n.m./adj.* pagan
ग़ैर-कानूनी **qgair-kānūnī** *adj.* illegal

गैलन **gailan** *n.m.* gallon
गैलरी **gailarī** *n.f.* gallery
गैस **gais** *n.m.* gas
गैसीय **gaisīy** *adj.* gassy
गोट **goṭ** *n.f.* hem
गोद **god** *n.f.* lap
गोद लेना **god lenā** *v.t.* adopt
गोता **gotā** *n.m.* dive
ग़ोता लगाना **qgotā lagānā** *v.t.* dive
ग़ोताख़ोरी **qgotāqhārī** *n.m.* diving
गोदाम **godām** *n.m.* warehouse
गोबर **gobar** *n.m.* dung
गोभी **gobhī** *n.f.* cauliflower
गोल **gol** *adj.* round
गोला **golā** *n.m.* sphere
गोली **golī** *n.f.* pill
गोली मारना **golī mārnā** *v.t.* shoot
गोल-मटोल **gol-maṭol** *adj.* plump
गोल्फ़ **golf** *n.m.* golf
गौरैया **gauraiyā** *n.m.* sparrow
ग्यारह **gyārah** *num.* eleven
ग्यारहवाँ **gyārahvāṁ** *adj.* eleventh
ग्रह **grah** *n.m.* planet
ग्रन्थका आकार **granthakā ākār** *n.m.* format
ग्राहक **grāhak** *n.m.* customer
ग्रिल में पकाना **gril meṁ pakānā** *v.t.* grill
ग्रीस लगाना **grīs lagānā** *v.t.* grease
ग्लोब **glob** *n.m.* globe

घ

घंटा **ghaṇṭā** *n.m.* hour
घंटी **ghaṇṭī** *n.f.* bell
घंटेवार **ghaṇṭevār** *adv.* hourly
घटक **ghaṭak** *n.m.* ingredient
घटना **ghaṭnā** *n.f.* occurrence; *v.i.* decrease
घटाई **ghaṭāī** *n.f.* shortening
घटाना **ghaṭānā** *v.t.* decrease
घटाव **ghaṭāv** *n.m.* reduction
घड़ा **ghaṛā** *n.m.* pitcher
घड़ी **ghaṛī** *n.f.* clock, wristwatch, watch
घबड़ाना **ghabaṛānā** *v.t.* embarrass
घबरा देना **ghabarā denā** *v.t.* agitate
घबरा देनेवाला **ghabarā denevālā** *adj.* upsetting
घबराहट **ghabarāhaṭ** *n.f.* confusion
घसीटना **ghasīṭnā** *v.t.* tug
घटित होना **ghaṭit honā** *v.t.* precede; *v.i.* occur
घनिष्ठ **ghaniṣṭh** *adj.* intimate
घन **ghan** *n.m.* cube
घर **ghar** *n.m.* home
घरघर करते हुए सांस लेना **gharghar karte hue sāns lenā** *v.i.* wheeze
घरेलू **gharelū** *adj.* domestic
घसीटना **ghasīṭnā** *v.t.* haul
घसीटनेवाला **ghasīṭnevālā** *n.m.* trailer
घाघरा **ghāgharā** *n.m.* skirt
घाट **ghāṭ** *n.m.* landing
घाटबन्धी **ghāṭbandhī** *n.f.* embargo
घाटी **ghāṭī** *n.f.* pass
घातक **ghātak** *adj.* fatal

घास **ghās** *n.f.* grass
घास-स्थली **ghās-sthalī** *n.f.* meadow
घायल **ghāyal** *adj.* injured
घायल करना **ghāyal karnā** *v.t.* injure
घाव **ghāv** *n.m.* wound, cut
घिरनी **ghiranī** *n.f.* pulley
घिसटते चलना **ghisṭate calnā** *v.i.* trail
घुँघराला **ghuṁgharālā** *adj.* curly
घुंघराला बनाना **ghuṁgharālā banānā** *v.t.* curl
घुटना **ghuṭnā** *n.m.* knee
घुटने टेकना **ghuṭne ṭeknā** *v.i.* kneel
घुमाव **ghumāv** *n.m.* turn
घुसेड़ना **ghuseṛnā** *v.t.* insert
घूमना **ghūmnā** *v.i.* spin
घूमते फिरना **ghūmte phirnā** *v.i.* wander
घूस **ghus** *n.m.* bribe
घृणा योग्य **ghṛnā yogya** *adj.* disgusting
घृणा **ghṛṇā** *n.m.* scorn
घेरघराहट **ghergharāhaṭ** *n.m.* wheeze
घेरा **gherā** *n.m.* enclosure
घेरा परिधि **gherā paridhi** *n.m.* circumference
घेरे में **ghere meṁ** *n.m.* radius
घोंघा **ghoṅhā** *n.m.* slug
घोंसला **ghonsalā** *n.m.* nest
घोंसला बनाना **ghonsalā banānā** *v.t.* nest
घोड़ा **ghoṛā** *n.m.* horse
घोड़ी **ghoṛī** *n.f.* mare
घोर व्यथा **ghor vyathā** *n.f.* agony
घोल **ghol** *n.m.* solution
घोषणा **ghoṣṇā** *n.f.* declaration
घोषणा करना **ghoṣaṇā karnā** *v.t.* announce, declare

च

चंगा हो जाना **caṅgā ho jānā** *v.i.* recover
चंगा कर देना **caṅgā kar denā** *v.i.* recuperate
चंदा **candā** *n.m.* subscription
चंदन की लकड़ी **candan kī lakaṛī** *n.f.* sandalwood
चक्की **cakkī** *n.f.* mill
चक्कीवाला **cakkīvālā** *n.m.* miller
चक्कर **cakkar** *n.m.* dizziness
चक्कर से आक्रांत **cakkar se ākrant** *adj.* dizzy
चक्र **cakr** *n.m.* wheel
चचेरा भाई **cacerā bhāī** *n.m.* cousin (*male on father's side*)
चटखनी **caṭkhanī** *n.f.* bolt
चटाई **caṭāī** *n.f.* mat
चटनी **caṭnī** *n.f.* sauce
चट्टान **caṭṭān** *n.f.* rock
चट्टानी **caṭṭānī** *adj.* rocky
चढ़ाई **caṛhāī** *n.f.* invasion; climb
चढ़ना **caṛhnā** *v.t.* climb
चढ़ाना **caṛhānā** *v.t.* offer
चढ़ना **caṛhnā** *v.i.* ride, mount
चढ़ाई करना **cāṛhāī karnā** *v.t.* invade
चढ़ाना **caṛhānā** *v.t.* mount
चतुर्थांश **catuthāṁś** *n.m.* quarter
चतुर **catur** *adj.* ingenious
चना **canā** *n.m.* gram
चन्द्र **candra** *n.m.* moon
चप्पल **cappal** *n.f.* sandal
चप्पू **cappū** *n.m.* oar
चबाना **cabānā** *v.t.* crunch
चमड़ा **camṛā** *n.m.* leather

चमड़ी **camṛī** *n.f.* skin
चमक **camak** *n.f.* glare
चमकना **camaknā** *v.t./v.i.* shine, glare, flash
चमत्कार **camatkār** *n.m.* miracle
चमत्कारी **camatkārī** *adj.* miraculous
चमकीला **camkīlā** *adj.* brilliant
चमेली **camelī** *n.f.* jasmine
चम्मच **cammac** *n.m.* spoon
चयन **cayan** *n.m.* selection
चर **car** *n.m.* variable
चरपरा **carparā** *adj.* tart
चरबी **carbī** *n.f.* grease
चरबीदार **carbīdār** *adj.* fatty
चर्मपत्र **carampatr** *n.m.* parchment
चलकी **calkī** *n.f.* strainer
चलता **caltā** *adj.* moving
चलता रहना **caltā rahnā** *v.t.* continue
चलती सीढ़ी **caltī sīṛhī** *n.f.* escalator
चलना **calnā** *v.t./v.i.* move
चल पड़ना **cal paṛnā** *v.t.* steer
चला जाना **calā jānā** *v.i.* retire
चलाना **calānā** *v.t.* launch; steer
चलनेवाला **calnevālā** *n.m.* walker
चश्मा **caśmā** *n.m.* glass
चश्मा बनानेवाला **caśmā banānvālā** *n.m.* optician
चाँदी **cāṁdī** *n.f.* silver
चाँदी के बरतन-भाँड़े **cāṁdī ke bartan-bhāṁṛe** *n.m.* silverware
चांद्र **cāndra** *adj.* lunar
चांदनी **cāndanī** *n.f.* moonlight
चाक **cāk** *n.f.* chalk
चाकलेट **cākleṭ** *n.f.* chocolate
चाकलेट रंग का **cākleṭ rang kā** *adj.* maroon

चाकू **cākū** *n.m.* knife
चाचा **cācā** *n.m.* uncle (*father's younger brother*)
चाची **cācī** *n.f.* aunt (*wife of father's brother*)
चादर **cādar** *n.f.* sheet
चापलूसी करना **cāpalūsī karnā** *v.t.* flatter
चाबी **cābī** *n.f.* key
चाय **cāy** *n.f.* tea
चायदान **cāydān** *n.m.* teakettle
चायदानी **cāydānī** *n.f.* teapot
चार **cār** *num.* four
चारा **cārā** *n.m.* bait
चारा देना **cārā denā** *v.t.* feed
चारों ओर **chāroṁ aor** *adv.* about
चाल **cāl** *n.f.* walk; speed; trick
चाल बढ़ाना **cāl baṛhānā** *v.i.* accelerate
चालीस **cālīs** *num.* forty
चालीसा **cālīsā** *n.m.* Lent
चालीसवाँ **cālīsvāṁ** *adj.* fortieth
चालन चक्का **cālan cakkā** *n.m.* steering
चालू **cālū** *adj.* current
चावल **cāval** *n.m.* rice
चाहना **cāhanā** *v.t.* desire
चाहिए **cāhiye** *v.i.* should
चिकित्सा **cikitsā** *n.f.* therapy
चिकित्सालय **cikitsālay** *n.m.* clinic
चिकित्सीय **cikitsīy** *adj.* therapeutic
चिकित्सक **cikitsak** *n.m.* therapist
चिकित्सक **cikitsak** *n.m.* physician
चिकोटी **cikoṭī** *n.m.* pinch
चिड़िया **ciṛiyā** *n.m.* bird
चिड़ियाघर **ciṛiyāghar** *n.m.* zoo
चिड़चिड़ा **ciṛciṛā** *adj.* fractious

चिड़चिड़ी **ciṛciṛī** *adj.* hasty
चित्ती **cittī** *n.f.* spot
चिढ़ **ciṛh** *n.m.* annoyance
चिढ़ाना **ciṛhānā** *v.t.* tease
चिढ़ानेवाला **ciṛhānevālā** *n.m.* tease
चित्र **citra** *n.m.* painting
चित्र सा **citra sā** *adj.* picturesque
चित्रण करना **citraṇ karnā** *v.t.* depict
चित्रकार **citrakār** *n.m.* painter
चित्रपट **citrapaṭ** *n.m.* tapestry
चिन्ता करना **cintā karnā** *v.t.* worry
चिन्तित **cintit** *adj.* worried, anxious
चिंतन करना **cintan karnā** *v.t.* reflect
चिंता **cintā** *n.f.* concern, worry
चिनगारियाँ निकलना **cingāriyāṁ nikalnā** *v.i.* sparkle
चिनगारी **cingārī** *n.f.* spark
चिन्ह **cinh** *n.m.* mark, trace
चिट्ठी **ciṭṭhī** *n.f.* letter
चिपटी **cipṭī** *n.f.* tack
चिपकना **cipkanā** *v.i.* cling
चिपकाना **cipkānā** *v.t.* paste
चिपचिपा **cipcipā** *adj.* adhesive
चिप्पी **cippī** *n.f.* chip
चित्र **citra** *n.m.* figure
चिमटा **cimṭā** *n.m.* tongs
चिमटी **cimṭī** *n.f.* tweezers
चिलम **cilam** *n.f.* pipe
चिलमची **cilmacī** *n.f.* basin
चिलाना **cilānā** *v.t.* cry
चिल्ला उठना **cillā uṭhnā** *v.t.* exclaim
चिल्लाना **cillānā** *v.t.* yell
चींटी **cīṁṭī** *n.f.* ant

चीख **cīkh** *n.f.* cry.
चीख़ना **cīqhnā** *v.t./v.i.* scream
चीज़ **cīz** *n.f.* thing
चीड़ **cīṛ** *n.m.* pine
चीड़ी का पत्ता **cīṛī kā pattā** *n.m.* club
चीन **cīn** *n.m.* China; china
चीनी **cīnī** *n.m./adj.* Chinese; *n.f.* sugar
चीनी बर्तन **cīnī bartan** *n.m.* china pot
चीमड़ **cīmaṛ** *adj.* tough
चीमड़पन **cīmaṛpan** *n.* toughness
चीर **cīr** *n.m.* rip
चील **cīl** *n.f.* kite
चुआना **cuānā** *v.t.* distill
चुंबक **cumbak** *n.m.* magnet
चुक़ंदर **cuqandar** *n.m.* beet
चुटकी **cuṭkī** *n.f.* pinch
चुथाना **cuthānā** *v.t.* stick
चुप **cup** *adj.* silent
चुप करना **cūp karnā** *v.t.* silence
चुप्पी **cuppī** *n.f.* silence
चुन लेना **cun lenā** *v.t.* select
चुन्ना **cunnā** *v.t./v.i.* choose, elect
चुनाव **cunāv** *n.m.* election
चुनौती **cunautī** *n.f.* challenge
चुनौती देना **cunautī denā** *v.t.* challenge
चुन्नट **cunnaṭ** *n.f.* crease
चुम्बकीय **cumbakīy** *adj.* magnetic
चुम्मा **cummā** *n.m.* kiss
चुलबुली **culbulī** *adj.* flirt
चुस्की **cuskī** *n.f.* sip
चुस्की लेना **cuskī lenā** *v.t.* sip
चूक **cūk** *n.f.* default

चूँकि **cūṁki** *conj.* since
चूकना **cūknā** *v.i.* fail
चूल्हा **cūlhā** *n.m.* stove
चूर्ण **cūrṇ** *n.m.* powder
चूसना **cūsnā** *v.t.* suck
चूहा **cūhā** *n.m.* rat
चूज़ा **cūzā** *n.m.* chick
चेक **cek** *n.m.* check
चेष्टा **ceṣṭā** *n.m.* move, gesture
चेन **cen** *n.f.* chain
चेरी **cerī** *n.m.* cherry
चेतावनी **cetāvanī** *n.f.* warning, alarm
चेतावनी देना **cetāvanī denā** *v.t.* warn
चेहरे का **cehare kā** *adj.* facial
चैली **cailī** *n.f.* splinter
चोंच **coṁc** *n.f.* beak
चोट **coṭ** *n.m.* hurt
चोट खाना **coṭ khānā** *v.t.* hurt
चोटी **coṭī** *n.f.* ridge
चोर **cor** *n.m.* thief
चोरी से जाना **corī se jānā** *v.t.* stalk
चोरी करना **corī karnā** *v.t.* steal
चौक **cauk** *n.m.* square
चौकी **caukī** *n.f.* chassis
चौकी मारना **caukī mārnā** *v.t.* smuggle
चौकीदार **caukīdār** *n.m.* watchman
चौकीमार **caukīmār** *n.m.* smuggler
चौकीमारी **caukīmārī** *n.m.* smuggling
चौकन्ना **cauknnā** *adj.* wary
चौखटा **caukhṭā** *n.m.* frame
चौखटा लगाना **caukhṭā lagānā** *v.i.* frame
चौड़ा **cauṛā** *adj.* wide

चौड़ा करना **cauṛā karnā** *v.t.* widen
चौड़ाई **cauṛāī** *n.m.* width
चौथा **cauthā** *adj.* fourth
चौदह **caudah** *num.* fourteen
चौदहवाँ **caudahvāṁ** *adj.* fourteenth

छ

छाँटना **chāṁṭnā** *v.t.* sort
छज्जा **chajjā** *n.m.* terrace
छड़ **chaṛ** *n.f.* rod
छड़ी **chaṛī** *n.f.* wand
छल **chal** *n.m.* spill
छलकाना **chalkānā** *v.t.* spill
छलाँग **chalāṁg** *n.f./v.i.* gallop
छलांग **chalāng** *n.m.* vault
छल्ला **challā** *n.m.* hoop
छलनी **chalnī** *n.f.* sieve
छपाई **chapāī** *n.f.* printing
छप्पर **chappar** *n.m.* shed
छपछप **chapchap** *n.m.* splash
छत **chat** *n.f.* roof
छतरी **chatarī** *n.f.* perch
छत्र **chatr** *n.m.* hood
छत्रक **chatrak** *n.m.* mushroom
छरहरा **charhrā** *adj.* slight
छाता **chātā** *n.m.* umbrella
छाती **chātī** *n.f.* chest
छात्र **chātra** *n.m.* pupil
छात्रवास **chātravās** *n.m.* boarding
छात्रवृत्ति **chātravr̥tti** *n.m.* scholarship
छान डालना **chān ḍālnā** *v.t.* ransack

छान-बीन करना **chān-bīn karnā** *v.t.* explore
छानना **chānnā** *v.t.* sift
छाप **chāp** *n.m.* stamp
छाप लगाना **chāp lagānā** *v.t.* impress
छापा **chāpā** *n.m.* raid
छापाभार **chāpābhār** *n.m./adj.* guerilla
छापना **chāpnā** *v.t.* print
छाया **chāyā** *n.f.* shadow, shade
छायादार **chāyādār** *adj.* shady
छाल **chāl** *n.f.* bark
छिछला **chichalā** *adj.* shallow
छिटपुट **chiṭpuṭ** *adj.* random
छिड़कना **chiṛaknā** *v.t.* sprinkle
छितराना **chitrānā** *v.t.* scatter
छिद **chid** *n.m.* slot
छिद्र **chidr** *n.m.* mesh
छिपकली **chipkalī** *n.f.* lizard
छिपाना **chipānā** *v.t.* hide
छिलका **chilkā** *n.m.* peel
छींक **chīṅk** *n.m.* sneeze
छींकना **chīṅknā** *v.i.* sneeze
छीलना **chīlnā** *n.m.* peel
छुटकारा **chuṭkārā** *n.m.* relief
छुट्टी **chuṭṭī** *n.f.* holiday, vacation
छुतहा **chuthā** *adj.* infectious
छूट **chūṭ** *n.f.* omission
छूट देना **chūṭ denā** *v.t.* exempt
छूना **chūnā** *v.t.* touch
छेद **ched** *n.m.* gap
छेदना **chednā** *v.t.* penetrate
छेदित करना **chedit karnā** *v.t.* pierce
छेनी **chenī** *n.f.* chisel

छेनी से काटना **chenī se kāṭnā** *v.t.* chisel
छोटा **choṭā** *adj.* small, little
छोटा चकोतरा **choṭā cakotrā** *n.m.* grapefruit
छोटा चम्मच **choṭā cammac** *n.f.* teaspoon
छोटा करना **choṭā karnā** *v.t.* shorten
छोटा-मोटा **choṭā-moṭā** *adj.* petty
छोटा-सा **choṭā-sā** *adj.* tiny
छोटी टहनी **choṭī ṭahnī** *n.f.* twig
छोड़कर **choṛkar** *v.t.* except
छोड़ देना **choṛ denā** *v.t.* quit
छोड़ना **choṛnā** *v.t.* leave, launch

ज

जंगल **jangal** *n.m.* wood
जंगला **jangalā̃** *n.m.* banister
जंगली **jangalī** *adj.* wild
जंगली जानवर **jangalī jānvar** *n.m.* wildlife
जंभाई **jambhāī** *n.f.* yawn
जंभाई लेना **jambhāī lenā** *v.i.* yawn
जहाँ तक कि **jahāṁ tak ki** *adv.* as far as
जग **jag** *n.m.* jug
जगह **jagah** *n.m.* space
ज़ंग **zaṅg** *n.m.* rust
ज़ंग लगना **zaṅg lagnā** *v.t.* rust
ज़ंग लगा हुआ **zaṅg lagā huā** *adj.* rusty
ज़बान **zabān** *n.f.* tongue
ज़र्दी **zardī** *n.f.* yolk
ज़माना **zamānā** *adj.* feminine
ज़मानत **zamānat** *n.f.* bail
ज़मानतदार **zamānatdār** *n.m.* surety
ज़मीन **zamīn** *n.f.* ground

जाँघ **jāṁgh** *n.f.* thigh
जज **jaj** *n.m.* judge
जटिल बनाना **jaṭil banānā** *v.t.* complicate
जड़ **jaṛ** *n.f.* root
जनजाति **janjāti** *n.f.* tribe
जननांग **jananāṅg** *n.m.* genitals
जनरल **janaral** *n.m.* journal
जनसंख्या **janamsaṅkhyā** *n.m.* population
जनवरी **janvarī** *n.f.* January
जनान संबंधी **janān sambandhī** *adj.* genital
जन्म-भूमि **janam-bhūmi** *n.f.* homeland, native land
जन्मदिन **janamdin** *n.m.* birthday
जन्मजात **janamjāt** *adj.* born
जब कभी **jab kabhī** *adv.* anytime
जब कि **jab ki** *adv.* as
जबड़ा **jabṛā** *n.m.* jaw
जब तक **jab tak** *prep.* until; *conj.* while
जब तक न **jab tak na** *conj.* unless
जब ... तब **jab ... tab** *adv.* when
जमना **jamnā** *v.i.* freeze
जमा करना **jamā karnā** *v.t.* gather
जुमा हुआ **jumā huā** *adj.* frozen
जमाना **jamānā** *v.t.* fix, freeze
जमा होना **jamā honā** *v.i.* gather
जमे रहना **jame rahnā** *v.i.* insist
जन्मस्थान **janamsthān** *n.m.* birthplace
जर्मन **jarman** *n.m./adj.* German
जर्मनी **jarmanī** *n.m.* Germany
जर्सी **jarsī** *n.f.* jersey
जलचर **jalcar** *adj.* aquatic
जलन **jalan** *n.f.* jealousy
जलपान **jalpān** *n.m.* refreshment

जलपानगृह **jalpāngṛha** *n.m.* café
जलयात्रा करना **jalyātrā karnā** *v.t.* sail
जलरंग **jalrang** *n.m.* watercolor
जलरंग का **jalrang kā** *adj.* watercolor
जलवायु **jalvāyu** *n.m.* climate
जलाना **jalānā** *v.t.* light, lighten
जलरूद्ध **jalrūddh** *adj.* waterproof
जलीय **jalīy** *adj.* watery
जल्दी **jaldī** *adv.* early, quickly, soon; *n.f.* haste
जल्दी करना **jaldī karnā** *v.t.* speed
जस्ता **jastā** *n.m.* zinc
जयन्ती **jayantī** *n.f.* anniversary
जवान **javān** *adj.* youthful
जवानी **javānī** *n.f.* youth
जवाब **javāb** *n.m.* response, reply
जवाब देना **javāb denā** *v.i.* reply
जवाहरात **javāharāt** *n.m.* jewelry
ज़हर **zahar** *n.m.* venom
ज़हरदार **zahardār** *adj.* poisonous
जहाँ **jahāṁ** *conj.* where
जहाज़ **jahāz** *n.m.* ship, vessel
जहाज़ पर चढ़ना **jahāz par caṛhnā** *v.t.* embark
जहाज़-घाट **jahāz-ghāṭ** *n.m.* wharf
जहाज़ी बेड़ा **jahāzī beṛā** *n.m.* marine
जहाज़ी मतली **jahāzī matlī** *n.f.* seasickness
जहाज़ी मतली से बीमार **jahāzī matlī se bīmār** *adj.* seasick
जाँच **jāṁc** *n.f.* scrutiny
जाँच करना **jāṁc karnā** *v.t.* examine
जाँचना **jāṁcnā** *v.t.* view
जाँच-पड़ताल **jāṁc-paṛtāl** *n.f.* investigation
जाँच-पड़ताल करना **jāṁc-paṛtāl karnā** *v.t.* inspect

जाकेट **jākeṭ** *n.f.* jacket
जागना **jāgnā** *v.i.* awake
जागरण **jāgaraṇ** *n.m.* wake
जाड़ा **jāṛā** *n.m.* winter
जातीय **jātīy** *adj.* racial
जादू **jādū** *n.m.* magic, charm
जादुई **jāduī** *adj.* magical
जादू कर देना **jādū kar denā** *v.t.* charm
जादूगर **jādūgar** *n.m.* magician
जानकार **jānkār** *adj.* conscious
जान बचाना **jān bacānā** *v.t.* save
जानबूझकर **jānbūjhkar** *adj.* deliberate
जानवर **jānvar** *n.m.* animal
जाना **jānā** *v.i.* go
जाना-आना **jānā-ānā** *adj.* round
जापानी **jāpānī** *n.m./adj.* Japanese
जायदाद **jāydād** *n.f.* estate
जाल **jāl** *n.m.* net
जालसाजी करना **jālasājī karnā** *v.t.* falsify
जाल तंत्र **jāl tantra** *n.m./v.t./v.i.* network
जाला **jālā** *n.m.* web
ज़िद्दी **ziddī** *adj.* wayward
जिन **jim** *n.m.* gin
ज़िन्दगी **zindagī** *n.f.* life
ज़िन्दा **zindā** *adj.* alive
ज़िन्दा **zindā** *n.m.* live
ज़िप **zip** *n.m.* zipper
ज़िप बंद करना **zip band karnā** *v.t.* zip
जिप्सी **jipsī** *n.m.* Gypsy
जिमख़ाना **jimqhānā** *n.m.* gymnasium
ज़िम्मेदार **zimmedār** *adj.* responsible
ज़िम्मेवार **zimmevār** *adj.* liable

ज़िला **zilā** *n.m.* county
जई **jī** *n.f.* oat
जई का दलिया **jī kā daliyā** *n.m.* oatmeal
जी उठना **jī uṭhnā** *v.t./v.i.* revive
जी बहलाना **jī bahalānā** *v.t.* amuse
जीत **jīt** *n.f.* victory
जीतना **jītnā** *v.t.* win
जीना **jīnā** *v.i.* live
जीवाणु **jīvāṇu** *n.m.* germ
जीवाणुहीन बना देना **jīvāṇuhīn banā denā** *v.t.* sterilize
जीवन के लिए आवश्यक **jīvan ke liye āvaśyak** *adj.* vital
जीवान्विक **jīvānvik** *adj.* bacterial
जीवाश्म **jīvāśam** *n.m.* fossil
जीवविज्ञान **jīvavigyān** *n.m.* biology
जीवन **jīvan** *n.m.* life
जीवन काल **jīvan kāl** *n.m.* lifetime
जीवन-स्तर **jīvan-star** *n.m.* standard
जीवनी **jīvanī** *n.f.* biography
जीवित **jīvit** *adj.* alive
जीवित रहना **jīvit rehnā** *v.i.* survive
जुआ **juā** *n.m.* yoke
जुटाना **juṭānā** *v.t.* furnish
जुड़वाँ **juṛvāṁ** *n.m.* twin
जुताई करना **jutāī karnā** *v.t.* cultivate
जुर्माना **jurmānā** *n.m.* fine
जुलाई **julāī** *n.m.* July
जुलाहा **julāhā** *n.m.* weaver
जूझना **jūjhnā** *v.i.* contend
जूता **jūtā** *n.m.* shoe
जूते का फ़ीता **jūte kā fītā** *n.m.* shoelace
जूतों का पालिश **jūtoṁ kā pāliś** *n.m.* shoe polish
जून **jūn** *n.m.* June

जूरी **jūrī** *n.f.* jury
जेट **jeṭ** *n.m.* jet
जेठ **jeṭh** *n.m.* brother-in-law (*husband's older brother*)
जेब **jeb** *n.f.* pocket
जेबकट **jebkaṭ** *n.m.* pickpocket
ज़ेबरा **zebarā** *n.m.* zebra
जेल **jel** *n.m.* jail
जेलख़ाना **jelqhānā** *n.m.* prison
जेली **jelī** *n.f.* jelly
जैक **jaik** *n.m.* jack
जैम **jaim** *n.m.* jam
जैव **jaiv** *adj.* organic
जैविक **jaivik** *adj.* biological
जैसा **jaisā** *adj.* such
जो **jo** *pron.* which
जोकर **jokar** *n.m.* joker
जोखिम **jokhim** *n.m.* venture, risk
जोखिम उठाना **jokhim uṭhānā** *v.t.* risk
जोड़ **joṛ** *n.m.* joint; total
जोड़ा **joṛā** *n.m.* pair
जोड़ना **joṛnā** *v.t.* unite, join, assemble
जोड़ निकालना **joṛ nikālnā** *v.t.* total
जो कोई **jo koī** *pron.* whoever
जो भी **jo bhī** *adv.* whatever
जौ **jī** *n.m.* barley
ज्ञान **gyān** *n.* knowledge
ज़्यादा **zyādā** *adj.* more
ज़्यादा पसंद करना **zyādā pasand karnā** *v.t.* prefer
ज्यों ही **jyoṁ hī** *adv.* soon
ज्वलन **jvalan** *n.m.* ignition
ज्वार-भाटा **jvār-bhāṭā** *n.m.* tide
ज्वलनशील **jvalanśīl** *adj.* inflammable

ज्वाला **jvālā** *n.f.* flame
ज्वालामुखी पहाड़ **jvālāmukhī pahāṛ** *n.m.* volcano

झ

झगड़ा **jhagṛā** *n.m.* quarrel
झटका **jhaṭkā** *n.m.* tug, jerk
झटकना **jhaṭkanā** *v.t.* jerk
झटके से खींचना **jhaṭke se khīṁcnā** *v.t.* yank
झण्डा **jhaṇḍā** *n.m.* flag
झपक **jhapak** *n.f.* nap
झपकी **jhapkī** *n.f.* wink
झपकाना **jhapkānā** *v.i.* wink
झपटना **jhapṭanā** *v.t.* rush
झबरा **jhabarā** *adj.* shaggy
झरना **jharnā** *n.m.* waterfall
झरोखा **jharokhā** *n.m.* ventilator
झलक **jhalak** *n.f./v.t.* glimpse
झाँसिया **jhāṁsiyā** *n.m.* swindler
झाग **jhāg** *n.m.* scum
झाड़ना **jhāṛnā** *v.t.* shed
झाड़ू देना **jhāṛū denā** *v.t.* sweep
झाड़न **jhāṛān** *n.m.* duster
झाड़ू **jhāṛū** *n.m.* mop
झाड़ूबरदार **jhaṛūbardār** *n.m.* cleaner
झाग **jhāg** *n.m.* scum
झींगा **jhīṅgā** *n.m.* prawn
झींगी **jhīṅgī** *n.m.* shrimp
झींगुर **jhīṅgur** *n.m.* cricket
झील **jhīl** *n.f.* lake
झुक जाना **jhuk jānā** *v.t.* submit
झुकना **jhuknā** *v.i.* crouch, incline

झुकाना **jhukānā** *v.t.* bend
झुकाव **jhukāv** *n.f.* trend
झुटपुटा **jhuṭpuṭā** *n.m.* twilight
झुण्ड **jhuṇḍ** *n.m.* swarm
झुनझुनी चढ़ना **jhunjhunī caṛhnā** *v.i.* tingle
झुनझुनी होना **jhunjhunī honā** *v.t./v.i.* tickle
झूठ **jhūṭh** *n.m.* lie
झूठा **jhūṭhā** *adj.* untrue
झूठा **jhūṭā** *adj.* counterfeit
झूला **jhūlā** *n.m.* seesaw
झूलना **jhūlnā** *v.t.* swing
झेंपना **jhoṁpnā** *v.i.* blush
झोंका **jhoṅkā** *n.m.* gust
झोपड़ा **jhopaṛā** *n.m.* hut
झोपड़ी **jhopaṛī** *n.f.* lodge
झोला **jholā** *n.m.* knapsack

ट

टंकी **ṭankī** *n.f.* tank, reservoir
टंकी भरना **ṭankī bharnā** *v.t.* tank
टंकी जहाज़ **ṭankī jahāz** *n.m.* tanker
टक्कर लगना **ṭakkar lagnā** *v.i.* collide
टखना **ṭakhnā** *n.m.* ankle
टगनी **ṭagnī** *n.f.* tag
टट्टू **ṭaṭṭū** *n.m.* pony
टन **ṭan** *n.m.* ton
टमाटर **ṭamāṭar** *n.m.* tomato
टमाटर का रस **ṭamāṭar kā ras** *n.m.* tomato juice
टहनी **ṭahanī** *n.f.* wicker
टहलुआ **ṭahluā** *adj.* tender
टाँका **ṭāṁkā** *n.m.* stitch

टाँका लगाना **ṭāṁkā lagānā** *v.t.* weld
टाँग **tāṁg** *n.m.* leg
टाँगना **ṭāṁgnā** *v.t./v.i.* hang
टाँड़ **ṭāṁṛ** *n.m.* shelf, rack
टाई **ṭāī** *n.f.* necktie
टाइप करना **tāip karnā** *v.t.* type
टाइपिस्ट **ṭāipisṭ** *n.m.* typist
टार्च **ṭārc** *n.f.* torch
टान्सिल **ṭānsil** *n.m.* tonsils
टापू **ṭāpū** *n.m.* island
टिकट **ṭikaṭ** *n.m.* ticket, stamp
टिक्का **ṭikkā** *n.m.* steak
टिड्डा **ṭiḍḍā** *n.m.* grasshopper
टिन **ṭin** *n.m.* tin
टिप्पणी **ṭippaṇī** *n.f.* comment, remark
टिप्पणी करना **ṭippaṇī karnā** *v.t.* comment
टिमटिमाना **ṭimṭimānā** *v.i.* twinkle
टिशू **ṭiśū** *n.m.* tissue
टीका **ṭīkā** *n.m.* inoculation
टीका लगाना **ṭīkā lagānā** *v.t.* inoculate
टीम **ṭīm** *n.f.* team
टीवी चैनल **ṭīvī cainal** *n.m.* channel
टीस **ṭīs** *n.f.* twinge
टुकड़ा **ṭukaṛā** *n.m.* piece
टुकड़े-टुकड़े **ṭukaṛe-ṭukaṛe** *n.m.* jigsaw puzzle
टुकड़े-टुकड़े कर देना **ṭukaṛe-ṭukaṛe kar denā** *v.i.* crumble
टुटे पैसे **ṭuṭe paise** *n.m.* change
टूथपेस्ट **ṭūthpesṭ** *n.m.* toothpaste
ट्यूब **ṭūyūb** *n.f.* tube
ट्यूलिप **ṭūlip** *n.f.* tulip
टेकन **ṭekan** *n.m.* support
टेढ़ा **ṭeṛha** *adj.* crooked

टेढ़ी-मेढ़ी रखा **ṭeṛhī-meṛhī rakha** *v.i.* zigzag
टेनिस **ṭenis** *n.m.* tennis
टेपरेकार्डर **ṭeprekārḍar** *n.m.* tape
टेलीफ़ोन करना **ṭelīfon karnā** *v.t.* dial
टैंक **ṭaink** *n.m.* tank
टैक्सी **ṭaiksī** *n.m.* taxi
टैल्क **ṭailk** *n.m.* talc
टोंटी **ṭoṁṭī** *n.f.* tap, faucet
टोकना **ṭoknā** *v.t./v.i.* interrupt
टोकरा **ṭokarā** *n.f.* wicker
टोपी **ṭopī** *n.f.* hat, cap
टोली **ṭolī** *n.f.* batch
ट्रक **ṭrak** *n.m.* truck
ट्रकटर **ṭraṭar** *n.m.* tractor
ट्राम **ṭrām** *n.f.* tram
ट्राइसिकल **ṭrāisikal** *n.f.* tricycle

ठ

ठंड **ṭhanḍ** *n.f.* chill
ठंडा **ṭhanḍā** *adj.* chilly
ठंडा करना **ṭhanḍā karnā** *v.t.* chill, cool
ठठरी **ṭhaṭharī** *n.f.* skeleton
ठहर जाना **ṭhahar jānā** *v.t.* pause
ठानी **ṭhānī** *v.t.* stand
ठिठुरना **ṭhiṭhurnā** *v.i.* shiver
ठीक **ṭhīk** *adj.* right, correct, appropriate, well, sound
ठीक करना **ṭhīk karnā** *v.t.* fix
ठीक-ठीक **ṭhīk-ṭhīk** *adj.* tidy
ठीक है **ṭhīk hai** *interj.* OK!
ठुड्डी **ṭhuḍḍī** *n.f.* chin

ठूसकर भरना **ṭhūskar bharnā** *v.t.* stuff
ठेलना **ṭhelnā** *v.t.* propel
ठेला **ṭhelā** *n.m.* cart
ठोकर खाना **ṭhokar khānā** *v.i.* stumble
ठोकर मारना **ṭhokar mārnā** *v.t.* kick
ठोस **ṭhos** *n.m./adj.* solid

ड

डंक **ḍaṅk** *n.m.* sting
डंक मारना **ḍaṅk mārnā** *v.t.* sting
डंठल **ḍaṇṭhal** *n.* stalk
डण्डा **ḍaṇḍā** *n.m.* stick, pole, shaft
डर **ḍar** *n.m.* fright, fear, terror
डरना **ḍarnā** *v.t.* fear, afraid
डराना **ḍarānā** *v.t.* frighten
डरा हुआ **ḍarā huā** *adj.* afraid
डलिया **ḍaliyā** *n.f.* basket
डाँटना **ḍāṁṭnā** *v.t.* scold
डाइन **ḍāin** *n.f.* witch
डाक **ḍāk** *n.f.* mail, post
डाकघर **ḍākghar** *n.m.* post office
डाका डालना **ḍākā ḍālnā** *v.t.* pirate
डाकिया **ḍākiyā** *n.m.* mailman
डाट **ḍāṭ** *n.m.* cork
डामर **ḍāmar** *n.m.* asphalt
डायरी **ḍāyarī** *n.f.* diary
डायल **ḍāyal** *n.m.* dial
डालर **ḍālar** *n.m.* dollar
डिब्बा **ḍibbā** *n.m.* bin; tin
डीज़ल **ḍizal** *n.m.* diesel
डुबाना **ḍubānā** *v.t.* drown; dip

डूब मरना **ḍubā marnā** *v.t.* drown
डेगची **ḍegacī** *n.f.* saucepan
डेरी **ḍerī** *n.f.* dairy
डोंगी **ḍoṁgī** *n.f.* canoe
डैश **ḍaiś** *n.m.* dash
डोल **ḍol** *n.m.* pail
डोलना **ḍolnā** *v.i.* swing, oscillate
डयोढ़ी **ḍyoṛhī** *n.f.* porch

ढ

ढंग **ḍhang** *n.m.* manner
ढाँपना **ḍhāṁpnā** *v.t.* cover
ढक लेना **ḍhak lenā** *v.t.* envelop
ढक्कन **ḍhakkan** *n.m.* lid, cover, cap
ढाल **ḍhāl** *n.f.* shield; incline
ढीला **ḍhīlā** *n.m.* cape
ढीला करना **ḍhīlā karnā** *v.t.* loosen
ढीली **ḍhīlī** *adj.* slack
ढेलवास **ḍhelvās** *n.* sling
ढेला **ḍhelā** *n.m.* lump
ढोना **ḍhonā** *v.t.* carry
ढोल **ḍhol** *n.m.* drum

त

तंग **taṅg** *adj.* narrow
तंग करना **taṅg karnā** *v.t.* harass
तंगघाटी **tangghāṭī** *n.f.* ravine
तंगहाली **tanghālī** *n.f.* misery
तंतु **tantu** *n.m.* fiber
तंदुरुस्त **tandurust** *adj.* well

तंबू **tambū** *n.m.* tent
तंबाकू **tambākū** *n.m.* tobacco
तंत्रिका **tantrikā** *n.f.* nerve
तंत्रिक्रान्ति **tantrikrānti** *n.f.* neuralgia
तंत्रका-विज्ञानी **tantrakā-vigyānī** *n.m.* neurologist
तंत्रिकीय **tantrikīy** *adj.* neural
तकनीकी **taknīkī** *adj.* technical
तकसाल **taksāl** *n.f.* mint
तकिया **takiyā** *n.m.* pillow
तकिये का गिलाफ़ **takiye kā gilāf** *n.m.* pillowcase
तख़्ता **taqhtā** *n.m.* board
तगड़ा **tagṛā** *adj.* stout
तटस्थ **taṭstha** *adj.* neutral
तटस्थता **taṭsthatā** *n.f.* neutrality
तटीय नगरभाग **taṭīy nagarbhāg** *n.m.* waterfront
तत्काल भाषण देना **tatkāl bhāṣaṇ denā** *v.t.* improvise
तत्त्व **tattva** *n.m.* element
तना **tanā** *n.m.* stem, trunk
तनाव **tanāv** *n.m.* tension
तनिक **tanik** *adj.* least
तनु **tanu** *adj.* tenuous
तन्ख़्वाह **tanqhvāh** *n.f.* wage
तपस्वी **tapasvī** *n.m.* monk
तब **tab** *adv.* then
तबीयत **tabīyat** *n.f.* health
तमाशा **tamāśā** *n.m.* show
तर करना **tar karnā** *v.t.* moisten
तर्क **tark** *n.m.* reason
तर्क करना **tark karnā** *v.i.* reason
तलना **talnā** *v.t.* fry
तलवा **talvā** *n.m.* sole (foot)
तलवार **talvār** *n.f.* sword

तला **talā** *n.m.* sole (shoe)
तलाक़ **talāq** *n.f.* divorce
तलाकशुदा **talākśudā** *adj.* divorced
तल्लीन करना **tallīn karnā** *v.t.* absorb
तश्तरी **taśtarī** *n.f.* saucer
तस्वीर **tasvīr** *n.f.* painting
तह **tah** *n.f.* fold
तहखाना **tahkhānā** *n.m.* cellar
तहाना **tahānā** *n.f./v.t.* fold
तथ्य **tathya** *n.m.* phenomenon
तरंग-दैर्ध्य **taraṅg-dairdhya** *n.m.* wavelength
तरह तरह **tarah tarah** *adj.* various
तर-बतर **tar-batar** *n.m.* soaking
तरबूज़ **tarbūz** *n.m.* watermelon
तर्कशास्त्र **tarkśāstra** *n.m.* logic
तर्कहीन **tarkhīn** *adj.* mindless
तर्कसंगत **tarksangat** *adj.* logical
तराजू **tarājū** *n.m.* balance
तला हुआ **talā huā** *adj.* fried
तवा **tavā** *n.m.* pan
ताँबा **tāṁbā** *n.m.* copper
ताक़ **tāq** *n.m.* niche
ताकत **tākat** *v.t.* strengthen
तागा **tāgā** *n.m.* thread
ताज **tāj** *n.m.* crown
ताज़ा **tāzā** *adj.* fresh
ताज़ा करना **tāzā karnā** *v.t.* refresh
ताड़ **tāṛ** *n.m.* palm
तानना **tānnā** *v.t.* extend
तापन **tāpan** *n.m.* heating
तापमापी **tāpmāpī** *n.m.* thermometer
तापस्थायी **tāpsthāyī** *n.m.* thermostat

ताबीज़ **tābīz** *n.m.* charm
ताबूत **tābūt** *n.m.* coffin
तारमीन **tārmīn** *n.m.* starfish
तार **tār** *n.m.* wire
तार लगाना **tār lagānā** *v.t.* wire
तारा **tārā** *n.m.* star
तारामंडल **tārāmaṇḍal** *n.m.* constellation
तारीख़ **tārīqh** *n.f.* date
तामचीनी **tāmcīnī** *n.f.* enamel
तामलेट **tāmleṭ** *n.f.* canteen
ताम्रवर्ण बनाना **tāmrvarṇ banānā** *v.t.* tan
तार **tār** *n.m.* cable
ताल **tāl** *n.m.* rhythm
ताला **tālā** *n.m.* lock
ताला लगाना **tālā lagānā** *v.t.* lock
तालाब **tālāb** *n.m.* pond
तालिका **tālikā** *n.f.* inventory
तालियाँ **taliyāṁ** *v.t.* applaud
ताली बजाना **tālī bajānā** *v.t.* clap
तिकोना **tikonā** *adj.* triangular
तिजौरी **tizaurī** *n.f.* safe
तितर-बितर होना **titar-bitar honā** *v.t.* scatter
तितली **titalī** *n.f.* butterfly
तिरछा **tirchā** *n.m.* italics
तिरछा देखना **tirchā dekhnā** *v.i.* squint
तिरछा **tirchā** *n.m.* slant
तिरछा होना **tirchā honā** *v.i.* slant
तीता **tītā** *adj.* hot (spicy)
तीन **tīn** *num.* three
तीर्थ मंदिर **tīrth mandir** *n.m.* shrine
तीर्थयात्रा **tīrthyātrā** *n.f.* pilgrimage
तीर्थयात्री **tīrthyātrī** *n.m.* pilgrim

तीस **tīs** *num.* thirty
तीसरा **tīsrā** *adj.* third
तीसरा पहर **tīsrā pahar** *n.m.* afternoon
तुक **tuk** *n.m.* rhyme
तुर्की **turkī** *adj.* Turkish
तुच्छ **tucch** *adj.* trivial
तुच्छ बातें **tucch bāteṁ** *n.m.* trivia
तुच्छ वस्तु **tucch vastu** *n.f.* trifle
तुम **tum** *pron.* you
तुम्हारा **tumhāra** *pron.* your
तुरत-पत्र **turat patr** *adj.* express
तुरत वितरण **turat-vitaraṇ** *v.t.* express
तुरूप का पत्ता **turūp kā pattā** *n.m.* trump
तुरूप चलना **turūp calnā** *v.t.* trump
तुलना **tulnā** *n.f.* comparison
तुलना करना **tulnā karnā** *v.t.* compare
तुला हुआ **tulā huā** *adj.* balanced
तुषार **tuṣār** *n.m.* frost
तूफ़ान **tūfān** *n.m.* storm
तूफ़ानी **tūfānī** *adj.* stormy
तृज्या **tr̥jyā** *n.m.* radius
तेज़ **tez** *adj.* fast, quick, loud, fiery, strong, bright
तेज़ दौड़ लगाना **tez dauṛ lagānā** *v.i.* streak
तेज़ी से **tezī se** *adj.* quick
तेज़ी-से घूमना **tezī-se ghūmnā** *v.i.* whirl
तेरह **terah** *num.* thirteen
तेरहवाँ **terahvāṁ** *adj.* thirteenth
तेल **tel** *n.m.* oil
तेल सा **tel sā** *adj.* oily
तैराक **tairāk** *n.m.* swimmer
तैनात करना **taināt karnā** *v.t.* station
तैयार **taiyār** *adj.* ready, set

तैयार करना **taiyār karnā** *v.t.* prepare
तैयारी **taiyārī** *n.f.* preparation
तैरना **tairnā** *v.i.* swim
तोंद **tond** *n.m.* paunch
तोता **totā** *n.m.* parrot
तोप **top** *n.f.* cannon
तोलना **tolnā** *v.t.* weigh
तोहफ़ा **tohfā** *n.m.* present
त्याग देना **tyāg denā** *v.t.* renounce
त्योरी **tyorī** *n.f.* frown
त्योरी चढ़ाना **tyorī caṛhānā** *v.i.* frown
त्योहार **tyohār** *n.m.* festival
त्वरित्र **tvaritra** *n.m.* accelerator

थ

थका **thakā** *adj.* tired
थकाऊ **thakāū** *adj.* tiresome
थका देना **thakā denā** *v.i.* exhaust
थका-माँदा **thakā-māṁdā** *adj.* weary, worn
थकावट **thakāvaṭ** *n.f.* tiredness
थप्पड़ **thappaṛ** *n.m.* slap
थान **thān** *n.m.* stall
थाम रखना **thām rakhnā** *v.t.* sustain
थाली **thālī** *n.f.* dish, plate
थाइम **thāim** *n.m.* thyme
थिएटर **thieṭar** *n.m.* theater
थीमाकार **thīmākār** *adj.* monstrous
थूकना **thūknā** *v.t./v.i.* spit
थैला **thailā** *n.m.* bag
थैली **thailī** *n.f.* pouch
थोड़ा **thoṛā** *adj.* minor

थोड़ा सा **thoṛā sā** *adj.* little
थोड़ी देर बाद **thoṛī der bād** *adv.* after

द

दंड देना **daṇd denā** *v.t.* punish
दंड का आदेश **daṇḍ kā ādeś** *n.m.* sentence
दंड का आदेश देना **daṇḍ kā ādeś denā** *v.t.* sentence
दंपती **dampati** *n.m.* couple
दंभी **dambhī** *n.m.* snob
दंभ-भरा **dambh-bharā** *adj.* snobbish
दख़ल **daqhal** *n.m.* occupancy
दर्ज़ी **darzī** *n.m.* tailor
ददोरा **dadorā** *n.m./adj.* rash
दण्ड **daṇḍ** *n.m.* penalty
दन्तचिकित्सक **dantcikitsak** *n.m.* dentist
दफ़्तर **daftar** *n.m.* office
दफ़्तरशाह **daftarśāh** *n.m.* bureaucrat
दबकना **dabaknā** *v.i.* crouch
दबाना **dabānā** *v.t.* depress, curb, squash
दबाया हुआ **dabāyā huā** *v.t.* depressed
दबाव **dabāv** *n.m.* stress
दमक **damak** *n.f.* flash
दमन **daman** *n.m.* oppression
दमन करना **daman karnā** *v.t.* oppress
दमपुख्त **dampukht** *n.m.* stew
दमा **damā** *n.m.* asthma
दमा का रोगी **damā kā rogī** *adj.* asthmatic
दया **dayā** *n.m.* pity, mercy
दया करना **dayā karnā** *v.i.* pity
दयालु **dyālu** *adj.* merciful
दर **dar** *n.m.* rate

दरवाज़ा **darvāzā** *n.m.* door
दरांती **darāntī** *n.f.* scythe
दरार **darār** *n.f.* crack
दर्जन **darjan** *n.m.* dozen
दर्जा **darjī** *n.m.* rank
दर्द **dard** *n.m./v.i.* ache
दर्दनाक **dardnāk** *adj.* painful
दर्पण **darpaṇ** *n.m.* mirror
दर्शक **darśak** *n.m.* spectator
दर्शन **darśan** *n.m.* appearance
दर्शन शास्त्र **darśan śāstra** *n.m.* philosophy
दल **dal** *n.m.* flock
दलदल **daldal** *n.f.* swamp
दवा **davā** *n.f.* medicine, remedy
दवा-ख़ाना **davā-qhānā** *n.m.* pharmacy
दवासाज **davāsāj** *n.m.* pharmacist
दशमिक **daśmik** *adj.* decimal
दशयता **daśyatā** *n.f.* visibility
दस **das** *num.* ten
दस लाख **das lākh** *n.m.* million
दसवाँ **dasvāṁ** *adj.* tenth
दस्त **dast** *n.m.* diarrhea
दस्तकारी **dastkārī** *n.f.* craft
दस्तखत **dastkhat** *n.m.* signature
दस्त बिन **dast bin** *n.m.* wastepaper
दस्ताना **dastānā** *n.m.* glove
दस्तावर **dastāvar** *n.m.* laxative
दस्तावेज़ **dastāvez** *n.m.* deed
दहिना **dahinā** *adj.* right
दही **dahī** *n.m.* yogurt
दहेज **dahej** *n.m.* dowry
दक्षिण **dakṣiṇ** *n.m.* south

दक्षिण-पश्चिम **dakṣiṇ-paścim** *n.m.* southwest
दक्षिण-पश्चिमी **dakṣiṇ-paścimī** *adj.* southwestern
दक्षिण-पूर्व **dakṣiṇ-pūrv** *n.m.* southeast
दक्षिण-पूर्वी **dakṣiṇ-pūrvī** *adj.* southeastern
दक्षिणहस्त **dakṣiṇhast** *adj.* right-handed
दक्षिणी **dakṣiṇī** *adj.* southern
दाँत **dāṁt** *n.m.* tooth
दाँत का **dāṁt kā** *adj.* dental
दाँत का दर्द **dāṁt kā dard** *n.m.* toothache
दाँत का ब्रश **dāṁt kā braś** *n.m.* toothbrush
दाँव **dāṁv** *n.m.* hazard
दाई **dāī** *n.f.* midwife
दाग़ डालना **dāq ḍālnā** *v.t.* stain
दाढ़ी **dāṛhī** *n.f.* beard
दादा **dādā** *n.m.* grandfather (*paternal*)
दादी **dādī** *n.f.* grandmother (*paternal*)
दान **dān** *n.m.* charity
दान में देना **dān meṁ denā** *v.t.* donate
दाब **dāb** *n.f.* pressure
दाम **dām** *n.m.* cost, price
दामाद **dāmād** *n.m.* son-in-law
दाय **dāy** *n.m.* inheritance
दाय पाना **dāy pānā** *v.t.* inherit
दायाँ **dāyāṁ** *n.m.* starboard
दालचीनी **dālcīnī** *n.f.* cinnamon
दावत **dāvat** *n.f.* banquet
दावा **dāvā** *n.m.* assertion
दावा **dāvā** *n.m.* claim
दावा करना **dāvā karnā** *v.t.* claim
दास **dās** *n.m.* slave
दासप्रथा **dāsprathā** *n.m.* slavery
दाह संस्कार **dāh sanskār** *n.m.* Hindi cremation rite, funeral

दिकसूचक **diksūcak** *n.m.* compass
दिखाई देने वाला **dikhāī dene vālā** *adj.* visible
दिखाना **dikhānā** *v.t.* show
दिखावा **dikhāvā** *n.m.* exposure
दिन **din** *n.m.* day
दिन का खाना **din kā khānā** *n.m.* lunch
दिल **dil** *n.m.* heart
दिल्चस्प **dilcasp** *adj.* interesting
दिलचस्पी **dilcaspī** *n.f.* interest
दिलचस्पी लेना **dilcaspī lenā** *v.t.* interest
दिलासा **dilāsā** *n.m.* consolation
दिलेर **diler** *adj.* bold
दिशा **diśā** *n.f.* direction
दिशाकोण **diśākoṇ** *n.m.* bearing
दिसेम्बर **disembar** *n.m.* December
दीघट-सूत्री **dīghaṭ-sūtrī** *adv.* slow
दीमक **dīmak** *n.f.* termite
दीवार **dīvār** *n.f.* wall
दुनिया **duniyā** *n.f.* world
दुपट्टा **dupaṭṭā** *n.m.* scarf
दुकान **dukān** *n.f.* store
दुकानदार **dukāndār** *n.m.* shopkeeper
दुख **dukh** *n.m.* affliction
दुख देना **dukh denā** *v.t.* afflict
दुखदायी **dukhdāyī** *adj.* troublesome
दुखना **dukhnā** *v.t.* sting
दुखी **dukhī** *adj.* unhappy
दुगुना **dugunā** *adj.* double
दुष्कर **duṣkar** *adj.* tough
दुष्कर्म **duṣkarm** *n.m.* misdeed
दुबला-पतला **dublā-patlā** *adj.* skinny
दुबारा **dubārā** *adv.* again

दुभाषिया **dubhāṣiyā** *n.m.* interpreter
दुरुपयोग **durupyog** *n.m.* abuse
दुरुपयोग करना **durupyog karnā** *v.t.* abuse
दुरूस्त करना **durūst karnā** *v.t.* refit
दुराग्रही **durāgrahī** *adj.* obstinate
दुर्गुण **durguṇ** *n.m.* vice
दुर्घटना **durghaṭnā** *n.f.* accident
दुर्भाग्य **durbhāgy** *n.m.* misfortune
दुर्भाग्यवश **burbhāgyavaś** *adj.* unfortunate
दुर्लभ **durlabh** *adj.* scarce
दुश्मन **duśman** *n.m.* enemy
दुम्बाल **dumbāl** *adj.* stern
दुहराना **duhrānā** *v.t.* revise
दुलारना **dulārnā** *v.t.* pet
दूज का चाँद **dūj kā cāṁd** *n.m.* crescent
दूल **dūl** *n.m.* messenger
दूतप्रेषण **dūtpreṣaṇ** *n.m.* legation
दूतावास **dūtāvās** *n.m.* consulate
दूध **dūdh** *n.m.* milk
दूध पिलाना **dūdh pilānā** *v.t.* nurse
दूध-बहन **dūdh behen** *n.f.* foster sister
दूध से बना **dūdh de banā** *n.m.* milk product
दूध-भाई **dūdh-bhāī** *n.m.* foster brother
दूर **dūr** *adv.* far
दूर का **dūr kā** *adj.* distant
दूरदर्शी **dūrdarśī** *adj.* farsighted
दूरदर्शिता **dūrdarśitā** *n.f.* foresight
दूरबीन **dūrbīn** *n.m.* telescope
दूरी **dūrī** *n.f.* distance
दूषित करना **dūṣit karnā** *v.t.* contaminate
दूसरा **dūsarā** *n.m.* second
दृष्टि **dṛṣṭi** *n.m.* sight; *adj.* optical

दृष्टिपटल **dṛṣṭipaṭal** *n.m.* retina
दृश्य **dṛśya** *n.m.* scene, view
दृश्यदर्शी **dṛśyadarśī** *n.m.* viewfinder
दृढ़ **dṛṛh** *adj.* tenacious
देखना **dekhnā** *v.t.* watch; *v.i.* behold
देखभाल **dekhbhāl** *n.m.* upkeep
देनदार होना **dendār honā** *v.t.* owe
देनदारी **dendārī** *n.f.* liability
देना **denā** *v.t.* give
देय **dey** *adj.* due
देर **der** *adj./adv.* late; *n.* delay
देरी करना **derī karnā** *v.t.* delay
देवदार **devdār** *n.m.* cedar
देवर **devar** *n.m.* brother-in-law (*husband's younger brother*)
देवी **devī** *n.f.* goddess
देश **deś** *n.m.* country
देशद्रोह **deśdroh** *n.m.* treason
देशभक्त **deśbhakt** *n.m.* patriot
देशभक्तिपूर्ण **deśbhaktipūrṇ** *adj.* patriotic
देशीय **deśīy** *n.f.* native
देहली **dehalī** *n.f.* sill
देहाती **dehātī** *adj.* rustic; *n.m.* peasant
देहाती बंगला **dehātī bangalā** *n.m.* villa
दैनिक **dainik** *adj.* daily
देशांतर **daiśantar** *n.m.* longitude
दो **do** *num.* two
दो बार **do bār** *adv.* twice
दोट **doṭ** *n.m.* castle
दोनो में से एक **dono meṁ se ek** *n.m.* either
दोपहर **dopahar** *n.m.* midday
दोबारा देना **dobārā denā** *v.t.* represent
दोष **doṣ** *n.m.* blame

दोषदर्शी **doṣdarśī** *adj.* cynical
दोषी **doṣī** *adj.* guilty
दोषी ठहराना **doṣī ṭharānā** *v.t.* accuse
दोस्त **dost** *n.m.* friend
दोस्ताना **dostānā** *adj.* friendly
दोस्ती **dostī** *n.f.* friendship
दौड़ **dauṛ** *n.m.* run
दौड़ना **daūṛnā** *v.t.* run
दौड़ाक **dauṛāk** *n.m.* runner
दौरा **daurā** *n.m.* stroke
दौरान **daurān** *adj.* during
द्रव **drav** *n.m./adj.* liquid
द्रवदाह **dravdāh** *n.m.* scald
द्विभाषी **dvibhāṣī** *adj.* bilingual

ध

धकेलना **dhakelnā** *v.t.* push
धक्का **dhakkā** *n.m.* shock, jog
धड़ **dhaṛ** *n.m.* fuselage
धड़कन **dhaṛkan** *n.f.* palpitation
धड़ाका **dhaṛākā** *n.m.* explosion
धन **dhan** *n.m.* wealth
धन राशि **dhan rāśi** *n.m.* plus
धन्यवाद **dhanyavād** *n.m.* thanks
धन्यवाद देना **dhanyavād denā** *v.t.* thank
धब्बा **dhabbā** *n.m.* stain
धमनी **dhamanī** *n.f.* artery
धमकी **dhamkī** *n.f.* threat
धमकी देना **dhamkī denā** *v.t.* threaten
धमाका **dhamākā** *n.m.* blast, crash
धमाके से गिरना **dhamāke se girnā** *v.t.* crash

धरती **dhartī** *n.f.* earth
धर्म **dharam** *n.m.* religion
धर्मनिष्ठ **dharmniṣṭh** *adj.* pious
धर्मपिता **dharampitā** *n.m.* godfather
धर्मपुत्र **dharmputra** *n.m.* godchild
धर्मपुत्री **dharamputrī** *n.m.* goddaughter
धर्ममाता **dharammātā** *n.m.* godmother
धागा **dhāgā** *n.m.* string
धातु **dhātu** *n.f.* metal
धातुकर्मी **dhātukarmī** *n.m.* smith
धार रखना **dhār rakhnā** *v.t.* sharpen
धारणा **dhārṇā** *n.f.* concept
धारा **dhārā** *n.f.* stream, current
धारी **dhārī** *n.f.* streak
धारीदार **dhārīdār** *adj.* striped
धाराप्रवाह **dhārāpravāh** *adj* fluent
धार्मिक **dhārmik** *adj.* religious
धावा मारना **dhāvā mārnā** *v.t.* raid
धीमे चलना **dhīme calnā** *v.t.* jog
धीरज **dhīraj** *n.m.* patience
धुंध **dhuṁdh** *n.f.* haze
धुआँ **dhuāṁ** *n.m.* smoke
धुआँकश **dhuā** *n.m.* chimney
धुँधला **dhundhlā** *adj.* dim
धुँधुआता **dhuṁdhuātā** *adj.* smoky
धुधलापन **dhudhlāpan** *n.m.* gloom
धुन्ध-कोहरा **dhum-koharā** *n.m.* smog
धुरी **dhurī** *n.f.* axle
ध्रुव **dhruv** *n.m.* Pole
धुलाई की मशीन **dhulāī kī maśīn** *n.f.* washing machine
धुलाई-सह **dhulāī-sah** *adj.* washable
धूप **dhūp** *n.f.* sunshine

धूप का चश्मा **dhūp kā caśmā** *n.m.* sunglasses
धूप खाना **dhūp khānā** *v.i.* sunbathe
धूपताम्रता **dhūptāgratā** *n.f.* suntan
धूप से जलना **dhūp se jalnā** *v.i.* sunburned
धूल **dhūl** *n.f.* dirt
धूल-धूसरित **dhūl-dhūsrit** *adj.* dusty
धूसर **dhūsar** *adj.* gray
धोखा **dhokhā** *n.m.* deceit
धोखा देना **dhokhā denā** *v.t.* deceive, trick
धोना **dhonā** *v.t.* wash
धोबीख़ाना **dhobīqhānā** *n.m.* laundry
ध्यान **dhyān** *n.m.* attention
ध्यान देना **dhyān denā** *v.t.* pay attention
ध्यान भंग करना **dhyān bhaṅg karnā** *v.t.* distract
ध्वनिविज्ञान **dhvanivigyān** *n.m.* phonetics
ध्वन्यात्मक **dhvanyātmak** *adj.* phonetic

न

नंगा **naṅgā** *adj.* bare
नंगा करना **nangā karnā** *v.t.* uncover
न **na** *adv.* not
नकल करना **nakal karnā** *v.t.* imitate
नक़ली **naqlī** *adj.* artificial
नकली **naklī** *adj.* counterfeit
नक़शा **naqśā** *n.m.* map
नक़्क़ाशी **naqqāśī** *n.m.* engraving
नक़्काशी **naqqāśī** *n.f.* carving
नक़ाब **naqāb** *n.m.* mask
नक़ाब लगाना **naqāb lagānā** *v.t.* mask
नकार देना **nakār denā** *v.t.* rebuff
नख **nakh** *n.m.* nail

नगर **nagar** *n.m.* town
नगरीय **nagrīy** *adj.* urban
नगरपालिका **nagarpālikā** *n.f.* municipality
नग्नता **nagntā** *n.m.* nudity
नज़र **nazar** *n.f.* vision
नटखट **naṭkhaṭ** *adj.* naughty
नटखटी **naṭkhaṭī** *n.f.* mischief
नथुना **nathu** *n.m.* nostril
नदी **nadi** *n.f.* river
नष्ट करना **naṣṭ karnā** *v.t.* ruin
नपुंसक **napunsak** *adj.* neuter
नफ़रत **nafrat** *n.m.* hate
नब्बे **nabbe** *num.* ninety
नम **nam** *adj.* moist
नम करना **nam karnā** *v.t.* dampen
नमक **namak** *n.m.* salt
नमक लगाना **namak lagānā** *v.t.* salt
नमकीन **namkīn** *adj.* salty
नमस्कार **namaskār** *n.m.* greeting, hello
नमस्कार करना **namaskār karnā** *v.t.* greet
नमूना **namūnā** *n.m.* pattern, sample
नमूना बनाना **namūnā banānā** *v.t.* designate
नमूना लेना **namūnā lenā** *v.t.* sample
नमी **namī** *n.f.* humidity
नया **nayā** *adj.* new
नया करना **nayā karnā** *v.t.* renew
नया कर देना **nayā kar denā** *v.t.* renovate
नया साल **nayā sāl** *n.m.* New Year
नर **nar** *n.m.* male
नरक **narak** *n.m.* hell
नरकट **narkaṭ** *n.m.* reed
नर्स **nars** *n.f.* nurse

नर्सरी **narsarī** *n.f.* nursery
नयीकरण **nayīkaraṇ** *n.m.* renewal
नलसाज़ **nalsāz** *n.m.* plumber
नली **nalī** *n.f.* tube
नवंबर **navambar** *n.m.* November
नवजात **navjāt** *n.m./adj.* newborn
नववर्ष **navvarṣ** *n.m.* New Year
नवीकरण **navīkaraṇ** *n.m.* renovation
नवीनता **navīntā** *n.f.* novelty
नशे में चूर **naṣṭ me chūr** *adj.* drunk
नष्ट करना **naṣṭ karnā** *v.t.* destroy
नस **nas** *n.f.* sinew
नहीं **nahīṁ** *adj.* no
नहर **nahar** *n.f.* canal
नहाना **nahānā** *v.t./v.i.* bathe
नाई **nāī** *n.m.* barber
नाई की दुकान **nāī kī dukān** *n.f.* barbershop
नाक **nāk** *n.f.* nose
नाका **nākā** *n.m.* barrier
नाग़ा करने वाला **nāqā karne vālā** *n.m.* truant
नागरिक **nāgarik** *n.m.* citizen
नाच **nāc** *n.m.* dance
नाचना **nācnā** *v.i.* dance
नाटक **nāṭak** *n.m.* drama, play
नाती **nātī** *n.m.* grandchild
नानबाई **nānbāī** *n.m.* baker
नाना **nānā** *n.m.* grandfather (*maternal*)
नानी **nānī** *n.f.* grandmother (*maternal*)
नाप **nāp** *n.f.* measure
नापसंद करना **nāpasand karnā** *v.t.* dislike
नाबालिग़ **nābāliq** *adj.* minor
नाभि **nābhi** *n.f.* navel

नाभिक **nābhik** *n.m.* nucleus
नामंज़ूर करना **nāmanzūr karnā** *v.t.* reject
नाम **nām** *n.m.* reputation
नामजद करना **nāmjad karnā** *v.t.* nominate
नामज़दगी **nāmzadagī** *n.m.* nomination
नामपत्र **nāmpatra** *n.m.* label
नाम देना **nām denā** *v.t.* christen
नामे **nāme** *n.m.* debit
नामे लिखना **nāme likhnā** *v.t.* debit
नारंगी **nārangī** *n.f.* orange
नारा **nārā** *n.m.* slogan
नाराज़ **nārāz** *adj.* angry
नाली **nālī** *n.m.* sink, drain
नाव **nāv** *n.f.* boat
नाशपाती **nāśpātī** *n.f.* pear
नाश्ता **nāśtā** *n.m.* breakfast
नास्तिकवाद **nāstikavād** *n.m.* atheism
नाइट्रजन **nāiṭrajan** *n.m.* nitrogen
निंदा करना **nindā karnā** *v.t.* damn
निबंध **nibandh** *n.m.* essay
निमंत्रण **nimantraṇ** *n.m.* invitation
निमंत्रण देना **nimntraṇ denā** *v.t.* invite
निकट **nikaṭ** *adj./adv.* nearby
निकट आना **nikaṭ ānā** *v.t.* approximate
निकटदर्शी **nikaṭdarśī** *adj.* nearsighted
निकटवर्ती **nikaṭvartī** *adj.* adjacent
निकल **nikal** *n.m.* nickel
निकल आना **nikal ānā** *v.i.* emerge
निकाल देना **nikāl denā** *v.t.* expel
निकालना **nikālnā** *v.t.* exclude
निकास **nikās** *n.m.* shaft
निकासनली **nikāsnalī** *n.m.* exhaust

निकासी **nikāsī** *n.f.* withdrawal
निगम **nigam** *n.m.* corporation
निगलना **nigalnā** *v.t.* swallow
निचला **niclā** *n.m.* bottom
निचला झरोखा **niclā jharokhā** *n.m.* hatch
निचोड़ **nicoṛ** *n.m.* extract
निचोडना **nicoḍnā** *v.t.* squash
निचोड़ना **nicoṛnā** *v.t.* extract
निजीलित **nijīlit** *adj.* dehydrated
नित्य **nitya** *adj.* eternal
नित्यक्रम **nityakram** *n.m.* routine
निदान **nidān** *n.m.* diagnosis
निदेशिका **nideśikā** *n.f.* directory
निधि **nidhi** *n.f.* fund
निधि में रखना **nidhi meṁ rakhnā** *v.t.* fund
निष्पादक **niṣpādak** *n.m.* executive
निष्यक्षता **niṣyakṣatā** *n.f.* equity
निष्क्रिय **niṣkriya** *adj.* inactive
निपटारा **nipṭārā** *n.m.* settlement
नियत करना **niyat karnā** *v.t.* constitute
नियति **niyati** *n.f.* destiny
नियन्त्रक **niyantrak** *n.m.* controller
नियम **niyam** *n.m.* rule
नियमित **niyamit** *n.m.* regular
नियमन **niyaman** *n.m.* regulation
नियुक्त करना **niyukt karnā** *v.t.* employ, appoint
नियोजक **niyojak** *n.m.* employer
नियोजन **niyojan** *n.m.* appointment
निरस्त्र **nirastra** *adj.* unarmed
निराकार **nirākār** *adj.* abstract
निरानन्द **nirānand** *adj.* dreary
निराला **nirālā** *adj.* extraordinary

निराश करना **nirāś karnā** *v.t.* frustrate
निराशा **nirāśā** *n.f.* frustration
निराशाजनक **nirāśājanak** *adj.* hopeless
निराशापूर्ण **nirāśāpūrṇ** *adj.* bleak
निराशावादी **nirāśāvādī** *adj.* pessimistic
निरीक्षक **nirīkṣak** *n.m.* inspector
निरीक्षण **nirīkṣaṇ** *n.m.* inspection
निरोधक **nirodhak** *n.m./adj.* contraceptive
निर्जीव **nirjīv** *adj.* lifeless
निर्णय करना **nirṇay karnā** *v.t.* award
निर्णायक **nirnāyak** *adj.* decisive
निर्दय **niarday** *adj.* merciless
निर्देशक **nirdeśak** *n.m.* director
निर्दोष **nirdoṣ** *adj.* innocent
निर्धारित करना **nirdhārit karnā** *v.t.* determine
निर्माण **nirmāṇ** *n.m.* make, manufacture
निर्माण करना **nirmāṇ karnā** *v.t.* manufacture, erect
निर्यात **niryāt** *n.m.* export
निर्यात करना **niryāt karnā** *v.t.* export
निर्वातक मशीन **nirvātak maśīn** *n.f.* vacuum
निर्वासित करना **nirvāsit karnā** *v.t.* deport
निर्वासन **nivarsan** *n.m.* ostracism, exile
निवारक **nivārak** *adj.* preventive
निवास **nivās** *n.m.* dwelling
निवासी **nivāsī** *n.m.* resident
निवेदन **nivedan** *n.m.* request
निवेदन करना **nivedan karnā** *v.t.* request
निलय **nily** *n.m.* ventricle
निश्चल **niścal** *adj.* still
निश्चायक **niścāyak** *adj.* definitive
निश्चयपूर्वक कहना **niścaypūrvak kahenā** *v.t.* affirm
निशाना **niśānā** *n.m.* aim

निशाना बाँधना **niśānā baṁdhnā** *v.t.* aim
निशानी **niśānī** *n.f.* souvenir
निश्चित **niścit** *adj.* certain
निश्चायक **niścāyak** *adj.* decimal
निश्चित करना **nìścit karnā** *v.t.* assign
नींद **nīnd** *n.f.* sleep
नींद की गोली **nīnd kī golī** *n.f.* sleeping
नींद की गोली देना **nīnd kī golī denā** *v.t.* sedate
नींद से जागना **nīnd se jāgnā** *v.t.* wake
नीचे **nīce** *adj.* down
नीचे **nīce** *prep./adv.* below
नीचे आना **nīce ānā** *v.i.* descend
नीचे पहनने के कपड़े **nīce pahenne ke kapṛe** *n.m.* underwear
नीबू **nībū** *n.m.* lemon
नीति **nīti** *n.f.* policy
नीतिपरक **nītiparak** *adj.* ethical
नीलम **nīlam** *n.m.* sapphire
नीला **nīlā** *adj.* blue
नीलाम **nīlām** *n.m.* auction
नीलाम करना **nīlām karnā** *v.t.* auction
नीलपुष्प **nīlpuṣp** *n.m.* violet
नेमी **nemī** *adj.* routine

प

पंक्ति **paṅkti** *n.f.* row
पंक्तिबद्ध करना **paṅktibaddh karnā** *v.t.* line
पंख **paṅkha** *n.m.* feather, wing, fan, plume
पंखुड़ी **paṅkhuḍī** *n.f.* petal
पंचम **pañcam** *adj.* fifth
पंचर **paṅkcar** *n.m.* puncture
पंचर करना **paṅcar karnā** *v.t.* puncture

पछताना **pachtānā** *v.t.* regret
पंजा **pañjā** *n.m.* claw, paw; tiptoe
पंजों के बल चलना **pañjoṁ ke bal calnā** *v.i.* tiptoe
पंद्रह **pandrah** *num.* fifteen
पंद्रहवाँ **pandrahvāṁ** *adj.* fifteenth
पंसारी **pansārī** *n.m.* grocer
पंसारी की दुकान **pansārī kī dukān** *n.m.* grocery
पंडित **paṇḍit** *n.m.* scholar
पकड़ **pakaṛ** *n.m.* grip
पकड़ना **pakaṛnā** *v.t.* clutch, catch
पका **pakā** *adj.* ripe
पकाना **pakānā** *v.t.* cook, bake
पक्का करना **pakkā karnā** *v.t.* confirm
पगडंडी **pagḍanḍī** *n.f.* trail
पचाना **pacānā** *v.t.* digest
पचास **pacās** *num.* fifty
पचासवाँ **pacāsvāṁ** *adj.* fiftieth
पच्चर **paccar** *n.f.* wedge
पटरी **paṭarī** *n.f.* rail
पटरी लगाना **paṭarī lagānā** *v.t.* track
पटरे पर लहरों पर खेलना **paṭare par laharoṁ par khelnā** *v.i.* surf
पट्टी **paṭṭī** *n.f.* tablet; bandage
पट्टा **paṭṭā** *n.m.* leash
पठन **paṭhan** *n.m* reading
पड़की **paṛkī** *n.f.* dove
पड़ना **paṛnā** *v.t.* must
पड़ा **paṛā** *adj.* horizontal
पड़ोस **paṛos** *n.m.* neighborhood
पड़ोसी **paṛosī** *n.m.* neighbor
पढ़ाना **paṛhānā.** *v.t.* teach, harness
पतंगा **pataṅgā** *n.m.* moth

पतझड़ **patjhaṛ** *n.m.* fall
पतवार **patvār** *n.f.* helm
पतला **patlā** *adj.* slim
पतलून **patlūn** *n.m.* pants
पता **patā** *n.m.* address
पता लगाना **patā lagānā** *v.t.* detect
पति **pati** *n.m.* husband
पत्थर **patthar** *n.m.* stone
पत्नी **patnī** *n.f.* wife
पत्ता **pattā** *n.m.* leaf
पत्तन **pattan** *n.m.* port
पथ **path** *n.m.* trail, path
पथिक **pathik** *n.m.* passerby
पद **pad** *n.m.* verse
पदक **padak** *n.m.* medal
पद की पोशाक **pad kī pośāk** *n.f.* robe
पदचारी **padacārī** *n.m.* pedestrian
पदच्युत करना **padcyut karnā** *v.t.* dismiss
पदयात्रा करना **padyātrā karnā** *v.t.* hike
पदाधिकारी **padādhikārī** *n.m.* officer
पनडुब्बी **panḍubbī** *n.f.* submarine
पनीर **panīr** *n.m.* cheese
पन्ना **pannā** *n.m.* page
पपड़ी **papaṛī** *n.f.* scar
पम्प **pamp** *n.m.* pump
पम्प करना **pamp karnā** *v.t.* pump
पर **par** *prep.* on
परखना **parakhnā** *v.t.* review
परचूनिया **parcūniyā** *n.m.* retailer
परजीवी **parjīvī** *n.m.* parasite; *adj.* parasitic
परदा **pardā** *n.m.* screen

परदार साँप **pardār sāṁp** *n.m.* dragon
परदेस जाना **pardes jānā** *v.i.* emigrate
परत **parat** *n.f.* crust
परम **param** *adj.* extreme
परमाणु **parmāṇu** *n.m.* atom
परमाण्विक **parmāṇvik** *adj.* nuclear
परवा करना **parvā karnā** *v.i.* care
परम्परा **paramparā** *n.f.* tradition
परवर्ती **parvarī** *adj.* latter
पहचान **pehcān** *n.f.* recognition
पत्र-व्यवहार **patr-vyavahār** *v.i.* correspond
पर्यटक **paryaṭak** *n.m.* tourist
पर्यटन **paryaṭan** *n.m.* tourism
पर्याप्त **paryāpt** *adj.* adequate
पर्यवेक्षक **paryaveikṣak** *n.m.* supervisor
पर्यवेक्षण **paryavekṣaṇ** *n.m.* observation
पर्यवेक्षण करना **paryavekṣaṇ karnā** *v.t.* supervise
पर्याय **paryāy** *n.m.* synonym
पर्वतमाला **parvatmālā** *n.m.* range
पर्स **pars** *n.m.* purse
पराकाष्ठा **parākāṣṭā** *n.f.* climax
पराबैंगनी **parābaiṅganī** *adj.* ultraviolet
परामर्शदाता **parāmarśdātā** *n.m.* consultant
परिक्रमा **parikramā** *n.f.* revolution
परिक्रमा करना **parikramā karnā** *v.t.* revolve
परिकल्पना **parikalpnā** *n.m./v.t.* design
परिचय **paricay** *n.m.* acquaintance, introduction
परिचय देना **paricay denā** *v.t.* introduce
परिचर **paricar** *n.m.* suite
परिचारिका **paricārikā** *n.f.* stewardess
परिचित **paricit** *adj.* familiar

परिचित करना **paricit karnā** *v.t.* acquaint
परित्याग करना **parityāg karnā** *v.t.* abandon
परिष्करण-शाला **pariṣkaraṇ-śālā** *n.f.* refinery
परिष्कार **pariṣkār** *n.m.* finish
परिष्कार करना **pariṣkār karnā** *v.t.* finish
परिपक्वत्ता **paripakvattā** *n.f.* maturity
परिभाषा **paribhāṣā** *n.f.* definition
परिमाण **parimāṇ** *n.m.* quantity
परियोजना **pariyojnā** *n.f.* project
परिरक्षण **parikṣaṇ** *n.m.* preserve
परिर्वतन **parivartan** *n.m.* change, alteration
परिवर्तन करना **parivartan karnā** *v.t.* modify
परिवर्तनीय **parivartanīy** *adj.* changeable
परिवर्ती **parivartī** *adj.* variable
परिवहन **parivahan** *n.m.* transport
परिवार **parivār** *n.f.* family
परिवार का नाम **parivār kā nām** *n.m.* surname
परिवेषिका **parivoṣikā** *n.f.* waitress
परिशिष्ट **pariśiṣṭ** *n.m.* supplement, appendix
परिषद **pariṣad** *n.f.* council
परिस्थिति **paristhiti** *n.f.* circumstance
परिहार **parihār** *v.t.* avoid
परित्राता **paritrātā** *n.m.* savior
परी **parī** *n.f.* fairy
परीक्षा **parīkṣā** *n.f.* examination
परीक्षण **parīkṣaṇ** *n.m.* trial
परेशान **pareśan** *n.m.* worry
परेशान करना **pareśān karnā** *v.t.* annoy
परेशानी **paeśānī** *n.f.* harassment
पल **pal** *n.m.* moment
पलक **palak** *n.f.* eyelid
पलस्तर **palstar** *n.m.* plaster

पलायन **palāpan** *n.m.* escape
पलायन करना **palāpan karnā** *v.t.* escape
पल्लेदार **palledār** *n.m.* porter
पवन-चक्की **pavan-cakkī** *n.m.* windmill
पवित्र **pavitra** *adj.* holy
पश्चिम **paścim** *n.m.* west
पश्चिमी **paścimī** *adj.* western
पशु **paśu** *n.m.* beast
पशुचिकित्सा **paśucikitsā** *adj.* veterinary
पशुचिकित्सक **paśucikitsak** *n.m.* veterinarian
पसंद आना **pasand ānā** *v.i.* appeal
पसंद करना **pasand karnā** *v.t.* like
पसली **paslī** *n.f.* rib
पसीना निकलना **pasīnā nikalnā** *v.i.* perspire
पसीना **pasīnā** *n.m.* sweat
पसीना बहाना **pasīnā bahānā** *v.t.* sweat
पहचानना **pahacānnā** *v.t.* identify
पहचान **pahacān** *n.f.* identification
पहचान लेना **pahacān lenā** *v.t.* spot
पहनकर देखना **pahenkar dekhnā** *v.t.* try
पहनना **pahannā** *v.t./v.i.* wear
पहनावा **pahnāvā** *n.m.* dress
पहला **pahalā** *n.m.* elementary
पहलू **pahalū** *n.m.* aspect
पहले **pahale** *adv.* before
पहले से **pahale se** *adv.* already
पहुँच **pahuṁc** *n.f.* reach
पहुँचना **pahuṁcnā** *v.t.* reach
पहुँचाना **pahuṁcānā** *v.t.* deliver
पहचानना **pahcānnā** *v.t.* recognize
पहाड़ **pahāṛ** *n.m.* mountain
पहाड़ी **pahāṛī** *n.f.* hill

पहेली **pahelī** *n.f.* riddle
पक्ष **pakṣ** *n.m.* fortnight
पत्रकार **patrakār** *n.m.* journalist
पत्र-केखक **patr-kekhak** *n.m.* correspondent
पत्र-व्यवहार **patr-vyavahār** *n.m.* correspondence
पत्राधान **patrādhān** *n.m.* portfolio
पत्रिका **patrikā** *n.f.* magazine
पाँच **pāṁc** *num.* five
पाँचा **pāṁcā** *n.* rake
पागल **pāgal** *adj.* crazy, insane, mad
पाचन **pācan** *n.m.* digestion
पाजामा **pājāmā** *n.pl.* pajamas
पाटा **pāṭā** *n.f.* trowel
पाठ **pāṭh** *n.m.* lesson
पाठक **pāṭhak** *n.m.* reader
पाठ्यक्रम **pāṭyakram** *n.m.* course
पाठ्यपुस्तक **pāṭhyapustak** *n.f.* textbook
पादरी वर्ग **pādrī varg** *n.m.* clergy
पाना **pānā** *v.t.* obtain, find; *n.m.* find
पानी **pānī** *n.m.* water
पाप **pāp** *n.m.* sin
पाप करना **pāp karnā** *v.i.* sin
पॉप संगीत **pāp sangīt** *n.m.* pop music
पायलट **pāylaṭ** *n.m.* pilot
पार **pār** *adv.* across, over
पारगमन **pārgaman** *n.m.* transit
पार्थिव **pārthiv** *adj.* terrestrial
पारसल **pārsal** *n.m.* parcel
पार्टी **pārṭī** *n.f.* party
पारम्परिक **pāramparik** *adj.* traditional
पाउन्ड **pāunḍ** *n.m.* pound
पाल **pāl** *n.m.* sail

पालक **pālak** *n.m.* spinach
पालतू **pāltū** *adj.* domestic (*animal*)
पालतू जीव **pāltū jīv** *n.m.* pet
पालतू बनाना **pāltū banānā** *v.t.* tame
पालन **pālan** *n.m.* maintenance
पालन करना **pālan karnā** *v.i.* comply
पालना **pālnā** *v.t.* cherish
पाल-नाव **pāl-nāv** *n.f.* sailboat
पालिश **pāliś** *n.m.* polish
पालिश करना **pāliś karnā** *v.t.* polish
पाली **pālī** *n.m.* shift
पट्टा **paṭṭā** *n.m.* lease
पट्टे पर देना **paṭṭe par denā** *v.t.* lease
पावरोटी **pāvroṭī** *n.f.* loaf
पास-पड़ोस **pās-paros** *n.m.* environs
पासपोर्ट **pāsporṭ** *n.m.* passport
पास **pās** *adj.* close
पास होना **pās honā** *v.t.* have
पात्र **pātra** *n.m.* vase
पिंजरा **piñjarā** *n.m.* cage
पिंड **piṇḍ** *n.m.* solid
पिण्ड़ली **piṇṛalī** *n.m.* calf (*part of leg*)
पित्त **pitt** *n.m.* gall
पिघलना **pighalnā** *v.i.* melt
पिचका देना **pickā denā** *v.t.* dent
पिचकारी **pickārī** *n.f.* syringe
पिचिण्डिका **piciṇḍikā** *n.f.* instep
पिछाड़ी **pichāṛī** *n.m.* rear
पिता **pitā** *n.m.* dad(dy)
पिता-जी **pitā-jī** *n.m.* father
पिन कोड **pin koḍ** *n.m.* PIN (Personal Identification Number)
पियानो **piyāno** *n.m.* piano

पिरैमिड **piraimiḍ** *n.m.* pyramid
पिल्ला **pillā** *n.m.* puppy
पिसा **pisā** *n.f.* ground
पिस्टन **pisṭan** *n.m.* piston
पिस्तौल **pistaul** *n.m.* pistol
पिस्सू **pissū** *n.m.* flea
पीछा **pīchā** *n.m.* chase
पीछा करना **pīchā karnā** *v.t.* chase
पीछे **pīche** *adv.* back; *prep./adv.* behind; *adj.* backward
पीछे-पीछे चलना **pīche-pīche calnā** *v.i.* follow
पीछे रह जाना **pīche rah jānā** *v.i.* lag
पीठ **pīṭh** *n.f.* back
पीड़ा **pīṛā** *n.m.* torment
पीड़ाहीन **pīṛāhīn** *adj.* painless
पीपा **pīpā** *n.m.* barrel
पीर **pīr** *n.m.* saint
पीरू **pirū** *n.m.* turkey
पीला **pīlā** *adj.* yellow
पीव **pīv** *n.m.* pus
पीसना **pīsnā** *v.t.* pound, grind
पुआल **puāl** *n.m.* straw
पुचारे से साफ़ करना **pucāre se sāf karnā** *v.t.* mop
पुरस्कार देना **purskār denā** *v.t.* recompense
पुराने ढंग का **purāne ḍhang kā** *adj.* antique
पुर्ल्लिंग **purlling** *adj.* masculine
पुस्तक **pustak** *n.f.* book
पूँजी **pūṁjī** *n.f.* stock, capital
पूजा करना **pūjā karnā** *v.t.* worship
पूछना **pūchnā** *v.t.* ask
पूरा **pūrā** *adj.* whole
पूरा करना **pūrā karnā** *v.t.* supplement, complete, satisfy
पूरी तरह से **pūrī tarah se** *adv.* altogether

पूला **pūlā** *n.m.* sheaf
पूरा **pūrā** *n.m.* total
पूर्ण **pūrṇ** *adj.* full, complete
पूर्ण-विराम **pūrṇ-virām** *n.m.* period
पूर्ण समझना **pūrṇ samajhnā** *v.i.* realize
पूर्व **pūrv** *adj.* East
पूर्व दिन **pūrv din** *n.m.* eve
पूर्वज **pūrvaj** *n.m.* ancestor
पूर्वाग्रह **pūrvāgrah** *n.m.* prejudice
पूर्वानुमान **pūrvānumān** *n.m.* forecast
पूर्ववर्ती **pūrvavartī** *adj.* previous
पूर्वसर्ग **pūrvasarg** *n.m.* preposition
पूर्वी **pūrvi** *adj.* Eastern
पृथक्करण **pr̥thakkaraṇ** *n.m.* insulation
पृष्ठांकन करना **pr̥ṣṭhāṅkan karnā** *v.t.* endorse
पृथक करना **pr̥thak karnā** *v.t.* insulate
पेंसिल **pensil** *n.f.* pencil
पेंट **penṭ** *n.m./v.t.* paint
पेच **pec** *n.m.* screw
पेचकस **peckas** *n.m.* screwdriver
पेट **peṭ** *n.m.* belly
पेट का दर्द **peṭ kā dard** *n.* stomachache
पेटी **peṭī** *n.f.* belt
पेट्रोल **peṭrol** *n.m.* gasoline
पेट्रोलियम **peṭroliyam** *n.m.* petroleum
पेड़ **peṛ** *n.m.* tree
पेनी **penī** *n.f.* penny
पेपरमिंट **peparminṭ** *n.m.* peppermint
पेय **pey** *n.m.* beverage
पेशा **peśā** *n.m.* occupation, profession
पेशाब **peśāb** *n.m.* urine
पेशाब करना **peśāb karnā** *v.t.* urinate

पेशीय **peśīy** *adj.* muscular
पेस्ट्री **pesṭrī** *n.f.* pastry
पैडल **paiḍal** *n.m.* pedal
पैक करना **paik karnā** *v.t.* pack
पैकेज **paikej** *n.m.* package
पैख़ाना **paiqhānā** *n.m.* lavatory
पैटर्न **paiṭarn** *n.m.* pattern
पैदल जाना **paidal jānā** *v.t.* walk
पैदल पार करना **paidal pār karnā** *v.i.* wade
पैदल सैर करना **paidal sair karnā** *v.i.* hike
पैदल सैर करने वाला **paidal sair karne vāl** *n.m.* hiker
पैना तेज़ **painā tez** *adj.* sharp
पैनिल **painil** *n.m.* panel
पैबंद **paiband** *n.m.* patch
पैबंद लगाना **paiband lagānā** *v.t.* patch
पैमफ़्लिट **paimfliṭ** *n.m.* pamphlet
पैर **pair** *n.m.* foot
पैर की उँगली **pair kī uṁgalī** *n.m.* toe
पैरिश **pairiś** *n.f.* parish
पैसा **paisā** *n.m.* cash
पैसे देना **paise denā** *v.t.* pay
पोछना **pochnā** *v.t.* wipe
पोता **potā** *n.m.* grandson (*son's son*)
पोती **potī** *n.f.* granddaughter (son's daughter)
पोतघाट **potghāṭ** *n.m.* dock
पोतड़ा कलोट **potaṛā kaloṭ** *n.m.* diaper
पोर्सिलेन **porsilen** *n.m.* porcelain
पोल्टरी **polṭarī** *n.f.* poultry
पोस्ट-कार्ड **posṭ-kārḍ** *n.m.* postcard
पोशाक **pośāk** *n.f.* costume
पोषण **poṣaṇ** *n.m.* nutrition
पोषण करना **poṣaṇ karnā** *v.t.* foster

पौधा घर **paudhā ghar** *n.m.* greenhouse
पौधा **paudhā** *n.m.* plant
पौराणिक **paurāṇik** *n.m.* myth
पौत्रा **pautrā** *n.m.* grandson
पौत्री **pautrī** *n.f.* granddaughter
प्लग **plag** *n.m.* plug
प्लैटिनम **plaiṭinam** *n.m.* platinum
प्यादा **pyādā** *n.m.* pawn
प्यार **pyār** *n.m.* love
प्यार करना **pyār karnā** *v.t.* love
प्रकट करना **prakaṭ karnā** *v.t.* express, reveal
प्रकटन **prakaṭan** *n.m.* revelation
प्रकट होना **prakaṭ honā** *v.i.* appear
प्रकार **prakār** *n.m.* sort, type
प्रकाश **prakāś** *n.m.* light
प्रकाशक **prakāśak** *n.m.* publisher
प्रकाशगृह **prakāśgṛha** *n.m.* lighthouse
प्रकाशन **prakāśan** *n.m.* publication
प्रकाशित करना **prakāśit karnā** *v.t.* publish
प्रकृति **prakṛti** *n.m.* nature
प्रकृतिक दृश्य **prakṛtik dṛśya** *n.m.* scenery
प्रक्रिया **prakriyā** *n.m.* process
प्रगति **pragati** *n.m.* progress
प्रगति करना **pragati karnā** *v.t.* progress
प्रगतिशील **pragatiśīl** *adj.* progressive
प्रचार **pracār** *n.m.* circulation
प्रचारित करना **pracārit karnā** *v.t.* circulate
प्रचंड **pracaṇḍ** *adj.* vehement
प्रचण्ड धारा **pracaṇḍ dhārā** *n.f.* torrent
प्रचूर **pracūr** *adj.* abundant
प्रचूरता **pracūratā** *n.f.* plenty
प्रति **prati** *pref.* anti-

प्रतिकार करना **pratikār karnā** *v.t.* remedy
प्रतिक्रिया **pratikriyā** *n.m.* reaction
प्रतिक्रिया लाना **pratikriyā lānā** *v.i.* react
प्रतिजैविक **pratijaivik** *n./adj.* antibiotic
प्रतिष्ठा **pratiṣṭhi** *n.f.* dignity
प्रतिष्ता **pratiṣtā** *n.f.* prestige
प्रतिष्ठित **pratiṣṭhit** *adj.* dignified
प्रतिध्वनि **pratidhvani** *n.f.* echo
प्रतिनिधि **pratinidhi** *n.m.* representative
प्रतिनिधिक **pratinidhik** *adj.* representative
प्रतिबंध **pratibandh** *n.m.* curb
प्रतिभाशाली **pratibhāśālī** *n.m.* genius
प्रतिभू **pratibhū** *n.m.* sponsor
प्रतिभू बनना **pratibhū bannā** *v.t.* sponsor
प्रतिमा **pratimā** *n.f.* icon
प्रतिलिपि **pratilipi** *n.m.* copy
प्रतिलिपि करना **pratilipi karnā** *v.t.* copy
प्रतिद्वन्द्वी **pratidvandvī** *n./adj.* rival
प्रतिद्वन्द्विता **pratidvanddvitā** *n.m.* rivalry
प्रतिरोधी **pratirodhī** *adj.* resistant
प्रतिस्थापित करना **pratisthāpit karnā** *v.t.* substitute
प्रतीक **pratīk** *n.m.* token
प्रतीकार्थ **pratīkārth** *adj.* symbolic
प्रतीक्षालय **pratīkṣālāy** *n.m.* lounge, waiting room
प्रतीत होना **pratīt honā** *v.i.* seem
प्रताप **pratāp** *n.m.* majesty
प्राथमिक **prāthmik** *adj.* primary
प्राथमिकता **prāthmiktā** *n.f.* priority
प्रदान करना **pradān karnā** *v.t.* grant
प्रदीपन **pradīpan** *n.m.* lighting
प्रदीप्त **pradīpt** *n.f.* illumination
प्रदूषण **pradūṣaṇ** *n.m.* pollution

प्रदूषित **pradūṣit** *adj.* polluted
प्रदूषित करना **pradūṣit karnā** *v.t./v.i.* pollute
प्रदर्शन **pradarśan** *n.m.* demonstration, display; *v.t.* demonstrate
प्रदर्शित करना **pradarśit karnā** *v.t.* display, exhibit
प्रदाही **pradāhī** *adj.* inflammable
प्रदेश **prades** *n.m.* province, state
प्रभाव **prabhāv** *n.m.* side
प्रशिक्षित करना **praśikṣit karnā** *v.t.* train
प्राकृतिक **prākṛtik** *adj.* natural
प्राप्ति **prāpti** *n.f.* gain, acquisition
प्राप्त करना **prāpt karnā** *v.t.* gain
प्रारंभिक **prarambhik** *n.m./adj.* initial
प्रेमी **premī** *n.m.* lover
प्रेमिका **premikā** *n.f.* lover, girlfriend
प्रेरित करना **prerit karnā** *v.t.* motivate
प्रेम **prem** *n.m.* love
प्रेमी **premī** *n.m.* boyfriend
प्रेम-लीला **prem-līlā** *n.m.* romance
प्रेरणा **prerṇā** *n.f.* inspiration, motive
प्रेरणा देना **prerṇā denā** *v.t.* inspire
प्रेषित रुपया **preṣit rupayā** *n.m.* remittance
प्रेषित करना **preṣit karnā** *v.t.* remit
प्रेस **pres** *n.m.* press
प्रसारण केंद्र **prasāraṇ kendra** *n.m.* station
प्लास्टिक **plāsṭik** *n.f./adj.* plastic
प्लाविका **plāvikā** *n.f.* plasma
प्लेटफ़ार्म **pleṭfārm** *n.f.* platform

फ

फंदा **phandā** *n.m.* trap
फुंसी **phunsī** *n.f.* pimple
फंसाना **phaṁsānā** *v.t.* trap
फाँक **phāṁk** *n.f.* slice
फाँक काटना **phāṁk kāṭnā** *v.t.* slice
फूँक **phūṁk** *n.f.* puff
फेंटना **phenṭnā** *v.t.* whip
फड़फड़ाना **faṛfaṛānā** *v.t.* flap
फ़ड़फ़ड़ाहट **faṛfaṛāhaṭ** *n.f.* flap
फटन **phaṭan** *n.f.* tear
फटकार **phaṭkār** *n.m.* reprimand
फटकारना **phaṭkārnā** *v.t.* reprimand
फटा-पुराना **phaṭā-purānā** *adj.* shabby
फफूँदी **phaphūṁdī** *n.f.* mold
फरहरा **pharharā** *n.m.* banner
फल **phal** *n.m.* blade; fruit
फलना-फूलना **phalnā-phūlnā** *v.i.* thrive
फलांग **phalāng** *n.m.* ramp
फलित-ज्योतिष **phalit-jyotiṣ** *n.m.* astrology
फली **phalī** *n.f.* pod
फलोद्यान **phalodyān** *n.m.* orchard
फ़ाइल **fāil** *n.f.* file
फ़ाइल में रखना **fāil meṁ rakhnā** *v.t.* file
फाटक **phāṭak** *n.m.* gate
फाड़ना **phāṛnā** *v.t.* rip
फावड़ा **phāvṛā** *n.m.* spade
फिरकी **phirkī** *n f.* reel
फिर भी **phir bhī** *adv.* however
फिर से दिखाई पड़ना **phir se dikhāī paṛnā** *v.i.* reappear

फिर से बनाना **phir se banānā** *v.i.* reform
फिर से भरना **phir se bharnā** *v.t.* refill
फिर से रखना **phir se rakhnā** *v.t.* reorganize
फिसलनी **phisalnī** *adj.* slippery
फीका पड़ना **phīkā paṛnā** *v.t.* fade
फीका पड़ गया **phīkā paṛ gayā** *v.i.* fade
फुटकर **phuṭkar** *n.f.* retail
फुटबाल **phuṭbāl** *n.m.* football
फुफकारना **phuphkārnā** *v.i.* snort
फुरतीला **phurtīlā** *adj.* agile, nimble
फुलाव **phulāv** *n.m.* swelling
फुहार **phuhār** *n.m.* spray
फुहार देना **phuhār denā** *v.t.* spray
फुहारा स्नान करना **phuhārā sna karnā** *v.i.* shower
फूफा **phūphā** *n.m.* uncle (*husband of father's sister*)
फूफी **phūphī** *n.f.* aunt (*father's sister*)
फूल **phūl** *n.m.* flower
फूलगोभी **phūlgobhī** *n.f.* broccoli
फूलना **phūlnā** *v.i.* bloom
फूल-वाला **phūl-vālā** *n.m.* florist
फेंकना **pheṁknā** *v.t.* cast
फेफड़ा **phephaṛā** *n.m.* lungs
फेल जाना **phel jānā** *v.i.* penetrate
फैलाना **phailānā** *v.t.* expand, spread
फैलाव **phailāv** *n.m.* spread
फैशन **phaiśan** *n.m.* fashion
फोड़ा **phoṛā** *n./adj.* sore

ब

बंडल **baṇḍal** *n.m.* bundle
बन्द **band** *adj.* closed
बदं करना **band karnā** *v.t.* enclose
बंदगोभी **bandgobhī** *n.f.* cabbage
बंद होना **band honā** *v.i.* cease
बन्दी **bandī** *n.m.* prisoner
बन्दी बनाना **bandī banānā** *v.t.* detain
बंदूक **bandūk** *n.m.* gun
बंजर **bañjar** *adj.* barren
बंदर **bandar** *n.m.* monkey
बंदरगाह **bandargāh** *n.m.* harbor
बंदरगाह में ले आना **bandargāh meṁ le ānā** *v.i.* dock
बंदोबस्त करना **bandobast karnā** *v.t.* arrange
बंधक **bandhak** *n.m.* mortgage
बंधन **bandhan** *n.m.* tie
बकरा **bakrā** *n.m.* goat
बक्सा **baksā** *n.m.* trunk
बगल **bagal** *n.m.* side
बगल का **bagal kā** *adj.* next
बगुला **bagulā** *n.m.* heron
बचकाना **backānā** *adj.* childish
बचपन **bacpan** *n.m.* childhood
बचत **bacat** *n.f.* saving
बचा-खुचा **bacā-khucā** *adj.* remaining
बचाना **bacānā** *v.t.* rescue
बचाव **bacāv** *n.m.* rescue
बच्चा **baccā** *n.m.* child
बच्चे **bacce** *n.m.pl.* children
बछड़ा **bachṛā** *n.m.* calf

बजट **bajaṭ** *n.m.* budget
बजाना **bajānā** *v.t.* play
बटन **baṭan** *n.m.* button
बटिया **baṭiyā** *n.f.* pebble
बटुआ **baṭuā** *n.m.* wallet
बटेर **baṭer** *n.m.* quail
बढ़ाना **baṛhānā** *v.t.* reinforce
बढ़ना **baṛhnā** *v.i.* swell
बढ़िया **baṛhiyā** *adj.* fine, great
बड़ा **baṛā** *adj.* major
बत्ती **battī** *n.f.* light
बताना **batānā** *v.t.* state
बदक़िस्मत **badqismat** *adj.* unlucky
बदनामी **badnāmī** *n.f.* disgrace
बदनामी का **badnāmī kā** *adj.* scandalous
बदबू **badbū** *adj.* smell
बदल देना **badal denā** *v.t.* alter
बदल जाना **badal jānā** *v.i.* vary
बदलना **badalnā** *v.t.* change, vary
बदला **badlā** *n.m.* revenge
बनाना **banānā** *v.t.* make
बनावट **banāvaṭ** *n.m.* make-up
बन्द करना **band karnā** *v.t.* close
बधाई हो **badhāī ho** *n.m.* congratulation
बरतन **bartan** *n.m.* vessel
बरताव करना **bartāv karnā** *v.t.* treat
बल **bal** *n.m.* strength
बल देना **bal denā** *v.t.* stress
बलात्कार **balātkār** *n.m.* rape
बलात्कार करना **balātkār karnā** *v.t.* rape
बली **balī** *adj.* strong
बल्कि **balki** *adv.* rather

बल्ब **balb** *n.m.* bulb
बहकाना **bahkānā** *v.t.* seduce
बहन **behen** *n.f.* sister
बहना **bahanā** *v.t.* flow
बहस **bahas** *n.m.* argument
बहस करना **bahas karnā** *v.t.* argue
बहादुर **bahādur** *adj.* brave
बहाना **bahānā** *v.t.* drain
बहाव **bahāv** *n.m.* flow
बहिष्कृता **bahiṣkṛtā** *n.m.* outcast
बहू **bahū** *n.f.* daughter-in-law
बहुत **bahut** *n.m./adj.* plural; *adj.* many, a lot
बहुत ज़्यादा **bahut zyādā** *adj.* numerous
बहुत पहले **bahut pahle** *adj.* long
बहुमत **bahumat** *n.m.* majority
बहुत शोर **bahut śor** *adj.* noisy
बहुतायत **bahutāyat** *n.f.* abundance
बहुवचन **bahuvacan** *n.m.* plural
बाँट देना **bāṁṭ denā** *v.t.* share
बाँटना **bāṁṭnā** *v.t.* deal, divide
बाँसुरी **bāṁsurī** *n.m.* reed
बाण **bāṇ** *n.m.* arrow
बारी **bārī** *v.t.* turn
बाल **bāl** *adj.* juvenile
बिगड़ाना **bigaṛānā** *v.t.* damage
बिजली के धक्के **bijalī ke dhakke** *v.t.* shock
बिना **binā** *adv.* without
बीमा की नीति **bīmā kī nīti** *n.f.* policy
बेकार **bekār** *adj.* vain
बैंगनी **baiṁganī** *n.m./adj.* violet
बैल **bail** *n.m.* ox
बोना **bonā** *v.t.* plant

भ

भंग **bhaṅg** *n.m.* violation
भंग करना **bhaṅg karnā** *v.t.* violate
भंगुर **bhungur** *adj.* fragile
भंडार **bhaṇḍār** *n.m.* storeroom
भंडार में माल होना **bhanḍār meṁ māl honā** *n.f.* stock
भंडारों का सिलसिला **bhaṇḍāroṁ kā silsilā** *n.f.* chain store
भंवर **bhanvar** *n.m.* whirlpool
भँडेहरी **bhṁḍeharī** *adj.* zany
भक्त **bhakt** *n.m.* devotee
भक्ति **bhakti** *n.f.* devotion
भगवान **bhagavān** *n.m.* God
भजन **bhajan** *n.m.* hymn
भला **bhalā** *n.m.* welfare
भट्ठी **bhaṭṭhī** *n.f.* furnace
भविष्य **bhaviṣya** *n.m.* future
भविष्यवाणी **bhaviṣyavāṇī** *n.f.* prophecy
भतीजी **bhatījī** *n.f.* niece (*brother's daughter*)
भरा हुआ **bharā huā** *adj.* crowded
भराई **bharāī** *n.m.* filling
भरना **bharnā** *v.t.* fill
भयंकर **bhayankar** *adj.* terrible
भय **bhay** *n.m.* fright
भयानक **bhayānak** *adj.* terrific
भरती करना **bharatī karnā** *v.t.* recruit
भराव **bharāv** *n.f.* filling
भस्मकलश **bhasmklaś** *n.m.* urn
भत्रिका **bhatrikā** *n.m.* nephew (*brother's son*)
भाई **bhāī** *n.m.* brother
भाग **bhāg** *n.m.* segment

भाग जाना **bhāg jānā** *v.i.* run
भाग देना **bhāg denā** *v.i.* divide
भाग लेना **bhāg lenā** *v.i.* participate
भागना **bhāgnā** *v.i.* flee
भाग्य **bhāgya** *n.m.* lot, luck
भांजा **bhāñjā** *n.m.* nephew (*sister's son*)
भाटक पर लेना **bhāṭak par lenā** *v.t.* charter
भाभी **bhābhī** *n.f.* sister-in-law (*brother's wife*)
भाड़ा **bhāṛā** *n.m.* freight
भात **bhāt** *n.m.* rice
भानजी **bhānjī** *n.m.* niece (*sister's daughter*)
भाप **bhāp** *n.m.* steam
भार **bhār** *n.m.* gravity, load
भार उठाना **bhār uṭhānā** *n.* weight
भारी **bhārī** *adj.* hoarse
भारी कर देना **bhārī kar denā** *v.t.* aggravate
भालू **bhālū** *n.m.* bear
भावना **bhāvnā** *n.m.* feeling
भाव-समाधि **bhāv-samādhi** *n.f.* trance
भाषा **ṭīkā bhāṣā** *n.f.* commentary
भाषा **bhāṣā** *n.m.* language
भावुक **bhāvuk** *adj.* passionate
भाषण **bhāṣaṇ** *n.m.* speech
भाषण देना **bhaṣhaṇ denā** *v.t.* address
भिगोना **bhigonā** *v.t.* soak
भिड़ंत **bhīrant** *v.t.* encounter
भिन्न **bhinn** *adj.* distinct
भिन्न-भिन्न **bhinn-bhinn** *adj.* diverse
भिक्षा माँगना **bhikṣā maṁgnā** *v.i.* beg
भिस्सा **bhissā** *n.m.* willow
भी **bhī** *adv.* too
भीकाय **bhīkāy** *n.m./adj.* giant

भीगना **bhīgnā** *v.i.* soak
भीड़ **bhīṛ** *n.f.* crowd
भीतर **bhītar** *adj.* indoor
भीतरी **bhītarī** *adj.* interior, internal
भुखमरी **bhukhmarī** *n.f.* starvation
भुगतान **bhugtān** *n.m.* payment
भुजाग्र **bhujāgr** *n.m.* forearm
भुना हुआ **bhunā huā** *adj.* roast
भूकंप **bhūkamp** *n.m.* earthquake
भूख **bhūkh** *n.f.* hunger
भूखंड **bhūkaṇḍ** *n.* lot
भूखा **bhūkhā** *adj.* hungry
भूगोल **bhūgol** *n.m.* geography
भूत **bhūt** *n.m.* ghost
भू-दृश्य **bhū-dṛśya** *n.m.* landscape
भूमिगत **bhūmigat** *adj.* underground
भूमिका **bhūmikā** *n.f.* role; introduction
भूमि **bhūmi** *n.f.* land
भूरा रंग **bhūrā rang** *adj.* tan
भूल **bhūl** *n.m.* lapse
भूल जाना **bhūl jānā** *v.t.* forget
भूल-भूलैया **bhūl-bhūlaiyā** *n.f.* maze
भूविज्ञान **bhūvigyān** *n.m.* geology
भृंग **bhṛṅg** *n.m.* beetle
भेजना **bhejnā** *v.t.* send, ship
भेजने वाला **bhejne vala** *n.* sender
भेंट **bheṇṭ** *n.f.* visit
भेड़ **bheṛ** *n.f.* sheep
भेड़िया **bheṛiyā** *n.m.* wolf
भेद **bhed** *n.m.* secret
भेद करना **bhed karnā** *v.t.* distinguish
भोज **bhoj** *n.m.* feast

भोजन **bhojan** *n.m.* meal
भोजन कक्ष **bhojan kakṣ** *n.m.* dining
भोजन करना **bhojan karnā** *v.i.* dine
भोला-भाला **bholā-bhālā** *adj.* naive
भोथरा **bhotharā** *adj.* blunt
भौंकना **bhauṁkn** *v.t.* bark
भौंह **bhauṁh** *n.f.* eyebrow
भौतिक **bhautik** *n.m.* physicist
भौतिकी **bhautikī** *n.f.* physics
भ्रमण करना **bhramaṇ karnā** *v.i.* ramble
भ्रष्ट **bhrṣṭ** *n.m.* corrupt
भ्रष्टाचार **bhraṣṭācār** *n.m.* corruption
भ्रान्ति **bhrānti** *n.m.* illusion

म

मंगलवार **mangalvār** *n.m.* Tuesday
मंच **mañc** *n.m.* stage
मंजरी **mañjarī** *n.f.* blossom
मंज़ूक करना **manzūk karnā** *v.t.* approve
मंज़ूरी **manzūrī** *n.f.* acceptance
मंत्रालय **mantrālay** *n.m.* ministry
मंत्री **mantrī** *n.m.* minister; secretary
मंद **mand** *adj.* sluggish
मंदिर **mandir** *n.m.* temple
मई **maī** *n.m.* May
मकड़ी **makaṛī** *n.f.* spider
मक्ड़ी के नाल **makṛī ke nāl** *n.m.* spider web
मकानमालिक **makānmālik** *n.m.* landlord
मक्खी **makkhī** *n.f.* fly
मक्खन **makkhan** *n.m.* butter
मख़मल **maqhmal** *n.f.* velvet

मगर **magar** *conj.* but
मचान **macān** *n.m.* scaffold
मच्छर **macchar** *n.m.* mosquito
मछली **machlī** *n.f.* fish
मछली पकड़ना **machlī pakaṛnā** *v.t.* fishing
मछुआ **machuā** *n.m.* fisherman
मज़बूत करना **mazbūt karnā** *v.t.* strengthen, reinforce
मज़दूर **mazdūr** *n.m.* worker, labor
मज़ा **mazā** *n.* zest
मज़ाक **mazāk** *n.m.* joke
मंज़ूरी **manzūrī** *n.f.* approval
मजिस्ट्रेट **majisṭreṭ** *n.m.* magistrate
मज्जा **majjā** *n.f.* marrow
मटर **maṭar** *n.f.* pea
मठ **maṭh** *n.m.* convent
मठवासिनी **maṭhvāsinī** *n.f.* nun
मणि **maṇi** *n.f.* jewel
मण्डप **maṇḍap** *n.m.* pavilion
मतदान **matdān** *n.m.* poll
मतदाता **matdātā** *n.m.* voter
मर्तबान **martabān** *n.m.* jar
मदद **madad** *n.m.* help
मदद करना **madad karnā** *v.t.* help
मदिरा **madirā** *n.f.* liqueur
मधु **madhu** *n.m.* honey
मधुमास **madhumas** *n.m.* honeymoon
मधुमेह **madhumeh** *n.m.* diabetes
मधुमेही **madhumehī** *adj.* diabetic
मधुमक्खी **madhumakkhī** *n.f.* bee
मध्यम **madhyam** *adj.* middle
मध्ययुग **madhyayug** *adj.* middle
मध्याह्नपूर्व **madhyāhrpūrv** *adj.* a.m.

मध्यांतर **madhyāntar** *n.m.* interval
मध्यरात्रि **madhyarātri** *n.f.* midnight
मन **man** *n.m.* mind
मना करना **manā karnā** *v.t.* forbid
मनाही **manāhī** *n.f.* prohibition
मनाना **manānā** *v.t.* persuade
मन-बहलाव **man-behlāv** *n.m.* recreation
मनद्र वायलिन **mandra vāyalin** *n.m.* violoncello
मन्दबुद्धि **mandbuddhi** *adj.* dull
मनश्चिकित्सक **manśicakitsak** *n.m.* psychiatrist
मन-माना **man-mānā** *adj.* arbitrary
मनोभाव **manobhāv** *n.m.* passion
मनोहर **manohar** *adj.* handsome, graceful, fancy, fair
मनोविज्ञान **manovigyān** *n.m.* psychology
मनोरंजक **manorañjak** *adj.* entertaining
मनोरंजन **manorañjan** *n.m.* entertainment
मनोरंजन करना **manorañjan karnā** *v.t.* entertain
मनोरंजन **manoranjan** *n.m.* sport
मनोरम **manoram** *adj.* elegant
मनोवृत्ति **manovr̥tti** *n.f.* attitude
मनोवैज्ञानिक **manovaigyānik** *adj.* psychological
मनोवैज्ञानी **manovaigyānī** *n.m.* psychologist
मनपसंद **manpasand** *adj.* favorite
मनसूखी **mansūkhī** *n.f.* cancellation
मफ़लर **maflar** *n.m.* muffler
ममेरा भाई **mamerā bhāī** *n.m.* cousin (*male on mother's side*)
ममेरी बहन **mamerī behen** *n.f.* cousin (*female on mother's side*)
मरगजा करना **maragjā karnā** *v.t.* mash
मरोड़ **maroṛ** *n.f.* twist
मरोड़ना **maroṛnā** *v.t.* twist
मरण **maraṇ** *adj.* dying

मरा हुआ **marā huā** *adj.* dead
मरदाना **mardānā** *n.m.* masculine
मरम्मत **marammat** *n.m.* repair
मरम्मत करना **marammat karnā** *v.t.* repair, restore
मरना **marnā** *v.i.* die
मरहम **marham** *n.m.* salve
मल टैंक **mal ṭaiṅk** *n.m.* septic
मसल **masal** *n.m.* mussel
मसाला **masālā** *n.m.* spice
मसालेदार **masāledār** *adj.* spicy
मसाना **masālā** *n.m.* bladder
मसूर **masūr** *n.m.* lentil
मस्सा **massā** *n.m.* wart
मस्तूल **mastūl** *n.m.* mast
मर्मस्पर्शी **maramsparśī** *adj.* touching
मलाई **malāī** *n.f.* cream
मलाई उतारना **malāī utārnā** *v.t.* skim
मलना **malnā** *v.t.* rub
मल्लाह **mallāh** *n.m.* sailor
मवेशी **maveśī** *n.f.* cattle
महंगा **mahangā** *adj.* expensive
महत्व **mahatva** *n.m.* importance
महत्वहीन **mahatvahīn** *adj.* unimportant
महत्वपूर्ण **mahatvapūrṇ** *adj.* important, vital, substantial
महत्वाकांक्षा **mahatvākāṇkṣā** *n.f.* ambition
महत्वाकांक्षी **mahatvākāṇkṣī** *adj.* ambitious
महल **mahal** *n.m.* palace
महसूल **mahsūl** *n.m.* postage
महसूस करना **mahasūs karnā** *v.t.* perceive
महाजन **mahājan** *n.m.* banker
महान **mahān** *adj.* great
महामारी **mahāmārī** *n.f.* epidemic

महामंदिर **mahāmandir** *n.m.* cathedral
महातरंग **mahātrang** *n.f.* swell
महाव्दीप **mahāvdīp** *n.m.* continent
महाराजधिराजा **mahārājādhirājā** *n.m.* emperor
महासभा **mahāsabhā** *n.f.* congress
महासागर **mahāsāgar** *n.m.* ocean
महिमा **mahimā** *n.f.* glory
महीना **mahīnā** *n.m.* month
मशीन **maśīn** *n.f.* machine
मस्जिद **masjid** *n.f.* mosque
माँ **māṁ** *n.f.* mom(my)
मांसपेशी **mānspeśī** *n.f.* muscle
मांस **māṁs** *n.m.* flesh; meat
माँद **māṁd** *n.m.* den
माँग **māṁg** *n.f.* demand
माँगना **māṁgnā** *v.t.* demand, request, require
माँजना **māṁjnā** *v.t.* scour, scrub
माँस **māṁs** *n.m.* beef
माइक **māik** *n.m.* microphone
माइल **māil** *n.m.* mile
माझोला **mājholā** *adj.* medium
माडल **mādal** *n.m.* model
माणिक्य **māṇiky** *n.m.* ruby
मात्रा **mātrā** *n.f.* dose
माता-पिता **mātā-pitā** *n.m.* parents
माता-जी **mātā-jī** *n.f.* mother
मातम **mātam** *n.m.* mourning
माथा **māthā** *n.m.* forehead
मादक **mādak** *adj.* alcoholic
मादा **mādā** *n.f.* female
माध्यम **mādhyam** *n.m.* medium
मान लेना **mān lenā** *v.t.* acknowledge

मानचित्र **māncitra** *n.* chart
मानचित्र बनाना **māncitra banānā** *v.t.* chart
मानव अधिकार **mānav adhikār** *adj.* human
मानसिक **mānsik** *adj.* mental
मानसिक सन्तुलन **mānsik santulan** *n.m.* sanity
मानक **mānak** *n.m.* standard
मानना **mānnā** *v.t.* regard
मानाना **manānā** *v.t.* confess
मानव जाति **mānav jāti** *n.m.* mankind
मानवीय **mānvīy** *n.m.* human
मानवोचित **mānvocit** *adj.* humane
मानवता **mānvatā** *n.f.* humanity
मानसिक तनाव **mānsik tanāv** *n.m.* stress
मानीटर **mānīṭar** *n.m.* monitor
मान्य **mānya** *adj.* valid
मान्यता **mānyatā** *n.m.* recognition
माप **māpa** *n.m.* gauge
मापना **māpnā** *v.t.* gauge
मापांक **māpānk** *n.m.* module
मामला **māmlā** *n.m.* affair
मामा **māmā** *n.m.* uncle (*mother's brother*)
मामी **māmī** *n.m.* aunt (*wife of mother's brother*)
मामूली **māmūlī** *adj.* ordinary
मार भगाना **mār bhagānā** *v.t.* repel
मार डालना **mār ḍālnā** *v.t.* kill
मारगरीन **mārgarīn** *n.m.* margarine
मारना **mārnā** *v.t.* hammer, hit
मार्टर **mārṭar** *n.m.* mortar
माल **māl** *n.m.* ware
माल ढोने की गाड़ी **māl ḍhone kī gāṛī** *n.f.* wagon
माल उतारना **māl utārnā** *v.t.* unload
माला **mālā** *n.f.* garland

माला विनती **mālā vinatī** *n.f.* rosary
मालिक **mālik** *n.m.* employer, boss, proprietor
मालिक होना **mālik honā** *v.t.* possess
मालिश **māliś** *n.f.* massage
मार्शल **mārśal** *n.m.* marshal
माफ़ी **māfī** *n.m.* excuse
माफ़ करना **māf karnā** *v.t.* excuse
मार्ग **mārg** *n.m.* avenue, track
मार्च **mārc** *n.m.* March
माहवारी **māhabarī** *n.m.* period
मिचली **micalī** *n.f.* nausea
मिचली आना **micalī ānā** *v.i.* nauseous
मिज़ाज **mizāj** *n.m.* temper
मिटाना **miṭānā** *v.t.* erase
मिट्टी **miṭṭī** *n.f.* soil
मिठाई **miṭhāī** *n.f.* candy
मितव्यय **mitvyay** *n.f.* thrift
मितव्ययी **mitvyayī** *adj.* thrifty
मित्र **mitra** *n.m.* ally
मिनट **minaṭ** *n.m.* minute
मिरगी **miragī** *n.m.* epilepsy
मिलाकर **milākar** *v.t.* plus
मिलाना **milānā** *v.t.* mix, join
मिलीमीटर **milīmīṭar** *n.m.* millimeter
मिश्रण **miśraṇ** *n.m.* mixture, mix
मीठा बनाना **mīṭhā banānā** *v.t.* sweeten
मीठा बिस्कुट **mīṭhā biskuṭ** *n.m.* cookie
मीठाई **mīṭhāī** *n.f.* sweet
मील-पत्थर **mīl-patthar** *n.m.* milestone
मीनार **mīnār** *n.f.* tower
मीनार का शिखर **mīnār kā śikhar** *n.m.* spire
मुँह **muṁh** *n.m.* mouth

मुँहासा **muṁhāsā** *n.m.* acne
मुकदमा **mukdamā** *n.m.* case
मुकदमा चलाना **mukdamā calānā** *n.m.* (*legal*) trial; *v.t.* (*legal*) try
मुक्का **mukkā** *n.m.* fist; punch
मुक्का मारना **mukkā mārnā** *v.t.* punch
मुक्केबाज़ी **mukkebāzī** *n.f.* boxing
मुकुट **mukuṭ** *n.m.* crown
मुक्त करना **mukt karnā** *v.t.* release
मुक्ति **mukti** *n.f.* salvation
मुखिया **mukhiyā** *n.m.* chief
मुख्य **mukhya** *adj.* main, chief, grand, major
मुख्य भू-भाग **mukhya bhū-bhāg** *n.m.* mainland
मुख्यालय **mukhyālay** *n.m.pl.* headquarters
मुझे **mujhe** *pron.* me
मुद्रक **mudrak** *n.m.* printer
मुद्रा-स्फीति **mudrā-sphıti** *n.m.* Inflation
मुफ़्त **muft** *adj.* free
मुबारक **mubārak** *n.m.* congratulation
मुट्ठा **muṭṭhā** *n.m.* roll
मुरदा **murdā** *adj.* dead
मुरब्बा **murbbā** *n.m.* marmalade
मुरगा **murgā** *n.m.* rooster
मुरली बजनेवाला **murlī bajanevālā** *n.m.* piper
मुरमुरी हड्डी **murmurī haḍḍī** *n.f.* cartilage
मुर्ख **murkh** *n.m.* fool
मुर्गी **murgī** *n.f.* chicken
मुलाकात **mulākāt** *n.f.* interview
मुलायम **mulāyam** *adj.* soft
मुलम्मा **mulammā** *n.m.* gilt
मुश्किल **muśkil** *adj.* difficult
मुश्किल से **muśkil se** *adv.* hardly

मुसलमान **musalmān** *n.m.* Muslim
मुसलमानी **musalmānī** *n.f.* Muslim
मुस्कराना **muskarānā** *v.i.* smile
मुस्कराहट **muskarāhaṭ** *n.f.* smile
मुहावरा **muhāvarā** *n.m.* phrase, idiom
मुहरा **muharā** *n.m.* facade
मुड़ना **muṛnā** *v.t.* turn
मूँड़ना **mūṁṛnā** *v.t./v.i.* shave
मूँगफली **mūṁgfalī** *n.f.* peanut
मूँछ **mūṁch** *n.f.* mustache
मूठ **mūṭh** *n.m.* handle
मूत्र-विज्ञानी **mūtr-vigyānī** *n.m.* urologist
मूत्रीय **mūtrīy** *adj.* urinary
मूर्ख **mūrkh** *adj.* silly
मूर्ति **mūrti** *n.f.* statue
मूर्ति बनाना **mūrti banānā** *v.i.* sculpt
मूर्तिकार **mūrtikār** *n.m.* sculptor
मूल **mūl** *n.m.* original
मूल भाषा **mūl bhāṣā** *adj.* native language
मूलवासी **mūlvāsī** *n.m.* native
मूल्य **mūly** *n.m.* value
मूल्यांकन **mūlyāṅkan** *n.m.* appreciation
मूल्यांकन करना **mūlyānkan karnā** *v.t.* valuation
मूल्यवान **mūlyavān** *n.m./adj.* valuable
मृत्तिका **mṛttiikā** *n.m./adj.* ceramic
मृगतृष्ण **mṛgatṛṣaṇ** *n.m.* mirage
मृदुल **mṛdul** *adj.* mild
मृत्यू **mṛtyū** *n.f.* death
में **meṁ** *prep.* into, inside, at
मेंढक **meṇḍhak** *n.m.* frog
मेघाच्छन **meghācchan** *adj.* cloudy
मेजर **mejar** *n.m.* major

मेज़ **mez** *n.f.* table
मेज़बान **mezbān** *n.m.* host
मेज़पोश **mezpoś** *n.m.* tablecloth
मेन्यू **menyū** *n.m.* menu
मेमना **memnā** *n.m.* lamb
मेयर **meyar** *n.m.* mayor
मेरा **merā** *pron.m.sing.* my
मेरे **mere** *pron.m.pl.* my
मेल **mel** *n.m.* conjunction
मेला **melā** *n.m.* fair
मेल-मिलाप **mel-milāp** *n.m.* reconciliation
मेल-मिलाप करना **mel-milāp karnā** *v.t.* reconcile
मेहमान **mehamān** *n.m.* guest
मेहमानशरिन **mehmānśarin** *n.m.* hostess
मेहनत **mehanat** *n.f.* toil
मेहनत करना **mehanat karnā** *v.t.* toil
मेहनती **mehnatī** *adj.* diligent
मेहमान **mehamān** *n.m.* guest
मेहराब **meharāb** *n.m.* arch
मैं **maiṁ** *pron.* I
मैकेनिक **maikenik** *n.m.* mechanic
मैडम **maiḍam** *n.m.* madam
मैदान **maidān** *n.m.* plain
मैनेजर **mainejar** *n.m.* manager
मैला **mailā** *adj.* filthy
मोच **moc** *n.f.* sprain
मोच आना **moc ānā** *v.i.* sprain
मोचन **mocan** *n.m.* release
मोज़ा **mozā** *n.m.* sock
मोटा **moṭā** *adj.* thick
मोटाई **moṭāī** *n.f.* thickness
मोटर **moṭar** *n.f.* automobile

मोटर साइकिल **moṭar sāikil** *n.m.* motorcycle
मोटल **moṭal** *n.m.* motel
मोडेम **moḍem** *n.m.* modem
मोती **motī** *n.m.* pearl
मोम **mom** *n.m.* wax
मोमोम लगाना **mom lagānā** *v.t.* wax
मोर **mor** *n.m.* peacock
मोरी **morī** *n.f.* sewer
मोल **mol** *n.m.* offer
मोह लेना **moh lenā** *v.t.* fascinate
मोहकता **mohktā** *n.f.* glamour
मोहर **mohar** *n.m.* postmark
मोहर लगाना **mohar lagānā** *v.t.* postmark
मौखिक **maukhik** *adj.* oral
मौतल **mautal** *n.m.* keel
मौसम **mausam** *n.m.* weather
मौसमी **mausamī** *adj.* seasonal
मौसा **mausā** *n.m.* uncle (*husband of mother's sister*)
मौसी **mausī** *n.f.* aunt (*mother's sister*)

य

यंत्र **yantra** *n.m.* machinery, appliance
यंत्रमानव **yantramānav** *n.m.* robot
यकृत-शोथ **yakṛt-śoth** *n.m.* hepatitis
यथार्थ **yathārth** *adj.* virtual
यथावत स्थिति **yathāvat sthiti** *n.m.* status
यदा-कदा **yadā-kadā** *n.m.* occasional
यदि **yadi** *conj.* if
यह **yah** *pron.* it
यहाँ **yahāṁ** *adv.* here
यहूदी **yahūdī** *adj.* Jewish

यहूदियों का मंदिर **yahūdiyoṁ kā mandi** *n.m.* synagogue
या **yā** *conj.* or
याट **yāṭ** *n.m.* yacht
यातायात **yātāyāt** *n.m./v.i.* traffic
यातना देना **yātnā denā** *v.t.* torment
यात्रा **yātrā** *n.m.* journey
यात्रा करना **yātrā karnā** *v.i.* journey
यात्री **yātrī** *n.m.* traveller
याद **yād** *n.f.* memory
याद करना **yād karnā** *v.t.* remember
याद दिलाना **yād dilānā** *v.t.* remind
यायावरी **yāyāvarī** *adj.* nomadic
युक्ति **yukti** *n.f.* device
युग **yug** *n.m.* era
युद्ध **yuddh** *n.m.* war
यूनानी **yūnānī** *n.m.* Greek
यूरोपियन **yūropiyan** *n.m./adj.* European
ये **ye** *pron.* these
योग **yog** *n.m.* yoga
योग्य **yogya** *adj.* qualified, deserving
योग्य बनाना **yogya banānā** *v.t.* enable
योग्य होना **yogya honā** *v.i.* qualify
योग्यता **yogyatā** *n.m.* competence
योजक चिन्ह **yojak cinh** *n.m.* hyphen
योजना **yojnā** *n.f.* plan
योजना बनाना **yojnā banānā** *v.t.* plan
यौगिक **yaugik** *n.m.* compound

र

रंग **rang** *n.m.* color, dye
रगं की मात्रा **rang kī mātrā** *n.f.* shade

रंग-विरंगा **rang-virangā** *adj.* fancy
रंगपट्टिका **raṅg-paṭṭikā** *n.m.* pallet
रंगत **raṅgat** *n.m.* tint
रंगत देना **raṅgat denā** *v.t.* tint
रंगना **rangnā** *v.t.* paint, dye
रंगरूट **rangrūṭ** *n.m.* recruit
रंगीन काँच **rangīn kāṁc** *n.m.* stain
रकसैक **raksaik** *n.m.* rucksack
रक्तचाप **raktacāp** *n.m.* blood pressure
रक़ाब **raqāb** *n.f.* stirrup
रक्षक **rakṣak** *n.m.* keeper; escort
रक्षार्थ साथ जाना **rakṣārth sāth jānā** *v.t.* escort
रक्षा **rakṣā** *n.f.* protection
रक्षा करना **rakṣā karnā** *v.t.* protect
रक्षा-नौका **rakṣā-naukā** *n.f.* lifeboat
रखकर भूल जाना **rakhkar bhūl jānā** *v.t.* mislay
रखना **rakhnā** *v.t.* keep, set, save, put; *n.m.* place
रखनेवाला **rakhnevālā** *n.m.* layer
रूखा **rūkhā** *adj.* sullen
रचना **racnā** *n.f.* composition
रचना करना **racnā karnā** *v.t.* compose
रचनास्वत्व **racnāsvatva** *n.m.* copyright
रजाई **rajāī** *n.f.* quilt
रज़ामंद **razāmand** *n.m.* willing
रजिस्टर **rajisṭar** *n.m.* register
रजिस्टरी डाक **rajisṭarī ḍāk** *n.f.* registered mail
रणनीति **raṇnīti** *n.f.* tactic
रण्डी **raṇḍī** *n.f.* prostitute
रत्न **ratn** *n.m.* gem
रद्द **radd** *adj.* null
रद्द करना **radd karnā** *v.t.* cancel, nullify
रद्दी **raddī** *n.f.* garbage

रफ़ू करना **rafū karnā** *v.t.* darn
रबर **rabar** *n.f.* rubber
रम **ram** *n.m.* rum
रवाना होना **ravānā honā** *v.t./v.i.* sail, depart
रविवार **ravivār** *n.m.* Sunday
रस **ras** *n.m.* juice, sap
रस लेना **ras lenā** *v.t.* enjoy
रसौली **rasaulī** *n.f.* tumor
रसायन विज्ञान **rasāyan vigyān** *n.m.* chemistry
रसीद **rasīd** *n.f.* receipt
रसीला **rasīlā** *adj.* mellow
रसोई-भंडार **rasoī-bhaṇḍār** *n.m.* pantry
रसोईघर **rasoīghar** *n.m.* kitchen
रस्सी **rassī** *n.f.* rope
रहना **rehnā** *v.i.* reside, stay, remain
रहने का कमरा **rehne kā kamrā** *n.m.* living room
रहने वाला **rahene vālā** *n.m.* inhabitant
रहस्य **rahasya** *n.m.* mystery
राई **rāī** *n.f.* rye
राक्षस **rakṣas** *n.m.* monster
राख **rākh** *n.f.* ash
राखदानी **rākhdānī** *n.f.* ashtray
राजा **rājā** *n.m.* monarch
राजकुमार **rājkumār** *n.m.* prince
राजकुमारी **rājkumārī** *n.f.* princess
राजकोष **rājkoṣ** *n.m.* treasury
राजदूत **rājdūt** *n.m.* ambassador
राजधानी **rājdhānī** *n.f.* capital
राजनयिक **rājnayik** *n.f.* diplomat
राजनीति **rājnīti** *n.pl.* politics
राजनीतिज्ञ **rājnītigya** *n.m.* politician
राजनेता **rājnetā** *n.m.* statesman

राजनैतिक **rājnaitik** *adj.* political
राजभवन **rājbhavan** *n.m.* palace
राजहंस **rājhans** *n.m.* swan
राजपथ **rājpath** *n.m.* highway
राजसी **rājsī** *adj.* majestic
राजशाही **rājśāhī** *n.m.* monarchy
राज्य **rājya** *n.m.* kingdom
राज्यपाल **rājypāl** *n.m.* governor
राज्यसभा **rājyasabhā** *n.f.* senate
रात **rāt** *n.f.* night
रात भर **rāt bhar** *adv.* overnight
रात का खाना **rāt kā khānā** *n.m.* supper
रानी **rānī** *n.f.* queen
राय **rāy** *n.f.* opinion
राल **rāl** *n.m.* resin
राष्ट्र **rāṣṭra** *n.m.* nation
राष्ट्रीय **rāṣṭrīy** *n.m.* national
राष्ट्रीयता **rāṣṭrīyatā** *n.f.* nationality
राष्ट्रपति **rāṣṭrapati** *n.m.* president
राष्ट्रपति **rāṣṭrapati** *n.m.* vice
राहदारी **rāhdārī** *n.f.* toll
राइफ़ल **rāifal** *n.f.* rifle
राशन **rāśan** *n.m.* ration
राशन से देना **rāśan se denā** *v.t.* ration
राशी **rāśī** *adj.* mass
राशी चक्र **rāśī cakr** *n.m.* zodiac
रासायनिक **rāsāynik** *adj.* chemical
रासायनिक पदार्थ **rāsāynik padārth** *n.m.* chemical
रास्ता **rāstā** *n.m.* path, way
रास्ते का फर्श **raste kā pharś** *n.* pavement
रीढ़ **rīṛh** *n.f.* (*anatomy*) spine
रीम **rīm** *n.f.* ream

रुकना **roknā** *v.t.* stop, pause
रुमाल **rumāl** *n.m.* handkerchief
रेंगना **reṅgnā** *v.i.* crawl
रेंगनेवाला **reṅganevālā** *n.m.* reptile
रेखाचित्र **rekhācitra** *n.m.* graph
रेखांकित करना **rekhāṅkit karnā** *v.t.* underline
रेगमाल **regmāl** *n.m.* sandpaper
रेगिस्तान **registān** *n.m.* desert
रेडियो **reḍiyo** *n.m.* radio
रेडियो स्टेशन **reḍiyo sṭeśan** *n.m.* station
रेस्तराँ **restarāṁ** *n.m.* restaurant
रेती **retī** *n.f.* file
रेलिंग **reliṇg** *n.f.* railing
रेल पटरी **rel paṭarī** *n.f.* railway
रेलगाड़ी **relgāṛī** *n.f.* train
रेलवे **relve** *n.f.* railroad
रेशम **reśam** *n.m.* silk
रैल स्टेशन **rail sṭeśan** *n.m.* station
रैली **railī** *n.f.* rally
रोआ **roā** *n.m.* fur
रोक **rok** *n.m.* stop, restriction
रोकना **roknā** *v.t.* stop
रोक रखना **rok rakhnā** *v.t.* withhold
रोकेट **rokeṭ** *n.m.* rocket
रोकना **roknā** *v.t.* restrain
रोकथाम **rokthām** *n.f.* prevention
रोग **rog** *n.m.* disease
रोगहर **roghar** *adj.* therapeutic
रोगी **rogī** *adj.* queasy; *n.m.* patient
रोगमुक्ति **rogmukti** *n.f.* cure
रोज़गार **rozgār** *n.m.* employment
रोगाणु नष्ट करना **rogāṇu naṣṭ karnā** *v.t.* disinfect

रोगाणुनाशक **rogāṇunāśak** *n.m.* disinfectant
रोटी **roṭī** *n.f.* bread
रोध **rodh** *n.m.* resistance
रोना **ronā** *v.i.* cry, weep
रोमानी **romānī** *adj.* romantic
रोम-कूप **rom-kūp** *n.m.* pore
रोष **roṣ** *n.m.* rage
रोशन **rośan** *n.m.* light

ल

लँगड़ी चाल **laṁgaṛī cāl** *n.f.* limp
लँगड़ना **laṁgaṛnā** *v.t.* limp
लंगर **laṅgar** *n.m.* anchor
लंगर डालना **laṅgar ḍālnā** *v.i.* anchor
लंबा **lambā** *adj.* tall
लंबा करना **lambā karnā** *v.t.* lengthen
लंबा मोज़ा **lambā mozā** *n.* stocking
लंबाई **lambāī** *n.m.* length
लकड़ी **lakaṛī** *n.f.* wood, log
लकड़ी का बुरादा **lakaṛī kā burādā** *n.* sawdust
लकवा **lakvā** *n.m.* paralysis
लकवा मारना **lakvā mārnā** *v.i.* paralyze
लक्ष्य **lakṣya** *n.m.* goal
लक्षण **lakṣaṇ** *n.m.* symptom, characteristic
लगड़ा **lagṛā** *adj.* lame
लगना **lagnā** *v.i.* suspect
लगभग **lagbhag** *adv.* nearly, about, approximate
लगा रहना **lagā rahanā** *v.t.* persist
लगाम **lagām** *n.f.* mouthpiece
लगाना **lagānā** *v.t.* install, spread
लघु **laghu** *adj.* less

लघुपथ **laghupath** *n.* short
लचीली **lacīlī** *n.m.* wicker
लज्जित **lajjit** *adj.* ashamed
लज्जा **lajjā** *n.f.* shame
लज्जीदार **lajjīdār** *n.m.* lye
लट **laṭ** *n.f.* strand
लटकन **laṭkan** *n.f.* flap
लड़ाई **laṛāī** *n.f./v.t.* battle
लड़ाका **laṛākā** *adj.* militant
लड़का **laṛkā** *n.m.* boy
लड़की **laṛkī** *n.f.* girl
लड़ना **laṛnā** *v.t./v.i.* fight
लपक **lapak** *n.m.* radiance
लपसी **lapsī** *n.f.* poridge
लपेटन **lapeṭan** *n.* wrap
लपेटना **lapeṭnā** *v.t.* roll, wrap
लबलब **lablab** *n.m.* ivy
लम्ब **lamb** *adj.* perpendicular
लम्बा **lambā** *adj.* long
लम्बी दौड़ **lambī dauṛ** *n.f.* marathon
लट्ठा **laṭṭā** *n.m.* log
ललक **lalak** *n.f.* urge
ललकना **lalaknā** *v.i.* yearn
लहर **lahar** *n.f.* wave
लहराना **lahrānā** *v.t.* wave
लहसुन **lahsun** *n.m.* garlic
लांच **lānc** *n.m.* launch
लाइन **lāin** *n.m.* line
लाइनर **lāinar** *n.m.* liner
लाइसेंस **lāisens** *n.m.* license
लाउडस्पीकर **lāuḍspīkar** *n.m.* loudspeaker
लाकर **lākar** *n.m.* locker

लागत **lāgat** *n.m.* cost
लागत लगाना **lāgat lagānā** *v.t.* cost
लागू करना **lāgū karnā** *v.t.* implement
लागू होना **lāgū honā** *v.i.* apply
लाटरी **lāṭarī** *n.f.* raffle
लादना **lādnā** *v.t.* load
लाबी **lābī** *n.f.* lobby
लाभ **lābh** *n.m.* profit, gain
लाभ पहुँचाना **lābh pahũcānā** *v.t.* benefit
लाभदायक **lābhdāyak** *adj.* beneficial
लाना **lānā** *v.t.* bring
ला-परवाह **lā-parvāh** *adj.* careless
लाल **lāl** *adj.* red, inflamed
लाल मिर्च **lāl mirc** *n.f.* chili pepper
लाल वाइन **lāl vāin** *n.f.* red wine
लालटेन **lālṭen** *n.f.* lantern
लली **lalī** *n.f.* glow
लालपन **lālpan** *n.m.* redness
लावा **lāvā** *n.m.* popcorn
लाश **lāś** *n.f.* corpse
लिंग **liṅg** *n.m.* penis; sex
लिखकर जोड़ना **likhkar joṛnā** *v.t.* writing
लिखना **likhnā** *v.t.* write
लिफ़्ट **lifṭ** *n.f.* elevator
लिफ़ाफ़ा **lifāfā** *n.m.* envelope
लुटेरा **luṭerā** *n.m.* robber
लुभाना **lubhānā** *v.t.* tempt
लू लगना **lū lagnā** *v.t.* stroke
लू लगने का रोग **lū lagne kā rog** *n.m.* sunstroke
लूट **lūṭ** *n.f.* robbery
लूटना **lūṭnā** *v.t.* rob
ले जाना **le jānā** *v.t.* take

लेई **leī** *n.f.* paste
लेकिन **lekin** *conj.* but
लेख **lekh** *n.m.* article
लेखक **lekhak** *n.m.* writer
लेखन सामग्री **lekhan sāmagrī** *n.f.* stationery
लेख्य प्रमाणक **lekhya pramāṇak** *n.m.* notary
लेखा कार्या **lekhā kāryā** *n.m.* accounting
लेखाकार **lekhākār** *n.m.* accountant
ले चलना **le calnā** *v.t.* lead
ले जाना **le jānā** *v.i.* lead
लेज़र **lezar** *n.m.* laser
लेनदार **lendār** *n.m.* creditor
लेन-देन करना **len-den karnā** *v.t.* deal
लेन्स **lens** *n.m.* lens
लेबल **lebal** *n.m.* tag
लेबल लगाना **lebal lagānā** *v.t.* label
लैंगिकता **laiṅgiktā** *n.m.* sexuality
लैटिन **laiṭin** *n.f.* Latin
लैस करना **laus karnā** *v.t.* equip
लोई **loī** *n.f.* dough
लोकतांत्रिक **loktāntrik** *adj.* democratic
लोकतंत्र **loktantra** *n.m.* democracy
लोग **log** *n.m.* people
लोमड़ी **lomṛī** *n.f.* fox
लोहे का सामान **lohe kā sāmān** *n.m.* hardware
लौकिक **laukik** *adj.* secular
लौट **lauṭ** *n.f.* lapel
लौटना **lauṭnā** *v.t.* return; *n.m.* refund

व

वकील **vakīl** *n.m.* lawyer
वक्त **vakt** *n.m.* time
वक्रता **vakratā** *n.f.* curve
वग़ैरह **vaqgairah** *n.m.* etcetera
वर्ग **varg** *n.m.* square
वर्ग-बोली **varg-bolī** *n.f.* slang
वर्गाकार **vargākār** *adj.* square
वर्गीकरण करना **vargirkaraṇ karnā** *v.t.* classify
वचन देना **vacan denā** *v.t.* undertake
वर्जित **varjit** *adj.* forbidden
वज़न **vazan** *n.m.* weight
वर्तिका **vartikā** *n.f.* suppository
वन **van** *n.m.* forest
वनभोज **vanbhoj** *n.m.* picnic
वफ़ादार **vafādār** *adj.* loyal
वयस्क **vyask** *n.m.* adult
वर्णमाला **varṇamālā** *n.f.* alphabet
वर्णन **varṇan** *n.m.* description
वर्णन करना **varṇan karnā** *v.t.* narrate
वर्दी **vardī** *n.f.* uniform
वसंत **vasant** *n.m.* spring
वस्तु **vastu** *n.m.* object
वस्तुगत **vastugat** *adj.* objective
वस्तुत **vastut** *adj.* virtual
वश में करना **vaś meṁ karnā** *v.t.* control
वश में लाना **vaś meṁ lānā** *v.t.* subdue
वह **voh** *pron.* it, that
वहाँ **vahāṁ** *adv.* yonder
वही **vahī** *adj.* identical

वांछनीय **vāñcnīy** *adj.* desirable
वाइरस **vāiras** *n.m.* virus
वाउचर **vāucar** *n.m.* voucher
वाक्य **vākya** *n.m.* sentence
वाक्यांश **vākyānś** *n.m.* phrase
वाक्यविन्यास **vākyavinyās** *n.m.* syntax
वाट **vāṭ** *n.m.* watt
वाट-संख्या **vāṭ-saṅkyā** *n.m.* wattage
वाणिज्य **vāṇijy** *n.m.* commerce
वातावरण **vātāvaraṇ** *n.m.* environment
वाद **vād** *n.m.* lawsuit
वादक **vādak** *n.m.* player
वादा **vādā** *n.m.* promise
वादा करना **vādā karnā** *v.t.* promise
वादी **vādī** *n.m.* suitor
वाद्य-वृत **vādyā-vṛt** *n.m.* orchestra
वापस बुलाना **vāpas bulānā** *v.t.* recall
वापस रख देना **vāpas rakh denā** *v.t.* replace
वापस लेना **vāpas lenā** *v.t.* reimburse
वापसी **vāpsī** *n.m.* return
वापसी करना **vāpsī karnā** *v.t.* send
वायलिन **vāyalin** *n.f.* violin
वायवीय **vāyviy** *adj.* aerial
वायु **vāyu** *n.f.* air
वायु सेना **vāyu senā** *n.m.* air force
वायु सेवा **vāyu sevā** *n.m.* air service
वायुदाबमापी **vāyudābamāpī** *n.m.* barometer
वायुयान **vāyuyān** *n.m.* aviation
वारंट **vāranṭ** *n.m.* warrant
वारनिश **vārniś** *n.m.* varnish
वारनिश लगाना **vārniś lagānā** *v.t.* varnish
वारिस **vāris** *n.m.* heir

वार्ता **vārtā** *n.m.* negotiation
वार्षिक **varṣik** *adj.* yearly
वाल्व **vālv** *n.m.* valve
वाशर **vāśar** *n.m.* washer
वास्तव में **vāstav meṁ** *adv.* indeed, in fact
वास्तविक **vāstavik** *adj.* actual
वास्तविकता **vāstaviktā** *n.m.* reality
वास्तुकला **vāstukalā** *n.f.* architecture
वास्तुकार **vāstukār** *n.m.* architect
वास्तुशिल्पीय **vāstuśīlpīy** *adj.* architectural
वाहक **vāhak** *n.m.* transporter
वाहन **vahan** *n.m.* transport
वाइन **vāin** *n.f.* wine
वाष्पकण **vāṣpkaṇ** *n.m.* vapor
विकर्ण **vikarṇ** *adj.* diagonal
विकलांग **viklāng** *adj.* handicapped
विकसित करना **viksit karnā** *v.t.* develop
विकल्प **vikalp** *n.m.* option
विकास **vikās** *n.m.* development
विकिरक **vikirak** *n.m.* radiator
विकृत करना **vikr̥t karnā** *v.t.* distort
विघटनाभिक **vighṭanābhik** *adj.* radioactive
विचलन **vicalan** *n.m.* deviation
विचार **vicār** *n.m.* thought
विचार करना **vicār karnā** *v.t.* consider
विचार-विमर्श **vicār-vimarś** *n.m.* discussion
विचारण **vicāraṇ** *n.m.* trial
विच्छेद **vicched** *n.m.* separation
विच्छेदन **vicchedan** *n.m.* amputation
विजय **vijay** *n.f.* win
विजय पाना **vijay pānā** *v.t.* conquer
विजेता **vijetā** *n.m.* winner

विटामिन **viṭāmin** *n.m.* vitamin
वितरण **vitaraṇ** *n.m.* distribution
वितरण करना **vitaraṇ karnā** *v.t.* distribute
विद्यालय **vidyālay** *n.m.* school
विद्यार्थी **vidyārthī** *n.m.* student
विधुत धारा **vidhut dhārā** *n.f.* current
विधवा **vidhvā** *n.f.* widow
विधुर **vidhur** *n.m.* widower
विध्न-डालना **vidhn-ḍālnā** *v.t.* hinder
विरूद्ध **virūddh** *adj.* contrary
विद्रोह **vidroh** *n.m.* revolt
विद्रोह करना **vidroh karnā** *v.i.* rebel
विदेश **videś** *adv.* abroad, overseas
विदेशी **videśī** *adj.* foreigner
विदेशी **vedeśī** *n.m.* alien
विदेशी भीति **vedeśī bhīti** *n.m.* xenophobia
विदूषक **vidūṣak** *n.m.* clown
विधिसम्मत **vidhisammat** *adj.* lawful
विनाश **vināś** *n.m.* disaster, ruin
विनिमय **vinimay** *n.m.* exchange
विनीत **vinīt** *adj.* humble
विनोदी **vinodī** *adj.* witty
विपणन **vipṇan** *n.m.* marketing
विपत्ति **vipatti** *n.f.* distress
विभाग **vibhāg** *n.m.* department
विभाजन **vibhājan** *n.m.* partition
विभिन्न रूप **vibhinn rūp** *n.m.* variation
विमान **vimān** *n.m.* jet
विमानशाला **vimānśālā** *n.m.* hangar
विरल **viral** *adj.* rare
विरले ही **virale hī** *adv.* seldom
विराम **virām** *n.m.* pause

विरामचिन्ह लगाना **virāmcinh lagānā** *v.t.* punctuate
विरामचिन्ह-विधान **virāmcinh-vidhān** *n.m.* punctuation
विरोध **virodh** *n.m.* opposition
विरोध करना **virodh karnā** *v.t.* oppose, resist, object
विरोधी **virodhī** *adj.* resistant
विलाप **vilāp** *n.m.* wait
विलायक **vilāyak** *n.m.* solvent
विलास **vilās** *n.m.* pleasure
विलासी **vilāsī** *adj.* luxurious
विलेप **vilep** *n.m.* ointment
विवाद **vivād** *n.m.* dispute
विवाहित **vivāhit** *adj.* married
विवेक **vivek** *n.m.* wisdom
विवेकी **vivekī** *adj.* scrupulous
विवेकशील **vivekśīl** *adj.* rational
विशद **viśad** *adj.* vivid
विशाल **viśāl** *adj.* immense
विशुध्द **viśudhd** *adj.* neat
विशेष **viśeṣ** *adj.* special, particular
विशेषण **viśeśaṇ** *n.m.* adjective
विशेषता **viśeṣtā** *n.f.* trait; *adj.* characteristic
विशेषज्ञ **viseṣagy** *n.m.* specialist
विशेषाधिकार **viśeṣādhikār** *n.m.* privilege
विश्लेषण **viśleṣaṇ** *n.m.* analysis
विश्लेषण करना **viśleṣaṇ karnā** *v.t.* analyze
विश्व **viśva** *n.m.* universe
विश्वकोश **viśvakoś** *n.m.* encyclopedia
विश्वविद्यालय **viśvavdyālay** *n.m.* university
विश्वव्यापी **viśvavyāpī** *adj.* worldwide
विश्व-संबंधी **viśv-sambandhī** *adj.* global
विश्वसनीय **viśvāsnīy** *adj.* faithful
विश्वास **viśvās** *n.m.* faith, trust

विश्वासघात करना **viśvāsghāt karnā** *v.t.* betray
विश्वासघाती **viśvāsghātī** *n.f.* traitor
विश्वास करना **viśvās karnā** *v.t.* believe, trust
विश्वास दिलाना **viśvās dilānā** *v.t.* assure
विश्राम-कक्ष **viśrām-kakṣa** *n.m.* lounge
विषमता **viṣamtā** *n.m.* contrast
विषय **viṣay** *n.m.* subject
विषयवस्तु **viṣayvastu** *n.f.* content
विषयक्षेत्र **viṣaykṣetra** *n.m.* scope
विषाक्त **viśākt** *n.m.* septic
विषाणु **viṣāṇu** *adj.* viral
विषाक्त हो जाना **viṣākt ho jānā** *adj.* septic
विषुवत रेखा **viṣukt rekhā** *n.f.* equator
विस्तार **vistār** *n.m.* extension
विस्तार देना **vistār denā** *v.t.* amplify
विस्मयकारी **vismaykārī** *adj.* amazing
विज्ञान **vigyān** *n.m.* science
विज्ञापन **vigyāpan** *n.m.* commercial
विज्ञापन करना **vigyāpan karnā** *v.t.* advertise
वीज़ा **vīzā** *n.m.* visa
वीणा **vīṇā** *n.f.* harp
वीर **vīr** *n.m.* hero; arrow
विरोचित **virocit** *adj.* heroic
वे **ve** *pron.* those
वेचैन **vecain** *adj.* impatient
वेदना **vednā** *n.m.* anguish
वेदी **vedī** *n.f.* altar
वेधशाला **vedhśālā** *n.f.* observatory
वेष्टन **veṣṭan** *n.m.* wrapper
वेबसाईट **vebsāīṭ** *n.m.* website
वेष **veś** *n.m.* disguise
वैकल्पिक **vaikalpik** *adj.* optional

वैज्ञानिक **vaigyānik** *n.m.* scientist
वैद्य **vaidy** *n.m.* physician
वैध **vaidh** *adj.* legitimate
वैधता **vaidhtā** *n.m.* legality
वैनिला **vainilā** *n.m.* vanilla
वैसा ही **vaisā hī** *adj.* as, same
वोट देना **voṭ denā** *n.m./v.i.* vote
वोल्ट **volṭ** *n.m.* volt
वोल्टता **volṭtā** *n.f.* voltage
व्यक्ति **vyakti** *n.m.* person, individual
व्यक्तिगत **vyaktigat** *adj.* individual, personal, private
व्यक्तित्व **vyaktitva** *n.m.* personality, individuality
व्याकरण **vyākaraṇ** *n.m.* grammar
व्याख्या **vyākhyā** *n.f.* explanation
व्याख्यान **vyākhyān** *n.m.* lecture
व्यग्य **vyagy** *n.m.* irony
व्यंग्यात्मक **vyangyātmak** *adj.* ironic
व्यंजन **vyañjan** *n.m.* consonant
व्यवहार **vyavyahār** *n.m.* treatment
व्यवहारक्षकौशल **vyavahārkṣkauśal** *n.m.* tact
व्यवहारकुशल **vyavahārkuśal** *adj.* tactful
व्यवस्थित **vyavasthit** *adj.* systematic
व्यवस्थित करना **vyavasthit karnā** *v.t.* arrange
व्यवसाय **vyavasāy** *n.m.* profession
व्यस्त **vyast** *adj.* busy
व्यापक **vyāpak** *adj.* widespread
व्यापार **vyāpār** *n.m.* business, trade
व्यापार करना **vyāpār karnā** *v.t.* trade
व्यापारी **vyāpārī** *n.m.* merchant
व्यापारी माल **vyāpārī māl** *n.m.* merchandise
व्यायामशाला **vyāyāmśālā** *n.m.* gymnasium
व्यायामी **vyāyāmī** *n.m.* athlete

व्यावसायिक **vyāvasāyik** *adj.* professional
व्यावहारिक **vyāvahārik** *adv.* practically
व्यास **vyās** *n.m.* diameter
व्रत **vrat** *n.m.* fast; vow
व्रत लेना **vrat lenā** *v.t.* vow

श

शंकु **śaṅku** *n.m.* cone
शक्ति **śakti** *n.m.* power, energy
शक्तिशाली **śaktiśālī** *adj.* powerful
शटल गाड़ी **śaṭal gāṛī** *n.m.* shuttle
शताब्दी **śatābdī** *n.f.* century
शतावरी **śatāvarī** *n.m.* strawberry
शतपद **śatpad** *n.m.* centipede
शत्रिक **śāstrik** *n.m.* jellyfish
शनिवार **śanivār** *n.m.* Saturday
शपथ **śapath** *n.f.* oath
शब्द **śabd** *n.m.* word
शब्दकोश **śabdkoś** *n.m.* dictionary
शब्दावली **śabdāvalī** *n.f.* vocabulary
शम्बूक **śambūk** *n.m.* scallop
शरण **śaraṇ** *n.f.* refuge, shelter
शरणार्थी **śarṇārthī** *n.m.* refugee
शरण-स्थान **śaraṇ-sthān** *n.m.* sanctuary
शरद **śarad** *n.f.* autumn
शराब **śarāb** *n.m.* liquor
शराब पीने से सरदर्द **śarāb pīne se sardard** *n.* hangover
शराबी **śarābi** *n.m.* alcoholic
शरीर **śarīr** *n.m.* body
शर्त **śart** *n.m.* bet
शर्त लगाना **śart lagānā** *v.t.* bet

शतरंज **śataranj** *n.m.* chess
शव-कक्ष **śav-kakṣ** *n.m.* vault
शव-परीक्षा **śav-parīkṣā** *n.f.* autopsy
शल्यचिकित्सा **śalycikitsā** *n.f.* surgery
शस्त्र **śāstra** *n.m.* weapon
शहर **śahar** *n.m.* city
शाकाहारी **śākākārī** *n.m./adj.* vegetarian
शादी **śādī** *n.f.* marriage
शादी करना **śādī karnā** *v.t.* marry
शानदार **śāndār** *adj.* magnificent
शान्त **śānt** *adj.* sedated
शान्ति **śānti** *n.f.* peace
शान्तिपूर्ण **śāntipūrṇ** *adj.* peaceful
शाप **śāp** *n.m.* curse
शाप देना **śāp denā** *v.t.* curse
शाबासी **śābāsī** *n.f.* applause
शाब्दिक **śābdik** *adj.* verbal
शाम **śām** *n.f.* evening
शामिल करना **śāmil karnā** *v.t.* include
शायद **śāyad** *adv.* perhaps
शायिका **śāyikā** *n.m.* sleeping
शारीरिक **śārīrik** *adj.* physical
शाल **śāl** *n.f.* shawl
शावर **śāvar** *n.m.* shower
शासन **śāsan** *n.m.* regime, administration
शासन करना **śāsan karnā** *v.t.* rule, govern
शासनपत्र **śāsanpatra** *n.m.* charter
शास्त्रीय **śāstrīy** *adj.* classical
शाही **śāhī** *adj.* royal
शिकार **śikār** *n.m.* victim
शिकारी **śikārī** *n.m.* hunter
शिकायत **śikāyat** *n.f.* grievance

शिकायत करना **śikāyat karnā** *v.i.* complain
शिक्षा **śikṣā** *n.m.* education
शिक्षा देना **śikṣā denā** *v.t.* instruct
शिक्षा-संबन्ध **śikṣā-sambandh** *adj.* educational
शिक्षक **śikṣak** *n.m.* schoolteacher
शिखा **śikhā** *n.f.* crest
शिरा **śirā** *n.f.* vein, vessel
शिल्प **śilp** *n.m.* handicraft
शिल्पी **śilpī** *n.m.* craftsman
शिल्पकृति **śilpkṛti** *n.f.* artifact
शिविर **śivir** *n.m.* camp
शिविर डालना **śivir ḍālnā** *v.i.* camp
शिष्ट **śiṣṭ** *adj.* polite
शिष्टाचार **śiṣṭācār** *n.m.* courtesy
शिष्टमंडल **śiṣṭmaṇḍal** *n.m.* mission
शीतदंश **śītadanś** *n.m.* frostbite
शीतल **śītal** *adj.* cool
शीशा **śīśā** *n.m.* glass
शीशी **śīsī** *n.f.* vial
शीर्षक **śīrṣak** *n.m.* headline
शुक्रवार **śukravār** *n.m.* Friday
शुक्रिया **śukriyā** *interj.* (*informal*) thanks
शुद्ध **śuddh** *adj.* pure
शुद्ध करना **śuddh karnā** *v.t.* purify
शुद्धिकरण **śuddhikaraṇ** *n.* purification
शुद्ध करना **śuddh karnā** *v.t.* refine
शुरू होना **śurū honā** *v.i.* commence
शुरू करना **śurū karnā** *v.i.* begin
शुभ **śubh** *adj.* auspicious, lucky
शुल्क **śulk** *n.m.* fee
शून्य **śūnya** *num./adj.* zero, void
शून्य स्थान **śūnya sthān** *n.m.* vacuum

शूरवीर **śūrvīr** *adj.* valiant
शेर **śer** *n.m.* tiger
शेयर दलाल **śeyar dalāl** *n.m.* stockbroker
शेयर बाज़ार **śeyar bāzār** *n.m.* stock market
शेष रह जाना **śeṣ reh jānā** *v.i.* remain
शैंपू **śaiṁpū** *n.m.* shampoo
शैतान **śaitān** *n.m.* devil
शैली **śailī** *n.f.* style
शोक मनाना **śok manānā** *v.t.* mourn
शोध **śodh** *n.m.* research
शोध करना **śodh karnā** *v.t.* research
शोध-प्रबन्ध **śodh-prabandh** *n.m.* thesis
शोर **śor** *n.m.* noise
शोरबा **śorbā** *n.m.* soup, broth
शोष **śoṣ** *n.m.* sequel
शौचालय **saucālay** *n.m.* latrine
शौक **śauk** *n.m.* hobby
शौकीन **śaukīn** *adj.* fashionable
श्रेणी **śreṇī** *n.m.* grade
श्रोता **śrotā** *n.m.* listener
श्रोतागण **śrotāgaṇ** *n.m.* audience
श्रुतलेख **śrutlekh** *n.m.* dictation
श्रद्धांजलि **śraddhānjali** *n.m.* tribute
श्रम **śram** *n.m.* labor
श्रमिक संघ **śramik saṅgh** *n.m.* union
श्रवण **śravaṇ** *n.m.* hearing
श्रीमती **śrīmatī** *n.f.* Mrs.
श्रीमान **śrīmān** *n.m.* mister, sir
श्रोणी **śroṇī** *n.f.* pelvis
श्रवण **ṣravaṇ** *adj.* auditory
श्वासनली-शोथ **śvāsnalī-śoth** *n.m.* bronchitis
श्वासनली **śvāsnalī** *n.f.* trachea

श्वासयंत्र **śvasyantra** *n.m.* respirator
श्वास निकालना **śvās nikālnā** *v.i.* exhale

ष

षडयंत्र **ṣaḍyantra** *n.m.* plot
षडयंत्र रचना **ṣaḍyantra racanā** *v.t.* plot

स

साँस खींचना **saṁs khīncnā** *v.t.* inhale
संकेत **saṅket** *n.m.* signal, crisis
संकल्प **sannkalp** *n.m.* determination
संकोचक **sankocak** *adj.* astringent
संकोची **saṅkocī** *adj.* shy
संक्रमित करना **sankramit karnā** *v.t.* infect
संकेत **sanket** *n.m.* hint
संकेत करना **sanket karnā** *v.i.* hint
संकेतक **sanketak** *n.m.* indicator
संबंध **sambandh** *v.t.* link
संबोधित करना **sambodhit karnā** *v.t.* direct
संक्षिपण **saṅkṣepaṇ** *n.m.* abbreviation
संक्षेप **saṅkṣep** *n.m.* résumé; summary
संक्षिप्त **saṅkṣipt** *adj.* concise
संक्षिप्त करना **saṅkṣipt karnā** *v.t.* abbreviate
संख्या **sankhyā** *n.m.* number
संगठन **saṅgaṭhan** *n.m.* organization
संगठित करना **sangaṭhit karnā** *v.t.* organize
संगत **sangat** *adj.* compatible
संगम **sangam** *n.m.* junction
संगमरमर **saṅgmarmar** *n.m.* marble
संगरोध **sangrodh** *n.m.* quarantine

संगति **saṅgati** *n.f.* companionship
संगीतकार **sangītkār** *n.m.* musician
संगीत समारोह **sangīt samāroh** *n.m.* concert
संग्रह करना **saṅgrah karnā** *v.t.* store
संग्रह क्रिया **saṅgrah kriyā** *n.m.* collection
संग्रहण **saṅgrahaṇ** *n.m.* storage
संग्राहलय **saṅgrāhalay** *n.m.* museum
संघ **saṅgha** *n.m.* union
संघर्ष **saṅgharṣ** *n.m.* struggle
संचालक **sañcālak** *n.m.* conductor, operator
संचालन **sañcālan** *n.m.* navigation
संचालन करना **sañcālan karnā** *v.t.* guide, conduct
संत **sant** *n.m.* saint
संतुष्ट **santuṣṭ** *adj.* satisfied
संतोष **santoṣ** *n.m.* satisfaction
संतोषजनक **santoṣjanak** *adj.* satisfactory
संत्रास **santrās** *n.m.* horror
संदर्श **sandarś** *n.m.* perspective
संदूषण **sandūṣaṇ** *n.m.* infection
संदेश **sandeś** *n.m.* errand
संदर्शिका **sandarśikā** *n.m.* guidebook
संदेहजनक **sandehjanak** *adj.* suspicious
संदेह **sandeh** *n.m.* doubt
संदेह करना **sandeh karnā** *v.t.* doubt
संदेहहर **sandehahar** *n.m.* messenger
संधि **sandhi** *n.f.* treaty
संज्ञा **sañgyā** *n.m.* noun
संपर्क **sampark** *n.m.* liaison
संपर्क **sparś** *n.m./v.t.* contact
संपत्ति **sampatti** *n.f.* property
संपादन करना **sampādan karnā** *v.t.* edit
संपूर्ण **sanpūrṇ** *adj.* perfect

संबंध **sambandh** *n.m.* reference
संबंध करना **sambandh karnā** *v.t.* associate
संबंध होना **sambandh honā** *v.t.* relate, concern
संभव **sambhav** *adj.* possible
संभावना **sambhāvnā** *n.m.* possibility
संयुक्त राष्ट्र **sanyukt rāṣṭra** *n.m.* United Nations
संयोग **sanyog** *n.m.* combination
संयोजन **sanyojan** *n.m.* addition
संयमी **sanyamī** *adj.* temperate
संरचना **sanracanā** *n.f.* structure
संरक्षण **sanrakṣaṇ** *n.m.* conservation
संरक्षक **sanrakṣak** *n.m.* patron
संवाद **sanvād** *n.m.* dialogue
संवाददाता **samvāddātā** *n.m.* reporter
संवाददाता सम्मेलन **sanvāddātā sammelan** *n.* press
संविधान **sanvihān** *n.m.* constitution
संवेदना **sanvednā** *n.m.* condolence
संवेदनात्मक **sanvedanātmak** *n.m.* narcotic
संशोधन **sanśodhan** *n.m.* amendment
संश्लिष्ट **sanśliṣṭ** *adj.* synthetic
संसद **sansad** *n.f.* parliament
संसदीय **sansadīy** *adj.* parliamentary
संसार **sansār** *n.m.* world
संस्कार **sanskār** *n.m.* ceremony, rite
संस्करण **sanskaraṇ** *n.m.* edition
संस्था **saṅsthā** *n.f.* association
संस्थान **sansthān** *n.m.* institute
संस्थापक **sansthāpak** *n.m.* founder
संस्मरण **sansmaraṇ** *n.m.* memoir
सकना **saknā** *v.aux.* can, be able to
सकारात्मक **sakārātmak** *adj.* positive
सक्रिय **sakriy** *adj.* active

सघन **saghan** *adj.* dense
सघनता **saghantā** *n.f.* density
सचमुच **sacmuch** *adv.* truly
सचित्र करना **sacitra karnā** *v.t.* illustrate
सच्चा **saccā** *adj.* earnest
सच्चाई **saccāī** *n.f.* truth, fact
सज़ा **sazā** *n.m.* punishment
सर्जन **sarjan** *n.m.* surgeon
सजाना **sajānā** *v.t.* decorate
सजावट **sajāvaṭ** *n.f.* decoration
सज्जन **sajjan** *n.m.* gentleman
सड़क **saṛak** *n.f.* road, street
सड़ना **saṛnā** *v.i.* rot, decay
सड़ा **saṛā** *adj.* rotten
सतह **satah** *n.f.* surface
सतही **sathī** *adj.* superficial
सतर्क **satark** *adj.* watchful
सताना **satānā** *v.t.* pester
सत्कारशील **satkārśīl** *adj.* hospitable
सत्तर **sattar** *num.* seventy
सत्यानाश **satyānāś** *n.m.* wreck
सत्यापन **satyāpan** *n.m.* verification
सत्यवादी **satyavādī** *adj.* truthful
समुद्र पार **samudra pār** *adv.* overseas
सत्र **satra** *n.m.* session
सत्रह **satrah** *num.* seventeen
सत्रहवाँ **satrahvāṁ** *adj.* seventeenth
सदस्य **sadsya** *n.m.* member
सादा **sādā** *n.m.* plain
सदा के लिये **sadā ke liye** *adv.* forever
सन **san** *n.m.* linen
सनक **sanak** *n.f.* fad

सन्त पिता **sant pitā** *n.m.* pope
सन्तान **santān** *n.m.* posterity
सन्तरा **santarā** *n.m.* orange
सन्निवेश **sanniveś** *n.m.* insert
सपना **sapnā** *n.m.* dream
सर्पमीन **sarpmīn** *n.m.* eel
सप्ताहांत **saptāhānt** *n.m.* weekend
सप्लाई **saplāī** *n.m.* supply
सप्लाई करना **saplāi karnā** *v.t.* supply
सफलता **saphaltā** *n.f.* success
सफलतापूर्वक **saphaltāpūrvak** *n.m.* accomplishment
सफलतापूर्वक पूरा करना **saphaltāpūrvak pūrā karnā** *v.t.* accomplish
सफ़ाई **safāī** *n.f.* plea
सफ़ाई का **safāī kā** *adj.* sanitary
सफ़ेद **safed** *adj.* white
सफ़ेद करना **safed karnā** *v.t.* whiten
सष **sab** *n.m.* all
सब कुछ **sab kuch** *pron.* everything
सब जगह **sab jagah** *adv.* everywhere
सबसे अच्छा **sabse acchā** *adj.* best
सबसे अधिक **sabse adhik** *adj.* top
सबसे ख़राब **sabse qharāb** *adj./adv.* worst
सबसे बुरा **sabse burā** *n.m.* worst
सबूत **sabūt** *n.m.* proof
सब्ज़ी **sabzī** *n.f.* vegetable
सब्से उपरला **sabse uparlā** *n.m.* top
सभा **sabhā** *n.f.* assembly, club
सभ्यता **sabhyatā** *n.m.* civilization
समाई **samāī** *n.f.* capacity
समकक्ष बनाना **samkakṣ banānā** *v.t.* coordinate
समझदार **samajhdār** *n.m.* understanding

समझना samajhnā *v.t.* understand
समझौता samjhautā *n.m.* agreement, settlement, treaty, compromise
समतल samtal *adj.* smooth
समर्पण samarpaṇ *n.m.* dedication
समर्पण करना samarpaṇ karnā *v.t.* dedicate
समर्थ samarth *adj.* competent
समर्थक samarthak *n.m.* supporter
समलैंगी samlaingī *n.m.* homosexual
सम्मान sammān *n.m.* regard
सम्मोहन sammohan *n.m.* fascination
सम्पादित करना sampādit karnā *v.t.* achieve
समय samay *n.m.* time
समय सारिणी samay sāriṇī *n.f.* timetable
समय से पहले samay se pahale *n.m.* early
समलैंगिक samalaiṅgik *adj.* gay
समस्या samasyā *n.f.* problem
समाचार samāchār *n.m.* news
समाचारपत्र samācārpatr *n.m.* newspaper
समाज samāj *n.m.* association
समाजवाद samājvād *n.m.* socialism
समाजवादी samājvādī *n.m.* socialist
समान samān *adj.* alike, equal
समान बनाना samān banānā *v.t.* equal
सामान रखना sāmān rakhnā *v.t.* stock
समानता samāntā *n.f.* similarity
समाप्त करना samāpt karnā *v.t.* consume
समाप्त हो जाना samāpt ho jāna *v.i.* terminate
समारोह samāroh *n.m.* function
समांतर samāntar *adj.* parallel
समायोजित करना samāyojit karnā *v.t.* adjust
समाविष्ट करना samāviṣṭ karnā *v.t.* comprise

सम्राट **samrāṭ** *n.m.* emphasis
समिति **samiti** *n.f.* committee
सम्मिलित करना **sammilit karnā** *v.t.* assimilate
समीक्षा **samīkṣā** *n.f.* review
समृद्ध **samṛaddh** *adj.* prosperous
समृद्धि **samṛddhi** *n.m.* prosperity
समुद्र **samudra** *n.m.* sea
समुद्र जल **samudra jal** *n.m.* seawater
समुद्रत्र तट **samudra taṭ** *n.m.* seacoast
समुद्र-पत्तन **samudra-pattan** *n.m.* seaport
समुद्री **samudrī** *adj.* marine
समुद्री चट्टान **samudrī caṭṭān** *n.f.* reef
समुद्री झींगा **samudrī jhīngā** *n.m.* lobster
समुद्री डाकू **samudrī ḍākū** *n.m.* pirate
समुद्री मछली **samudrī machlī** *n.f.* seafood
समुद्री यात्रा करना **samudrī yātrā karnā** *v.t.* navigate
समुद्री लहरें **samudri laharem̐** *n.f.* surf
समुद्री शैवाल **samudrī śaivāl** *n.f.* seaweed
समूह **samūh** *n.m.* group
सफ़ेद वाइन **safed vāin** *n.f.* white wine
सरकार **sarkār** *n.m.* government
सरकन **sarkan** *n.m.* slide
सरकस **sarkas** *n.m.* circus
सरल **saral** *adj.* simple
सरल बना देना **saral banā denā** *v.t.* simplify
सरल बनाना **saral banānā** *v.t.* facilitate
सरसों **sarsom̐** *n.f.* mustard
सरसरी नज़र **sarsarī nazar** *n.m./v.i.* glance
सराहना **sarāhnā** *v.t.* appreciate
सराय **sarāy** *n.f.* inn
सरेस **sares** *n.m.* glue

सरेस लगाना **sares lagānā** *v.t.* glue
सर्वस त्मक **sarvasttātmak** *adj.* totalitarian
सर्वसम्मति **sarvsammati** *adj.* universal
सपिलाकार **sapilākār** *adj.* spiral
सलाद **salād** *n.m.* salad
सलाद का मसाला **salād kā masālā** *n.m.* mayonnaise
सलाद पत्ता **salād pattā** *n.m.* lettuce
सलाह **salāh** *n.f.* advice
सलाहकार **salāhkār** *n.m.* adviser
सलाह देना **salā denā** *v.t.* advise
सवा घंटा **savā ghaṇṭā** *n.m.* quarter
सवार **savār** *n.m.* rider
सवारी करने की सैर **savārī karnē kī sair** *n.f.* ride
सवाल **savāl** *n.m.* question
सवाल करना **savāl karnā** *v.t.* question
सवेरा **saverā** *n.m.* morning
सर्वतोमुखी **sarvatomukhī** *adj.* versatile
सर्वनाम **sarvanām** *n.m.* pronoun
ससुर **sasur** *n.m.* father-in-law
ससुराल **sasurāl** *n.m.* in-laws' home
सस्ता **sastā** *adj.* inexpensive
सहज **sahaj** *adj.* feasible
सहनशीलता **sahanśīltā** *n.f.* tolerance
सहना **sahnā** *v.i.* endure
सहपाठी **sahpāṭhī** *n.* schoolmate
सहमति **sahmati** *n.f.* consent
सहमत होना **sahamat honā** *v.t.* agree
सहयोग **sahyog** *n.m.* collaboration
सहयोग देना **sahyog denā** *v.t.* contribute
सहयोग करना **sahyog karnā** *v.i.* cooperate
सहयोगी **sahayogī** *n.m.* associate
सहराज्य **sahrājy** *n.m.* condominium

सहलाना **sahlānā** *n.m.* stroke
सहानुभूति जताना **sahānubhūti jatānā** *v.i.* sympathize
सहारा **sahāra** *n.m.* support
सहारा देना **sahārā denā** *v.t.* support
सहायक **sahāyak** *n.m.* lieutenant
सहायता **sahāyatā** *n.f.* assistance, aid
सहायता देना **sahāyatā denā** *v.t.* aid, accommodate
सहायता करना **sahāyatā karnā** *v.t.* assist
सही **sahī** *adj.* true
सर्वतत्र **sarvatatra** *adj.* all over
सांविधिक **sānvidhik** *adj.* statutory
सांस्कृति **sanskṛti** *n.m.* culture
सांस्कृतिक **sanskṛtik** *adj.* cultural
साँचा **sāṁcā** *n.m.* cast
साँप **sāṁp** *n.m.* snake
साँस लेने की नली **sāṁs lene kī nalī** *n.f.* snorkel
साइकिल **sāikil** *n.m.* cycle
साइकिल चलाना **sāikil calānā** *v.t.* cycle
साइडर **sāiḍar** *n.m.* cider
साकेट **sākeṭ** *n.m.* socket
साक्षय **sākṣya** *n.m.* testimony
साज़ **sāz** *n.m.* harness
साज़-सामान **sāz-sāmān** *n.m.* equipment
साठ **sāṭh** *num.* sixty
सार्डीन **sārḍīn** *n.m.* sardine
सात **sāt** *num.* seven
सातवाँ **sātvāṁ** *adj.* seventh
साथ काम करना **sāth kām karnā** *v.i.* collaborate
साथ साथ **sāth sāth** *adv.* accompany
साथी **sāthī** *n.m.* mate
सादगी से **sādgī se** *adv.* simply
सादृश्य **sādṛśya** *n.m.* analogy, resemblance

साधारण **sādhāraṇ** *adj.* usual, regular
साफ़ **sāf** *adj.* clean
साबुन **sābūn** *n.m.* soap
सामाजिक **sāmājik** *adj.* social
सामान **sāmān** *n.m.* luggage
सामान निकालना **sāmān nikālnā** *v.t.* unpack
सामान्य **sāmānya** *adj.* normal
सामान्यत: **sāmānyatah** *adv.* generally
साम्राज्य **sāmrājya** *n.m.* empire
सामग्री **sāmgrī** *n.f.* stuff
सामना करना **sāmnā karnā** *v.t.* withstand
सामने आना **sāmne ānā** *v.t.* against
सामने का **sāmne kā** *adj.* front; *n.m./adj.* opposite
सामंत **sāmant** *n.m.* knight
सामुद्रिक **sāmudrik** *n.m.* seagull
साम्यवाद **sanyavād** *n.m.* communism
साम्यवादी **sāmyavādī** *n.f.* communist
साया **sāyā** *n.m.* phantom
सार **sār** *n.m.* essence
सारजेंट **sārjenṭ** *n.m.* sergeant
सारस **sāras** *n.m.* crane
साल **sāl** *n.m.* year
साला **sālā** *n.m.* brother-in-law (*wife's brother*)
साली **sālī** *n.f.* sister-in-law (*wife's sister*)
सावधान **sāvdhān** *adj.* careful
सावधानी **sāvdhānī** *n.m.* caution
सावधानी से जाइये **sāvdhānī se** *adv.* carefully, with caution
सार्वजनिक **sārvjanik** *adj.* public
सास **sās** *n.m.* mother-in-law
साहस **sāhas** *n.m.* courage; dare
साहस करना **sāhas karnā** *v.t.* dare
साहसिक **sāhasik** *adj.* daring

साहित्य **sāhity** *n.m.* literature
साहित्यिक **sāhityik** *adj.* literary
साहूकार **sāhūgkār** *n.m.* banker
सिंचाई **siñcāī** *n.f.* irrigation
सिंडर **sinḍar** *n.m.* cinder
सिंदूरी **sindūrī** *adj.* scarlet
सिंह **sinha** *n.m.* lion
सिहासन **sihāsan** *n.m.* throne
सिकुड़ना **sikuṛnā** *v.t.* shrink
सिकुड़ाना **sikuṛānā** *v.i.* shrink
सिक्का **sikkā** *n.m.* coin
सिखाना **sikhānā** *v.t.* teach
सिगार **sigār** *n.f.* cigar
सिगरेट **sigareṭ** *n.f.* cigarette
सिग्रेट पीना **sigreṭ pīnā** *v.t.* smoke
सिझाना **sijhānā** *v.t.* tan
सिझाया हुआ चमड़ा **sijhāyā huā camaṛā** *n.m.* suede
सिटकिनी **siṭkinī** *n.f.* latch
सितंबर **sitambar** *n.m.* September
सिद्धांत **siddhānt** *n.m.* principle, theory
सिद्धांतसंबंधी **siddhāntsambandhī** *adj.* theoretical
सिनेमा **sinemā** *n.m.* cinema
सिपाही **sipāhī** *n.m.* soldier
सिर्फ़ **sirf** *adv.* only
सिफ़ारिश **sifāriś** *n.m.* recommendation
सिफ़ारिश करना **sifāriś karnā** *v.t.* recommend
सिमसिमाना **sigsimānā** *v.i.* simmer
सिम्फ़नी **simfanī** *n.f.* symphony
सिर **sir** *n.m.* head
सिर चढ़ाना **sir caṛhānā** *v.t.* spoil
सिरका **sirkā** *n.m.* vinegar
सिरप **sirap** *n.m.* syrup

सिर्फ़ **siraf** *adj.* only
सिर्फ़ **sirf** *adv.* just
सिलसिला **silsilā** *n.m.pl.* series
सिलाई **silāī** *n.f.* sewing
सिलाई की मशीन **silāi kī maśīn** *n.f.* sewing machine
सिलाई करना **silāī karnā** *n.* tailor
सिसकना **sisaknā** *v.i.* sob
सींग **siṅg** *n.m.* horn
सींचना **sīñcnā** *v.t.* irrigate
सीख **sīkh** *n.f.* moral
सीखना **sīkhnā** *v.t.* learn
सीटी **sīṭī** *n.f.* whistle
सीटी बजाना **sīṭī bajānā** *v.t.* whistle
सीगड़ा **sīgṛā** *n.m.* shoehorn
सीढ़ी **sīṛhī** *n.f.* stair
सीढ़ियाँ **sīṛhiyāṁ** *n.f.* staircase
सीध मिलाना **sīdh milānā** *v.t.* align
सीधा **sīdhā** *adj.* direct, straight
सीनेटर **sījneṭar** *n.m.* senator
सीने वाला **sīnen vālā** *n.m.* sewer
सीने की सुई **sīne kī suī** *n.f.* sewing needle
सीप **sīp** *n.f.* oyster
सीमा **sīmā** *n.f.* limit
सीमा शुल्क **sīmā śulk** *n.m.* tariff
सीमित करना **sīmit karnā** *v.t.* restrict
सीमेंट **sīmenṭ** *n.m.* cement
सीरम **sīram** *n.m.* serum
सील मछली **sīl machlī** *n.m.* seal
सीवन **sīvan** *n.f.* seam
सीसा **sīsā** *n.m.* lead
सुंदर **sundar** *adj.* beautiful
सुअर का मांस **sūar kā māṁs** *n.m.* bacon

सुअर की चरबी **suar kī carbī** *n.f.* lard
सुख **sukh** *n.m.* enjoyment
सुखकर **sukhkar** *adj.* pleasant
सुखाने वाला यंत्र **sukhāne vālā yantra** *n.m.* dryer
सुखान्त **sukhānt** *n.m.* comedy
सुगन्ध **sugandh** *n.f.* perfume
सुझाव देना **sujhāu denā** *v.t.* suggest
सुन्दर **sundar** *adj.* pretty
सुन्दरता **sundartā** *n.f.* beauty
सुधार **sudhār** *n.m.* reclamation
सुधारना **sudhārnā** *v.t.* improve
सुधार होना **sudhār honā** *v.i.* improve
सुनवाई **sunvāī** *n.f.* hearing
सुनहला **sunhalā** *adj.* gilt
सुनना **sunnā** *v.t.* hear
सुनाना **sunānā** *v.t.* relate
सुन्न **sunn** *adj.* numb
सुपरबाज़ार **suparbāzār** *n.m.* supermarket
सुपुर्द करना **supurd karnā** *v.t.* refer
सुरंग **suraṅg** *n.f.* tunnel
सुरंगपथ **suraṅgpath** *n.m.* subway
सुर **sur** *n.m.* tune
सुर मिलाना **sur milānā** *v.t.* tune
सुरक्षा **surakṣā** *n.m.* safety
सुरक्षित **surakṣit** *n.m.* secure
सुरक्षित कर देना **surakṣit kar denā** *v.t.* ensure
सुराक्षित करना **surākṣit karnā** *v.t.* secure
सुरक्षित रखना **surkṣit rakhnā** *v.t.* preserve
सुवाच्य **suvācy** *adj.* legible
सुविधा **suvidhā** *n.f.* convenience
सुव्यवस्थित **suvyavsthit** *adj.* methodical
सुसाध्य **susādhy** *adj.* benign

सुस्पष्ट **suspaṣṭ** *adj.* noticeable
सूँघना **sūṁghnā** *v.t.* smell
सूई **sūī** *n.f.* needle
सूई लगाना **sūī lagānā** *v.t.* inject
सूअर **sūar** *n.m.* pig
सूअरी **sūarī** *n.m.* sow
सूखी घास **sūkhī ghās** *n.f.* hay
सूखना **sūkhnā** *v.t.* dry
सूखारोगी **sūkhārogī** *adj.* rickety
सूचना **sūcnā** *n.f.* communication
सूचना देना **sūcnā denā** *v.t.* notify
सूचना-पत्र **sūcnā-patr** *n.m.* news
सूचित करना **sūcit karnā** *v.t.* inform
सूची **sūcī** *n.m.* list
सूची बनाना **sūcī banānā** *v.t.* list
सूची-पत्र **sūcī-patr** *n.m.* catalog
सूजन **sūjan** *n.f.* inflammation
सूत **sūt** *n.m.* yarn
सूती **sūtī** *n.m.* cotton
सूत्र **sūtra** *n.m.* formula
सूरजमुखी का बीज **sūrajmukhī kā bīj** *n.f.* sunflower
सूर्य **sūrya** *n.* sun
सूर्योदय **sūryoday** *n.m.* sunrise
सूर्यास्त **sūryast** *n.m.* sunset
सूली **sūlī** *n.f.* cross
सूस **sūs** *n.m.* dolphin
सूक्ष्म **sūkṣam** *adj.* subtle
सूक्ष्म भेद **sūkṣam bhed** *n.m.* nuance
सूक्ष्मदर्शी **sūkśamdarśī** *n.m.* microscope
सृष्टि **sṛṣṭi** *n.f.* creation
से **se** *prep.* from
से अधिक **se adhik** *adj.* better

सेट **seṭ** *n.m.* set
सेनटीमीटर **senṭīmīṭar** *n.m.* centimeter
सेना **senā** *n.f.* troops
सेब **seb** *n.m.* apple
सेम **sem** *n.m.* bean
सेवा **sevā** *n.f.* service
सेवा करना **sevā karnā** *v.t.* serve
सेवानिवृती **sevānivr̥ti** *adj.* retired
सैकड़ा **saikaṛā** *n.* cent
सैकरिन **saikarin** *n.m.* saccharin
सैंडविच **saiṅḍvic** *n.m.* sandwich
सैर **sair** *n.m.* hike
सैर करना **sair karnā** *v.t.* tour; *v.i.* hitchhike
सोंटा **soṇṭā** *n.m.* staff
सोच निकालना **soc nikālnā** *v.t.* devise
सोचना **socnā** *v.i.* think
सोडा **soḍā** *n.m.* soda
सोडियम **soḍiyam** *n.m* sodium
सोता **sotā** *n.m.* fountain
सोना **sonā** *v.i.* sleep; *n.m./adj.* gold
सोना चढ़ाना **sonā caṛhānā** *v.t.* gild
सोने का **sone kā** *adj.* golden
सोने का कमरा **sone kā kamrā** *n.m.* bedroom
सोने का थैला **sone kā thailā** *n.m.* sleeping bag
सोफ़ा **sofā** *n.m.* sofa
सोमवार **somvār** *n.m.* Monday
सोया **soyā** *n.m.* soy
सोया बीन **soyā bīn** *n.m.* soybean
सोयाा हुआ **soyā huā** *adj.* asleep
सोलह **solah** *num.* sixteen
सोलहवाँ **solahvāṁ** *adj.* sixteenth
सौंपना **saumpnā** *v.t.* entrust

सौ **sau** *num.* hundred
सौतेला भाई **sautelā bhāī** *n.m.* stepbrother
सौतेला बाप **sautelā bāp** *n.m.* stepfather
सौतेला बेटा **sautelā beṭā** *n.m.* stepson
सौतेली बेटी **sautelī beṭī** *n.m.* stepdaughter
सौतेली बहन **sautelī behen** *n.f.* stepsister
सौतेली माँ **sautelī māṁ** *n.f.* stepmother
सौदा **saudā** *n.m.* bargain, deal
सौदागर **saudāgar** *n.m.* trader
सौभाग्यवश **saubhāgyaśālī** *adj.* fortunate
सौर **saur** *adj.* solar
सौवां **sauvāṁ** *adj.* hundredth
स्कैब **skaib** *n.m.* scab
स्की **skī** *n.m.* ski
स्कूटर **skūṭar** *n.m.* motorbike
स्कूली लड़का **skūlī laṛkā** *n.m.* schoolchild
स्कूली लड़की **skūlī laṛkī** *n.f.* schoolchild
स्केट **skeṭ** *n.m.* skate
स्केट पर चलना **skeṭ par calnā** *v.i.* skate
स्टाफ़ **sṭāf** *n.m.* staff
स्टाल **sṭāl** *n.m.* stall, stand
स्टार्च **sṭārc** *n.m.* starch
स्टीरियो **sṭīriyo** *n.m.* stereo
स्टीमर **sṭīmar** *n.m.* steamship
स्टूल **sṭūl** *n.m.* stool
स्ट्रेचर **sṭrecar** *n.m.* stretcher
स्टेडियम **sṭeḍiyam** *n.m.* stadium
स्टेपल **sṭepal** *n.m.* staple
स्टेपल निकालने वाला **sṭepal nikālne vālā** *v.t.* staple
स्टेपल से बाँधना **sṭepal se bāṁdhnā** *v.t.* staple
स्टेथास्कोप **sṭethāskop** *n.m.* stethoscope
स्टेशन **sṭeśan** *n.m.* station

स्तंभ **stambh** *n.m.* column, shaft
स्तमभक **stambhak** *n.m.* astringent
स्तनपायी **stanpāyī** *n.m.* mammal
स्तर **star** *n.m.* standard
स्त्रायु-रोगी **strāyu-rogī** *adj.* neurotic
स्त्री **strī** *n.f.* female
स्त्रोत **strot** *n.m.* (*origin*) source
स्थगित करना **sthagit karnā** *v.t.* postpone
स्थल **sthal** *n.m.* site
स्थापित करना **sthāpit karnā** *v.t.* found
स्थायित्व **sthāyitva** *n.m.* permanence
स्थान **sthān** *n.m.* place, post
स्थायी **sthāyī** *n.m.* standing
स्थायी आदेश **sthāyī ādeś** *adj.* standing
स्थिर **sthir** *adj.* stable
स्नान **snān** *n.m.* bath
स्नान टब **snān ṭab** *n.m.* bathtub
स्नान करना **snān karnā** *v.i.* bathe
स्नातक **snātak** *n.m.* graduate
स्नातक होना **snātak honā** *v.i.* graduate
स्नेही **snehī** *adj.* affectionate
स्नेहमान **snehamān** *n.m.* cod
स्नैपशाट **snaipśāṭ** *n.m.* snapshot
स्पंज **spañj** *n.m.* sponge
स्पष्ट **spaṣṭ** *adj.* evident, clear
स्पष्ट करना **spaṣṭ karnā** *v.t.* explain
स्पर्श **sparś** *n.m.* feel, touch
स्पर्शक **sparśak** *n.m.* tentacle
स्फटिक **spaṭik** *n.m.* crystal
स्फुलिंग-प्लग **sphuliṅg-plag** *n.m.* spark
स्याही **syāhī** *n.f.* ink
स्लाइड **slāiḍ** *n.m.* slide

स्लेटी पत्थर **sleṭī patthar** *n.m.* slate
स्लीपर **slīpar** *n.m.* slipper
स्वयं **svayam** *pron.* itself, myself
स्वयं सेवक **svayaṁ sevak** *n.m.* volunteer
स्वयं-सेवा **svayam-sevā** *n.m./adj.* self-service
स्वचालित **svacālit** *adj.* automatic
स्वचलन **svacalan** *n.m.* automation
स्वेटर **sveṭar** *n.m.* sweater
स्वत **svat** *adj.* spontaneous
स्वतंत्र **svatantra** *adj.* independent
स्वतंत्रता **svatantratā** *n.f.* independence
स्वत्व **svatva** *n.m.* possession
स्वत्वबोधक **svatavbodhak** *adj.* possessive
स्वर **svar** *n.m.* tone
स्वर का **svar kā** *adj.* vocal
स्वर्ग **svarg** *n.f.* heaven
स्वस्थ **svasth** *adj.* healthy
स्वस्थचित **svasthcit** *adj.* sane
स्वागत **svāgat** *n.m.* reception
स्वागतक **svāgatak** *n.m.* receptionist
स्वागतम **svāgatam** *n.m.* welcome
स्वागत करना **svāgat karnā** *v.t.* welcome
स्वाद **svād** *n.m.* flavor, taste
स्वाद मिलाना **svād milānā** *v.t.* flavor
स्वादिष्ट **svādiṣṭ** *adj.* savory
स्वभाव **svabhāv** *n.f.* nature
स्वाभाव से **svābhāv se** *adv.* naturally
स्वामिनी **svāminī** *n.f.* mistress
स्वामी **svāmī** *n.m.* lord, master
स्वास्थय **svāsthy** *adj.* sanitary
स्वायत शासन **svāyat śāsan** *adj.* autonomous
स्वीकार करना **svīkār karnā** *v.t.* accept

स्विच **svic** *n.m.* switch
स्विच खोलना **svic kholnā** *v.t.* switch
स्थिति **sthiti** *n.m.* situation
स्थिर **sthir** *adj.* steady

ह

हँसी **haṁsī** *n.f.* laughter
हँसना **haṁsnā** *v.i.* laugh
हैंड बैग **haiṇḍbaig** *n.m.* handbag
हैंगर **haingar** *n.m.* hanger
होंठ **hoṁṭh** *n.m.* lip
हकलाना **haklānā** *v.i.* stammer
हकलाहट **haklāhaṭ** *n.m.* stammer
हजामत का ब्रश **hajāmat kā braś** *n.m.* shaving brush
हजामत क्रीम **hajāmat krīm** *n.f.* shaving cream
हज़ार **hazār** *num.* thousand
हज़ारवाँ **hazārvāṁ** *adj.* thousandth
हटना **haṭnā** *v.i.* shift
हट जाना **haṭ jānā** *v.t.* withdraw
हटा देना **haṭā denā** *v.t.* eliminate
हटाना **haṭānā** *v.t.* move, shift, withdraw
हठीला **haṭhīlā** *adj.* stubborn
हड्डी **haḍḍī** *n.f.* bone
हड़बड़ी **haṛbaṛī** *n.f.* rush
हड़ताल **haṛtāl** *n.m.* strike
हड़ताली **haṛtālī** *adj.* striker
हताहत **hatāhat** *n.m.* casualty
हताश करना **hatāś karnā** *v.t.* disappoint
हताशा **hatāśā** *n.f.* disappointment
हतोत्साहित होना **hatotsāhit honā** *adj.* frustrated
हत्या **hatyā** *n.f.* murder

हत्यारा **hatyyārā** *n.m.* murderer
हथौरा **hathaurā** *n.m.* hammer
हथेली **hathelī** *n.f.* palm
हर्निया **harniyā** *n.f.* hernia
हर **har** *n.m.* every
हर एक **har ek** *adj.* each
हर कोई **har koī** *pron.* everybody
हरा **harā** *adj.* green
हफ़्ता **haftā** *n.m.* week
हम **ham** *pron.* we
हमको **hamko** *pron.* us
हमदर्द **hamdard** *adj.* sympathetic
हमदर्दी **hamdardī** *n.f.* sympathy
हमला **hamlā** *n.m.* attack
हमला करना **hamlā karnā** *v.t.* attack
हमारा **hamārā** *pron.* our
हमेशा **hameśā** *adv.* always
हर रोज़ **har roz** *adj.* every
हराना **harānā** *v.t.* defeat
हरी मिर्च **harī mirc** *n.f.* pepper
हर्ष **harṣ** *n.m.* delight
हल **hal** *n.m.* solution; plow
हल चलाना **hal calānā** *v.t.* plow
हल करना **hal karnā** *v.t.* solve
हलके रंग **halke rang** *adj.* blond
हलका **halkā** *adj.* pale
हल्का नाशता **halkā nāśtā** *n.m.* appetizer
हल्का सा **halkā sā** *n.m.* minute
हल्ला **hallā** *n.m.* racket
हवा **havā** *n.m.* air
हवाई अड्डा **havāī aḍḍā** *n.m.* airport
हवा निकालना **havā nikālnā** *v.t.* deflate

हवादार **havādār** *adj.* windy
हवादार बनाना **havādār banānā** *v.t.* ventilate
हवादारी **havādārī** *n.f.* ventilation
हवाई डाक **havāī ḍāk** *n.m.* airmail
हवाई अड्डा **havāī aḍḍā** *n.m.* airport
हवाई जहाज़ **havāī jahāz** *n.m.* airplane
हवाई कम्पनी **havāī kampanī** *n.f.* airline
हवाई छतरी **havāī chatarī** *n.f.* parachute
हवेली **havelī** *n.f.* mansion
हशिया **haśiyā** *n.m.* margin
हस्ताक्षर करना **hastākṣar karnā** *v.i.* subscribe
हस्तलिपि **hastlipi** *n.m.* manuscript
हाँ **hāṁ** *adv.* yes
हाँगर **hāṁgar** *n.m.* shark
हाकी **hākī** *n.f.* hockey
हाथ **hāth** *n.m.* hand
हाथ-पैर मारना **hāth-pair mārnā** *v.t.* struggle
हाथ में होना **hāth meṁ honā** *v.t.* attend
हाथी **hāthī** *n.m.* elephant
हाथी दाँत **hāthī dāṁt** *n.m.* ivory
हार्दिक **hārdik** *adj.* hearty
हानि **hāni** *n.f.* harm
हानि सहना **hāni sahanā** *v.t.* sacrifice
हानिकर **hānikar** *adj.* harmful
हाफ़पैंट **hāfpainṭ** *n.m.pl.* shorts
हार **hār** *n.f.* defeat
हार मानना **hār mānnāl** *v.t.* submit
हार्दिक रूप से **hārdik rūp se** *adv.* cordially
हाल का **hāl kā** *adj.* recent
हालत **hālat** *n.m.* state
हाल में **hāl meṁ** *adv.* lately
हालाँकि **halāṁki** *conj.* although

हास्य **hāsya** *n.m.* humor
हास्यपद **hāsyapad** *adj.* ridiculous
हास्यकर **hāsyakar** *adj.* funny
हिंसा **himsā** *n.f.* violence
हिंसापूर्ण **himsāpūrṇ** *adj.* violent
हिचकिचाहट **hickicāhaṭ** *n.f.* hesitation
हिचकिचाना **hickicānā** *v.t.* hesitate
हिच्की **hickī** *n.f.* hiccup
हिचकना **hicknā** *v.i.* waver
हिज्जे करना **hijje karnā** *v.t.* spell
हितकर **hitkar** *adj.* wholesome
हिदायत **hidāyat** *n.f.* gospel
हिम झंझावात **him jhamjhāvāt** *n.m.* snowstorm
हिमलव **himlav** *n.m.* snowflake
हिन्दी **hindī** *n.m.* Hindi
हिन्दू **hindū** *n.m./adj.* Hindu
हिरन **hiran** *n.m.* deer
हिलना **hilnā** *v.i.* shake
हिलाना **hilānā** *v.t.* shake, agitate
हिलसा **hilsā** *n.f.* herring
हिसाब **hisāb** *n.m.* calculation
हिसाब लगाना **hisāb lagānā** *v.t.* calculate
हिस्सा **hissā** *n.m.* share
हिस्सेदार **hissedār** *n.m.* partner
हीटर **hīṭar** *n.m.* heater
हीरा **hīrā** *n.m.* diamond
हुकुम का पत्ता **hukum kā pattā** *n.m.* spade
हेकड़ **hekaṛ** *adj.* arrogant
हेकड़ी **hekaṛī** *n.m.* arrogance
हेलिकॉप्टर **helikāpṭar** *n.m.* helicopter
हेलमिट **helmiṭ** *n.m.* helmet
हैरान करना **hairān karnā** *v.t.* amaze

हो जाना **ho jānā** *v.i.* become
हो सकना **ho saknā** *v.aux.* may
होटल **hoṭal** *n.m.* hotel
होटिस **hoṭis** *n.m.* suspenders
होना **honā** *v.i.* be; consist
होने देना **hone denā** *v.t.* let
होश **hoś** *n.m.* wit
हो-हल्ला **ho-hallā** *n.m.* riot
हौसला **hausalā** *n.m.* morale

Geographical Appendix

Rivers in India

	Transliteration	हिन्दी
Brahmaputra	brahmāputra	ब्रह्मापुत्र
Ganges	gangā	गंगा
Mahanadi	mahānadī	महानदी
Godavari	godāvarī	गोदावरी
Krishna	kṛṣṇā	कृष्णा
Kaveri	kāverī	कावेरी
Tapi	tāpī	तापी
Narmada	narmadā	नर्मदा
Indus	sindhu	सिन्धु
Yamuna	yamunā	यमुना
Chenab	cenāb	चेनाब
Ravi	rāvī	रावी
Sutlej	satluj	सतलुज
Jhelum	jhelam	झेलम

Indian States

	Transliteration	हिन्दी
Andhra Pradesh	andhra pradeś	अंध्र प्रदेश
Arunachal Pradesh	aruṇācal pradeś	अरुणाचल प्रदेश
Assam	asam	असम
Bihar	bihār	बिहार
Chhattisgarh	cattīsagaṛh	चत्तीसगढ़
Goa	goā	गोआ

INDIAN STATES *(continued)*

	Transliteration	हिन्दी
Gujarat	gujarāt	गुजरात
Haryana	hariyāṇā	हरियाणा
Himachal Pradesh	himācal pradeś	हिमाचल प्रदेश
Jammu and Kashmir	jammū aur kaśmīr	जम्मू और कश्मीर
Jharkhand	jhārkhanḍ	झारखंड
Karnataka	karnāṭak	कर्नाटक
Kerala	kerala	केरल
Madhya Pradesh	madhya pradeś	मध्य प्रदेश
Maharashtra	mahārāṣṭra	महाराष्ट्र
Manipur	maṇipūr	मणिपूर
Meghalaya	meghālaya	मेघालय
Mizoram	mizoram	मिज़ोरम
Nagaland	nāgālainḍ	नागालैण्ड
Orissa	uṛīsā	उड़ीसा
Punjab	panjāb	पंजाब
Rajasthan	rājsthān	राजस्थान
Sikkim	sikkim	सिक्किम
Tamil Nadu	tamilnāḍu	तमिलनाडु
Tripura	tripūrā	त्रिपूरा
Uttar Pradesh	uttar pradeś	उत्तर प्रदेश
West Bengal	paścim bangāl	पश्चिम बंगाल

Major Cities of India

	Transliteration	हिन्दी
Mumbai (Bombay)	mumbaī	मुम्बई
Delhi	dillī	दिल्ली
Kolkata (Calcutta)	kolkātā	कोलकाता
Chennai (Madras)	cennaī	चेन्नई
Bengaluru (Bangalore)	bangalaur	बंगलौर
Hyderabad	haidarābād	हैदराबाद
Ahmedabad	ahmadābād	अहमदाबाद
Pune	puṇe	पुणे
Kanpur	kānpur	कानपुर
Surat	sūrat	सूरत
Jaipur	jaypur	जयपुर
Lucknow	lakhnaū	लखनऊ
Nagpur	nāgpur	नागपुर
Patna	paṭnā	पटना
Indore	indaur	इन्दौर
Meerut	meraṭh	मेरठ
Bhopal	bhopāl	भोपाल
Vadodara (Baroda)	vadodarā	वदोदरा
Ludhiana	ludhiyānā	लुधियाना
Bhubaneshwar	bhuvaneśvar	भुवनेश्वर
Coimbatore	koyambaṭūr	कोयम्बटूर
Agra	āgarā	आगरा
Nashik	nāsik	नासिक
Kochi (Cochin)	kocci	कोच्चि
Visakhapatnam	viśākhāpaṭṭanam	विशाखापट-टनम
Varanasi (Benares)	vārāṇasī	वाराणसी

MAJOR CITIES OF INDIA (*continued*)

	Transliteration	हिन्दी
Rajkot	rājkoṭ	राजकोट
Madurai	madurai	मदुरै
Asansol	āsansol	आसनसोल
Jabalpur	jabalpur	जबलपुर
Allahabad	ilāhābād	इलाहाबाद
Jamshedpur	jamśedpur	जमशेदपुर
Dhanbad	dhanbad	धनबद
Amritsar	amṛtsar	अमृत्सर
Aurangabad	aurangabād	औरंगबाद
Vijayawada	vijayavāṛā	विजयवाड़ा
Mysore	maisūr	मैसूर
Srinagar	śrīnagar	श्रीनगर
Solapur	solāpur	सोलापुर
Bhilai	bhilāe	भिलाए
Ranchi	rām̐cī	राँची
Thiruvananthapuram (Trivandrum)	tiruvanantapuram	तिरुवनंतपुरम
Guwahati	guvāhāṭī	गुवाहाटी
Chandigarh	caṇḍīgaṛh	चण्डीगढ़
Kozhikode (Calicut)	kozikoḍ	कोज़िकोड़
Gwalior	gvāliyar	ग्वालियर
Salem	selam	सेलम
Tiruchirapalli	tirūccirāpallī	तिरूच्चिरापल्ली
Jalandhar	jālandhar	जलन्धर

Countries in the Region

	Transliteration	हिन्दी
Afghanistan	afgānistān	अफ़गानिस्तान
Bangladesh	bānglādeś	बांग्लादेश
Bhutan	bhūṭān	भूटान
India	bhārat	भारत
Iran	īrān	ईरान
Maldives	māldvīp	मलव्दीप
Myanmar (Burma)	myānmār	म्यांमार
Nepal	nepāl	नेपाल
Pakistan	pākistān	पाकिस्तान
Sri Lanka	śri lankā	श्री लंका
Tibet	tibbat	तिब्बत

Major Oceans in South Asia

	Transliteration	हिन्दी
Arabian Sea	arab sāgar	अरब सागर
Bay of Bengal	bangāl kī khāṛī	बंगाल की खाड़ी
Indian Ocean	hind mahāsāgar	हिंद महासागर

Other South Asian Interest Titles from Hippocrene Books...

LANGUAGE GUIDES

Hindi-English/English-Hindi Dictionary & Phrasebook
Todd J. Scudiere
Hindi is one of the most widely spoken languages in the world and one of the two official languages of India. This guide provides the traveler or student with essential resources for communication. It presents the Hindi script with a comprehensive pronunciation guide and basic grammar. Each entry in the two-way dictionary features the script and romanized Hindi. The phrasebook contains cultural information (such as why eating with the left hand is considered rude), as well as a section on problems a traveler may encounter.
3,400 entries · 280 pages · 3¾ x 7½ · 0-7818-0983-5 · $12.95pb

Teach Yourself Hindi
Mohini Rao
This book combines a direct conversational style with vocabulary, grammar, phrases, and sentences, to make learning Hindi easy and pleasurable.
207 pages · 4⅜ x 7 · 0-87052-831-9 · $14.95pb

Hindi-English/English-Hindi Standard Dictionary
30,000 entries · 800 pages · 6 x 9 · 0-7818-0470-1 · $27.50pb

Hippocrene Hindi Children's Picture Dictionary
625 entries · 108 pages · 8½ x 11 · 0-7818-1129-5 · $14.95pb

Bengali (Bangla)-English/English-Bengali (Bangla) Dictionary & Phrasebook
4,000 entries · 4 ¾ x 7 ½ · 978-0-7818-1252-8 · $14.95pb

Bengali (Bangla)-English/English-Bengali (Bangla) Practical Dictionary
13,000 entries · 4 3/8 x 7 · 978-0-7818-1270-2 · $24.95pb

Marathi-English/English-Marathi Dictionary & Phrasebook
2,000 entries · 4 ¾ x 7 ½ · 978-0-7818-1142-2 · $14.95pb

Nepali-English/English-Nepali Dictionary & Phrasebook (*Romanized*)
1,500 entries · 130 pages · 4¾ x 7½ · 0-7818-0957-6 · $13.95pb

Punjabi-English/English-Punjabi Dictionary
25,000 entries · 782 pages · 5 x 7 · 0-7818-0940-1 · $24.95pb

Concise Sanskrit-English Dictionary
18,000 entries · 366 pages · 5 x 7 · 0-7818-0203-2 · $14.95pb

Tamil-English/English-Tamil Dictionary & Phrasebook
6,000 entries · 222 pages · 3¾ x 7½ · 0-7818-1016-7 · $14.95pb

Urdu-English/English-Urdu Dictionary & Phrasebook (*Romanized*)
3,000 entries · 175 pages · 3¾ x 7½ · 0-7818-0970-3 · $13.95pb

CULTURE

India: An Illustrated History
Prem Kishore & Anuradha Kishore Ganpati
234 pages · 5 x 7 · 50 photos/illus/maps · 0-7818-0944-4 · $14.95pb

CUISINE

Menus and Memories from Punjab
Veronica "Rani" Sidhu
288 pages · 6 x 9 · 16-page color photo insert · 0-7818-1220-8 · $29.95hc

The Kerala Kitchen: Recipes and Recollections from the Syrian Christians of South India
Lathika George
256 pages · 8 x 9 · 16-page color photo insert · 0-7818-1184-8· $35.00hc

Healthy South Indian Cooking, ***Expanded Edition***
Alamelu Vairavan & Patricia Marquardt
350 pages · 5½ x 8½ · 16-page color photo insert ·
0-7818-1189-9 · $35.00hc

Flavorful India: Treasured Recipes from a Gujarati Family
Priti Chitnis Gress
147 pages · 5 ½ x 8 ½ · 0-7818-1207-0 · $14.95pb

Rice & Curry: Sri Lankan Home Cooking
S.H. Fernando Jr.
208 pages · 7 ¼ x 9 · color photos throughout ·
978-0-7818-1273-3 · $19.95pb

Prices subject to change without prior notice. **To purchase Hippocrene Books** contact your local bookstore, visit www.hippocrenebooks.com, call (212) 685-4373, or write to: HIPPOCRENE BOOKS, 171 Madison Avenue, New York, NY 10016.